Language and

The relationship between language and power has been an important subject of study in the social sciences, linguistics, and philosophy. This volume examines how language and politics interact and mutually reproduce and reinforce scales of social hierarchies, political power, and cultural and economic inequalities in the Indian context. It offers diverse viewpoints to contextualize the inter-linkages of culture and power, and situates language politics within an interdisciplinary framework.

The introduction provides an overview of the key aspects of the language question in India. The essays address the relationship between language, community, and nation; the interaction between language, culture, and state; and the complex interplay between language and identity politics in India.

The *Themes in Politics* series presents essays on important issues in the study of political science and Indian politics. Each volume in the series brings together the most significant articles and debates on an issue, and contains a substantive introduction and bibliography.

Language and Politics in India

edited by

Asha Sarangi

OXFORD
UNIVERSITY PRESS

OXFORD
UNIVERSITY PRESS

YMCA Library Building, Jai Singh Road, New Delhi 110 001

Oxford University Press is a department of the University of Oxford.
It furthers the University's objective of excellence in research, scholarship,
and education by publishing worldwide in

Oxford   New York
Auckland   Cape Town   Dar es Salaam   Hong Kong   Karachi
Kuala Lumpur   Madrid   Melbourne   Mexico City   Nairobi
New Delhi   Shanghai   Taipei   Toronto

With offices in
Argentina   Austria   Brazil   Chile   Czech Republic   France   Greece
Guatemala   Hungary   Italy   Japan   Poland   Portugal   Singapore
South Korea   Switzerland   Thailand   Turkey   Ukraine   Vietnam

Oxford is a registered trademark of Oxford University Press
in the UK and in certain other countries.

Published in India
by Oxford University Press, New Delhi

ISBN-13: 978-0-19-806422-0
ISBN-10: 0-19-806422-5

Typeset in Minion 10.5/13
by Eleven Arts, Keshav Puram, Delhi 110 035
Printed in India at De-Unique, New Delhi 110 018
Published by Oxford University Press
YMCA Library Building, Jai Singh Road, New Delhi 110 001

Dedicated to the memory of my parents
who taught me the languages of honesty, love, and truth.

Contents

Figures

Tables

Acknowledgements

While preparing this volume, I have been fortunate in having the support of a number of friends, colleagues, and family members who have been generous, cooperative, and helpful in all ways possible. I developed the initial intellectual curiosity in the subject of language and politics during my graduate studies at the University of Chicago. For several years at Chicago and afterwards, my teachers and intellectual mentors Lloyd and Susanne Rudolph continued to provide me with tremendous intellectual support and encouragement. Susanne's careful reading of the introduction with her rigorous queries helped me to improve it further. Lloyd nourished and nurtured several key ideas in this area with his outstanding qualities of an intense researcher, a uniquely dedicated and affectionate teacher, and a generous donor of intellectual rigour. To them, I owe more than can be said in words. Leela Fernandes has remained a committed friend sharing the universe of ideas on both sides of the world. Her incisive comments and suggestions on the introduction helped me to think through some of the issues central to the theme of this volume. I am especially grateful to Selma Sonntag for pointing out a few ambiguities and omissions in the introduction initially. Her close reading of the text helped me in writing the introduction more precisely. Despite his countless responsibilities, Udaya Narayana Singh took time to read and comment on the introduction without any delay. D.P. Pattanaayak promptly searched and sent his book to me from Bhubneshwar. My special thanks to both of them. I would like to thank all the contributors of this volume. It is due to their promptness and continuing interest in the subject that I was able to put together this volume. Discussions with students and colleagues at the Centre for Political Studies of Jawaharlal Nehru University, New Delhi, made reading and writing for the book a pleasant task. I would particularly like to thank Ram Advani, Ayhan Akman, Hanna Kim, and Manoranjan Satpathy. Their friendship has sustained life and work over the last several years. Family members in Dehradun, Dhenkanal, and Delhi have always provided their unbound affection and care at every stage of the work for this volume. I am grateful to the New Ink Publications and particularly to Prakash for his help in digitizing the maps. It was pleasure to work with the editorial team at the Oxford University Press, New Delhi, who were always ready to help and advice needed at various stages for the volume. Most of all, Prabhat has always remained a dedicated and honest co-thinker in life and work providing the intellectual world of ours with his unique capacity to search truth and honesty. Finally, Madhav and Raghav brought in a new world of happiness, humour, and love along with their everyday innovations in learning the languages of the world today.

Publisher's Acknowledgements

The publisher acknowledges the following for permission to include articles/extracts in this volume.

Modern Asian Studies for Sumathi Ramaswamy, 'Sanskrit for the Nation', 33 (2), May 1999, pp. 339–81.

Oxford & IBH Publishing Company Pvt. Ltd. for Joseph E. Schwartzberg, 'Factors in the Linguistic Reorganization of Indian States', in Paul Wallace (ed.), *Region and Nation in India*, New Delhi, 1985, pp. 155–82.

Ethnic and Racial Studies for Paul R. Brass, 'Elite Interests, Popular Passions, and Social Power in the Language Politics of India', 27 (3), May 2004, pp. 353–75.

Journal of Commonwealth and Comparative Politics for Selma K. Sonntag, 'The Political Saliency of Language in Bihar and Uttar Pradesh', 34 (2), July 1996, pp. 1–18.

Har-Anand Publications under the auspices of Himalayan Research and Cultural Foundation for K. Warikoo, 'Language and Politics in Jammu and Kashmir: Issues and Perspectives', in P.N. Pushp and K. Warikoo (eds), *Jammu, Kashmir and Ladakh: Linguistic Predicament*, New Delhi, 1996, pp.183–221

xvi   Publisher's Acknowledgements

Sage Publications for D.L. Sheth, 'The Great Language Debate: Politics of Metropolitan versus Vernacular India', in Upendra Baxi and Bhiku Parekh (eds), *Crisis and Change in Contemporary India*, New Delhi, 1995, pp. 187–215.

Franz Steiner Verlag for Sudipta Kaviraj, 'Writing, Speaking, Being: Language and the Historical Formation of Identities in India', in Dagmar Hellmann-Rajanayagam and Dietmar Rothemund (eds), *Nationalstaat and Sprachkonflikte in Sudund Sudostasien*, Stuttgart, Germany, 1992, pp. 25–68.

Sage Publications for David Lelyveld, 'Talking the National Language: Hindi/Urdu/Hindustani in Indian Broadcasting and Cinema', in Sujata Patel, J. Bagchi, and M.K. Raj (eds), *Thinking Social Science in India: Essays in Honour of Alice Thorner*, New Delhi, 2002, pp. 355–66.

Introduction
Language and Politics in India

Asha Sarangi

The relationship between language and power has for long remained a subject of inquiry in various fields of the social sciences, linguistics, and philosophy. The subject has been analysed from a variety of analytical and philosophical perspectives within specific social, anthropological, historical, economic, cultural, and political contexts. Owing to the complex and dense interlinkages between language and power, a number of fields and subfields have emerged focusing on this relationship with newer methodological approaches and thematic concerns. They have established zones of interdisciplinary and multidisciplinary foci to the field. The relationships between language and history (historical linguistics), language and society (sociolinguistics), language and cognitive system (psycholinguistics), language and literature (literary studies or stylistics), language and philosophy (philosophy of language), and language and anthropology (linguistic anthropology) have continued to occupy scholarly attention in all major disciplines of the social sciences throughout the world.

It is important to explore and examine the sites where language and politics interact. They mutually reproduce and reinforce scales of social hierarchies, political power, cultural and economic inequalities. The problematic of the *language question* needs to probe into the deep structures of relationships between language, history, culture, ideology, power, economy, and politics. I use the term language question to refer to those multiple domains where language and politics interact and result in tangible historical and political outcome of a certain kind. The language question should not be reduced simply to the problem of language planning, policy, and programmes but should take into account the ideological power of language(s) and its various forms of domination and subordination. Furthermore, we need to pay attention to how discourses of linguistic rights, identities, and interests are at times located within the broader fields of culture, education, economy, law, politics, and administration. In this regard, the field of linguistic politics shows us not only the dynamics between language and politics in a given context but also alerts and draws attention to the alternative, non-conventional, and, at times, radical social and political histories underneath the discourses of community, culture, region, nation, and state. It will be important to keep in mind the 'empirical and analytical distinction between language as a pattern of meanings and language as a means of communication'[1] to illustrate the relationship between language and politics.

The relationship among languages, regions, territories, cultures, and literatures is an intensely overlapping one. Sheldon Pollock emphasizes that the 'universe of literary cultures in the history of South Asia is plural, multi-faceted and richly diverse'. For Pollock, 'if languages come to distinguish nations, it is in part because nations are made by turning languages into distinctive national markers'.[2] He, therefore, urges us to explore the complex internal and at times hierarchical relationships that exist in the cultural and literary histories of multilingual societies where 'borders of place and borders of language were as messy as they were elsewhere'.[3] The history of early modern Europe shows us the compact relationship between languages and empires, the rise of vernaculars, the political economy of 'specialized languages in reproducing monopolies of knowledge, and the

---

[1]Miguel A. Cabrera, 'On Language, Culture and Social Action', *History and Theory*, 40 (4), December 2001, pp. 82–109.

[2]Sheldon Pollock (ed.), *Literary Cultures in History: Reconstructions from South Asia* (New Delhi: Oxford University Press, 2003).

[3]Ibid., p. 17.

implications of linguistic imperialism and colonialism'.[4] There are strong interlinkages between language and political economy dealing with 'symbolic, linguistic aspects of power, domination and global political economy', suggesting a link between language and the material world.[5] Gal reminds us about the intricate relationship between language and social inequality visible in relations of colonial domination and subordination. Similarly, Judith Irvine argues that the Saussurean theory of linguistic signs 'may refer to aspects of an exchange system; differentiated ways of speaking may index social groups in a social division of labor; and linguistic 'goods' may enter the marketplace as objects of exchange.'[6]

The rise of modern nation-states in Europe cannot be understood without taking into account the historical reconstruction of languages and their uses as a marker of differences. A number of linguistic practices were prescribed and legitimized to enforce the processes of social, cultural, and political differentiation among people belonging to distinct racial and cultural communities. Grillo calls them *communicative practices*, which are ideologically structured and institutionally imposed over a long historical period of time. These linguistic practices reflect the broader social and cultural hierarchies through which 'the politics of language incorporates a multiple struggle on one terrain— about language, in language, for language'.[7] The struggle over expansion, retention, or loss of languages has been waged alongside the spread of

[4]Ian Parker, 'The Rise of Vernaculars in Early Modern Europe: An Essay in the Political Economy of Language', in Bruce Bain (ed.), *The Sociogenesis of Language and Human Conduct* (New York: Plenum Press, 1983). Few theorists have tried to establish a close relationship between language and labour and how both of them produce commodities, one in the form of words, vocabularies, meanings, and narratives, and another in the form of goods and products. Rossi-Landi has convincingly tried to establish the theory of exchange and use value in the fields of linguistics and economics. See F. Rossi-Landi, *Linguistics and Economics* (The Hague: Mouton, 1975).

[5]Susan Gal, 'Language and Political Economy', *Annual Review of Anthropology*, 18, 1989, pp. 345–67.

[6]Judith T. Irvine, 'When Talk isn't Cheap: Language and Political Economy', *American Ethnologist*, 16 (2), May 1989.

[7]R.D. Grillo, *Dominant Languages: Language and Hierarchy in Britain and France* (Cambridge: Cambridge University Press, 1989). Grillo shows how through a process of linguistic centralization, both French and English languages began to be identified with the national identity of French and English nations and states. In both cases, Grillo argues, sites of linguistic struggle were religion and education.

empires and their colonies. Histories of Habsburg, Ottoman, French, English, and Spanish empires are replete with accounts of imperial possession over their own languages and their subsequent import overseas. The political economy of imperialism needs to be examined by looking at the relationship between language, land, and labour more closely.[8] Ostler reminds us that not all languages can become languages of empires and colonies because 'reasons of military annexation, capitalist expansion, religious warfare, evangelical and educational expansion and several others can arguably account for the global rise or decline of a few languages over numerous others'.[9] The emergence of linguistic nationalism in nineteenth-century Europe had its 'intellectual roots in renaissance humanist thoughts', which established the relationship between language and politics, whereby the former provided the symbol and source of social and political power.[10] Historically, different languages were considered markers of different ethnic groups and nations, and boundaries of languages and nations converged periodically in European history.[11] Modern states have used the 'modus operandi' of market to create symbols and forms to institutionalize the national language and to delegitimize the patois, creoles, pidgins, and common non-standard languages because it is the state which controls, promotes, and even promulgates an intricate system of langue and parole, of written and spoken forms, and also the correct pronunciation of the language through a variety of official sanctions and cultural practices.[12]

Languages become cultural capitals to provide instantly a sense of belonging to communities—religious and linguistic—which need to be integrated within the territorial limits of nations and nationalities.

[8]There has not been much work done in this important area which can critically examine the relationship between language, labour (economy), and land (territoriality). However, writings of Susan Gal and Rossi-Landi have opened up this new field of study.

[9]Nicholas Ostler, *Empires of the Word: A Language History of the World* (New York: Harper Collins, 2005).

[10]Alan Patten, 'The Humanist Roots of Linguistic Nationalism', *History of Political Thought*, 27 (2), Summer 2006.

[11]Stephen Barbour and Cathie Carmichael (eds), *Language and Nationalism in Europe* (New York: Oxford University Press, 2001).

[12]Pierre Bourdieu, *Language and Symbolic Power* (Cambridge: Harvard University Press, 1991). Bourdieu emphasizes the class formation of official language(s) which, used as cultural capital on the part of the elites, work in reinforcing the class hierarchies and distinctions in a society.

This overwhelming ideology of nationalism not just equates nation with a linguistic community but, as Jespersen argues, 'nation means a linguistic unit, a linguistic community'.[13] The modern nations do require, according to Bhabha, the 'performativity of language' in constructing the narratives of the nation.[14] The language question is obviously related to group and community rights and identities. It is a question of rights, representations, and resources drawn on the social and political privileges and powers enjoyed by some languages and their users over others. Political theory in recent years has brought forth the tension between individual and group rights, and has argued for multicultural perspectives. Questions of 'linguistic diversity' and 'language rights' have not been central to the field of 'normative political theory' which has rather focused on issues of race, immigration, nationalism, and citizenship.[15] Alan Patten's argument suggests that the principle of 'liberal neutrality' can provide a significant 'role in the construction of a normative theory of language politics'.[16] He further suggests that 'for maintaining the diversity of cultures and languages, "liberal neutrality" model is combined with a policy of official multilingualism to defend and protect the minority rights and their claims for representation and recognition in the public institutions'. Any form of public recognition of a language, in Patten's views, should serve three distinctive interests of 'communication, symbolic affirmation, and identity promotion'[17] of various language groups in a multilingual society.

In order to understand the complex character of linguistic politics in India, it is important to note the colonial state's interventions related to various policies pertaining to the study and teaching of Indian languages by colonial officials, institutionalization of English language in the Indian universities and colleges, publication of school textbooks for teaching Indian and English languages, and the uses of Indian languages in colonial administration, legislation, and education. Indian languages, in Cohn's words, were used as 'languages of command' by

[13]Otto Jespersen, *Mankind, Nation and Individual from a Linguistic Point of View* (London: George Allen and Unwin Ltd, 1954).

[14]Homi K. Bhabha (ed.), *Nation and Narration* (London: Routledge, 1990).

[15]Will Kymlicka and Alan Patten (eds), *Language Rights and Political Theory* (New York: Oxford University Press, 2003).

[16]Alan Patten, 'Liberal Neutrality and Language Policy', *Philosophy and Public Affairs*, 31 (4), 2003.

[17]Alan Patten, 'Political Theory and Language Policy', *Political Theory*, 29 (5), October 2001.

the colonial officials for establishing a certain degree of communicability with the natives. The institutionalization of English language was, as Viswanathan has argued persuasively, part of the hegemonic power apparatus between the colonizers and the colonized. Ayesha Jalal has rightly pointed out that 'the role of language as culture and ideology in the politics of South Asia has remained curiously understudied'.[18] This, in her views, has to do with the given-ness of language as a category of analysis. She underlines the need to problematize and conceptualize the language question not simply in terms of linguistic loyalties, consciousness, geo-linguistic boundaries and regions but to situate it historically.[19] The colonial state's inability to comprehend language as culture and ideology, Jalal argues, accounts in some ways for the rise of intense nationalist discourse on it. The latter had to deal with the internal dynamics played out between language and territory, language and caste, language and religion, and language and nation. This was, as Washbrook thinks, because 'the new ideology (of modern linguistic ethnicity) dictated that territorial space itself must be culturally (or at least linguistically) homogeneous' and thus India became 'a society of language jatis much as it has previously been one of the caste jatis competing for honor and status within a continuing multi-jati social order'.[20] A number of scholars have correlated different languages with their distinctive world views, habitus, and potentials for creating distinctive social-cultural formations necessary for the idea of national communities and their identities. Ananthamurthy observes the symbiotic ideological relationship between languages and cultures in his inimitable phrases of 'world of frontyard' and the 'world of backyard', identifying them with languages of literates and illiterates, of learned and less learned, of men and women, global and local, and of Sanskrit and vernacular literatures, respectively.[21]

In India, the territorial location and distribution of castes and languages can be considered significant bases for defining the cultural

[18]Ayesha Jalal, *Democracy and Authoritarianism in South Asia: A Comparative and Historical Perspective* (Cambridge: Cambridge University Press, 1995), pp. 223–4.

[19]Ibid., p. 224.

[20]David Washbrook, '"To Each a Language of His Own": Language, Culture, and Society in Colonial India', in Penelope J. Corfield (ed.), *Language, History and Class* (London: Basil Blackwell, 1991).

[21]U.R.Ananthamurthy, 'Towards the Concept of a New Nationhood: Languages and Literatures in India', in Peter de Souza (ed.), *Contemporary India* (New Delhi: Sage Publications, 2001).

regions. Regional identities based on linguistic affiliation can at times marginalize the dominant caste identities and can thus create 'para-communities' of those speaking the same language or a dominant speech of the region. Caste distinctions are used to demarcate the spheres of purity and impurity, and high and low levels of speech. The Maithil Brahmans of Mithila, Burghart tells us, have defined, delimited, and distinguished the purity of Maithili language from its localization characterized in the speech of the lower-caste people. Unlike others, calling oneself a Maithil is to denote being a Maithil Brahman because the 'named languages are geographically centred and socially hierarchical'.[22] The characterization of a language, according to Burghart, is significantly determined by the political culture. The power of representation constructs both language and culture in a mutually reinforcing manner because 'patterns of speech and political culture mutually reinforce one another, and this mutuality, in turn, sustains language representations in southern Asia'.[23] It is not always the grammar, speech, communication, and vocabulary that determine the life and death of a language, but how people live in and through languages and their worldviews.

Cameron underlines the relationship between language and ideology as a mutually reinforcing one whereby 'language is not simply a vehicle for other ideological processes but is itself shaped by ideological processes'. These ideological positions about languages, in her views, are culturally and historically specific as well as contextually contested at a particular historical moment.[24] The question of language ideology is as much about group and individual identities and their linkages to the social institutions of education, law, and administration, which in turn are affected by the 'ideologization of language use'.[25] State- and nation-building exercises have more often struck a relationship between dominant political ideologies and language policies, which

[22]Richard Burghart, 'Quarrel in the Language Family: Agency and Representations of Speech in Mithila', *Modern Asian Studies*, 27 (4), 1993, p. 771.

[23]Ibid.

[24]Deborah Cameron, 'Ideology and Language', *Journal of Political Ideologies*, 11 (2), June 2006. It is in this context that a subfield of 'language ideologies' has emerged that has occupied itself with the beliefs, status and position adopted by a particular language community towards its own or others' languages while using their own or others languages.

[25]Kathryn A.Woolard and Bambi B. Schieffelin, 'Language Ideology', *Annual Review of Anthropology*, 23, 1994, pp. 55–82.

have tried to rationalize the multilingual diversity in various ways.[26] The question of multiculturalism needs to be understood within this relationship of language, culture, and national identity that has existed historically in both European and non-European contexts.[27]

Multilingual societies need to be more careful in framing their policies and programmes for language planning, which affect and regulate the linguistic behaviour of people directly.[28] Language planning has to be integrated within the broader processes of social change dealing with issues of minority rights, representation and redistribution of resources, national integration, social and cultural development, and the modernization of traditional elites.[29] Each of the distinct forms of language planning involves a distinctive set of activities and functions involving a number of governmental agencies, non-state actors, state organizations, policy makers, administrators, linguists, voluntary groups, individuals, and language leaders.[30] It is important to note how the question of language planning is related to the 'planning and development of some culture in place of some other(s)'.[31] Language policy can at times be part of cultural and ethnic

[26]William Safran, 'Language, Ideology and State-Building: A Comparison of Policies in France, Israel, and Soviet Union', *International Political Science Review,* 13 (4), 1992, pp. 397–414.

[27]Eric Hobsbawm, 'Language, Culture and National Identity', *Social Research,* 63 (4), Winter 1996.

[28]Joan Robin (ed.), *Language Planning: Current Issues and Research* (USA: Georgetown University Press, 1973).

[29]Robert L. Cooper, *Language Planning and Social Change* (New York: Cambridge University Press, 1989). He considers various questions such as the revival of Hebrew as a spoken language, sexist biases in the use(s) of languages, ideology of adult literacy programmes and campaigns, language movements related to spelling reforms, purging and purifying the words and vocabulary of a language, and indigenization of languages and their writing systems being part of the language planning.

[30]Cooper considers corpus planning, status planning, and acquisition planning as three distinct forms of planning. Each of these three forms not only involves a large number of state and societal functionaries but aims at achieving numerous goals such as coining new words and vocabulary, reforming spelling and script, and broader processes of language standardization, codification, and purification (corpus planning), official recognition of language(s), using them as medium of instruction, as print languages, as languages of administration, education, and economy (status planning), and processes related to actual expansion and spread of languages (acquisition planning).

[31]Ronald Breton, 'The Dynamics of Ethnolinguistic Communities as the Central Factor in Language Policy and Planning', *International Journal of the Sociology of Language,* 118, 1996, pp. 163–79. He considers that language planning is linked up with two other crucial processes— recognition of official (state) languages and the categorization of minority languages.

cleansing, and, hence, it is important to explore the relationship between political regimes and language regimes.[32] But as Laitin suggests, unconditional voluntary assimilation of minority language groups in a linguistically and culturally diverse society still remains a remote possibility, and, therefore, 'a unified national language, achieved through persuasion and combined with a diligent work ethic, is no guarantee of peace and prosperity, but it may be a way to promote a nation's development culturally, politically and economically'.[33]

Dasgupta considers that language planning is distinctly different from economic planning as the former has to deal with the strategies of reconciliation with various linguistic groups and communities who affect the political processes in a significant manner.[34] Any policy regarding the official language rights granted to different language communities—minorities, immigrants, indigenous, tribal—should be universalistic and inclusive. But as Alan Patten has argued, the official language policies should 'rest on both a normative principle (what would or would not be "desirable") and on a set of empirical conjectures (what would occur if rights were universalized).'[35] Patten's analysis of the cultural and language rights of immigrants in Canada can be applicable to the understanding of minority linguistic communities' rights to their language maintenance and representation of their culture in other multilingual countries also.

However, there is a close relationship working between linguistic culture and language planning in various multilingual nation-states. It is in this regard that Harold Schiffman's study of France, India, and the United States clearly indicates variation in language policies 'ultimately grounded in *linguistic culture*, the latter including a set of behaviours, beliefs, myths, cultural values, and ways of thinking about a particular language.'[36] Rather than reducing the one to the other, it is

[32]Uldis Ozolins, 'Language Policy and Political Reality', *International Journal of the Sociology of Language*, 118, 1996.

[33]David Laitin, *Language Repertoires and State Construction in Africa* (Cambridge: Cambridge University Press, 1992) and David Laitin, 'Review of Brian Weinstein', *Language Problems and Language Planning*, 16 (3), 1992.

[34]Jyotirindra Dasgupta, 'Practice and Theory of Language Planning: The Indian Policy Process', in William M. O' Barr and Jean F. O'Barr (eds), *Language and Politics* (Paris: Mouton, 1976).

[35]Alan Patten, 'Who Should Have Official Language Rights?', *Supreme Court Law Review*, 31, 2006.

[36]Harold F. Schiffman, *Linguistic Culture and Language Policy* (New York: Routledge, 1996).

vital to regard language as a kind of cultural construct embedded within specific political, social, and historical conditions. Some have argued for the 'political economy of language' and language choice being a matter of both individual as well as collective decision.[37] Considering the state agenda behind the institutionalization of official language(s), Bourdieu argued that 'the official language is bound up with the state, both in its genesis and in its social uses. It is in the process of state formation that the conditions are created for the constitution of a unified linguistic market dominated by the official language. Obligatory on official occasions and in official places (schools, public administration, political institutions etc.); this state language becomes the theoretical norm against which all linguistic practices are objectively measured.'[38]

Language and politics in India as a field of study has received much less scholarly attention. Though there have been a few seminal writings related to the relationship between language-group demands and politics, the field has overwhelmingly been dominated by the subfield of sociolinguistics, which is an 'inter-face of sociology and linguistics.'[39] Other arenas such as the 'sociology of language', 'language planning', 'language policy', 'ethnography of speaking', and 'discourse analysis' have been integral parts of the field of linguistic politics. Singh rightly claims that 'language enjoys a prestige in a plural community in direct proportion to the expressive needs of the community it serves', and it is therefore imperative that 'new agenda of sociolinguistics could emerge'.[40] The question of national language, its recognition and representation over and above the colonial language and other regional languages has remained central to the making of language policy in

---

Schiffman associates the notion of linguistic culture with the complex interaction between language and politics while analysing the language policies in France, India, and the USA.

[37] Abram De Swaan, *Words of the World: The Global Language System* (Cambridge: Polity Press, 2001). Swaan lucidly argues about the global language system being part of the global political economy, which also determines the status and importance of various languages as languages of power and economy in the world. The language system has its own hierarchical structure whereby languages of the world are tied to one another. Languages characterized as imperial, colonial, national, regional, peripheral, and minority languages are situated within this global language system, which affects the rise, death, or revival of languages historically.

[38] Pierre Bourdieu, *Language and Symbolic Power* (Cambridge: Harvard University Press, 1991), pp. 45–6.

[39] Udaya Narayan Singh, 'Social Aspects of Language', in Veena Das (ed.), *The Oxford India Companion to Sociology and Social Anthropology* (New Delhi: Oxford University Press, 2003).

[40] Ibid., p. 728.

independent India.[41] At times, the problematic of the politics of language has been viewed in the broader context of 'elite competition', and different language movements are seen as 'political strategies pursued by emerging elites in multinational states...(whose) goal is to replace the existing, established elites at the center of political power'.[42] The field of language and society is a multidisciplinary one, and it should move away from 'quantitative paradigm' to have the 'demythologized sociolinguistics' which would 'examine the linguistic practices in which members of a culture regularly participate or whose effects they are exposed to.'[43]

Language movements of various kinds have emerged in India since the late nineteenth century. They have raised issues of script reform, language purism, standardization of a language or its dialect, sanskritization and/or romanization of the script, and the official recognition of a language with its inclusion in the Eighth Schedule (ES) of the Constitution. Other demands such as making some languages the media of instruction, redrawing of geolinguistic boundaries of a state, and using distinctive linguistic signs on particular occasions have been brought up by a number of ethnolinguistic movements from time to time. It is important to note the overlapping hierarchies of caste, religion, class, region, and gender embedded within these movements. In the early writings on this question, language was viewed more in an instrumentalist manner and was interpreted as a means of effective social communication. The language question was considered an internal part of the process of the modernization project that the new developing countries were destined to follow. Dasgupta, therefore, considers that 'linguistic cleavage is a politically generated cleavage'.[44] In his views, the language policy of two decades (1950–70) has been somewhat revivalist in nature, and language loyalties during this period

[41]Hans R. Dua, 'The National Language and the Ex-Colonial Language as Rivals: The Case of India', *International Political Science Review*, 14 (3), 1993, pp. 293–308.

[42]Selma K. Sonntag, 'Elite Competition and Official Language Movements', in James W.Tollefson (ed.), *Power and Inequality in Language* (Cambridge University Press, 1995), p. 92.

[43]Deborah Cameron, 'Demythologizing Sociolinguistics: Why Language Does not Reflect Society', in John E. Joseph and Talbot J. Taylor (eds), *Ideologies of Language* (London: Routledge, 1990).

[44]Jyotirindira Dasgupta, *Language Conflict and National Development Group Politics and National Language Policy in India* (Berkeley: University of California Press, 1970), p. 65.

promoted the growth and consciousness of national community based on an idea of political development and 'linguistic modernization.' The demand for the formation of linguistic states immediately after independence was due to the political interests, symbols, and their manipulation on the part of the elites.[45] The 'partition-migration' effect on languages and their territorial contiguity has been most intensely felt among the linguistic communities belonging predominantly to Urdu, Hindi, Punjabi, Bengali, and Sindhi languages.[46] Deustch's model of social communication and modernization seems to have provided a blueprint for these early writers on the language question.[47] The institution of the state, in these writings, has to act as a modernizing arbiter having decisive effects in the realms of society, economy, and polity to ensure a certain degree of political integration, unity, and sustainability. Paul Brass's essay in this volume clearly brings out the complexities of various language movements that show us the intriguing aspects of elite interests, popular passions, and social forms of power in the language politics of India. His writings on this subject have continued to provide newer insights and perspectives. In his long-standing engagement with the subject of language and politics that Brass has been writing on for more than three decades, this is a fresh look at the phenomenon of language politics in independent India. In his understanding, the resolution of language question has been a success story in India.

Various themes can be included in the wider context of language and politics of India since independence. I take up a few of them here to highlight the complex character of this relationship. The essays contributed to this volume aim at expanding the field in a variety of ways. All of them approach the problematic of language politics using important methodological and analytical substantiations in the field.

[45]Ram Gopal, *Linguistic Affairs of India* (New York: Asia Publication House, 1966).

[46]A.R. Kamat, 'Ethno-Linguistic Issues in Indian Federal Context', *Economic and Political Weekly*, 4–21 June, 1980. Kamat calls the dominant regional languages of the states as the 'home state languages' particularly after the process of the reorganization of states was partially completed in 1956.

[47]The model of modernization and political development was applied to examine the phenomenon of linguistic conflicts and group loyalties in India in the decades of the 1950s and 1960s. The early writings of Paul Brass (1974), Jyotirindra Dasgupta (1970) and Baldev Raj Nayyar (1969) opened up this new field of study.

LINGUISTIC DIVERSITY AND ITS POLITICAL PREDICAMENT

India is considered to be one of the linguistically most diverse and complex societies in the world. This linguistic diversity was speculated to lead to the break-up of the country in the initial years immediately after independence.[48] Norman Brown considered language as 'an internally disruptive force in both India and Pakistan' serving a secondary function to more important and pressing needs such as economic development, industrial progress, and equality of economic and political opportunities in newly independent countries of South Asia.[49] Brown thinks that both language and religion have given a 'thin sort of unity to groups' and have played as divisive forces in the state-building exercises. On the other hand, rich and varied Indian multilingualism is at times celebrated to understand the specific cultural and historical ethos of multiculturalism and social pluralism in India.[50] It is almost impossible to count the total number of languages, mother tongues, dialects, and speech varieties spoken throughout the country. In order to understand the linguistic-cultural composition of India, the British colonial state used a number of enumerative strategies to classify and categorize the linguistic demography of the country. Censuses, gazetteers, linguistic survey reports, and ethnographical accounts recorded the linguistic diversity for purposes of colonial control over the vast and heterogeneous Indian social structure. This kind of ethnolinguistic classification of India has remained a subject of continuous debate among scholars contesting the enumerative strategies and techniques to map the linguistic diversity of the country. The varied concerns and constraints of colonial and postcolonial states have had an impact on the choice of enumerative tactics which result in tangible political and social effects.

[48]Selig Harrison, *India: The Most Dangerous Decades* (New Jersey: Princeton University Press, 1960).

[49]W. Norman Brown, 'Religion and Language as Forces Affecting Unity in Asia', *Annals of the American Academy of Political and Social Sciences*, 318, July 1958, pp. 8–17.

[50]Lachman Khubchandani's writings have continued to focus on this aspect from the vantage point of language as culture and its relevance for the nation-building exercise. He has interlinked the field of sociolinguistics within the broader field of language planning and policy while analysing the questions of multilingualism, minority language education, communicational pattern and mother tongue instruction, etc.

A quick glance through the official classification of the linguistic diversity will help us understand better the political economy and cultural power of various linguistic communities and the rationale behind state patronage or lack of it towards them. George Grierson's twelve volume project of *Linguistic Survey of India* published between 1903 and 1923 identified 179 languages and 544 dialects.[51] The number of mother tongues and languages has varied from census to census since 1881. The category of mother tongue has been the most controversial one since the 1961 census, which counted, 1,652 as the total number of mother tongues out of which 184 mother tongues had fewer than ten thousand speakers each.[52] The total number of languages listed in the census records since 1951 has not been uniform or exact because there has been a considerable loss of minority languages to the majority or dominant languages. The category of mother tongue, and its inclusion or exclusion from the census records, has created considerable discontent and anxiety in the minds of state officials, linguists, and the linguistic communities concerned. These, 1,652 mother tongues were grouped into 114 languages in the census report of 1991, showing a considerable reduction in the number of actual languages spoken, and thus reflecting the loss of minority languages to the majority languages.[53] Anvita Abbi

---

[51]Grierson's monumental survey, known as *Linguistic Survey of India* (*LSI*), was the first of its kind to be carried out in colonial India. The survey was used by subsequent census commissioners to compile adequate data on the linguistic classification of the country. It has been considered a storehouse of details about linguistic-cultural communities and their social characteristics. *LSI* has also remained a subject of scholarly contestation regarding its methodological and conceptual classification of languages and dialects used in early twentieth-century colonial India.

[52]Different census operations have used different enumerative criteria to count and classify the total number of mother tongues which have at times been conflated and combined with local regional dialects including caste, community, village, or even locality names. Furthermore, the minimum number of speakers, i.e., 10,000 for a mother tongue to be listed in the census, has also created much confusion and ambivalence in the categorization of mother tongues as well as languages. For example, the total number of mother tongues returned in the 1961 and 1971 censuses was about 3,000 which increased to 7,000 in 1981 and 10,000 in 1991. The 1961 census indicated a sharp decline from the first census of 1881 which had counted 3,000 mother tongues. There is no coherent and clear data available on the criteria used to distinguish mother tongues from languages, and therefore their numbers have been drastically varied in each of the decennial census records. For example, the 1991 census listed 1,576 mother tongues without explaining the reasons for the decline in the total number of mother tongues from the 1961 census.

[53]Anvita Abbi, *Vanishing Diversitites and Submerging Identities: An Indian Case* (Chapter 8, this volume).

counts more than 47 languages within the fold of the Hindi language alone. This clearly indicates the loss and absence of several minor and secondary languages which are not being counted separately from Hindi. The case of Maithili and its inclusion under Hindi language in two censuses of 1951 and 1961 is worth mentioning here.[54]

At the bottom are those languages whose speakers are less than 10,000 in number and thus omitted from the census enumeration by the government. It is the last category of languages that are on the verge of extinction and disappearance.[55] In Abbi's view, minority languages consist of non-scheduled languages, dialects of non-scheduled languages, and those languages represented by less than 10,000 speakers. It would not be wrong to say, as Oommen puts it, that languages listed in the census returns are 'expressions of socio-cultural affinities'.[56] Abbi's essay in this volume alerts us to the rapid decline of existing linguistic diversity in India as a result of larger processes of cultural homogenization and its impact on the social lives of linguistic communities affected. Tribal languages as well as the Andamanese languages deserve special attention in this regard.

For the first time, the government of India published the *Language Atlas of India* in the year 2004. As a first language atlas in independent India, the linguistic data was compiled to understand the notion of 'ethnicity' to measure the degree of bilingualism, trilingualism, and multilingualism through the actual number of mother tongue speakers in independent India. Based on the 1991 census, it counted the total number of languages to be 114. This census also recorded the total

---

[54]It is important to note the footnote from the 1951 census of volume 6, point 2A:28 which mentions that 'the small number shown against Maithili, Bhojpuri, Magahi ... should not be understood to mean that these dialects have gone out of vogue. In actual fact, vast majority of the population still used them but they referred to their mother tongue simply as Hindi'. Since the same method was used for the 1961 census also, the number of Maithili speakers went up to five million approximately. Even the next two censuses of 1971 and 1981 took Maithili speakers as Hindi speakers.

[55]Abbi, *Vanishing Diversities.*

[56]T.K. Oommen, *Nation, Civil Society and Social Movements: Essays in Political Sociology* (New Delhi: Sage Publications, 2004). Oommen thinks that listing of languages like Reddy Bhasha, Muslim Pahari, Ahiri Hindi, Rajputi, Ad Dharmis and Islami, etc., are simply expressions of ethnolinguistic, sociocultural and geolinguistic expressions. Similarly, the inclusion of caste name (Teli), sect name (Haridasi), place name (Bilaspuria), and immigrant status (Pardeshi) as mother tongues in the census records are actually variants of a dominant regional language, and thus affect the actual count of mother tongues in the census records.

number of mother tongues to be at 10,400, out of which 3,372 were counted as the rationalized names of mother tongues. Out of these, 1,576 were classified and the names of 1,796 mother tongues remained unclassified and relegated to 'others' mother tongue category.[57]

The People of India (POI) project counted 700 languages belonging to four dominant families.[58] The POI identified seventy-five major languages out of a total number of 325 languages used in Indian households. It is estimated that about 44 per cent of the population speaks Hindi as their mother tongue followed by Telugu, Bengali, Marathi, and Tamil ranking next with at least five per cent of these being used as mother tongues, followed by Urdu, Gujarati, Malayalam, Kannada, and Oriya, which are claimed to be spoken by two or three per cent of the population, and lastly Bhojpuri, Punjabi, and Assamese spoken by less than one per cent of the speakers. The POI reported that the number of mother tongues was decreasing rapidly because of the census practice of clubbing and conjoining minor and smaller languages into the dominant and well-known ones. If the 1881 census had reported about 237 languages (188 languages and forty-nine dialects), the 1991 census listed only 114 languages, whereas the ethnographic survey conducted by POI identified 325 languages spoken at home and for larger social communication. It has been suggested that about thirty-four languages have speakers exceeding 100,000. These include well-developed literary languages like Awadhi, Bhojpuri, Bundelkhandi, Chattisgarhi, Dhundhari, Garhwali, Harauti, Haryanavi, Kangri, Kumauni, Magahi, Maithili, Mewari, Pahari, and Rajasthani. Out of these 114 languages, forty-seven of them have been considered as dialects of Hindi and thus have contributed to the increasing strength of Hindi speakers in the country. In the 1951 census,

[57]*Language Atlas of India, 1991* (Delhi: Controller of Publications, Government of India, 2004).

[58]The People of India project was started under the auspices of the Anthropological Survey of India in 1985 by its director K.S.Singh, a well-known administrator and ethnographer. It compiled data of various kinds and grouped them together under various ethnological categories with their territorial spread in different states and union territories. The enumeration of mother tongues proved extremely helpful in knowing the exact status of languages, dialects and regional languages in the country. The total number of scripts counted by the POI was twenty-five with eleven major scripts of the languages listed in the ES and thirteen of them listed as minor scripts.

Hindi speakers were only 42 per cent, though it included forty-six dialects and speakers of Punjabi, Urdu, Hindustani, Maithili, Magahi, and Bhojpuri. Similarly, in the 1961 census, Hindi speakers constituted only 30 per cent of the total speakers as Maithili, Urdu, and Punjabi were listed separately. It was in 1981, after a hundred years of census operations in India, that attempts were made to differentiate 'mother tongue' from the household languages—a differentiation that made substantial difference to the actual number of languages recorded.

The POI project has put together data on linguistic communities and not just on the number of language speakers, the latter having been done regularly by decennial censuses from 1881 onwards. It identified 4,635 communities which, as cultural communities, give us a profile about the nature and form of the linguistic communities' spread throughout the country. The important finding of POI has been a refutation of any unproblematic correspondence established between linguistic groups and culturally homogeneous communities. In fact, linguistic heterogeneity exists among culturally homogeneous communities and vice versa. The dense and complex linguistic diversity existing in India defies any easy correspondence set up between language and culture that otherwise seems to be suggestive of linguistic ethnicity in multilingual societies. The POI data also show the territorial spread of various languages, degree of bilingualism, and an extensive mapping of the mother tongue distribution in the country. The linguistic heterogeneity, as K.S. Singh suggests, 'becomes an instrument of integration in a multi-language and multi-cultural situation'.[59] On the other hand, newspapers and periodicals are published in about ninety-seven languages, sixty-seven languages are used for primary education, national literacy mission imparts literacy in eighty languages, All India Radio broadcasts in 104 languages and twenty-two languages are used at the level of state administration. This kind of functional multilingualism has its own dynamics of elite and mass socialization, mobilization, and acculturation. An important question to pose here is whether multilingualism in India is socially and politically protected and promoted. The differences of languages

[59]K.S. Singh and S. Manoharan, *Languages and Scripts*, People of Indian Project, Vol. 9 (New Delhi: Oxford University Press, 1993), p. 31.

and cultures have been considered as illustrating 'pattern of interaction of living together separately' to characterize their multiplicities and diversities.[60] Annamalai suggests that the 'maintenance' of multilingualism among various linguistic communities through the roles of state, community, and the individual is not a question of the degree of learning or using many languages in one's daily life but reflective of the universe of linguistic repertoire that accounts for the essence of multilingualism. Language learning both formally (in the school) and socially (at home or workplace) of different languages (that is, English, Hindi, and dominant regional languages) is in a way tied up with the scale of social power, prestige, identity, and solidarity that individuals and communities feel part of.[61] The constant shift and switch between less dominant and more dominant languages is oftentimes indicative of political compulsions than simply an outcome of social volunteerism and autonomy to choose and use a particular language over another. Under such circumstances, language planning as an important social exercise gets politicized to an extent that languages and language communities are perceived in newer hierarchical relations that gradually affect their social, cultural and economic ties significantly. The choice of national language for purposes of broadcasting and cinema primarily was part of the national identity as David Lelyveld tracks the crucial historical journey of this subject in his essay. Sanitization of Hindustani by purging it of Arabic-Persian vocabulary and making it more sanskritized was a part of the larger process of linguistic sanskritization that the Indian state embarked on immediately after independence. The official policies of the All India Radio and the Ministry of Information and Broadcasting have been part of this project, which Lelyveld neatly summarizes. The media politics and policy have played a significant role in mandating the use of Hindi as a national language on the public radio system of India much before the liberalization of the media world began.

[60]Annie Montaut, 'Colonial Language Classification, Post-Colonial Language Movements, and the Grassroot Multilingualism Ethos in India', in Mushirul Hasan and Asim Roy (eds), *Living Together Separately: Cultural India in History and Politics* (New Delhi: Oxford University Press, 2005).

[61]E. Annamalai, *Managing Multilingualism in India: Political and Linguistic Manifestations* (New Delhi: Sage Publications, 2001).

LINGUISTIC STATE FORMATION IN INDEPENDENT INDIA

The state formation process in independent India began with the territorial reorganization of the then existing states. The reorganization of states in 1956 was based on the partial fulfilment of recommendations made in the States Reorganization Commission (SRC) set up in the year 1953. Even much before this, since the 1920s when Congress reorganized its Provincial Congress Committees on a linguistic basis, the demand for linguistic states as custodians of linguistic-cultural uniformity began to intensify. Nationalist leaders debated and argued passionately for redrawing the state boundaries corresponding with their regional linguistic and cultural homogeneity to promote regional solidarity as well as national unity.[62] The category of language began to be used politically but not without taking into account other criteria such as geographical contiguity, economic viability, sociocultural distinctiveness, and caste, region, and class alliances to redraw the territorial boundaries of the Indian state. The demands for linguistic states and their regional specification could not be completed for the entire country in 1956.[63] Since then, the reorganization process has continued with the latest addition of Chattisgarh, Jharkhand, and Uttarakhand states formed in the year 2000. Joseph Schwartzberg's essay on the linguistic reorganization of Indian states included in this volume delineates the historical trajectory of administrative changes introduced in response to the demands for linguistic states and their territorial reconfiguration after 1956. In his lucid analysis of the states reorganization process, he rightly draws attention to the phenomenon of linguistic minorities and its institutionalization as part of the state

---

[62]Nationalist leaders had varying views on this question. For Gandhi, the language question was integrally a part of *swaraj*. Nehru, Patel, Azad, Rajgopalachari, and several others intensely debated over the choice of a national-official language for independent India. See Asha Rani, 'Language as a Marker of Religious Difference', in Imtiaz Ahmad and Helmut Reifeld (eds), *Lived Islam in South Asia: Adaptation, Accommodation and Conflict* (Delhi: Social Science Press, 2004).

[63]There were dissenting voices among these nationalists, some of whom disapproved the idea of 'one language, one state', and preferred to accept a broader framework of 'one state, one language'. Ambedkar and Nehru shared this dilemma for some time. For elaboration of Ambedkar's critical views on this subject, see Asha Sarangi, 'Ambedkar and the Linguistic States: A Case for Maharashtra', *Economic and Political Weekly*, 14 January 2006.

rationale in independent India. His close scrutiny of the states reorganization reveals the intensities of newer hierarchies that emerged, with newer alliances formed around languages and ethnicities of caste, class, and region undermining the exclusive criterion of linguistic homogeneity as an unworkable solution to the territorial reconfiguration of India. The reorganization process was an exercise in initiating the democratic order in independent India. The colonial state's arbitrary separation and amalgamation of regions and boundaries was much opposed by people, giving rise to the demands for the formation of culturally unified states in various parts of the country.

The question of political identity of a region and state in India is intricately tied up with the historical development of Indian nationalism.[64] The language question in India is tied up with an idea of a 'community'—community of the users of language (s)—but, as Leaf suggests, it is not to be interpreted as a 'communal issue in the sense proscribed by the Indian Constitution ... rather the idea of community is widely used in secular politics'.[65] He suggests that this can link up the language issue with economic policies, common good, idea of a Sikh community and identity based on the notion of sacrifice and so on. In case of the Punjabi Suba, Leaf argues, 'the regions, that the language issue was separating, had quite different needs, and were obviously competing for priorities in development resources, economic policies, and foreign currency allocations. It was reasonable for the voters of Ropar, mainly farmers and those they depended upon and who depended on them in turn, to see their interests in division into two states along linguistic lines, with the concomitant creation of a government in a more uniform region sharing their local problems, using their religious literature as a means of teaching the official language in the schools and as a fund of ethical principles and historical precedents to refer to in working out solutions.'[66]

[64]In recent years, a number of writings have focused on this form of Indian nationalism in different parts of the country in late nineteenth-and early twentieth-century colonial India. Vasudha Dalmia (1998), Christopher King (1994), Veena Naregal (2001), Francesca Orsini (2002), Alok Rai (2000), and Harish Trivedi (2004) have analysed this question historically using important historical, literary, and political narratives.

[65]Murray J. Leaf, 'Economic Implications of the Language Issue: A Local View in Punjab', *The Journal of Commonwealth and Comparative Politics,* 14 (1), March 1976. Leaf situates the language movement of Punjabi Suba in the state of Punjab in independent India to illustrate this point.

[66]Ibid. p. 203.

What was true of Punjab was also true of several other states in other parts of the country. The partition of the country in 1947 into two nation-states was also a partition of two languages—Hindi and Urdu—whose national identities were more firmly asserted with India and Pakistan as states. The category of language aroused passions and violence of emotions. Nationalists feared that Hindi's dominance could communalize the language question, and hence cautioned alertness to the linguistic demands emerging from different parts of the country. With the formation of Andhra Pradesh on the basis of language, the agenda of linguistic states had already been settled to some extent.[67] The case of the formation of Andhra Pradesh clearly brought out the interrelationship between language and political identity. The case of Andhra, according to R.V.R. Chandrasekhara Rao, in terms of its integration with Telengana could be seen to be like the problem of the Punjab-Haryana integration.[68] In his account, the idea of the political identity of Andhra was primarily based on the recognition of the Telegu language, which had to be reconciled with the dominant position earlier taken by the Urdu language in the state.

The case of the Kannada identity is intimately tied up with the politics of culture, community, and linguistic nationalism of the early twentieth-century modern India. This reveals to us the relationship between Kannada nationalism and Indian nationalism, between Lingayats and Kannadigas, and the construction of an identity of modern Karnataka as different from princely Mysore. In this, the questions of caste, script, and dialectal differences were also involved while choosing the languages of the upper-caste men of the Mysore region for purposes of standardization.[69] Janaki Nair's excellent essay on the Kannada language question alongside the emergence of Kannada nationalism points out the hierarchies of caste, region, class, and labour to understand the distinctiveness of Kannada identity as not simply derived from the princely state of Mysore but also shaped by the Bombay-Karnataka

[67]Prakash Karat examined this by considering the language and nationality question as being interconnected particularly in the case of Tamil Nadu politics. See Prakash Karat, *Language and Nationality Politics in India* (Delhi: Orient Longman, 1973).

[68]R.V.R. Chandrasekhara Rao, 'Conflicting Roles of Language and Regionalism in an Indian State: A Case Study of Andhra Pradesh', in David Taylor and Malcolm Yapp (eds), *Political Identity in South Asia* (London: Curzon Press, 1979).

[69]V.B. Tharakeshwar, 'Translating Nationalism: The Politics of Language and Community', *Journal of Karnataka Studies*, 1, November 2003–April 2004.

region in early twentieth-century colonial India. Nair's persuasive argument clearly unfolds the complex historical dynamics underlying the coexistence of Kannada linguistic nationalism within a hegemonic Tamil nationalism during this period. Even in 1991, the dispute over the Cauvery waters, which resulted in violent attacks on Tamil labourers and landholders in parts of southern Karnataka, the relationship between language and labour was clearly evident.

The field of cultural politics has often centred on the language question in various ways. The phenomena of NTR in Andhra Pradesh, MGR in Tamil Nadu, and of Rajkumar in Karnataka indicate powerful uses of language and its symbolic significance in the cinematic and political life of their particular societies. Guha suggests that 'Rajkumar embodied the pride of Kannadigas'.[70] On the other hand, linguistic affinity sometimes can potentially promote a more inclusive and secular orientation since different religious groups can possibly belong to the same linguistic community.[71] Language and territory, Oommen thinks, provide the central bases for the formation of modern state systems as it is through language that the communicative network is established without which human beings cannot relate to one another. But the complex overlap between linguistic and religious differences has also contributed to the communalization of linguistic identity as in the instances of Hindi-Urdu, Punjabi-Hindi, and Urdu-Bengali conflicts in early twentieth-century modern India.

The criterion of linguistic homogeneity was considered to be most appropriate for redrawing the boundaries of the existing states immediately after independence. But such a territorial re-demarcation could not use the principle of linguistic homogeneity uniformly throughout the country. Brass suggests that the boundaries of the southern states were organized in close conformity with traditional linguistic regions.[72] The border disputes between neighbouring states,

---

[70]Ramachandra Guha, 'Passions of the Tongue', *The Hindu,* April 2006.

[71]T.K. Oommen, *Nation, Civil Society and Social Movements.* Oommen considers that human communities are primarily linguistic communities. He thinks that it is due to the linguistic pluralism that the possibility of containing inter-linguistic conflicts is higher as compared with interreligious conflicts. Since a particular religious identity can be linguistically plural, all religious communities, in his view, are drawn from a multiplicity of linguistic communities (p. 104).

[72]Paul R. Brass, *The Politics of India Since Independence* (Cambridge: Cambridge University Press, 1990).

which earlier seemed to be linguistic-cultural in origin, began to take more complicated forms after the reorganization process was over. Whether language ideology would remain as sustainable as religion and caste based ideologies was something to wait for. Kaviraj in his essay engages and argues well about the pluralities of worldview inherent in a multilingual society like India, where achieving cultural homogenization through the primacy of one language is not possible or even desirable. The linguistic identification of people with their regions, Kaviraj points out, was a sign of a democratic upsurge in independent India.

Indian Constitution and the Language Question

The Constituent Assembly debated for almost six weeks over the choice of national and/or official language (s) in independent India.[73] It witnessed controversies with respect to the questions of link language, official language, and the choice and retention of the national language of independent India. After independence, the language of the nation had to be institutionalized and ritualized as national and/or official language as a mark of national sovereignty.[74] The famous Munshi-Ayyangar formula providing for Hindi in the Devanagari script to be an official language of the Indian union along with the continuation of the English language for a period of fifteen years from the commencement of the Constitution was a result of this intense debate.[75] Ambedkar said that 'there was no article which proved more controversial than article 115 which deals with the (Hindi) question.

[73]After a prolonged discussion, when the question was put, the vote was 78 against 78. The tie could not be resolved. When the question was put to the Assembly once more, the result was 77 against 78 for Hindi. Hindi won its place as national language by one vote only.

[74]Mahadev L. Apte, 'Multilingualism in India and Its Socio-Political Implications: An Overview', in William O'Barr (ed.), *Language and Politics* (Paris: Mouton, 1976).

[75]It was a historic moment for the Hindi language which had only 78 votes in favour and 77 against it. The one vote margin has been seen as a sign of disapproval for Hindi more than any undisputed victory for it. The national-official language status accorded to Hindi in the Constitution gave way to considerable resentment among non-Hindi states, particularly the Tamil language speakers. Subsequently, the Official Language Act of 1963 stipulated that English would remain alongside Hindi as an official language. The Official Language Amendment Act of 1967 guaranteed that English would continue as an associate official language indefinitely with the provision that the state governments, if they desire, have a veto power to displace English by Hindi as an official and link language.

No article produced more opposition. No article, more heat.'[76] Austin, in his classic work on the Indian Constitution, referred to this confusion and dilemma existing among various leaders in the Constituent Assembly debates. In a detailed account of the proceedings, Austin characterizes the language solution as a 'half-hearted compromise'. The debate continued with contesting positions taken on the choice of national and official languages particularly with regard to Hindi, Hindustani, and English. The language question in the Assembly debates continued to be overshadowed by the effects of partition, and, in Austin's words, 'problems of language were an everyday affair.'

Various language provisions of the Indian Constitution are contained in Part Seventeen in the Articles 343–51. Article 343 declares that the official language of the Indian union would be Hindi in the Devanagari script. It is Article 345 that allows different states of the Indian union to have their own official language acts to adopt some language 'to be used for all or any of the official purposes' of the states. Here, 'language in use' means that at least 15 per cent of the population should be speaking that language in the state. The North-Eastern states and some union territories have declared English as their official language under this article. If we read through these various constitutional provisions related to language rights and representation, we can understand the question of linguistic minorities and their predicament in the Indian political structure. For example, Article 350 states that the language for grievances could be followed using provisions enshrined under article 350(A), which was inserted by an amendment act of 1956, directing the states to 'provide adequate facilities for instruction in mother tongue at the primary stage of education to children belonging to linguistic minority groups'. This article states that any representation for the redress of any grievance to any officer or authority of the central or state government can be made in any of the languages used in the state or in the central government. Article 350(B) provides the appointment of a special officer for linguistic minorities to submit special report to the president and to submit and table an annual report to the parliament. In consonance with it, the office of the Commissioner for Linguistic

---

[76]Quoted in Selig Harrison, *India: The Most Dangerous Decades*, p. 282.

Minorities was created in July 1957. Article 351 states that 'it shall be the duty of the union to promote the spread of Hindi language ... so that it may serve as a medium of expression for all the elements of the composite culture of India'. Article 29 of the Indian Constitution confers on cultural and linguistic minorities the right to conserve their languages and cultures. It is under this very article that scheduled tribes are provided constitutional protection to preserve their languages, dialects, and cultures. Furthermore, under this article, it is ensured that the state would abstain from imposing any particular linguistic or cultural identity on them. Article 29 has to be read along with Article 350(A) which provides for facilities of instruction through the mother tongue at the primary stage of education.

Regarding the administrative uses of a language, the Indian Constitution has also provided certain safeguards. Articles 345 and 346 provide that the 'legislature of a State may by law adopt any one or more of the languages in use in the State or Hindi as the language or languages to be used for all or any of the official purposes of that State'. It also stipulates that 'provided that until the Legislature of the State otherwise provides by law, the English language shall continue to be used for those official purposes within the State for which it was being used immediately before the commencement of this Constitution'. Thus Article 346 clearly states that 'if two or more States agree that the Hindi language should be the official language for communication between such States, that language may be used for such communication'. Furthermore, Article 347 has 'special provisions to be made by the President, if he is satisfied that a substantial proportion of the population of a State desire the use of any language spoken by them to be recognized by that State, direct that such language shall be officially recognized throughout that State or any part thereof for such purposes as he may specify.' For the third rung of the administration where people of a state have to correspond with the state, the Constitution has an Article 350 which stipulates the provision that any citizen can submit a petition to the state or central government in any language used in the territory under the state government or in the case of the central government 'in any language spoken in the country'.[77]

[77]D.D. Basu, *Shorter Constitution of India* (New Delhi: Prentice-Hall of India Private Limited, 1996).

The Indian Constitution adopted several safeguards to protect linguistic minorities in the country. Articles 350 (A) and 350 (B) were adopted in addition to the earlier Articles 29(1), 30, 347, and 350 in order to preserve the interests of the minorities. Article 29(1) clearly guarantees the right of minorities to conserve their cultural as well as linguistic traditions. The first clause of Article 30 guarantees all minorities, based on religion or language, the right to establish and administer educational institutions of their own in order to preserve their linguistic and/or cultural heritage. The second clause of Article 30 prohibits the state from discriminating against minority educational institutions. Thus minorities are allowed to secure state funds for their educational institutions. Article 347 allows the use of minority languages for official purposes. Accordingly, a state should be recognized as unilingual only if one language group constitutes 70 per cent or more of the total population. Moreover, where there is a minority of over 30 per cent of the total population, the state should be recognized as bilingual for administrative purposes. A similar principle applies at the district level.[78] It is under this constitutional provision that Urdu has been declared by law a second official language in the states of Bihar, Uttar Pradesh, Andhra Pradesh, and Delhi.

The peculiar predicament of the Urdu language in independent India has been a result of populist political agenda adopted in different states from time to time. Selma Sonntag probes into the dilemma of political identity marked out in the political programmes in two states of Bihar and Uttar Pradesh in the 1980s and 1990s. Even though both states have the largest concentration of Urdu speakers, they have followed different routes to its adoption as the second official language, primarily in the realms of education and administration. She rightly argues how the Urdu issue remained more contentious in Uttar Pradesh than in Bihar for reasons of political identity forged over issues of language, religion, and community identities. On the other hand, in the state of Jammu and Kashmir, Urdu has been declared an official language of the state despite the speakers of Kashmiri being in majority in the state. Warikoo's essay in this volume about the language and

[78]Rajeshwari V. Pandharipande, 'Minority Matters: Issues in Minority Languages in India', *MOST: Journal of Multicultural Societies*, 4 (2), 2002, (Paris: UNESCO).

politics in Jammu and Kashmir engages with this aspect, bringing out the contestation over language as a marker of cultural and religious differences between Hindus and Muslims. In this case, religion and not language has been a 'mobilizing factor' in the demands for state autonomy. The notion of 'ture Kashmiriat' woven around the linguistic identity of Kashmiri has been marginalized. Several other languages have also been considered either regional or minor languages of the state. Warikoo argues how Kashmiri has been displaced from a position of significance from schools, administration, and even the judiciary. Such a change in 'linguistic geography', in his view, is symptomatic of the 'displaced minority of Hindus disinherited from their own language and dialect'—a phenomenon of ethnic cleansing as other linguistic identities such as Pahari and Gujari have not been recognized in the multilingual state of Jammu and Kashmir.

EIGHTH SCHEDULE: A CASE OF POLITICAL COMPROMISE

Since its inclusion in the Indian Constitution in 1950, the ES has been seen as a powerful source to provide formal and constitutional recognition to various languages and their communities in the spheres of administration, education, economy, and social status. Languages of the ES acquire a certain degree of cultural capital since they play a crucial role in social mobility. To begin with, there were only fourteen languages in the schedule recognized as the official languages of the Indian state. Numerous other languages, which were spoken by a large majority of people and which had a well-established canon and literary traditions, were not included in the schedule. On the other hand, Sanskrit not spoken widely and limited only to a few hundred people was included in the ES. Sindhi too was added in 1967 after a sustained movement for it was carried on for several years. The English language, though made an associate official language in 1967, has not been included in the schedule. The move to include English in the ES in 1959 was resisted on the grounds of English not being an Indian language. Nehru too considered this move inappropriate. It was during the debate on the Official Languages Amendment Bill, 1967, that a member of parliament pointed out that 'the languages in the schedule should be the languages of the country, languages used for communication, for conduct of business affairs'.[79] Several linguists have pointed out that the ES covers more than 90 per cent of the total population of India because the majority of languages in the schedule belong to Indo-Aryan and Dravidian families.

At present, there are twenty-two languages in the schedule. The demand from various language groups for inclusion in the ES has been increasing. Manipuri, Konkani, and Nepali were added in 1992 through the Seventy-One Amendment. Again, in February 2004, three more languages—Dogri, Maithili, and Santhali—were included in the ES after a series of long and sustained cultural and social movements carried out by leaders for each of these languages since the early twentieth-century onward. The important question to consider in case of the ES is the state rationale and criteria used to include more languages in it. Is it the linguistic specificity of a geographical area, numerical majority of language speakers, rich cultural past, or classical and standardized form of a language that determines the inclusion of a particular language or its variant in the ES? How do we explain the exclusion of Rajasthani, Braj, Bhojpuri, or Awadhi from or inclusion of Sindhi, Sanskrit, and Konkani in the ES?[80] Bodo, Bhotia, Lepcha, Mizo, Nicobari, Sambhalpuri, and Tulu language groups have been agitating for their inclusion in the ES. Now that the Bodo people have attained an Autonomous Council and the Mizo language has the backing of the state, there is demand for the inclusion of Bodo and Mizo in the ES. The numerical majority as a criterion for inclusion of a language in the ES does not seem to be a sufficient criterion. The new demands for the inclusion of Rajasthani, Bhojpuri, and Pahari in the ES have to be evaluated properly, since they are subdivided into Marwari, Mewari, Mewati, Mandiali, Chambiali, Sirmouri, Himachali, and Kulvi. D.P. Pattanayak has even argued that owing to the inconsistency in the criteria used for the inclusion of languages in the ES, it should be abolished.[81] In his view, languages listed in this schedule have 'relevance

[79]Proceedings of the Official Languages Amendment Bill, 1967, p. 6092.

[80]R.S. Gupta, Anvita Abbi, and Kailash S. Aggarwal (eds), *Language and the State: Perspectives on the Eighth Schedule* (New Delhi: Creative Books, 1995).

[81]D.P. Pattanayak, 'The Eighth Schedule: A Linguistic Perspective', in Gupta, Abbi, and Aggarwal (eds), *Language and the State: Perspectives on the Eighth Schedule* (New Delhi: Creative Books, 1995).

for drawing up the state boundaries, declaration of official languages within a State, and for use as media of communication at different levels'. He, therefore, thinks that 'article 344 (1) being inoperative and article 351 recommendatory, the intents of which can be best achieved by listing languages prevalent in the country, the ES itself has become anachronistic'.[82] Sanskrit, Sindhi, Nepali, and Urdu are not limited to any territorial boundaries of a state. Despite the resistance to Sanskrit's inclusion in the ES by some members in the Constituent Assembly, Sanskrit was included, as Sumathi Ramaswamy shows in her essay, for nationalizing the Indian past and its continued presence in the new Indian nation. Drawing her argument on the close reading of the Sanskrit Commission set up in 1956, she elucidates and cogently sets up the logic of the relationship between language and nation in independent India. Ramaswamy's essay explains the historical trajectory of Sanskrit with the life and times of the making of the Indian nation.

LINGUISTIC MINORITIES

The category of linguistic minorities in India has to be understood within the hierarchies of caste, class, region, religion, and gender relations. More specifically, it is the complex relationship between caste and language, characteristic of various tribal languages and their communities. Tribal languages as recorded in the census are spoken by less than 10,000 people.[83] Conceptually, the notion of tribal languages is considered a case of minority languages. Tribal languages have been in contact with the dominant regional languages for centuries and have thus been affected by them in their vocabularies and speech forms. To understand them properly, as Emeneau argued,

[82]Ibid., p. 53.

[83]Though the census uses the limit of 10,000 speakers for recognizing a language in its list of languages, such a classification is based purely on numbers and does not take into account the social, cultural, economic, and political capital of languages. It also ignores the fact as to why and how some languages and their communities, despite being large in number, may be perceived as belonging to the minority communities. Languages like Urdu, Sindhi, and Sanskrit can be included in this list. Since tribal languages are displaced and marginalized from the domains of administration, economy, education, and law, they are clearly a case of linguistic minorities.

would require a deep ethnographic analysis and understanding about the relationship between tribes and castes in India. The Indian Constitution refers to minorities as 'based on religion or language'. There are four articles in the Constitution which protect the rights of linguistic minorities. Only one of these articles specifically refers to the protection of the mother tongue. Articles 20, 30, and 350 refer to languages and the rights of linguistic minorities to preserve their 'distinct language, script or culture'. No separate attention has been paid to tribal languages which are included within the category of scheduled tribe communities defined under Article 342 of the Constitution safeguarding the interests of scheduled tribes in general.

The tribal movements of various kinds in India have had a strong linguistic dimension to them. Jharkhand, Naga, Mizo, and Khasi movements have tried to define their agenda of ethnic identity through strong linguistic dimensions. An important question that needs to be asked is what is tribal in the tribal languages? Can we delineate their specific geolinguistic locations which can clearly mark their differences from non-tribal languages? Annamalai suggests that the 'term "tribal" in tribal languages does not have any linguistic connotation'[84], and, rather, it needs to be understood within the larger cultural, social, and historical context which defines and delimits the notion of a tribal community. Tribal languages are oftentimes understood as being closer to dialects or speech variety and not neatly codified or regulated by grammar as in a rigid system of rules. Such a view of the tribal languages is wrong and easily misses the complexities of the scripts and grammars of the tribal languages. Annamalai has argued persuasively how tribal languages have added to India's linguistic diversity genetically.[85] The distinction between scheduled and non-scheduled languages among the tribal languages in the census records makes the case of tribal languages more complicated in terms of their legal and administrative classification, identification, and

[84]E. Annamalai, 'Questions on the Linguistic Characteristics of the Tribal Languages of India', in Anvita Abbi (ed.), *Languages of Tribal and Indigenous People of India* (Varanasi: Motilal Banarsidas Publishers Pvt Ltd, 1997).

[85]Ibid., p. 17. In Annamalai's views, out of the four language families that India has, Austro-Asiatic and Sino-Tibetan languages are mostly tribal. These tribal languages share certain commonalities with one another.

characterization. Tribal languages also perform the task of 'either bridge or buffer between the more powerful politico-cultural entities'.[86] Tribal communities like Bhil, Bhuyan, Bhumij, Muriyas, Gond, Malpaharia, Lodha have either given up their languages or accepted the dominant regional languages for their survival. Kui, a Dravidian language of Orissa, and the Kurux—a tribal language spoken in four states of Bihar, Madhya Pradesh, Orissa, and West Bengal—have shifted towards the dominant languages in these states.[87] Speakers of Kurux have tried to shift to other dominant regional languages such as Hindi, Oriya, and Bengali. Anvita Abbi suggests that 'tribal languages should not be equated with primitive or underdeveloped languages'.[88] Different states have followed different programmes to initiate assimilationist, interventionist, pluralist, reformist, or even segregationist policies with respect to the tribal languages.

Another important question is the choice of script and writing system of the tribal languages. The Bodo community initially accepted the script used for Bengali and Assamese till the Assam agitation made them think that acceptance of the script of a dominant language was a form of domination. They demanded to use the Roman script, which in turn agitated the Assamese, who wanted to retain their linguistic hegemony over the Bodos. Finally, at the instance of the central government, the Bodos were asked to accept the Devanagari script as a kind of political solution. There are controversies whether Saurashtri and Badaga should be written using the Tamil script, and whether languages like Konkani and Santhali written in five scripts each should be rewritten using a single script. The case of Sindhi here is noteworthy to understand the conflicting claims over the choice of a script for a language which has multireligious and

[86]B.K. Roy Burman, 'Distribution of the Scheduled Tribes of India: An Exploratory Geo-Cultural Appraisal', in A. Chandra Shekar (ed.), *Economic and Socio-Cultural Dimensions of Regionalisation: An Indo-USSR Collaborative Study* (New Delhi: Office of the Registrar General, 1972).

[87]S. Imtiaz Hasnain, 'Linguistic Consequences of Ethnicity and Nationalism', in Mrinal Miri (ed.), *Tribal India: Continuity and Change in Tribal Society* (Shimla: IIAS, 1993).

[88]Anvita Abbi, 'Introduction', in Anvita Abbi (ed.), *Languages of Tribal and Indigenous People of India* (Varanasi: Motilal Banarsidas Publishers Pvt Ltd, 1997). There has not been a consensus on the exact number of tribal languages spoken. K.S.Singh in his People of India project counted 449 languages spoken by various tribal communities.

multicultural speakers.[89] Like Sindhi, which should be written either in Devanagari or Perso-Arabic script, Konkani can be written in Devanagari, Kannada, Malayalam, or Roman scripts.[90] Similarly, Santhali, spoken in four states of Madhya Pradesh, Orissa, Bengal, and Bihar, can be written in Devanagari, Oriya, and Bengali scripts or the Roman script. This makes the task of recognizing one script for one language particularly difficult when the language has already entered the ES. Similarly, there has been contestation over the choice of script for the Manipuri language—whether it should have a Meitei, Bengali, or Roman script.

Some regions have developed local creolized and hybrid forms of languages. Sadri, Bhojpuri, Magahi, Mundari in Bihar and Madhya Pradesh, Halabi—a mixture of Chhatisgarhi, Marathi, and Gondi in Madhya Pradesh and Maharashtra, Nagamese, hybrid of Assamese and Sylhet Bengali are a few such cases. The textbooks in predominant Santhali schools are in Bengali, though Santali textbooks have been introduced in a number of missionary and other unrecognized schools in different districts for teaching Santhali as a language subject. In Bihar, on the recommendations of the Tribes Advisory Council, a committee was appointed to prepare readers and primers in Santhali, Oraon, Mundari, Ho, and Kharia languages.[91] The fate of Dangi, tribal language of the adivasi district of Dang, had to establish its own linguistic identity and not just be either a dialect of Marathi or Gujarati after the two states of Maharashtra and Gujarat were reorganized in 1960. Both Marathi and Gujarati had been introduced as medium of instruction in Dang adivasi districts after independence. Bili and Dangi are two adivasi languages that have received some attention in the last few years from the state government.[92] Xaxa draws attention to the residual

[89]D.P. Pattanayak, *Language and Social Issues* (Mysore: Central Institute of Indian Languages, 1981).

[90]The question of the choice of a script has been a very contentious one in India, and several languages and their communities of speakers have identified themselves with specific scripts as symbolic of their historical, cultural, and religious identifications. It is in this regard that the Konkani speakers using Malayalam script are demanding special status for themselves.

[91]A number of non-governmental organizations have been working towards preparing school primers and textbooks in tribal and minority languages. The *Sanhtal Paharia Seva Mandal* of Bihar has published a set of books in Santhali and in Devanagari scripts. The *Christian Mission* of Santhal Parganas has published a large number of books in Santhali.

[92]Achyut Yagnik, 'My Mother Tongue', *Seminar*, 470, October 1998.

understanding of tribes as a conceptual category, and points out that the distinctive ethnic characteristics of tribes have been primarily linguistic-cultural in nature. However, 'this aspect of the labeling of tribals has been overlooked in sociological discourse on tribes'.[93]

LANGUAGE AND EDUCATION: INTERLINKAGES

The language question has to be contextualized within the larger domain of education, since the latter is an active site of linguistic ideology production and its consolidation. In a multilingual country, the choice of learning through a particular language is not always freely available but subject to the hierarchies of class, caste, race, gender, and region. The British colonial state institutionalized teaching of the English language through a formal educational structure. Learning to read and write in a particular language is to imbibe and inculcate the worldview of that language and its community. The question of first and second languages has been a question of much contestation in a multilingual educational and cultural context.[94] Probal Dasgupta illustrates how the modernization of polity and democratization of political culture in postcolonial India have been associated with the continuity of the English language and its cultural hegemony in multiple spheres of daily life.[95] The first two education commissions— the Radhakrishnan Commission of 1947 and the Kothari Commission (1964–6)—recommended that Indian languages should be the media of instruction at the level of universities so that the gap between English-knowing and non-English-knowing people is minimized. The close relationship between language and education has been confirmed in the Constitution itself. Article 51(A) of the Constitution enjoins

[93]Virginius Xaxa, 'Politics of Language, Religion and Identity: Tribes in India', *Economic and Political Weekly*, 26 March 2005.

[94]The policy makers in India have not paid sufficient attention to the historical and political uses of the term first or second language. The term second language indicates a kind of formal scaling of any language which is not the first native language learnt after birth.

[95]Probal Dasgupta, *The Otherness of English: India's Auntie Tongue Syndrome* (New Delhi: Sage Publications, 1993). A number of works in the recent past have focused on the relationship between the colonial and postcolonial predicament of English language teaching in independent India. Writings of Svati Joshi (1994), Rajeshwari Sunder Rajan (1993), and Gauri Viswanathan (1989) have been particularly noteworthy in this field.

upon the citizens of India to uphold the composite culture of India. The Indian Constitution also guarantees all citizens the right to 'conserve' their language, and all religious and linguistic minorities to have the right to establish and administer educational institutions of their choice. On the other hand, the English language was initially considered unfit to be a national or official link language, as Nehru, too, said that 'it had no relation to the problem of mass education and culture'. In order to provide facilities and encouragement for reading, writing, and teaching in the minority languages, the Education Ministry in consultation with the states formulated a three language formula (TLF), which consisted of mother tongue or regional language, official language of the union, or the associate official language of the union so long as it exists, and a modern Indian or foreign language not covered under either of these two and other than used as the medium of instruction. It provides that Hindi, English, and modern Indian languages, preferably one of the southern languages, should be taught in the Hindi-speaking states, whereas Hindi, English, and a regional language should be taught in the non-Hindi speaking states at various stages of the school education. This has worked adversely against those languages which are not designated as regional languages such as Sindhi, Urdu, and Sanskrit. TLF provides choices only from among the languages listed in the ES. An important aspect in the TLF is to what extent it increases the burden of learning languages by the linguistic minorities whose language is not included in the educational curricula of the state. Minorities will have to learn one more language in addition to the three languages. Different states and union territories accepted the norm of the three language formula differently.

LANGUAGE AND POLITICS: A LONG VIEW

There are multiple domains where language and politics interact. One such domain is the relationship between law and language in a multilingual society. The complex network of relationships existing among lawyers, litigants, and defendants affect the actual procedural functioning of legal process in the Indian courts. The difficult question that Kidder poses for his query is 'whether and in what ways linguistic diversity influences their structure and functioning'.[96] In this context, one has to examine carefully to what extent the English language is used by the litigants and judges as their linguistic capital in the law courts and offices at various levels. How does the use of the English language reinforce elitism, denigrating and misrecognizing the value of vernaculars in the legal processes? Bailey, however, emphasizes the significance of verbal behaviours, linguistic codes and communication in the institutional sites of courts, councils, and committees.[97] He locates how this kind of frequent code switching and shifting in language forms and patterns was indicative of the shifts in power and legitimacy in the state of Orissa. The gradation, as Kidder suggests, between high court and *munsif* courts in India is also indicative of the gradation of language usages. Kidder further uses the twin terms 'linguistic and legalistic blackout' as being complementary processes.[98] English in this context, he tells us, becomes 'the language of mystification of elite discourse', and 'an adjunct of elitism'.[99]

Another important field of study within the language politics is the relationship between language and caste. The subject of distinctiveness of dalit literature and its deep association with dalit expressions and articulations has emerged as central to most of the dalit writings in the past two decades. Its uniqueness has much to do with a distinct literary tradition based on the historical trajectory and genealogy of caste oppressions in the lives of the dalits themselves. Some have even argued that the question of dalit hegemony needs to be recast in terms of the linguistic control over English, and not simply in the use of dominant regional languages, to counter the effects of Sanskrit and other classical languages used as forms of domination.[100] The use and appropriation of the English language is seen as a new way of going beyond the caste oppression and exclusion on the part

[96]Robert L. Kidder, 'Language and Litigation in South India', in William M.O'Barr and Jean F.O'Barr (eds), *Language and Politics* Kidder uses Banglore as the site of his intensive research on the relationship between law and language in the years of 1969–70.

[97]F.G. Bailey, '"I-Speech" in Orissa' in *Language and Politics*, O'Barr (ed.).

[98]Kidder, *Language and Litigation*, p. 240.

[99]Ibid., pp. 249–50.

[100]Probal Dasgupta, 'Sanskrit, English and Dalits', *Economic and Political Weekly*, 15 April 2000.

of the oppressed social groups. The English language is perceived, by the dalit intelligentsia, to be capable of providing a sense of solidarity to establish a communicative network among them across regions and states. On the other hand, we also see the growing importance of the English language as its becoming a natural ally of the globalizing world and new middle class. The English language becomes cultural capital in this global world. Joshua Fishman argues about the 'new linguistic order' combining both globalization and localization of languages throughout the world in our contemporary times. It is imperative to resist the hegemony of the global language, English, on the one hand, and to spread and maintain linguistic heterogeneity in terms of the survival and protection of smaller languages on the other.[101] The conflict between global and national languages will not minimize the fight for the recognition and rights of vernacular languages which, as David Laitin has suggested, 'will use all political resources to stem the tide of globalization', particularly in the newly independent and postcolonial states that continue to live with 'the maintenance of multilingual repertoires'.[102] The conflict between metropolitan versus vernacular India, as Sheth describes in his essay included in this volume, is indicative of the conflict over resources, interests, and rights between English and vernacular elites in the democratic polity of India. It is not simply, in Sheth's views, a conflict of languages but conflict in worldviews and in ideologies of the agenda of development in the nation-building exercise. He rightly points out that it is not simply a question of intra-elite conflict but the divide between India and Bharat, and between languages of modernity (English) and tradition (indigenous languages) since the time of independence. Modern Indian political discourses are multivocal, articulated in languages of English, Hindi, regional, vernacular, and indigenous languages—all of which inhabit distinct worldviews.

The relationship between gender and language is another complex arena where the interface between language and power is played out in a more complex and intricate manner. Historians, anthropologists, and cultural theorists have tried to analyse the gendered discourses of

[101]Joshua A. Fishman, 'The New Linguistic Order', *Foreign Policy*, Winter 1998–9.

[102]David Laitin, 'The Game Theory of Language Regimes', *International Political Science Review*, 14 (3), 1993.

the language question in various European and non-European contexts. The uses of rhetoric, satire, symbols, metaphors, and icons are played out to illustrate this relationship. As a new field of study, this requires unique and even newer methodological and analytical tools to examine the historical narratives and texts of gendered linguistic discourses. The discourse of linguistic nationalism in India has been a gendered discourse, identifying language with woman in the images of mother, deity, goddess, and wife. Sumathi Ramaswamy examines this aspect of the language politics in a conceptually nuanced manner by looking at the symbolic iconisation of land and language in the form of motherland, and its articulation in the form of *Tamilttay* (Tamil Goddess) in early twentieth-century colonial India. The battle was actually between Tamil and Hindi as two rival languages.

In the last two decades, in the disciplines of mainly history, sociology, and political science, language as an identity marker has been examined to situate the discourses of ethnicity, culture, and community as one that is a mutually sustainable and reproducible one. The linguistic repertoire of a community is clearly an indicator of its multifaceted identity preserved in its sociolinguistic life.[103] T.K. Oommen argues that language is the 'most appropriate basis for the cultural renewal of a multinational polity like India'.[104] He suggests that to 'establish an uncritical relationship between language and religion in case of India such as Tamil with Dravidian Hinduism, Sanskrit with Aryan Hinduism, Pali with Buddhism, Urdu with Islam, Punjabi with Sikhism and English with Christianity is to undermine the diversity of social relations and identities based on the categories of religion and language in a heterogeneous plural society like India'. The language question is tied up with the community identity and the political formation of it in numerous ways.[105]

The linguistic politics has to be contextualized within the larger phenomenon of linguistic nationalism and its political economy. It, at

[103]Sonia Ryang, 'How to Do or Not Do Things with Words: The Case of Koreans in Japan', *Asian Ethnicity*, 6 (3), (Oct.) 2005.

[104]T.K. Oommen, *Nation, Civil Society and Social Movements*.

[105]I have discussed this in detail with regard to the Hindi-Urdu linguistic community identity formation in colonial north India in my Phd thesis. See Asha Rani, *Politics of Linguistic Identity and Community Formation in Colonial North India: 1900–1947* (Department of Political Science, University of Chicago, 2002).

times, masquerades as different forms of cultural nationalism. Language conflicts in various parts of the world have tried to imagine the notion of a political community through a long process of political mobilization, at times resulting in different forms of linguistic separatism.[106] Swaan suggests that the political economy and political sociology of language can possibly provide an analytical framework for understanding the multilingual social order better.[107] The 'politics of language' and 'language of politics' are intertwined and densely overlapping in multilingual countries where linguistic conflicts have intensified, from time to time, over the hegemonic control of English versus indigenous languages.[108] There have been numerous riots and violent incidents over support and opposition to the English and Hindi languages as the link languages in independent India. As lingua franca, they can be used by both elite groups and the common people.[109] It is important to understand the complex nature of state politics and its diversity through the standpoint of the 'language question', and to further comprehend the field and arenas of scholarly attention on it. The phenomenon of linguistic nationalism needs to be examined as a form of political nationalism in Indian historiography, because language is much more than simply a descriptive marker of the identity of community, ethnicity, race, region, state, and nation.

[106]Ronald F. Inglehart and Margaret Woodward, 'Language Conflicts and Political Community', *Comparative Studies in Society and History*, 10, October–July 1967–8. Inglehart and Woodward take into account cases of India, Canada, Belgium, and Nigeria to illustrate the point that 'in the early phases of social mobilization and economic modernization, linguistic nationalism was seized upon by reactionary elements (such as the feudal nobility) as a means by which they might isolate themselves from cosmopolitan influences'. Ibid., p. 37.

[107]Abram De Swaan, *Words of the World*.

[108]S.J. Tambiah, 'The Politics of Language in India and Ceylon', *Modern Asian Studies*, 1 (3), 1967, pp. 215–40.

[109]Partha S. Ghosh, 'Language Policy and National Integration: The Indian Experience' in *Ethnic Studies Report*, 14 (1), January 1996.

PART I
LANGUAGE, HISTORY, AND NATION

1

Language and the Constitution
The Half-Hearted Compromise*

Granville Austin

How shall we promote the unity of India and yet preserve the rich diversity of our inheritance?

—Jawaharlal Nehru

What India needed most was unity. What would most effectively unite her was a common language. But in India there were a dozen major regional languages—each written in a different script—and none of them was spoken by a majority of the population. Even Hindustani, defined in the broadest terms as a bazaar language comprised of Hindi, Urdu, Punjabi, and words from other Indian languages as well as English, was spoken by only approximately 45 per cent, of the population.[1] The common tongue of India in 1946 was the language of the conqueror, English.

---

*Originally published as 'Language and the Constitution—The Half-Hearted Compromise', in Granville Austin, *The Indian Constitution: Cornerstone of a Nation* (New Delhi: Oxford University Press, 1966), pp. 265–307.

[1] The 1951 Census of India reported that nearly 150 million, or about 42 per cent of India claimed to have as their native tongue Eastern and Western Hindi, Urdu, Hindustani, and Punjabi, collectively known as Hindustani. India has also over 700 minor languages and dialects. See *Census of India* (New Delhi: Government of India, 1951), Paper No. 1, pp. 2ff. Of the fourteen languages recognized by the Eighth Schedule of the Constitution, one, Kashmiri, is spoken by less than 100,000 people, and another, Sanskrit, is a dead language.

Yet the strong emotional appeal of a national language, of an Indian language for Indians, could not be denied. It was politically and psychologically necessary that the Assembly should find a solution to the problem despite the apparent impossibility of the task. Not only did the emotional void have to be filled, but, it was self-evident, Indians must be able to communicate with one another. And the speakers of each of the regional languages were clamouring for recognition and status for their languages.

Faced with this situation, what were the members of the Constituent Assembly to do? What language should the Assembly designate as the means of communication between Indians generally, between provincial governments, between the provinces and the union, and within the countrywide structure of the union government? Could any of the Indian languages be given precedence over the others? If so, which? And then, what would be the status of the other languages? If an Indian language was given special status, what would be the position of English?

The members of the Constituent Assembly did not attempt the impossible; they did not lay down in the language provisions of the Constitution that one language should be spoken over all India. Yet they could not avoid giving one of the regional languages special status, so they provided, not that there be a 'national' language, but, using a tactful euphemism, that Hindi should be the 'official language of the Union'.[2] Hindi would also be used for inter-provincial communication. For an initial period of fifteen years, however, English was to continue to serve as the official language. After this time, Hindi would supplant English unless parliament legislated otherwise; but English would be retained for use in the courts and for official texts after the expiration of the fifteen-year period and until parliament otherwise legislated. The provincial governments were permitted to choose one of the regional languages, or English, for the conduct of their own affairs and the major regional languages were listed in a schedule to the Constitution. Finally, the members also attempted a definition of Hindi, and provided for language commissions to report on the language situation and on how to further the spread of the 'official language'.

[2]The language provisions are to be found in the *Constitution*, Part XVII, and comprise Articles 343–51.

The language provisions are thus a compromise. Although from the first Assembly members favoured adopting Hindi or Hindustani, and finally decided this in near unanimity, they split into bitterly contending factions over the other issues. The central points of the controversy were the length of time English should continue to be used as the language of government and the status to be accorded the other regional languages. A third major issue proved to be the definition of Hindi. A group of Hindi-speaking Assembly members from the provinces of north-central India, led by a hardcore of linguistic extremists, whom we shall call the Hindi-wallahs, constituted one faction.[3] This group believed that Hindi should be not only the 'national' language by virtue of an inherent superiority over other Indian languages, but that it should replace English for official union purposes immediately or in a very short time. It also held that Hindi should soon replace English as the second language of the provinces. In opposition were the moderates, who believed that Hindi—which they defined much more broadly—might be declared the 'official' language of the union because the largest number of Indians spoke it, but that it should be simply the first among equals, the other regional languages having national status. And the moderates demanded that English, as the *de facto* national language, should be replaced very, very slowly and cautiously. Nehru, joined by several other Assembly leaders, led this group. The other moderates came largely from south India, Bombay, and Bengal, areas where Hindi was not spoken and where English had been the only link between the speakers of the regional languages. But as the controversy grew hotter, a number of Hindi-speakers joined the ranks of the moderates.

The Assembly was not separated into such distinct factions in its early days. At first, the general sentiment in favour of an Indian national language blinded all concerned to the problems involved. But as the members framed the language provisions, they became aware of the difficulties and of their disagreements. Then the split began to grow slowly and steadily. The Hindi-wallahs, unremittingly militant, pressed

[3]The *Concise Oxford Dictionary* defines 'wallah' as meaning a 'person or thing employed about or concerned with something, (a) man'. 'Wallah' is a common word in India: a 'Delhi-wallah' is a man from Delhi; a 'carpet-wallah' sells carpets, a 'khabadi-wallah' is the old-clothes man.

their demands. The moderates retreated in an attempt to preserve national unity and peace within the Assembly. Doing so gained them nothing. And by August 1949 their resistance was hardening. They had realised that acceptance of the Hindi-wallahs' demands would lead to the destruction, not the creation, of unity. In August and September they rallied to a last-ditch defence against the final attacks of the extremists. As a result, the moderates preserved much of their position, but largely in the negative form of exceptions to the overall intent of the language provisions, which bore the stamp of the Hindi-wallahs. Parliament, for example, could extend the use of English by an act, but if it failed to do so, Hindi was automatically to replace English in 1965. During the interim period, the union was to promote the spread of Hindi and the president could authorize its use by the union in addition to English. The presence of Nehru as prime minister from 1950 to 1964 kept the hard core of Hindi speakers from using these provisions to force their language on the rest of the country. Nehru, supported by moderate opinion, also used the loopholes in the provision—for example, that parliament may provide for the use of English after fifteen years, etc.—to prevent the use of English from lapsing and to preserve national unity.

The Hindi-wallahs were ready to risk splitting the Assembly and the country in their unreasoning pursuit of uniformity. They thus denied the Assembly's belief in the concept of accommodation and in decision making by consensus. Assembly members preferred to take decisions by consensus or by as near to unanimity as possible. Not only was this method deeply embedded in the Indian tradition, it was manifestly the most practical way to frame the Constitution. A system of government would not work effectively, Assembly members knew, if large segments of the population were opposed to it. Every attempt had to be made, therefore, to achieve the broadest possible agreement. The Hindi-wallahs, however, announced that they would impose Hindi on the country if they had a one-vote majority. To prevent this, the moderates went to great lengths to find a compromise. They ultimately acquiesced in the language provisions, although they were not happy with them, in the hope that they would provide a framework within which an amicable settlement could be reached. The moderates' fears that the extremists had not accepted the provisions in the spirit of consensus have, unfortunately, been borne out. Since 1950 the extremists have continued to scorn this spirit and have pursued their original aims on the basis of the letter of the Constitution, ignoring the intention of the compromise, which was to resolve the language issue without unduly harming the interests of any linguistic group.

According to the concept of accommodation, apparently incompatible principles can co-exist because they operate in different spheres, on different levels, and thus do not conflict.[4] The Hindi-wallahs held that the use of English was incompatible with India's independence and therefore Hindi must become the national language. They preached that multilingualism was incompatible with Indian unity and that for this reason, also, the nation should adopt Hindi. The moderates, however, did not consider the question as one of *either* English *or* Hindi. They believed that English and all the regional languages could be effectively utilized in their proper spheres, like liquids seeking their own levels. Hindi—broadly defined—might be given a special place because it was spoken by a relatively larger number of persons, but the use of English, they believed, was not incompatible with Indian nationalism. The extremists, although finally forced into a compromise by the resistance of the moderates, spurned accommodation as they had consensus. Theirs was a half-hearted compromise, and the issue of language thus remained a source of great danger to Indian unity.

Language assumed such surpassing importance in the Assembly because, like fundamental rights, it touched everyone. The power of the executive or the judiciary would rarely affect most individuals. Federalism was a question for politicians. But in a nation composed of linguistic minorities, where even provinces were not linguistically homogenous and there were, for example, Tamil enclaves existing in Oriya-speaking areas,[5] problems of language were an everyday affair. Language meant the issue of mother tongue instruction in primary schools—an issue well known in every country where there are substantial minority groups—as well as the question of the medium of instruction in universities. The language of the union and provincial civil services meant money and social status to the middle and upper classes, for the services were their primary source of prestigious

[4]For a further discussion of consensus and accommodation, see Granville Austin, *The Indian Constitution: Cornerstone of a Nation*, 1966, chapter 13.

[5]Such enclaves were to a large extent removed and most states made more nearly unilingual by the States Reorganization of 1956.

employment. Politicians and administrators would be no less affected by the language provisions. The language issue was also made real because it involved the cultural and historical pride of the linguistic groups, and, in the case of Muslims and Sikhs particularly, religious sentiments. Finally, there was one aspect that proved to be especially important, affecting even Hindi-speakers themselves, namely, the definition of Hindi.

If Hindi became too narrowly defined by 'purifying' it of words derived from other Indian languages, particularly Urdu and English, and by coining modern technical and scientific terms on the basis of archaic Sanskrit roots, it would become the language of a learned coterie. Not only would everyday communication be impeded, but progress towards a social revolution would be greatly retarded, perhaps stopped. Nevertheless, the Hindi-wallahs made insistent attempts in this direction in the Assembly. This, as much as their efforts to eliminate English, brought the Assembly to the verge of a public split. It revealed the lengths to which the extremists' zealotry was leading them. In the end, the extremists succeeded in getting a partial expression of their view placed in the language provisions of the Constitution, which lay down that Hindi, for its vocabulary, must draw 'primarily on Sanskrit and secondarily on other languages'.[6] For their part, the moderates exacted a quid pro quo to the effect that Hindi must serve as an expression of the 'composite culture of India' and should assimilate 'the forms, style, and expression used in Hindustani' and in the other major languages of India.[7] Neither faction believed in this compromise definition, either then or today. The Hindi-wallahs show no tendency towards broadening their views on Hindi, and the majority of Indians realize that to sanskritize Hindi would make it the language of the few. This issue declined in importance, however, as the time came closer for parliament to decide on the future status of English as the second official language of India.

The language issue in other major federations, such as Pakistan, Canada, and Switzerland, and in South Africa, despite its importance to the framing and working of their constitutions, cannot be compared in intricacy or dimensions with that faced by India. Although its language problem is an especially difficult one, Pakistan has, basically, only Bengali, Punjabi, and Urdu (little different in its spoken form from Punjabi)

[6]*Constitution*, Article 351.
[7]Ibid.

to contend with—Pushtu being spoken by only a very small minority, and Sindhi, which is dying out, being much like Urdu. Because Urdu and Bengali speakers rarely learn each other's language, Pakistan uses English as the common language at the federal government level. Canada and South Africa also have only two languages, and compared with India, linguism is a small issue. Six million more persons speak Tamil, for example, than there are people in all Canada. Switzerland has three major languages, but they are spoken by a population of only six million in an area only slightly larger than Kerala, India's smallest state. In each of these countries it is possible for government officials and many citizens to speak each of the major languages. It was found possible, therefore, to give all the major languages the status of official languages either in the Constitution or in practice.[8] As such a solution obviously was out of the question in India, the Constituent Assembly had to find its own solution to the nation's most delicate problem.

The Assembly actually framed the language compromise during the six weeks from 1 August to 14 September 1949. The negotiations will be treated in the latter half of this chapter. The language issue appeared in the Assembly, however, within several days of its convening, and its roots reach back many years. It is to this background and to the development of the various aspects of the problem that the first portion of the chapter will be devoted.

FROM THE COMING OF GANDHI TO THE CONSTITUENT ASSEMBLY

Gandhi placed the language issue at the heart of the independence movement. 'It is my humble but firm opinion', he said in 1918, 'that unless we give Hindi its national status and the provincial languages their due place in the life of the people, all talk of Swaraj is

---

[8]For comment on the language provisions of these constitutions, one may consult Keith Callard, *Pakistan* (London: Macmillan, 1957); R.M. Dawson, *The Government of Canada* (Toronto: University of Toronto Press, 1958); E.H. Walton, *The Inner History of the National Convention of South Africa* (Cape Town: T.M. Miller, 1912); C. Hughes, *The Federal Constitution of Switzerland* (London: Clarendon Press, 1953); and texts of the various constitutions. It should be noted how far the Swiss were willing to go on the language issue for the sake of national unity. The language of the majority of the inhabitants of Switzerland is Swiss-German. Yet because the speakers of French, Italian, and Romanche would learn high-German in school, it has become a convention that high German and *not* Swiss-German must be spoken in the Federal Parliament. See Hughes, op. cit., p. 128.

useless.'[9] India must assert its real self if it was to regain its soul and thus truly become independent. It had lived too long 'under the spell of English' and as a result its people 'were steeped in ignorance'.[10] Therefore English must no longer be used in legislatures and on public platforms. Two years later Gandhi asserted that 'as political knowledge and education grows, it will become more and more necessary to use a national language'.[11] Under Gandhi's urging, the Congress changed to a mass movement in 1920, and the party went to the people in their own languages. The new constitution, adopted at Nagpur that year, formed the party into Provincial Congress Committees based on linguistic areas instead of—as had previously been the case—on the administrative boundaries of existing provinces. The new Provincial Congress Committees were encouraged to use the local language in their affairs. The Cocanada Congress of 1923 amended the party constitution, laying down that the proceedings of the annual sessions should be conducted as far as possible in Hindustani. Yet it proved impossible to avoid using English, and the party constitution provided that English and the provincial languages could also be used.[12]

The *Nehru Report* continued to support this policy. Its authors were 'strongly of the opinion that every effort should be made to make Hindustani the common language of the whole of India as it is today of half of it'.[13] As to the provincial languages, they were to be the instruments for achieving national democracy. Culture depends on language, said the report. 'It becomes essential therefore to conduct the business and politics of the country in a language which is understood by the masses. So far as the provinces are concerned, this must be in the provincial language.... Provincial languages will have to be encouraged.'[14] But again English proved inescapable: the

---

[9]In a speech to the Hindi Sahitya Sammelan at Indore, reproduced in *Thought on National Language* (Ahmedabad: Navajivan Press, 1956), p. 14. Gandhi, as we shall see, used the words Hindi and Hindustani at different times for several reasons, but he was always speaking of the same tongue, that is, broad Hindustani written in both the Urdu and Devanagari scripts.

[10]Ibid., p. 9.

[11]From an article in *Young India*, 1920; ibid., p. 17.

[12]Chakrabarty and Bhattacharya, *Congress in Evolution* (Calcutta: The Book Co. Ltd, 1940), p. 220. Azad later seemed to take the credit for the introduction of Hindustani into the Congress Constitution; see *Constituent Assembly Debates (CAD)*, IX, 34, 1454. Cocanada was in Madras at that time and is now in Andhra.

[13]*Nehru Report*, p. 62.

[14]Ibid.

members of the Nehru Committee discussed their report and wrote it in English.

This pattern continued during the 1930s and early 1940s. Purushottam Das Tandon wrote that 'India's real self must assert itself through her own languages'.[15] For Nehru, it was 'axiomatic that the masses can only grow educationally and culturally through the medium of their own languages'. But he approached the question of the status of English more realistically and cautiously than some others. He wrote in 1937 that 'English will inevitably remain an important language for us because of our past associations and because of its present importance in the world.' But it was 'manifestly impossible' for English to serve as a common tongue in India 'if we think in terms of the masses'.[16] The general view of this formative period was well summed up by Z. Ahmad in 1941 in a book entitled *National Language for India*. 'All sensible persons', Ahmad wrote, 'are agreed that we have to forge a medium of thought and expression which can cement our common efforts and urges for the rehabilitation and development of our national life.'[17] Throughout these years, English remained the language of the independence movement, at least in its upper echelons. Little attention was paid to the details of the language question, and the exact position of English in independent India seems not to have been discussed, nor the status of the regional languages, nor other details that would confront the Constituent Assembly, such as the language of the courts, of parliament, and of the Constitution itself. Even the difficulties that the choice of Hindustani as the national language would pose to north-south relations could be glossed over, because the issue could not be put to the vital test of action. It was enough at this time to proclaim that Indians must speak an Indian language.

The Congress had made Hindustani, at least on paper, its official language.[18] Gandhi had hundreds of times said that Hindustani should be the national language, and Nehru said it was 'bound to become the

---

[15]In an article contributed to Z. Ahmad, *National Language for India* (Allahabad: Kitabistan, 1941), p. 93.

[16]In 'The Question of Language', written in 1937. Included in Nehru, *The Unity of India* (London: Lindsay Drummond, 1948), pp. 243–4.

[17]Ahmad, op. cit., p. 7—Ahmad's Introduction to the compilation of articles.

[18]The Congress Constitution of 1934, 'for the first time in Congress and Indian history', prescribed Hindustani as the language of all Congress proceedings. See N.V. Rajkumar, *Development of the Congress Constitution* (New Delhi: Indian National Congress, 1948), p. 70.

all-India medium of communication'.[19] Why did the Congress choose Hindustani? What qualifications had it for a national role? What effect did the choice have on the non-Hindustani-speaking areas, and particularly on the south? What, indeed, did Hindustani mean?

Hindustani meant what Gandhi said it meant and for him it was the language of the masses of north India.[20] Only four months before his death, Gandhi summed up his life-long views about Hindustani:

This Hindustani (Gandhi wrote) should be neither Sanskritized Hindi nor Persianised Urdu but a happy combination of both. It should also freely admit words wherever necessary from the different regional languages and also assimilate words from foreign languages, provided that they can mix well and easily with our national language. Thus our national language must develop into a rich and powerful instrument capable of expressing the whole gamut of human thoughts and feelings. To confine oneself exclusively to Hindi or Urdu would be a crime against intelligence and the spirit of patriotism.[21]

Congress leaders, especially the Oligarchy, had long accepted this definition. And Rajagopalachari suggested broadening Hindustani even furthering by writing it in the regional scripts as well as in the Devanagari script of Hindi and the Persian-like Urdu script of Urdu.[22]

This choice of a simple bazaar language posed certain problems, however. Hindustani might be the language of the masses, but was it sufficiently developed to meet the needs of science, technology, and politics? Bengali and Tamil were much more developed and better met the needs of a modern state; yet even they were not wholly adequate to the task, and were far less widely spoken than Hindustani. Hence the problem. What language should be chosen: one less well developed, but more widely spoken, or vice versa? In pre-independence days this issue received little attention. For the Assembly, however, it was of major importance, particularly in the light of the Hindi-wallahs' campaign to purge Hindustani of Urdu and English—the major source of technical terms as well as many other words and phrases—and to substitute unknown, Sanskrit-derived words in their place.

The widespread use of Hindustani was what first attracted the Congress leadership to it. Gandhi claimed in 1928 that 120 million

[19]Nehru, *Unity of India*, pp. 20–1.
[20]See, for example, his speech to the Hindi Sammelan at Indore in 1918; ibid., p. 10.
[21]From *Harijansevak* of 12 October 1947; see Gandhi, *Thoughts*, p. 174.
[22]In an article included in Ahmad, op. cit., p. 201.

persons spoke Hindustani and that 80 millions more understood it.[23] Nehru used the same figures in 1937. These estimates, in the light of the 1931 census, appear to be somewhat high, but nevertheless Hindustani speakers outnumbered Tamil speakers (20 millions) six to one and Bengali speakers (53 millions, halved by partition) by more than two to one.

The Congress leadership also chose Hindustani as the language of the independence movement, because it bridged the widening gulf between Hindus and Muslims. Hindustani, as the leadership understood it, drew its vocabulary from both Sanskrit and Arabic-Persian roots. It could be written in either the Devanagari (Nagari) or Urdu scripts. Muslims, on one side, might be expected to use a more Persianized vocabulary and the Urdu script—which had religious overtones for them because of its relationship to Arabic, the holy language of the Koran. Hindus, would, in general, use the Nagari script and a more sanskritized vocabulary both of which had links with Hindu scripture. This was commonly called the Hindi language. But except for the extremists on each side, north Indians shared the vernacular speech, and many intellectuals wrote in both scripts. Many Hindus, Nehru among them, considered Urdu their mother tongue. Hindustani provided a happy example of cultural synthesis sorely needed in an atmosphere of increasing communal tension.

Gandhi and Nehru emphasized time after time that only Hindustani could link the two communities. In 1945, for example, Gandhi wrote to Purushottam Das Tandon that he intended to resign from the Hindi Sahitya Sammelan because it preached that only Hindi in the Nagari script could be the national language.[24] Tandon replied that he could not agree that all Indians should learn Urdu and Hindi and he believed, instead, that it was more important to oust English from its position and to convert the speakers of regional languages to Hindi.[25] Several days later, Gandhi resigned from the sammelan saying, 'my definition of Rashtra Bhasha (national language) includes a knowledge of both Hindi and Urdu and both the Nagari and Urdu scripts. Only thus can a happy fusion of Hindi and Urdu take place'.[26] For his part, Nehru summed up the situation thus: 'Scratch a separatist in language and

[23]Gandhi in *Young India*, 23 August 1928; cited in Gandhi, *Thoughts*, p. 30.
[24]Gandhi to Tandon, 28 May 1945. See Gandhi, *Thoughts*, p. 133.
[25]Tandon to Gandhi, letters of 8 June and 11 July 1945; ibid., p. 134, pp. 136–7.
[26]Gandhi to Tandon, 15 July 1945; ibid., p. 141.

you will invariably find that he is a communalist and very often a political reactionary.'[27]

The choice of Hindustani as the official language of the Congress and as the prospective national language affected north-south relations very little before independence—largely because the issue was not forced. But on one occasion in 1937 when Rajagopalachari, as premier of Madras, and P. Subbarayan, his education minister, introduced Hindustani as a compulsory subject in the first three forms of high schools, there was a violent reaction. For weeks afterwards, according to Subbarayan, he left his house to cries of 'Let Hindi die and let Tamil live. Let Subbarayan die and Rajagopalachari die.'[28] It was one of the unfortunate coincidences of Indian history that Hindustani was a northern language and that it was given special status by north Indians, like Nehru, Prasad, and Azad and by north-oriented Gujaratis like Gandhi and Patel, who held the balance of power in the Congress. These men were above choosing Hindustani because they were born to it or had adopted it, but nevertheless Hindustani became forever tarred with the brush of northern power in the party. And after independence, politicians from the north would have little more success in spreading Hindi in the south than had party leaders in previous years.

Early Skirmishes in the Assembly

Through the Framing of the Draft Constitution

The language issue entered the Assembly through the door of the Rules Committee. The committee, under Prasad's chairmanship, decided on 14 December 1946 that in the Assembly, business should be 'transacted in Hindustani (Hindi or Urdu) or English' and that, with the president's permission, a member could address the house in his mother tongue. Records of the Assembly were to be kept in Hindustani (Hindi or Urdu) and English.[29] This rule remained unchanged

[27]Nehru, *Unity of India*, p. 248.
[28]*CAD* IX, 33, 1401.
[29]Minutes of the meeting, 14 December 1946, in *Orders of the Day* for that date; *INA*. The rule in question was numbered 18 during the debate. It was number 30 in the first edition of the Rules, and was renumbered 29 in subsequent editions. For the membership of the Rules Committee, see Appendix II of Granville Austin, *The Indian Constitution: Cornerstone of a Nation*.

throughout the life of the Assembly. The Assembly debate on the draft rules, held 'in camera' on 22 December, demonstrated clearly how controversial was the continuance of English and the antagonism the subject could arouse between Hindi extremists and south Indians. The two principle amendments proposed to the rule on language bore the names of Seth Govind Das, a Hindi extremist from Mahakoshal in the Central Provinces, and K. Santhanam, a prominent Madrassi. Govind Das had moved that the language of the Assembly should be Hindustani and that anyone not able to speak it could use his mother-tongue or English. Speaking on his amendment, Govind Das said it was 'painful' that the Constituent Assembly of free India 'should try to make English its national language'. (Govind Das had expressed a common equation: whatever was designated the language of the Assembly or, later, of parliament, equalled the national language). He continued: 'I want to tell my brethren from Madras that if after twenty-five years of efforts on the part of Mahatma Gandhi they have not been able to understand Hindustani, the blame lies at their door. It is beyond our patience that because some of our brethren from Madras do not understand Hindustani, English should reign supreme in a Constituent Assembly ... assembled to frame a Constitution for a free India.'[30]

Santhanam's amendment to the rules provided that all motions and amendments in the Assembly be tabled in English, and that English should be spoken on the floor of the house whether or not the member knew Hindustani. Supporting his provision and replying to Govind Das' speech, Santhanam remarked that in time all India would learn Hindustani, but he doubted the ability of many persons to use it in technical discussions.[31] As if to emphasize Santhanam's point, A.K. Ayyar had requested that Govind Das's speech, which had been made in Hindustani, be translated into English for him. Prasad had agreed that the substance of the speech be translated because Ayyar was too old to learn Hindustani. Speaking after the closure motion, K.M. Munshi said that no one doubted that Hindustani was the national language and that in the Assembly it would have precedence, but, said Munshi, English

[30]*CAD* I, 11, 233. This number of the CAD was kept confidential at the time—for other reasons than the rules debate, it seems most likely because the budget of the Assembly was under discussion. It is now available in the Indian National Archives. For the texts of both Santhanam's and Govind Das's amendments, see *Orders of the Day*, 22 December 1946; *INA*.

[31]Ibid., p. 235.

could not be omitted altogether.[32] The Assembly passed the rule relating to language unamended by a large majority.

Three months later, the language issue was again under discussion, this time in the Fundamental Rights Sub-Committee. At two meetings in late March 1947, the members debated the necessity of including a clause on language in the rights. They decided in favour of a language clause 'in view of the peculiar conditions of this country'—meaning, primarily, the Hindu-Muslim conflict.

The clause read:

Hindustani, written at the option of the citizen either in the Devnagari (sic) or the Persian script, shall, as the national language, be the first official language of the Union. English shall be the second official language for such period as the Union may by law determine.[33]

In their report to the advisory committee of 16 April, the Rights Sub-Committee members recommended this provision and, additionally, that the records of the union be kept in Hindustani, in both the scripts and in English.[34]

The sub-committee's recommendation was not moderate enough for Masani and Mrs Mehta. They submitted a minute of dissent, reiterating their earlier suggestions that Roman be an optional script for the writing of Hindustani, along with Urdu and Nagari, in view of 'the lakhs of Indians ... particularly in the South' who were not familiar with the two northern scripts.[35]

The advisory committee considered the rights sub-committee's report during the latter half of April. At the meeting of 22 April it postponed consideration of the language provision, and subsequently the clause was dropped from the rights. This had been done, Patel informed the Assembly, because responsibility for the matter had been assumed by the Union Constitution Committee (UCC).[36] Although this

[32]Ibid., p. 327.

[33]Minutes of the meetings, 24 and 25 March 1947; *Prasad Papers*, File 1-F/47. Present when the decision was made were: Kripalani, Ayyar, Harnam Singh, Shah, Munshi, Kaur, Masani, and Mrs Mehta. Absent were Azad, Panikkar, Daulatram, and Ambedkar.

[34]See report of the Fundamental Rights Sub-Committee to the Advisory Committee, dated 16 April 1947; ibid.

[35]See their joint minute, dated 14 April 1947; *Prasad Papers*, File 1-F/47.

[36]*CAD* V, 11, pp. 361–2. See also Supplementary Report of the Advisory Committee on Fundamental Rights; *Reports, Second Series*, p. 47.

was in fact the case, it may have been equally true that the party leaders wished to preserve harmony and to avoid muddying the waters of the rights debate with so controversial a subject as language.

There is no evidence that the UCC devoted much time or thought to the language question beyond recommending in its report that the language of the union parliament should be Hindustani (Hindi or Urdu) and English, with the members permitted to use their mother tongue if necessary. This provision descended directly from the Assembly Rules by way of Rau's memorandum on the union Constitution. The Provincial Constitution Committee took up the question of language during the same period as the UCC. Its report recommended that in provincial legislatures, business should be conducted in the provincial language or languages, or in Hindustani, or in English. Unexceptional as this provision appears, it was much more moderate than that suggested by Rau, who granted the provincial languages no status even in their own legislatures. According to his model Provincial Constitution, the languages were to be Hindustani or English.[37]

The opening of the fourth Assembly session on 14 July 1947 began a new phase in the language controversy. Meeting under the shadow of partition, the Assembly witnessed a concerted attack, led by the Hindi-wallahs, on Hindustani, English, and the provincial languages. On the first day of the session, Patel introduced the report of the Provincial Constitution Committee. The next day the order paper carried five amendments that would have substituted 'Hindi' for Hindustani as an alternative language in provincial legislatures.[38] That day and the next the order paper also carried amendments that would have prevented English from being spoken in the provincial legislatures; only the provincial language and Hindi could be used, according to these amendments. The evening of the third day, the Congress Assembly Party took up the issue and there occurred 'the rare phenomenon of

[37]See Benegal Marsing Rau, in B. Shiva Rao (ed.), *India's Constitution in the Making* (Calcutta: Orient Longman, 1960), pp. 147–8. There is reason to believe that Munshi shared this view, for he made a handwritten note to this effect in the margin of his suggested minority rights. See a draft of rights provisions dated 15 April 1947; *Munshi Papers*.

[38]Amendments 92–95 and 98, *Orders of the Day*, 15 July 1947; *INA*. Moving these amendments were Balkrishna Sharma, Purushottam Das Tandon, H.V. Pataskar, D.P. Khaitan, who would later become a member of the Drafting Committee, and H.J. Khandekar. Others submitting strongly pro-Hindi amendments at this time were Guptanath Singh, R.V. Dhulekar, and S.L. Saksena.

the Congress leaders and the rank and file being ranged in opposite camps and the leaders being heavily outvoted'.

The meeting voted sixty-three to thirty-two that Hindi, not Hindustani 'should be the national language of India'. In a second vote, the meeting designated Nagari the national script by a majority of sixty-three to eighteen. English was favoured as a second language.[39] In the Assembly the following morning, Patel asked that the question of the language in provincial legislatures be held over.

Less than a week later, this pattern recurred in regard to the UCC report. Several amendments by Hindi-wallahs would have changed the name of the language of parliament from Hindustani to Hindi. Other amendments went much further, however, providing that Hindi should be the national language and Nagari the national script and that only Hindi might be used in parliament,[40] that Hindi be the official language of the state but that English might be used for five or ten years, and that Hindi should be the national language but that English might be used in parliament if parliament so decided. There is no evidence that these amendments were discussed in the Assembly Party meeting, and the Assembly did not debate the provision in the UCC report naming Hindustani as the language of parliament. Contrary to the National Convention of South Africa, which considered the language issue one that 'must be dealt with and settled satisfactorily before any real progress (in constitution-making) could be hoped for',[41] the Constituent Assembly was apparently postponing coming to grips with the problem in the belief that the enmities roused by debating it might endanger other aspects of the Assembly's work.

In the two months between the third and fourth sessions, the Assembly had passed a watershed in the language controversy. This watershed was partition. Partition killed Hindustani and endangered the position of English and the provincial languages in the Constitution. 'If there had been no Partition, Hindustani would without doubt have been the national language,' K. Santhanam believed, 'but the anger against the Muslims turned against Urdu.'[42] Assembly members 'felt

[39]*The Hindustan Times*, 17 July 1947.

[40]Amendment 305, submitted by Seth Govind Das, List 2, *Orders of the Day*, 22 July 1947; *INA*.

[41]Walton, *Inner History*, p. 97.

[42]K. Santhanam in an interview with the author.

that the Muslims having caused the division of the country, the whole issue of national language must be reviewed afresh', said an article in The *Hindustan Times*.[43] Having seen the dream of unity shattered by partition, by the 'treachery' of the Urdu (Hindustani) speakers, the Hindi extremists became even more firmly committed to Hindi and to achieving national unity through it. Speakers of the provincial languages must learn Hindi and the regional languages must take second place, the Hindi-wallahs believed. And as for English, it should go as Urdu had gone. Were not both un-Indian?

Hindustani might have been eliminated as a term, but its spirit still lived. Gandhi, Nehru, and other members of the Assembly who had believed in Hindustani would in the future support 'broad' Hindi. Many would remember the words Gandhi had written just two weeks after the Assembly party meeting had rejected Hindustani:

The Congress has always kept a broad vision.... The omens of today seem to point to the contrary. During the crisis the Congress must stand firm like a rock. It dare not give way on the question of the *lingua franca* for India. It cannot be Persianized Urdu or Sanskritized Hindi. It must be a beautiful blend of the two simple forms written in either script.[44]

When the Draft Constitution appeared in February 1948, it had no separate language provision, but it established that the language of parliament was English or Hindi and that these languages could be used in the provincial legislatures as alternatives to the provincial languages. It is not clear why the members of the Drafting Committee changed Hindustani to Hindi without the official sanction of the Assembly. According to the committee's own version, it did so by a majority vote after being informed by Munshi of 'the Congress Party's resolution for the changing of the words "Hindustani (Hindi or Urdu)" to "Hindi"'.[45] The resolution alluded to must have been that of the previous July. One presumes that the Oligarchy had agreed to the change, and that it again did so to postpone conflict. 'Hindustani became a

---

[43] *The Hindustan Times*, 17 July 1947.

[44] Gandhi in *Harijan*, 10 August 1947, but written on 31 July; Gandhi, *Thoughts*, p. 170.

[45] See comments by the Drafting Committee on amendments suggested to Article 99 of the Draft—written in March 1948, preparatory to the meeting of the Special Committee in April; *Prasad Papers*, File 1-M/48. The committee took the original decision on 10 December 1947; see minutes of the meeting, *Prasad Papers*, File 1-D/47.

bad word after Partition,' as one observer put it, 'and the party leaders were reluctant to divide the party over it.'[46]

Events of 1948

Nineteen forty-eight was a busy year for the Hindi-wallahs. They seemed at the beginning to hold views that a large number of Assembly members could support—sixty-three members had voted to replace Hindustani by Hindi. But by the end of the year many members had come to distrust their 'linguistic fanaticism'. Alienating their erstwhile followers was their attack on the provincial languages and on English, and their attempts to sanskritize Hindi. The Hindi-wallahs made their views clear not only in amendments to the Draft Constitution but during the framing of the new Congress constitution and in their attempts to have the nation's Constitution adopted in Hindi as well as in English.

The Hindi extremists submitted twenty-nine amendments to the Draft Constitution between February and November 1948.[47] Some of these would have revised the articles concerning the language of parliament and the legislatures; others would have added new language provisions to the draft. Compressed into one provision, the amendments would have read somewhat like this:

NATIONAL LANGUAGE

Hindi (Bharati) shall be the national (official) language of India.

Devanagari shall be the national script of India.

In provinces where Hindi is not spoken or Nagari used, the language to be used may be decided by the local legislature.

Provinces may use English as a second official language so long as the legislatures so desire (or, in several amendments, for seven or five years only).

English may be used as a second official language of the Indian Union for as long as Parliament may determine. (In a variety of amendments the use of English was to be limited to five or seven years.)

[46]K. Santhanam in an interview with the author.

[47]Sponsoring these provisions were several new figures on the language scene—G.S. Gupta, Dr Raghuvira, Algurai Shastri, and B.A. Mandloi—as well as Govind Das, Tandon, S.L. Saksena, V.D. Tripathi, and Balkrishna Sharma. Oddly absent was Ravi Shankar Shukla, who, by the following summer, was to emerge as one of the most militant leaders of the group.

In Parliament, business shall be transacted in Hind, in Nagari. But for as long as Parliament may prescribe, English may be used. (Or, in several versions English might be used for only five or seven years.)[48]

The members of the group who believed that English should not be used after a five—or seven-year period were Gupta, Govind Das, Saksena, and Tripathi.

To these amendments, there were counter-amendments. With the exceptions of two submitted by K.T. Shah and the venerable Sachchidananda Sinha (both supporting Hindustani), they came from Muslims and south Indians. The Muslims all supported Hindustani in both scripts as a national language, but ignored the problem of English. The south Indians were willing to use the term Hindi, but believed that the official language should be English for fifteen years, after which Hindi should be recognized as the official language, and Hindi and English would be the language of parliament.

The Congress's decision to redraft its constitution gave the Hindi-wallahs an opportunity to attack both Hindustani (and the spirit of broad Hindi) and the regional languages. In November 1947, the All-India Congress Committee (AICC) appointed a new drafting committee, the drafts of several previous committees having proved unacceptable.[49] On 7 April 1948, the convenor of the committee sent a draft constitution prepared by the committee and an accompanying circular to all AICC members. The language provision of the draft, much as in the past, laid down that Hindustani in the Nagari script was the language of Congress proceedings, but that provincial languages or English could be used. In Provincial Congress Committee (PCC) proceedings, the provincial language, Hindustani, or English could be used.[50] The draft also listed, in accordance with long practice, the names, headquarters-cities, and the languages of various PCCs. For such PCCs as those of the United Provinces, Bihar, and Mahakoshal (Central Provinces) the language listed in the 1948 draft was Hindustani.

Tandon, however, objected to Hindustani being the language of Congress proceedings, Kishore explained in the circular letter; he

[48]See *Amendment Book* 1, pp. 19–25. See especially pp. 19–21 and 30.

[49]The members of the new committee were Sitaramayya, Tandon, Narenda Dev, Diwakar, S.K. Patil, S.M. Ghose, and Jugal Kishore, convenor.

[50]Article XXVI of the Draft Congress Constitution. Sent under cover of Congress Circular Letter of 7 April 1948; *Prasad Papers*, File 3-A/48.

wanted Hindi to be used. The tone of the letter indicated that the committee supported Hindustani. Discussing the draft later in April, the AICC meeting in Bombay passed over the language provision as too controversial. When the draft came before the Jaipur Congress in December—and was approved—all mention of language had been removed—even the list of regional languages used by the PCCs had been deleted. Evidently, the high command had again temporized in the interests of party unity. Tandon's success in forcing Hindustani from its place of political birth (it had been named the language of Congress proceedings and placed in the 1920 constitution as a result of Gandhi's advocacy) was a blow to moderation. More than anything else, it was a reminder that a few months previously the greatest champion of linguistic moderation had been killed by a member of a Hindu communalist organization that detested Hindustani.[51]

The Congress presidential election of 1948 also played a part in the development of the language controversy, although the question of language was not directly involved, by embittering north-south relations. The election was to take place in October 1948, less than a month before the beginning of the seventh Assembly session, when Rajendra Prasad's year of office expired. Who should replace him? Pattabhi Sitaramayya, a Telegu speaker from Madras province, very much wanted to do so, and he believed that he had the support of the south. The other major candidate was Purushottam Das Tandon. It is doubtful if Tandon decided to stand for the presidency because of the language issue; ideological conflicts and the desire for greater power in the party were more important. But Tandon may have decided to remain a candidate—instead of withdrawing his name as Prasad requested—in part to uphold his views on language. Certainly, many opposed him on language grounds. In any case a contest between a northerner and a southerner at this time was bound to have linguistic overtones. Prasad, for example, did not like the prospect of an election in which Sitaramayya would be opposed by a candidate from the north. 'I have a feeling', he wrote, 'that the sentiments of South Indians that they do not get full recognition in the Congress deserves consideration ... I think that a contest against Dr Pattabhi, who is the only candidate

---

[51]The RSS. See, for example, articles printed in *Organizer* in 1947–8, which was the publication of the Rashtriya Swayamsevak Sangh (the RSS).

from the South, will assume the form of a contest between the North and the West on the one hand and the South on the other, and I think it would be a most unfortunate thing to have that kind of contest.'[52] Despite all efforts to get him to do so, Tandon refused to withdraw so that Sitaramayya might be elected unanimously. In the election Sitaramayya won by a small majority. And although it was not a central issue, the question of language, according to *Harijan's* post-mortem on the election, affected the vote.[53]

The efforts of the Hindi-extremists to have the Constitution adopted in a Hindi version produced resentment among both southerners, who could not speak Hindi, and among Hindi speakers who found that the Hindi versions had been so sankritized as to make them unintelligible. Vernacular versions of the Constitution were not only feasible but necessary if the general public was to understand its government. A sanskritized translation, however, would not only be unintelligible, except to a tiny group of the initiates, but it was doubtful if a sanskritized Constitution could be superimposed on the base of parliamentary government and the British common-law tradition to which the nation was accustomed and which Assembly members wanted to retain. Having become aware of these obstacles, the Assembly framed and adopted the Constitution in English. There is today no version of the Constitution with legal standing in any Indian language.[54]

The possibility of framing it in the national language had been considered as early as January 1947. The matter first achieved prominence, however, in early May that year when Prasad asked in the Assembly (of no one in particular) if India 'forever in future' should have a constitution in English and have to rely on English-speaking judges to interpret it. Perhaps, he suggested, 'we could have a translation made of this Constitution as it is drafted as soon as possible, and ultimately adopt that as our original Constitution. (Cheers.)'[55] Prasad

---

[52]Prasad to P.C. Ghosh, 1 October 1948; *Prasad Papers*, File 1-A/48.

[53]*Harijan*, 7 November 1948.

[54]In an only slightly similar situation, South Africa had chosen an English original version for its Constitution, instead of versions in Dutch and English, which would have conflicted. See Walton, op. cit., pp. 108ff. The Burmese, however, have made both English and Burmese language versions of the Constitution 'authentic' versions, and in cases where the meaning is in doubt, both versions are consulted. See Maung Maung, *Burma's Constitution* (The Hague: Martin Nighoff, 1959), pp. 206–7.

[55]*CAD* III, 5,533–4.

pursued the idea through the summer, apparently thinking in terms of only a Hindi translation. On 1 November 1947, the Hindi translation committee met for the first time with Prasad present. Later Hindustani and Urdu committees would be created.

The two chief members of the Hindi committee were G.S. Gupta and Dr Raghuvira. Gupta was the Speaker of the Legislative Assembly in the Central Provinces and a Hindi purist who opposed the incorporation of international political and legal terms into Hindi. New words should be coined from a Sanskrit base, he believed.[56] Raghuvira, a Punjabi from Lahore residing in Nagpur, was the author of *The Great English-Indian Dictionary*. He opposed taking 'Hindustani people' onto the Hindi translation committee.[57] In the autumn of 1947, neither Gupta nor Raghuvira were Assembly members. They believed that they should be, apparently the better to pursue their aim of a Hindi constitution, and succeeded in getting themselves seats with the aid of Ravi Shankar Shukla, the prime minister of the Central Provinces, who also was a Hindi extremist.

By the summer of 1948, the Hindi translation, as well as the Urdu and Hindustani translations, had been completed. Nehru saw a copy and wrote to Prasad 'that he did not understand a word of it'.[58] Sanskritization, as even Hindi speakers later charged, had made the translation incomprehensible. Continuing his campaign, Gupta sent a resolution to the Steering Committee saying that because English 'cannot and must not' long remain the language of India, the Constitution should be framed in Hindi 'side by side' with English. For five years, English would be recognized as the authoritative version and then it would yield to Hindi.[59] S.L. Saksena took this a step further, recommending that the English and Hindi versions be framed jointly and that the Hindi version passed by the Assembly should be considered the original version of the Constitution.[60] The

[56]Gupta expressed these views many times. See, for example, Government of India, *Verbatim Record of the Educational Conference*, 16–18 January 1948, pp. 62–5.

[57]Raghuvira to C. Sharan, private secretary to Prasad, in a letter dated 7 October 1947. Raghuvira was almost demanding that he be made a member of the Hindi committee. *Prasad Papers*, File 1-H/47–8–9.

[58]Related by Prasad to G.S. Gupta in a letter, 29 June 1948; ibid.

[59]Agenda for Steering Committee meeting of 25 October 1948; *Munshi Papers*. When Hindi became the authorized version, the English version would remain 'valid', said Gupta.

[60]See agenda for Steering Committee meeting of 10 November 1948; *Munshi Papers*.

Steering Committee decided that the resolutions should be held over until the Assembly had considered the provision on the language of parliament.

The views of the Hindi-wallahs, or at least one section of them, were also made brutally plain in three recommendations by a committee of the C.P. and Berar Legislative Assembly. Headed by Ravi Shankar Shukla, the premier, and with G.S. Gupta as one of its members, the committee recommended that the official language of the union should be Hindi and Nagari with English optional during a transitional period, that a knowledge of Hindi should be mandatory for entrants into the Union Public Service (and Hindi-speaking entrants should know a provincial language), and that the Constitution should be framed in Hindi. Elucidating these basic tenets, the committee said that the grace period for English should be five years and that Hindi's source of 'learned terms ... can only be Sanskrit'. The committee did not recognize Urdu as an Indian script and said of Hindustani: 'Hindustani by itself is no language...As a vehicle of learned thought it is non-existent ... The highest dictates of nationalism require that our terms of any technical value must be based on Sanskrit. This way lies the linguistic unity of India.'[61] These recommendations were printed on 22 October 1948 and copies were forwarded by Gupta to all members of the Constituent Assembly.

When the Assembly reconvened on 4 November, the effect of the Hindi-wallahs' activities became evident. Speakers referred to the intolerance, thoughtlessness, and fanaticism of the Hindi campaign. It was 'no use repeating *ad nauseam*', one member said, 'the new dictum that independence will be meaningless if we all do not start talking in Hindi or conducting official business in Hindi from tomorrow'.[62] G.G.S. Musafir, who favoured framing the Constitution in Hindi, accused the Hindi-wallahs of sanskritizing the language and called for the use of simple words that everyone could understand. Two speeches sum up the adverse reaction to the extremists. T.T. Krishnamachari of Madras told the Assembly:

I would, Sir, convey a warning on behalf of the people of the South for the reason that there are already elements in South India who want separation

[61] *Report of the Committee of the Whole*, dated 18 October 1948, *Munshi Papers, INA*.
[62] *CAD* VII, 2, 249; L.K. Maitra.

and it is up to us to tax the maximum strength we have to keeping those elements down, and my honourable friends in U.P. do not help us in any way by flogging their idea 'Hindi-Imperialism' to the maximum extent possible.[63]

L.K. Maitra of Bengal warned the Hindi-wallahs 'not in their over-zealousness (to) mar their own case'. He continued:

This is a sort of fanaticism, this is linguistic fanaticism, which if allowed to grow and develop will ultimately defeat the very object they have in view. I therefore plead to them for a little patience and forbearance towards those who, I for the time being, cannot speak the language of the North.[64]

The battle over language was not to be joined at this time, however. Assembly leaders, desirous of a just and lasting solution to the controversy, refused to permit debate. Neither consensus nor accommodation could be achieved in the heat of the moment. Prasad told the Assembly that, for the very reasons the extremists wanted immediate discussion of the language issue, he intended to delay it and to turn to other aspects of the Draft. 'I suggest', he said, 'that it is much better to discuss at any rate the fundamentals of the Constitution in a calm atmosphere before our tempers get frayed.'[65] Nehru agreed that debate on language at that time might delay completion of the Constitution. 'Urgency may ill serve our purposes', he counselled. And he warned the Assembly to seek consensus. 'If we proceed in an urgent matter to impose something, maybe by a majority, on an unwilling minority in parts of the country, or even in this House, we do not really succeed in what we have started to achieve.'[66]

At least half the Assembly were against the Hindi-wallahs, who nevertheless were prepared to ignore the major concepts of consensus and accommodation in order to force their will upon the Assembly and the nation. Their intolerance and cohesiveness never faltered. What were the bonds or similarities of background, if any, that impelled these extremists to pursue this course in concert? They all were, of course, Hindi speakers. Although three of the group (Tandon among them) had attended Christian mission schools, which might have increased

[63]Ibid., p. 235.
[64]Ibid., p. 249.
[65]CAD VII, 1, 21.
[66]CAD VII, 4, 321.

their dislike of English and its alien culture, the majority had received a university education at the famous Hindu institutions of Allahabad and Benares. None had been educated outside India or outside Hindi areas. Few of these men, if any, could be called orthodox Hindus: they would dine with Muslims, for example. But several were revivalists— Balkrishna Sharma, Tandon, Govind Das—and envisaged the new India in terms of the glories of ancient Hindu kingdoms. Tandon also led the opposition to the Hindu Code Bill. G.S. Gupta had for many years been a member of the fundamentalist Arya Samaj. And Dr Raghuvira ran for parliament in 1962 on the ticket of the communalist Jan Sangh Party. Others among the extremists, however, like Algurai Shastri, V.D. Tripathi, and S.L. Sakxena were quite secular in outlook and had socialist political views. Although each of these men would have claimed that he was not anti-Muslim, there can be little doubt that their attitudes were at least tinged with communalism. There would be little other reason to attempt to purge Hindustani of words of Arabic and Persian origin. Only on the language question did these men act as a group, so presumably religious conservatism was not the unifying force—although such sentiments must not be entirely discounted. The extremists' attitude towards English and the regional languages supported this view. The principal motive, then, was apparently a narrow nationalism generating its own fervour and tolerating no deviation from its own vision of what was truly Indian.

Events of 1949, January to August

The language controversy continued to develop along these lines in 1949. Outside the Assembly, groups like the Socialists called for the gradual introduction of a national language, and this was to be 'simple Hindustani using one script only'.[67] The Hindi extremists conducted themselves in such a way that Nehru condemned the 'narrow-minded', near-communal tone of the controversy. 'Everybody knows', he said; 'that obviously Hindi is the most powerful language of India...But it is the misfortune of Hindi that it has collected round it some advocates who continually do tremendous injury to its cause by advocating it in

[67]Socialist Party, *Resolutions of the 7th Annual Socialist Party Conference*, March 1949, p. 25.

a wrong way.'[68] The question of a Hindi Constitution continued to agitate the Assembly during the first half of the year. Most important as background to the events of August and September was the steadily increasing assertiveness of regional language speakers, not only towards the Hindi extremists, but often towards each other. This spirit was manifest particularly in multilingual areas and in the field of education.

The 'original version' question was reopened in January and, as spring arrived, it developed into a contest between Prasad and Nehru. Nehru agreed that the Constitution should be translated, but he favoured having this done by experts and not Assembly members,[69] and he continued to oppose adopting the Constitution in a Hindi version. On 5 January 1949, apparently inflicting a defeat on the Hindi-wallahs, the Steering Committee empowered Prasad to appoint an expert committee to prepare a translation that would 'as far as possible be precise and easily understood by the common man'.[70] Prasad, however, still argued in support of a Hindi original version, although he was willing to have the Constitution passed also in English, and the English version would be the authoritative one for an initial period.

Prasad pressed his view in a series of letters and memoranda. He wrote to the secretary of the Assembly on 4 June that the Assembly should appoint a committee to examine the expert committee's translation so that the Assembly might pass it. The Hindi version could then, after fifteen years, 'become the authoritative version of the Constitution',[71] On the same day, he wrote to Nehru that when the Assembly's committee had examined the translation, he proposed to ask the house to set aside a day a week to pass it article by article. After ten to fifteen years, wrote Prasad, the Hindi version would become 'crystallized', the language of the union would 'become more and more Hindi or Hindustani, and people from the South will get an opportunity

---

[68]At a ceremony at the Central Institute of Education, New Delhi, 18 April 1949; *Charka*, May 1949.

[69]Munshi in a letter to Satyanarayan Sinha, the Chief Whip, 2 January 1949; *Munshi Papers*.

[70]Minutes of the meeting, 5 January 1949; *Munshi Papers*. Present at this meeting were: Patel, Satyanarayan Sinha, M.A. Ayyangar, Durgabai, P.G. Merlon, Nalavade, J.N. Lal, and S.M. Ghose. There by special invitation were: Nehru, Pant, Ambedkar, Kher, and B.G. Reddi.

[71]Prasad to H.V.R. Iyengar, 4 June 1949; *Law Ministry Archives*.

of adjusting themselves'. To support his arguments, Prasad cited the precedent of the Irish Constitution.[72]

Nehru's reply to Prasad's manoeuvres throughout the spring had been that the Constitution might be translated, that an Assembly committee could examine the translation, and even that it could be accepted as 'an original text'.[73] He rejected Prasad's other views. Consideration of the Hindi version in the Assembly, he believed, would 'give rise to fierce argument at every step and on almost every word. It will thus tend to raise passions which will be reflected in the consideration of the English version and delay matters there.'[74] The English version of the Constitution must inevitably be authoritative, Nehru told Prasad—although 'many years after' a Hindi version might have equal or greater authority. As to the Irish experience, he had discussed it with De Valera and had been informed that the Irish had found Gaelic 'hard going' and were reverting more and more to English.[75] Despite Nehru's opposition, Prasad placed his ideas before the Steering Committee meeting of 10 June 1949. The committee, no doubt, wisely decided that 'no decision should be taken at this stage'.[76] The issue never again assumed serious proportions in the Assembly.

Prasad's adamant stand on translation presents an odd contrast to his moderation on other aspects of the language issue. Sensitive to the feelings of both Muslims and other Hindustani speakers, he had advocated first Hindustani and then broad, inclusive Hindi. He had, it is true, said that technical terms could be drawn from Sanskrit, but he had not objected to the incorporation of English words. Aware of the belief among south Indians that they occupied an inferior position in the Congress, he helped Pattabhi Sitaramayya gain presidency of the party. He had supported the use of English as the language of the Constituent Assembly. Yet his efforts to have the Constitution adopted in either an authoritative or an original Hindi version directly opposed the interests of non-Hindi speakers. The reason he pursued this course so strongly was apparently that he believed, like Gandhi, whose thought

[72]Prasad to Nehru, 4 June 1949; *Prasad Papers*, File, RP-5/49.
[73]Nehru to Prasad, 24 May 1949; ibid.
[74]Nehru to Prasad, 5 June 1949; ibid.
[75]Ibid.
[76]Minutes of the meeting, 10 June 1949; *Munshi Papers.*

he understood so well, that Indians would not be truly independent so long as they relied upon English.

The agitation over the national language quite obviously involved the status of the regional languages in relation to Hindi. Long before this became a burning question in the Constituent Assembly, however, language in multilingual areas and in education—issues that themselves overlapped—had been a source of conflict involving the pride of the various linguistic groups. In the closing months of the Assembly the resurgence of these sub-issues fuelled the fires of the central controversy.

India, as has been pointed out, was a land of linguistic minorities, where no one language was spoken by a majority of the population, and where there were not only true linguistic minorities but also relative minorities—groups of speakers of one of the more important languages living in enclaves controlled by the speakers of other major languages. This was one of the basic facts of Indian political life, and, recognizing it as such, the Congress laid down in the 'Karachi Rights' of 1931 that 'the culture, language, and scripts of the minorities and of the different linguistic areas should be protected'.[77] In 1938, a committee of the Central Advisory Board of Education supported one of the perpetual demands of linguistic minorities by espousing the principle of mother tongue instruction in primary schools, and official support for this, and for the use of mother tongue instruction at higher educational levels, increased during the years 1940-5.[78]

The Congress Experts Committee in the summer of 1946 suggested that the Constitution should protect linguistic minorities by providing that the members of a group not speaking the language of their area should not be restricted in developing their language and culture and that, in areas where a considerable proportion of the population used a language other than the provincial language, public authority must provide facilities for mother tongue education.[79] Munshi recommended

[77]See Chakrabarty and Bhattacharya, op. cit., p. 28. Nehru wrote, in 1937 that state education should be given in the language of the student and that minority groups of sufficient size could demand education in their own language. See 'Question of Language', in Nehru, *Unity of India*, p. 256.

[78]See for the period, Government of India, *Reports and Proceedings of the Central Advisory Board of Education*, 1938–49 (Delhi).

[79]See draft fundamental rights prepared by the Experts Committee; *Prasad Papers*, File, 16-P/45–6–7.

a similar provision to the Minorities Sub-Committee of the Advisory Committee in mid-April 1947. Neither suggestion was accepted. Instead, the advisory committee drafted a set of provisions that, generally speaking, provided that minorities should have the right to conserve their language, script, and culture; that no minority could be discriminated against on language grounds in regard to entrance into state educational institutions; that minorities could establish and maintain their own educational institutions; and that, when providing aid for schools, the state could not discriminate against schools maintained by language minorities.[80] To ensure that all types of minorities were protected by these rights, including speakers of major languages residing in an area where another major language was spoken, special phraseology was used.[81]

These were negative rights: neither the state nor society should prevent a minority from using its own language. But had linguistic minorities any positive rights in the educational field? Munshi and Ambedkar held that they did not. Explaining the minority provisions, Munshi said:

This minority right is intended to prevent majority controlled legislatures from favouring their own community to the exclusion of other Communities ... Is it suggested that the State should be at liberty to endow schools for minorities? Then it will come to this, that the minority will be a favoured section of the public. This destroys the very basis of a fundamental right.[82]

Ambedkar agreed that the provisions cast 'no burden upon the State'. But he believed that the state had a moral, if not a political, obligation to linguistic minorities. He held that because the state was not prohibited from legislating on such matters, provided the legislation was not oppressive, and because mother tongue education was 'such a universal principle', no provincial government could justifiably abrogate

[80]See advisory committee report, *Reports, First Series*, p. 33; also *CAD* V, 11, 365–71; also the *Constitution*, Arts. 29–30.

[81]Instead of using an earlier form 'Minorities in every Unit shall be protected' relative to language, etc., Ambedkar chose 'Any section of citizens residing in the territory of India or any part thereof having a distinct language ...' shall, etc. The purpose of the change, Ambedkar explained, was to include groups which 'although not minorities in the technical sense, (were) cultural minorities'—meaning Tamil-speaking Madrassis living in Bombay, for example. *CAD* VII, 22, 922.

[82]*CAD* V, 11, 367.

the principle 'without damage to a considerable part of the population in the matter of its educational rights'.[83] By the time Ambedkar made this speech in the Assembly (8 December 1948), these views had already been expressed in a policy statement by the union government. Mother tongue instruction for children, said a government resolution, was an accepted principle. And to achieve this, as well as administrative efficiency, the resolution continued, most provinces must be to some degree multilingual. Provincial governments must not force linguistic conformity on minorities.[84]

These principles were severely tested by a variety of conflicts during the autumn of 1948, and, in 1949, conflicts that had a direct bearing on the language issue in the Assembly. In Oriya-speaking Orissa, for example, the large Telegu-speaking minority in Ganjam and Koraput districts charged that although both Oriya and Telegu were recognized languages, Oriya-speaking court officers were refusing to accept documents written in Telegu. In the Manbhum district of Bihar, the large Bengali-speaking minority claimed that Hindi was being used to the detriment of Bengali in schools.[85] In the Central Provinces, Nagpur University announced its intention to make Hindi the compulsory medium of instruction, starting in the autumn of 1949,[86] even though it was in a largely bilingual province and in a division of the province where Marathi speakers outnumbered Hindi speakers two to one.

To try to meet these and like situations, the Congress Working Committee drafted the well-known Resolution on Bilingual Areas, which was published on 5 August 1949. The resolution, although, as the name suggests, devoted primarily to problems in multilingual areas, also tried to weave together into a coherent—and conciliatory—policy statement the party's ideas on the issue of language generally. A further reason for publishing the resolution was to dampen the linguistic provinces' agitation. The leaders of the major language groups were demanding that the problems of multilingual areas should be solved

[83]*CAD* VII, 22, 923.

[84]Government of India, Ministry of Education, *Resolution Number* D.3791/48-D.I, dated 3 August 1948.

[85]See note by the Working Committee, approximate date 20 May 1949, and memorandum prepared for the W.C. by P. Mishra and P.C. Ghosh, 7 June 1949; *Prasad Papers*, File 4-A/49.

[86]Government of India, Ministry of Education, *Report of the Committee on the Medium of Instruction at the University Stage*, p. 3. Report published November 1948.

by territorial readjustment. But the working committee had no intention, at this time at least, of approaching the problem in this way. Pressed on the issue, it had, therefore, to suggest a positive alternative.

The resolution, largely drafted by Prasad,[87] laid down that certain 'principles' might be applied to the various aspects of the language controversy. For example, each province should choose its own language, which should be used in the courts and for administrative purposes and as the medium of instruction at all educational levels. Bilingual areas were the only exceptions to this. In these 'fringe' areas, if the minority was 'of a considerable size, i.e. 20 per cent of the population', public documents should be in both languages.[88] This was followed by other recommendations regarding education at various levels.

On the subject of the national language, the resolution laid down that there should be 'a State language in which the business of the Union will be conducted'. And, the resolution continued, the state language,

will be the language of correspondence with the Provincial and State Governments. All records of the Centre will be kept and maintained in that language. It will also serve as the language for inter-Provincial and inter-State commerce and correspondence. During a period of transition, which shall not exceed fifteen years, English may be used at the Centre and for inter-Provincial affairs provided that the State language will be progressively utilized until it replaces English.[89]

Several aspects of the resolution deserve comment. First, its generality. Compared with the language provisions of the Constitution, the terms of the 5 August resolution were very broad. Perhaps it could not have been otherwise, but the detail of the Constitution demonstrates the great lengths to which the extremists and the moderates thought it

[87]Minutes of the Working Committee meeting, 31 Jury 1949; *Prasad Papers*, File 4-A/49. Present during the drafting of the resolution were: Sitaramayya, Prasad, Patel, Azad, Nehru, Pant, P.C. Ghosh, Kamaraj Nadar, Deo, Ram Sahai, Patil, Pratap Singh, Debeshwar Sharma, Sucheta Kripalani, K.V. Rao, and Nijalingappa. Eight of the group were Hindi speakers. The native tongue of the other members were: Patel, Gujarati; Ghosh, Bengali; Patil and Deo, Marathi; Rao and Sitaramayya, Telegu; Nijalingappa, Kannada; Kamaraj, Tamil.

[88]For the text of the resolution, see Indian National Congress, *Resolutions on Language Policy* (1949–57) (New Delhi: 1958), pp. 1–3. The working committee went to special pains to point out that Urdu was one of the languages recognized for all purposes mentioned in the resolution.

[89]Ibid.

necessary to go in order to give fullest expression to their own views and to protect their interests from the insidious intentions of their opponents. The working committee's resolution suggested, for example, that the provincial language should be used in the courts. If by this the members meant the subordinate, district courts, etc., they were on relatively safe ground. Yet the courts in a province included the High Court, and in the Constitution the uses of English in the High Courts and the Supreme Court would be set out in some detail. The resolution also indicates that Congress leaders had decided that it would be impolitic to single out any tongue for the honour of being the 'national' language, and that the Hindi-Hindustani dispute remained so sensitive that they avoided specifying what the state language should be.

The working committee also recommended that during a fifteen-year grace period, when English might be used by government, Hindi could progressively be employed. In the Assembly the Hindi-wallahs would make this their position, while south Indians, particularly, would fight fiercely against it. That the working committee found it necessary to publish the language resolution shows the temperature to which the controversy had risen under the pressure of the Hindi-wallahs and how unaccustomed the party leadership was to facing opposition of such militancy. The resolution also testifies to a strong belief in the necessity for a national language. As one observer later wrote, many Indians of the time believed that 'India lacked that linguistic unity which was thought to be so vital for a free people'.[90] Most of all the resolution, particularly the fifteen-year grace period for English, reflected the hopeful belief that within a few years most difficulties could be ironed out and that the 'next generation' could settle the language issue once and for all.[91] This hope has been rudely shattered.

THE BATTLE IS JOINED

The reaction to the 5 August Resolution began immediately. Although the Assembly did not sit on 6 or 7 August, the Congress Party's office

[90]S.K. Chatterji in his Minority Report to the *Report of the Official Language Commission* (New Delhi: 1956), p. 282.
[91]B. Shiva Rao and K.M. Munshi in interviews with the author have testified to the commonness of this belief.

was reported to be flooded with 'thousands' of letters about language policy, especially as it applied to bilingual areas. And on these two days the Hindi Sahitya Sammelan, under President Seth Govind Das, held a National Language Convention in New Delhi, to 'obtain a considered decision about the national language'.[92] Although the sponsors of the convention claimed that prominent litterateurs representing all Indian languages would be present to produce this decision, few of the writers who attended were well known.[93] The convention was intended, in fact, to be a claque for Hindi and for Govind Das. At the end of its discussions, it demanded that 'Sanskritized Hindi' and the Nagari script be made the national language of India and said that Hindi should progressively replace English for union and inter-governmental correspondence during a period not to exceed ten years. 'This arrangement was quite in accordance with the nation's will', proclaimed Govind Das subsequently.[94] But the convention, in fact, must have hurt rather than helped the cause of unity.

In a public speech in Delhi on 7 August, Purushottam Das Tandon made the Hindi-wallah's position even clearer. 'Those who oppose acceptance of Hindi as the national language and Nagari as the single national script', he said, 'are still following a policy of anti-national appeasement and are catering to communal aspirations.'[95] When the Assembly met on 8 August, the order paper bristled with language amendments to the Draft Constitution. Postponement was over, the battle had begun. Many of the amendments embodied the commonly-known views of the extremists, including a provision that during a ten-year transition period, parliament could provide for the use of *either or both* Hindi and English for union purposes. The moderates opposed this wording, recognizing it as a loophole that would permit the immediate exclusion of English. One such amendment bore the names of eighty-two members, forty-five of whom were from Bihar, the Central Provinces, and the United Provinces, and of whom at least

---

[92]Seth Govind Das, *Self Examination (An Autobiography)*, 3 volumes (Delhi: Bhartiya Vishva Prakashan), p. 124. This book is written in Hindi and was translated for the author.

[93]For a list of those attending, see Das, *Self-Examination*, Appendix.

[94]Ibid., p. 126. The convention was also reported in the press; see *The Hindu* and *The Hindustan Times* of these days. The convention dismissed Urdu as the language of military 'camps'; *The Hindustan Times*, 8 August 1949.

[95]*The Hindustan Times*, 8 August 1949.

fifty-eight were Hindi speakers. The name of Acharya Jugal Kishore, a general secretary of the Congress in 1948, headed this list, and several southerners, surprisingly enough, were also among the sponsors.[96] This amendment clearly demonstrated the support that the extremists had at this time from many Hindi-speaking backbenchers and, to some extent, among non-Hindi speakers. Other amendments would have reduced the grace period for English to five years, and yet others would have lengthened it or have given parliament the authority to provide for the continued use of English at its expiration—a provision that would appear in the Constitution.

The next day the non-Hindi bloc, led by the southerners, protested against these amendments and launched a counter-attack. At the Assembly Party meeting in the afternoon, they insisted that English should be used as the official language for at least fifteen years and they flatly refused to agree to the progressive substitution of Hindi during this time. They did concede, however, that by a two-thirds majority, parliament could authorize the use of Hindi *in addition to* English in the transitional period. The Hindi-wallahs objected, saying that the complete replacement of English by Hindi at the end of fifteen years would only be possible by progressive substitution.[97]

The meeting was able to agree unanimously, however, that 'Hindi should be the official language of the Indian union and that Devanagari should be the script'.[98] That Hindi should have this special status was never again in doubt. But there was, predictably, a 'divergence of opinion' over the meaning of Hindi. Nehru explained that Hindi should be defined as having the style and form of Hindustani—a phrase that would appear in the Constitution—and he and Prasad criticized the Hindi extremists for trying to purge Urdu from the language.[99] With an easy and peaceful solution of the controversy out of the question, the members at the meeting decided to appoint a committee to draft a compromise provision. It consisted of the members of the Drafting Committee (N.G. Ayyangar, T.T. Krishnamachari Ayyar, Munshi,

[96]Amendment number 4, *Orders of the Day*, 8 August 1949; *INA*.

[97]*The Hindu*, 12 August 1949.

[98]Ibid. According to *The Hindustan Times*, 12 August 1949, the meeting agreed that 'Hindi, as understood by the common man, should be chosen the national language'.

[99]*The Hindustan Times*, 12 August 1949.

Ambedkar, Saadulla, and N.M. Rau), plus Azad, Pant, Tandon, Balkrishna Sharma, S.P. Mookerjee, and Santhanam.[100]

That evening, after the party meeting, the non-Hindi speakers gathered together to draft an amendment to answer those proposed the day before by the Hindi supporters. The result was an amendment signed by forty-four members, twenty-eight of whom came from Madras; the remainder were also from the south with the exception of two Assamese and three Biharis. K. Santhanam's name headed the list of supporters, which included T.T. Krishnamachari, Mrs Durgabai, A.K. Ayyar, and M.A. Ayyangar. The amendment itself closely resembled a recommendation made by Santhanam a month earlier. It accepted Hindi with Nagari as the official language and proposed that English continue in use for fifteen years and for a further period if so determined by both houses of parliament. During the transition period, Hindi could be used in addition to English, and the union government should make funds available for teaching Hindi. Up to this point, both factions had talked in generalities. But the forty-four members now inserted a vital detail, probably at Santhanam's behest. They provided that 'For all official purposes of the Union or any State, numbers shall be indicated by Arabic numerals'.[101] The question of numerals was to become the sorest point in the language controversy.

The week from 10 to 17 August saw the language issue debated in 'stormy meetings' of the Assembly Party, according to the press; Prasad was reported to have said that the official language must be the language that is generally understood in northern India, and that although there should be a fifteen-year grace period for English, Hindi should be

---

[100]Ibid. According to *The Hindustan Times*, 12 August 1949, G.S. Gupta, Moti Satyanarayana, and Amrit Kaur were also members. In most cases, references to *The Hindu* have been cross-checked with *The Hindustan Times*.

[101]Amendment 52, *Orders of the Day*, 10 August 1949; *INA*. While the southerners were at work, Dr Raghuvira was drafting an amendment that was nearly the ultimate in extremist sentiment. It appeared on the same order paper. It laid down that Hindi with Nagari constituted the national and the official language and listed recruitment to the Union Public Services as one of the areas in which Hindi should be used. Within three to five years, English should be replaced 'totally, entirely, and absolutely', wrote Raghuvira. After five years, English could no longer be used either in parliament or in the legislatures or in the administration of the provinces, where the regional language or Hindi must be used. And the English version of the Constitution would be valid for only five years. Amendment 36; ibid.

progressively introduced for use 'in all-India matters'.[102] An editorial in *The Hindu* expressed the contrary view, saying that south Indian, Assamese, and Bengali members of the Assembly had 'good reason' to oppose the progressive substitution of Hindi because Hindi must be developed before it could attain the stature of a national language. Cultural changes take centuries not years, said the editorial.[103] In Delhi, a female sanyasi promised to fast to the death unless Hindi was adopted as the national language and India renamed Bharat. Nehru, among others, visited her. She broke her fast on 12 August, claiming that Nehru and other Congress leaders had assured her that Hindi would be adopted. And Pandit Pant was reported to have made a suggestion that, had it been accepted, would have avoided years of bitterness. Pant suggested that 'it should be left to the non-Hindi speaking regions to suggest the time limit' for the replacement of English by Hindi in union affairs.[104]

The special committee presented its report to the party meeting on 16 August. It pleased no one and was particularly offensive to the moderates. According to the most important of its provisions, English would be the sole official language for ten years and for five more if parliament agreed by a two-thirds majority. If Hindi replaced English at the end of ten years, parliament could, by a simple majority, provide for the continued use of the 'International numerals'. This tactful change from 'Arabic numerals' unfortunately did not mollify the Hindi extremists, who demanded the adoption of Nagari numerals. An 'influential section' of the committee, it was also reported, desired that Hindustani and Urdu as well as Sanskrit be named as sources of Hindi vocabulary.[105] Azad had resigned from the committee over this issue, claiming that the members would neither accept the word Hindustani nor 'accept any such interpretation which can widen the scope of Hindi'.[106] S.P. Mookerjee accurately labelled the committee a failure. The swing of moderates among the Hindi speakers away from the extremists appears to date from this time.

The special committee's efforts having been of no avail, the party meeting left it to the Drafting Committee to produce a compromise

[102]A Press Trust of India (PTI) dispatch in *The Hindu*, 17 August 1949.

[103]*The Hindu*, 13 August 1949. The editorial also said that the term Hindi must mean broad and inclusive, not sanskritized, Hindi.

[104]*The Hindu*, 11 August 1949; reported in *The Hindustan Times* of the same date.

[105]*The Hindu*, 17 August 1949.

[106]*CAD* IX, 34, 1456. See also ibid., p. 1452.

article. On 22 August, Ambedkar presented this newest in the series of attempted compromises. It provided that English would be used for fifteen years for official union purposes and that parliament could extend the period. The question of numerals, however, was left unresolved. In the interim, the president could provide for the use of Hindi in addition to English; English was to be the language of the courts, and the regional languages were to be protected and listed in a schedule to the Constitution. After the inauguration of the Constitution, a language commission would be established to study such matters as the progressive use of Hindi, the choice of numerals, etc.[107]

Numerals and the fifteen-year transition period dominated the debate in Assembly Party meetings during the succeeding ten days. During this time, the language provisions were hammered out in greater and greater detail until they became what was called the 'Munshi-Ayyangar formula', which was the basis of the language provisions of the Constitution. On 26 August, the debate over numerals lasted a tense and acrimonious three hours. Sitaramayya was in the chair. Ultimately the question came to a vote. The result, by a show of hands, was sixty-three in favour of international numerals and fifty-four in favour of Nagari numerals. The Hindi-wallahs called for a division. The count in the lobbies yielded a seventy-four/seventy-four tie. At this the Hindi side claimed that it had had seventy-five votes when the voting first commenced, but that one of its members had left the house after the show of hands.[108] The meeting decided, however, evidently on Sitarammayya's and Nehru's urging, that Nagari numerals could not be forced on the country by such a narrow margin. In two other moves, the meeting agreed that Hindi-speaking provinces might use Hindi rather than English as the inter-provincial language during the transition period and removed English from the list of fourteen languages that would be named in the schedule to the Constitution.

For the next few days, the Hindi-wallahs under Tandon's leadership continued to refuse to accept the international numerals and maintained that English must not be used beyond fifteen years. Other members of the Hindi bloc pressed for a reduction in the transition period and for the progressive substitution of Hindi as well as for the

[107]*The Hindu*, 23 August 1949.
[108]For reports of this meeting see *The Hindu* and *The Hindustan Times* of 27 August 1949. The reports are substantially the same.

use of Hindi in the civil services, etc. The pressure of the extremists, particularly on the numerals issue, drove many Gujarati, Marathi, Bengali, and even Bihari Assembly members from the Hindi group into the ranks of the moderates. The south Indians among the moderates, as might be expected, took the strongest stand. Their views were expressed by *The Hindu*, which editorially condemned the stupidity and uselessness of the fight over numerals and cited the frequently used arguments that the international numerals were of Indian origin (which was true) and that they must be retained for the sake of efficiency in such matters as the census, federal statistics, commerce, and so on.[109]

Nehru and Azad now led the moderates quite openly. Patel, although not deeply interested in the language issue, brought his influence for compromise to bear from his sickbed in Bombay. He wrote to Nehru, who read the letter at the party meeting, that fifteen years was sufficient for the changeover to Hindi, but that in the interim period, when Hindi might be authorized as an additional language to English, care should be taken not to upset administrative procedures.[110] Patel, conservative by nature, seems to have been, in general, sympathetic to Tandon's position and somewhat annoyed by the southern resistance to Hindi.[111] Yet he was sufficiently Gandhian for us to assume that he opposed sanskritized Hindi, and, as the practical man, he must simply have wanted above all a settlement of the dispute. For this reason he probably supported the Munshi-Ayyangar formula.

On 2 September, this was ready, and its authors (who included Ambedkar) presented it to the party meeting held, as usual, in the afternoon at Constitution House on Curzon Road. This compromise, generally speaking, suited everyone but the Hindi extremists, who opposed it two weeks later in one of the bitterest debates in the Assembly's history. Barring a few changes, the formula closely

[109]*The Hindu*, 30 August 1949.

[110]*The Hindu*, 24 August 1949. The Home Ministry, presumably on Patel's direction, had earlier recommended that the official language of the union (whether it be Hindi or English) should be the language of the High Courts, not the regional language. Home Ministry letter 11-a/48, dated 16 May 1948; *R.S. Shukla Papers*.

[111]An article published in *Harijan*, 21 November; 1948 (Vol. XII, No. 38), indicated that Patel was displeased because Congress proceedings still had to be in English 'because of the South Indian bloc'.

resembled Part XVII of the Constitution, and it is worthwhile here to review its major provisions.

The formula provided that the official language of the union was to be Hindi with the Nagari script but that international numerals would be used.[112] Notwithstanding this, English was to be used for union affairs for fifteen years and parliament could extend the period. The president could, during this period, order the use of Hindi and the Nagari numerals in addition to English and the international numerals. The language of the Supreme Court and the High Courts, the authoritative texts of bills, acts, ordinances, etc., should be in English, and for fifteen years no bill to alter this provision could be introduced in parliament without the sanction of the president. It was the duty of the union to promote the spread and development of Hindi so that it could serve as a medium of expression for the 'composite culture of India' and to secure Hindi's enrichment by seeing that it assimilated the 'forms, style, and expressions used in Hindustani and in the other languages of India'. For its vocabulary, Hindi should draw 'primarily on Sanskrit and secondarily on other languages'. An attached schedule listed thirteen living Indian languages, but not English or Sanskrit.

States could adopt any language used in the state, or Hindi, as their official language, the formula laid down, but English was to be used until the state legislature otherwise provided. The language in use by the union was to be the language of union-state and inter-state communications but Hindi-speaking states could use Hindi. The formula called for the formation of language commissions in 1955 and 1960 to survey the progress of Hindi. When drawing up its recommendations, the commission was to have due regard, among other things, for 'the just claims and the interests of the non-Hindi speaking areas in regard to the public services'.[113]

The roots of the Munshi-Ayyangar formula are apparent in the debates of the previous weeks and years. Two aspects of the compromise, however, included for the benefit of regional language speakers, deserve special comment. They are: the listing of regional languages in the

---

[112]The Munshi-Ayyangar formula was, officially, Amendment 65 'Relating to Language' on the Fourth List of Amendments, *Orders of the Day*, 5 September 1949; *INA*. For the text, see also *CAD* IX, 32, 1321–23. Listed as its sponsors were N.G. Ayyangar, Munshi, and Ambedkar.

[113]Ibid.

Constitution and the reference to the interests of non-Hindi speakers in regard to the public services. The services provided one of the largest sources of prestige employment for the middle and upper classes in India. They exerted 'a disproportionate pull on the educated youth of the country'.[114] Any move that would detrimentally affect the chances of Bengali or Tamil speakers, for example, entering the services would therefore be furiously resisted. Making Hindi the language of the services by the rapid replacement of English, as the Hindi-wallahs frequently advocated, was such a move.[115] For even if Hindi speakers, were obliged to learn a regional language, as some Hindi supporters were willing to agree, having the entrance examinations for the services in Hindi would place non-Hindi speakers at a great disadvantage. And so long as English remained the medium of instruction in universities (as it must for 'some time' in the view of the Universities Education Commission[116]), it would be unrealistic to demand that non-Hindi speaking university graduates should have a command of Hindi equalling that of native Hindi speakers—hence the provision of the Constitution protecting the interests of the non-Hindi speakers.

The plan to list thirteen living Indian languages in the Constitution was unique, yet what was its significance? The Munshi-Ayyangar formula provided that each language should be represented on the language commission; later it was agreed that these languages should be the sources from which Hindi should broaden itself.[117] But these were the

[114]*Report of the Official Language Commission*, p. 186. The other aspect of the provisions regarding the public services that interested the Assembly was the matter of minority representation. The minorities sub-committee, at its July 1947 meetings, voted that places should be reserved in the services for certain minorities. The advisory committee rejected this decision several weeks later, however, and no such provision was included in the Constitution. But by the Fundamental Rights the state is permitted to reserve places for 'backward classes' of citizens.

[115]Some examples of this: G.S. Gupta submitted a resolution to the Steering Committee on 25 October 1948 that all candidates to the union services pass tests in Hindi and one other Indian language; *Munshi Papers*. Mahavir Tyagi moved an amendment in the Assembly that provided that 'all tests, examinations, and competitions' held to select candidates for the union services should be in the official language. *CAD* IX, 28, 1106.

[116]Government of India, *Report of the Universities Education Commission*, p. 325. The report, although dated January 1950, was completed and presented to Nehru and Azad—as Minister of Education—on 24 August 1949. Radhakrishnan, the chairman, was quoted as saying at a press conference held the next day that 'We have also recommended that there must be no attempt at hasty replacement of English as a medium of instruction.' See *The Hindu*, 26 August 1949.

[117]See *Constitution*, Article 351.

only tangible advantages accruing to the regional languages from being listed in the Constitution. As the first language commission observed, 'there is no particular distinction bestowed on a language' because it is named in, Schedule VIII.[118] The languages were not made either national or official languages on the pattern of the Swiss, Pakistan, and South African Constitutions, the only constitutions in which the languages of the country are given by name.[119] Why, then, was such a list included in the formula, and why did its inclusion assume such importance in the eyes of regional language speakers?

The answer was: 'for psychological reasons and to give these languages status', according to Durgabai Deshmukh. 'We had these languages listed in the Constitution to protect them from being ignored or wiped out by the Hindi-wallahs.'[120] According to Nehru the regional languages should be enumerated so that they would be assured 'their due place' in the new India.[121] And he once suggested that they be called 'Officially Recognized Languages' instead of regional languages.[122] That the fears of the regional-language speakers were far from baseless was borne out by the attitude of Ravi Shankar Shukla, who opposed the listing of the languages in the Constitution as 'wholly unnecessary in view of the precarious conditions in the country'. Listing the languages, he believed, was a 'reactionary provision' because a commission representing these languages would 'delay the introduction of Hindi as the Official Language of the Union'.[123]

With such opinions current among the Hindi-wallahs, no wonder the speakers of other languages feared for the status of their tongues. As Mrs Durgabai from Madras said:

... The people of the non-Hindi speaking areas have been made to feel that this fight or this attitude on behalf of the Hindi-speaking areas is a fight for

[118]*Report*, op. cit., p. 51.

[119]The Canadian Constitution lists no languages, although it does accord special status to French as well as English. The Soviet Constitution (1936) does even less, providing in Article 40 only that laws passed by the Supreme Soviet must be published in the languages of the Republics of the Union.

[120]Mrs Durgabai (now Durgabai Deshmukh), in an interview with the author. This explanation has been corroborated by T.T. Krishnamachari, also in an interview with the author.

[121]The *Hindustan Times*, 24 August 1949.

[122]Nehru letter to Ambedkar, Munshi, and N.G. Ayyangar regarding their new language formula, dated 23 August 1949; *Law Ministry Archives*, File CA/19(11)/Cons/49.

[123]Shukla letter to the chairman of the Drafting Committee, 1 September 1949; *Shukla Papers*.

effectively preventing the natural influence of other powerful languages of India on the composite culture of the nation.[124]

S.P. Mookerjee, a former president of the communal Hindu Mahasabha, but a Bengali, welcomed the listing of the regional languages. Why, he asked, have 'many people belonging to non-Hindi speaking provinces ... become a bit nervous about Hindi?' Because 'people speaking other languages, not inferior to Hindi by any means, have not been allowed the same facilities which even the much-detested foreign regime did not dare deprive them of'.[125]

Pattabhi Sitaramayya occupied the chair on the afternoon of 2 September when the Munshi-Ayyangar formula was debated. He requested the meeting to treat the formula as a whole and as a compromise designed to satisfy the major points of view. The heated discussion revolved about two points: the content of the formula and how the formula was to be sponsored on the Assembly floor. The debate on the compromise itself covered familiar ground. The debate on the sponsorship of the formula—which, it will be recalled, took the form of an amendment to the Draft Constitution—involved an important matter of policy. If the party meeting voted to endorse the formula and it was then moved in the Assembly, it would be an official amendment, recognized as expressing Congress policy, and thus be binding on Congress members. If moved on the floor by its sponsors without the Assembly Party's sanction, it would have only the status of a member's private amendment. The moderates fought for passage by the party meeting; the Hindi-wallahs opposed it.[126] Finally the issue came to a division. On the side of the moderates, it was reported, voted members from Bombay (primarily Gujaratis), Bengal, Assam, Madras, and the south, plus Nehru, many ministers of the union government, and

[124]*CAD* IX, 34, 1426.

[125]*CAD* IX, 33, 1391. The speakers of the regional languages had reason for pride. Nearly all these languages were older, more developed tongues than Hindi—particularly Bengali and Tamil. Hindi was a relative newcomer, dating from the later half of the eighteenth century; S.K. Chatterji, *Languages and the Linguistic Problem*, Oxford Pamphlets on Indian Affairs (Bombay: Oxford University Press, 1943), p. 18. Even the Official Language Commission noted that Hindi lacked 'such natural ascendancy over the other provincial languages as to incline inhabitants of these provinces to accept secondary position for the language in their own regions' (*Report*, op. cit., p. 320.)

[126]The following account is based on reports in *The Hindu* and *The Hindustan Times* of 3 September 1949.

members of the Drafting Committee. Opposing the party's adoption of the amendment were Assembly members from the United Provinces, the Central Provinces, the East Punjab, Bihar, and Rajasthan. The result was a tie vote, seventy-seven to seventy-seven. Sitaramayya declined to use his casting vote, and the deadlock remained unresolved.

The question that continued to defy solution was numerals. The Hindi-wallahs had opposed the adoption of the formula because it recognized the international numerals. The moderates, in the face of extremist insistence on Nagari numerals, had threatened to break off negotiations entirely.[127] The language dispute thus went to the Assembly unresolved. There was to be no whip, and the vote in the Assembly would be free.

We may pause here to bury a minor controversy. The closeness of the votes on language in the party meetings has given rise to the legend that Hindi became the official language of India by a majority of only one vote.[128] This seems very doubtful. Issues of *The Hindu* on 12 and 28 August 1949 reported that two meetings of the Congress Assembly Party 'unanimously' named Hindi as the official language. The *Hindustan Times* throws no doubt on this and in its report of 12 August on the previous day's party meeting said that it had been agreed to make Hindi as spoken by the common man the national language. Had this been decided by one vote, it presumably would have been reported in the same manner as the one-vote margins on numerals and the sponsorship of the Munshi-Ayyangar formula. Moreover, there seems never to have been any doubt that either Hindi or Hindustani would be given all-India status, and the choice of the word Hindi instead of Hindustani was apparently made in July 1947 by a large majority.[129]

One is left with the conclusion that the 'one-vote' legend is based on the events at the party meeting of 26 August 1949, when there may have existed briefly a one-vote majority in favour of Nagari over international numerals. Accounts of the language controversy by Ambedkar and Seth Govind Das in fact support this view, although they apparently uphold the legend. In his *Thoughts on Linguistic States*, Ambedkar wrote:

[127]Ibid. Also Durgabai Deshmukh in an interview with the author.

[128]See for example, Harrison, *Dangerous Decades*, p. 9—in which Harrison cites an article published in 1958 in *The Hindu*. Selig Harrison, *India: The Most Dangerous Decades* (New Jersey: Princeton Univeristy Press, 1960).

[129]See above, p. 277.

... There was no Article which proved more controversial than Article 115, which deals with the (Hindi) question. No Article produced more opposition. No Article more heat. After a prolonged discussion, when the question was put, the vote was 78 against 78. The tie could not be resolved. After a long time when the question was put to the meeting once more, the result was 77 against 78 for Hindi. Hindi won its place as the national language by one vote.[130]

Govind Das, in his autobiography, has written:

... When the votes were taken, 78 were in favour of Hindi and 77 in favour of Hindustani ... This was not liked by the supporters of Hindustani and they descended to rowdyism ... Kaka Bhagwant Rai (Roy) of Patiala, having cast his vote in favour of Hindi and knowing the result to have been in favour of Hindi left the Assembly due to some urgent work. When votes were again taken, on the matter being pressed by the supporters of Hindustani, the Hindi side had one less vote and therefore both sides were equal at 77. A wave of enthusiasm ran through the opposition group.[131]

Neither of the authors gives a date for the events recounted. But they bear sufficient resemblance to the 26 August party meeting for it to be assumed that that is what they describe. The *Hindustan Times* also reported that the departure of a Patiala representative reduced the one-vote majority to a tie. The most reasonable conclusion one can draw is that Ambedkar and Govind Das have confused the facts or have interpreted the one-vote majority for Nagari numerals, if such there was, as a victory for Hindi, but this would in no way justify the claim that Hindi became the official language of India by one vote. And in the context of the Assembly Party's belief in consensus, the one-vote legend loses all meaning. For the close voting in the party meeting produced not decisions, but only further attempts at compromise in order that the controversy might be settled with maximum agreement or, if possible, unanimously.

During the week following the 2 September party meeting, the Assembly continued, as it had during the past month, to devote its time to problems of federalism, special minority provisions, tax matters, and so on. Off the floor of the House, the Hindi-wallahs persisted in

---

[130]Ambedkar, *Thoughts on Linguistic States* (Delhi: Published by Ambedkar, 1955), p. 14. In none of the many draft versions of the Constitution does an Article 115 deal even remotely with the language question.

[131]Govind Das, *Self Examination*, pp. 128–9.

their attacks on the Munshi-Ayyangar formula while the moderates stood firm on it. The debate on language in the Assembly was scheduled to open on 12 September. On 10 September, the dammed waters of extremist fury burst upon the compromise formula. The order paper bulged with forty-five pages of language amendments, most of them submitted by the Hindi-wallahs. They would have wiped out, or made unrecognizable, the provisions by which the formula intended to save Indian unity.

The amendments by Govind Das conveyed the tone of extremist sentiment. One of them, which would have replaced the formula with a wholly new language section, provided that states adopting Hindi as their language could print the texts of bills, acts, and the judgments of courts in Hindi and could use it instead of English in High Court proceedings.[132] This amendment omitted mention of international numerals, provided that Hindi should replace English as the official language after ten years (or after fifteen if Hindi had been used additionally to English for all purposes during the interim). It made no provision for parliament to extend this period, nor for Hindi to have a composite, all-India character. Another amendment by Govind Das (like provisions were submitted by Shukla, Mandloi, Gupta, and others) would have deleted from the formula the schedule naming the regional languages. Amendments by other extremists called for the complete replacement of English in five years and for the progressive substitution of Hindi.

The disgust and dismay with which many Assembly members by this time looked on the controversy was shown by the amendments that would have made Sanskrit the official language. Heading the list of twenty-eight members who submitted such amendments were the names of Ambedkar and T.T. Krishnamachari.[133] Neither could have believed that their amendment would be accepted, but they would have agreed with L.K. Maitra, who told the Assembly that choosing Sanskrit would put all the regional languages on an equal footing and

---

[132]Fourth List of Amendments, *Orders of the Day*, 10 September 1949; *INA*.

[133]Amendment 71, *Orders of the Day*, 10 September 1949; *INA*. Ambedkar had at one time expressed a strong belief in linguistic homogeneity for India. He had suggested that the language chosen as the national language by the Assembly should be 'the language of the State, i.e. of the Union as well as the Units.' Ambedkar, minute of dissent to the Fundamental Rights Sub-Committee, 19 April 1947; *Prasad Papers*, File 1-F/47.

put an end to the 'jealousies' aroused by the choice of Hindi.[134] The *Hindustan Times* called the suggestion 'a council of despair'.[135]

The final confrontation on language began late in the afternoon of 12 September, the morning session having been devoted to the finale of the compensation issue, and in a short time the pattern of the debate became established. President Prasad opened the proceedings by enjoining a calm approach and temperate language. Speakers, he said, 'should not let fall a single word or expression which might hurt or cause offence'. And he further called for the decision on the language provisions of the Constitution to be taken by consensus. 'The decision of the House should be acceptable to the country as a whole,' he said. '... Therefore, members will remember that it will not do to carry a point by debate in this House.'[136]

N.G. Ayyangar then introduced the Munshi-Ayyangar formula, saying that it embodied not his or his co-sponsors' ideas, but that it was 'a compromise between opinions which were not easily reconcilable'. There were two basic principles behind the formula, Ayyangar explained. One was that 'we should select one of the languages in India as the common language of the whole of India'. Yet this could not be achieved immediately and English must continue to be used because Hindi 'is not today sufficiently developed and must be given time to establish itself'. The second principle was 'that the numerals to be used for all official Union purposes should be what have been described as the all-India forms of Indian numerals'. For the sake of compromise, Ayyangar said, the drafters of the formula had made two concessions on the latter principle. The first was that the president could order the use of Nagari numerals in addition to international numerals; the second, that the language commission might make recommendations on the subject of numerals. Otherwise, said Ayyangar, the basic principles of the compromise must stand.[137]

Seth Govind Das, speaking in Hindi, replied to Ayyangar. The distance between his views and those of Prasad and Ayyangar was great. He rejected Prasad's appeal for consensus, although he called for reaching decisions 'in an amicable spirit'.

[134]*CAD* IX, 33, 1352–60.
[135]*Hindustan Times*, 19 September 1949.
[136]*CAD* IX, 32, 1312.
[137]Ibid., pp. 1317–19.

We have accepted democracy (Govind Das said) and democracy can only function when majority opinion is honoured. If we differ on any issue, that can only be decided by votes. Whatever decision is arrived at by the majority must be accepted by the minority respectfully and without any bitterness.[138]

Govind Das also rejected international numerals and the idea that English might not be completely replaced by Hindi in fifteen years. To the charge that the extremists were narrowing the scope of Hindi and behaving in a communal and revivalist fashion, he replied, 'It is a great injustice to accuse us of communalism'. He then charged that 'Urdu has mostly drawn inspiration from outside the country' and used *Bulbul* instead of *Koyal* to mean cuckoo. India, he said, had had one cultural tradition for thousands of years. 'It is in order to maintain this tradition that we want one language and one script for the whole country. We do not want it to be said that there are two cultures here.'[139]

That evening, the leaders of the Hindi-wallahs met and drew up an amendment that may be regarded as their 'official' position. Signed by Tandon, Shukla, Balkrishna Sharma, Govind Das, Govind Malaviya, and six others, it appeared on the next day's order paper. The amendment provided that the official union language would be Hindi with the Nagari script and with both Nagari and international numerals. It laid down, however, that during a fifteen-year interim period in which English would be used, the president could authorize the use of *either or both* forms of numerals for official purposes and could also authorize the use of Hindi in addition to English in all fields 'other than auditing, accounting, and banking'. Parliament was empowered to extend the use of English.[140] Here the amendment ended. It made no mention of language in the states or in the courts, and it contained no schedule of regional languages and no directive that Hindi should absorb the style and forms of Hindustani and the other Indian languages.

The debate of the following day was marked by speeches for S.P. Mookerjee and Nehru. Mookerjee repeated the call for a decision based on consensus.

If it is claimed by anyone (he said) that by passing an article in the Constitution of India one language is going to be accepted by all by a process of coercion,

---

[138]Ibid., p. 1325.

[139]Ibid., p. 1328.

[140]Amendment 333 of the Eighth List of Amendments, *Orders of the Day*, 13 September 1949; *INA*.

I say, Sir, that that will not be possible to achieve. (Hear, Hear.) Unity in diversity is India's keynote and must be achieved by a process of understanding and consent and for that a proper atmosphere has to be created.[141]

Nehru, speaking thoughtfully, rambled typically to the heart of the matter. The Munshi-Ayyangar formula was the best solution under the circumstances, therefore he supported it, he said. Although English must continue to be a most important language in India, no nation could become great on the basis of a foreign language. The language India chose for itself must be 'a language of the people, not a language of a learned coterie', he continued. Gandhi had used the word Hindustani to represent the people's language, to represent 'the composite culture of India', and it was the references to Hindustani that had allowed him to support the Munshi-Ayyangar formula. Had those references not been made, he said, 'then it would have been very difficult for me to accept this Resolution'.[142] Nehru criticized the 'tone of authoritarianism' in the speeches of the Hindi-wallahs, and told them they could not force a language on the people. In conclusion he attacked the attempts to narrow and to sanskritize Hindi, the attempts to cut India off from the English language aspects of its heritage.

We stand on the threshold of a new age (Nehru said) ... What sort of India do we want? Do we want a modern India—with its roots steeped in the past ... in so far as it inspires us—do we want a modern India with modern science and all the rest of it, or do we want to live in some ancient age, in some other age which has no relation to the present? You have to choose between the two. It is a question of approach. You have to choose whether you look forward or backward.[143]

The third day of the debate Dr Raghuvira attacked Urdu, and Jaipal Singh deprecated 'the puritanical fanaticism that has gripped so many people'.[144] Tandon, Maulana Azad, and Shankarrao Deo made long contributions. Although Deo, a general secretary of the Congress, supported the Munshi-Ayyangar formula, international numerals, and broad Hindi, he said that the very aims of the formula conflicted: 'I cannot understand how these things can go together', he said. 'We

[141]CAD IX, 33, 1389.
[142]Ibid., pp. 1410–11.
[143]Ibid., p. 1416.
[144]CAD IX, 34, 1440.

cannot hope to have one language for the whole country and at the same time work for the enrichment of the regional languages.' Deo hoped that India could retain its cultural diversity. He was an Indian, he said, but his language was Marathi. If having Hindi as the official language meant 'one language for the whole country, then I am against it', he said.[145]

Tandon, not surprisingly, objected to the formula at nearly every point. He had hoped that the substitution of Hindi for English would begin immediately, and spoke, therefore, of the 'hard provision in regard to Hindi not being used at all except in addition to English for five years, and more until a commission makes a recommendation and that recommendation is accepted by the President'. He called the continued use of English in the provinces 'palpably retrograde'. He described the Nagari numerals as 'an ancient heritage', and said that 'Hindi, with the backing of Sanskrit can face all the difficulties of vocabulary with ease.'[146]

Azad replied to Tandon in a speech noteworthy for its reasonableness and perceptiveness. He explained how he had come to realize the need for a gradual approach to the replacement of English. 'The Union of North and South', he said, 'has been made possibly only through the medium of English. If today we give up English, then this linguistic relationship will cease to exist,' Azad closed by expressing the hope that 'the present atmosphere of narrowmindedness' would give way to an atmosphere 'in which people freeing themselves from all sorts of sentiments would see the problem of language in its real and true perspective'.[147]

This was 14 September. The sitting adjourned at 1 p.m. for lunch. Most members must have eaten a sober meal. Decision was due that afternoon, but the debate had brought agreement no closer. The members in general looked forward with distaste to a division. The Assembly Party met at 3 p.m. to try to break the deadlock. Sitaramayya presided over two hours of 'strenuous and stormy discussion' that brought no result. Just at five o'clock, when the Assembly was scheduled to reconvene, the members reached an agreement. They trooped into the Assembly room and requested the Chair for a further hour to work

[145]Ibid., pp. 1430–1.
[146]Ibid., pp. 1443–9.
[147]Ibid., pp. 1453 and 1459.

out details. At six o'clock the work was done. The members breathed 'a genuine sigh of relief' that the matter had been settled.[148]

The compromise consisted of five amendments to the Munshi-Ayyangar formula, each of which was a concession to the extremist bloc. These provided that after fifteen years, parliament could legislate on the use of Nagari numerals as well as on the continued use of English, that Hindi might be used in the proceedings of a High Court with the sanction of the president, that bills, acts, ordinances, etc., could be issued in the official language of a state if an official English translation was published, and that Sanskrit be added to the list of languages in the schedule.[149]

With the final compromise on paper, the party meeting agreed that the members should withdraw the nearly 400 language amendments they had submitted and support the final version of the formula. A whip was issued to this effect. Back in the Assembly chamber, the members heard Munshi read the agreed amendments, and all but five members withdrew their own amendments. Three of them were Congressmen, Brajeshwar Prasad, S.L. Saksena, and Tandon. The two others were League Muslims, Naziruddin Ahmad and Z.H. Lari.[150] The Assembly rejected their amendments by overwhelming majorities. The new Munshi-Ayyangar formula was then put to the vote, to be carried 'amidst deafening cheers'.

EPILOGUE

'We have done the wisest possible thing', Prasad told the Assembly immediately after the adoption of the language provisions, 'and I am

---

[148]This account of the meeting was taken from *The Hindu* of 15 September 1949. It has been largely corroborated by interviews.

[149]For the texts of the amendments as finally moved, and for the formula as amended, see *CAD* IX, 34, 1486–9. The Drafting Committee on its own initiative later changed the last article of the formula so that the sources of Hindi were to be the 'other languages of India specified in the Eighth Schedule', and not simply the 'other languages of India', as had been the earlier wording; see *Constitution,* Article 351.

[150]Tandon resigned from the Assembly Party 'as a protest against the mandate' (*The Hindu,* 16 and 17 September 1949), apparently in the meeting of 14 September, so that he would be free to press his amendments on the floor of the House. The Congress two days later requested that he withdraw his resignation, and he did so; ibid. Z.H. Lari resigned from the Assembly because Hindustani and the Urdu script were not mentioned in the language provisions; *The Hindu,* 17 September 1949.

glad, I am happy, and I hope posterity will bless us for this.' He predicted that a common language would 'forge another link that will bind us all together from one end (of the country) to the other'.[151]

Yet India, even north India, despite the increasing efforts of the extremists, has not rushed to embrace Hindi. An editorial written in *The Hindu* at the time foresaw the future more closely than had Prasad when it said that fifteen years was more like a minimum than a maximum for the replacement of English. In the fifteen years since the inauguration of the Constitution, the union government has put Hindi to only minor uses in the conduct of its affairs. Only the Hindi-speaking states have been using Hindi, and then not always widely. The regional languages in other states, generally speaking, have replaced English as the language of subordinate courts and of legislative proceedings, but otherwise English has continued to be the principal language of state as well as of union affairs.[152]

The principal reason for this is that India has produced very little feeling of linguistic nationalism. It was not, and is not, generally speaking, un-Indian to speak English. The Congress (as apart from Gandhi himself) proclaimed the virtues of speaking Hindustani, yet continued to use English at all but the local level. In the Constituent Assembly, speeches were made calling for a national language and emphasizing its importance to national unity as a 'cement' to hold the various parts of India together. Yet more than half the members of the Assembly, one may reasonably estimate, voted for the Munshi-Ayyangar formula because it did not make inevitable the de facto adoption of an Indian tongue as the national language. The element of linguistic nationalism—or, better, linguistic chauvinism—was injected by the Hindi extremists. Since the coming into force of the Constitution, the official language of the union has not replaced English, and the use of English after 1965 has been provided for by the Official Languages Act of 1963.[153]

India's problem has been and is, rather, one of sub-national sentiment and sub-national competition, which often take the form of linguistic

[151]*CAD* IX, 34, 1490–1.

[152]For a description of the language situation after the first five years of the language provisions, see Government of India, *Report of the Official Language Commission*, 1956, esp. pp. 442–62.

[153]*The Official Languages Act*, 1963, Government of India, Act No. 19 of 1963.

rivalries.[154] In the Assembly, these rivalries had not assumed their present proportions or many of their present guises; they were expressed as resistance to the linguistic chauvinism of another sub-national group, the Hindi speakers—who came, unfortunately, to be represented by a group of extremists. The language provisions of the Constitution were designed, in a typically Indian fashion, to meet such a situation: Assembly members believed that India should, ideally, have an indigenous national language; Hindi (or Hindustani) was the most suitable, so it was named for the role. Yet for Hindi to be in practice the national language was impossible, for the only language in national use was English. Moreover, the other sub-nations feared the introduction of Hindi and had pride in their own languages. Hence the Constitution makes clear what the national ideal is, and then, realistically compromises, laying down how the nation is to function, linguistically speaking, until the ideal is achieved. More than this, as the furious controversy among the members testifies, the Assembly was unable to do. Yet the language provisions are not just an unhappy compromise; they have a more positive side. They show that the large majority of the Assembly believed that the use of many Indian languages and of English was compatible with national unity and with the evolution of a national spirit.

[154]For a comprehensive treatment of the forms interprovincial competition has taken—over allocation of funds for development plans, etc.—and how this often expresses itself in language rivalries, see Harrison, *Dangerous Decades*.

2

Sanskrit for the Nation*

Sumathi Ramaswamy†

> ... the people of India love and venerate Sanskrit with a feeling
> which is next only to that of patriotism towards Mother India.
>
> *Report of the Sanskrit Commission, 1956–57*

LANGUAGE IN THE REGIMES OF THE NATION

This essay raises the language question in its relationship to the wider problematic of the nationalization of pasts by focusing on the curious and puzzling status accorded to Sanskrit in the nationalization of the Indian past in this century. I use the words 'curious' and 'puzzling' deliberately, for the Sanskrit issue unsettles many well-entrenched assumptions about language and nationalism that circulate in scholarly circles and popular imagination. Just as crucially, Sanskrit's (mis)adventures in the past century or so draw our attention to the

*Originally published as 'Sanskrit for the Nation', in *Modern Asian Studies*, 33 (2), May 1999, pp. 339–81; published by Cambridge University Press.

†I am very grateful to a number of Sanskrit scholars who so graciously shared with me their thoughts on the subject of this essay: George Cardona, Robert Goldman, Wilhelm Halbfass, Hans Hock, Sheldon Pollock, Ludo Rocher and Rosane Rocher. I also thank Dipesh Chakrabarty and Rich Freeman for their suggestive critiques. This essay was originally intended for a volume on nationalizing the Indian past. I wish to thank the editors for their programmatic statement on this subject which inspired me to write this.

troubling linguistic turns taken by the nationalization process in India with its disquieting complicity with colonial categories and certitudes. The concerns of this paper have thus been shaped by three related issues pertaining to language, nationalism, and modernity.

First, since at least the 1950s, the Government of India has invested an unusual amount of energy and time, not to speak of money, in regulating Sanskrit through creating supervisory agencies, inaugurating new centres of Sanskritic learning, and reopening old ones. It has also financed publications, cultural events, and radi (and more recently, television) broadcasts for nationwide consumption, all centred round the promotion of the language. The state's Sanskrit policy (if we may call it that) was forged by the Sanskrit Commission which was set up in 1956, and which in turn derived its authority from the Constitution of India. While much of this essay examines the remarkable report issued by this commission, and considers some of its implications for independent India's linguistic politics, this examination itself is provoked by the following question—what can we say about the modernity of the Indian nation that it needs the crutches of an ancient language, a language that many argue is known to few of its citizens and spoken by a mere handful? Existing theories of language and nationalism, themselves largely based on the normative western European experience, would have us think that the very emergence of the nation-state leads to a jettisoning of archaic 'classical' languages from positions of prestige, profit, and power, and to the empowering of the modern 'vernacular' that is deemed to be spoken by a majority of its citizens—their 'mother tongue'—as the 'national' language. Yet in India, the demand which has periodically surfaced over the past century for instituting Sanskrit as the national language has been couched in exactly the opposite terms. Sanskrit deserves this status, in the view of its advocates, precisely because it is the most ancient language of the nation, and precisely because it is nobody's 'mother tongue'. Does this demand therefore amount to a rejection of a 'western' model of the nation imagined around a modern spoken language, or is it a reflection of the orientalist and colonial inflections of the Indian nation? Or does it suggest an alternate imagination about the place of language in nation and modernity?

Second, and following from this first set of questions, what is the fate of ancient languages which get entangled in the regimes of the modern nation-state? To date, some of the more interesting work on this subject has been done on Hebrew whose relationship to Israeli and Jewish nationalism shows some fascinating parallels with the place of Sanskrit in Indian and Hindu nationalism. Robert Alter has argued that the 'normalization' of Hebrew in modern Israel under the 'ideological impulse' of Israeli nationalism necessitated the secularization of what had hitherto been the 'holy tongue' of Jews and its transformation from a 'dead' liturgical and literary language into a spoken medium. This process also fostered a 'ruthlessness' towards non-Hebraic, especially Yiddish, manifestations in Israeli national culture.[1] His work reminds us that the nationalization of a language, ancient or otherwise, does not merely involve the standardization of its linguistic forms, vocabularies, and meanings; just as significantly, or perhaps more so, it also calls for a standardization (and sanitization) of cultural notions about the language that have gathered through time. In other words, the nationalization of language is never just a linguistic or grammatical project, but is always an ideological one in which old assumptions have to be rethought or discarded, and new meanings assigned to enable the national project at hand. As we shall see, Sanskrit is made to take on new meanings—and abandon some old ones—in relationship not just to its own past, but to the past(s) of the nation, its languages, and their speakers. To anticipate one of the fundamental contentions of this paper, I will suggest that the nationalization of Sanskrit transforms it into a metonym of the nation, as voiced in the formulation 'Sanskrit is India'.[2] Here, a putative whole that is 'India' is reduced metonymically to one of its constitutive parts, namely, Sanskrit. The part comes to stand for the whole through erasure or absorption of other parts that make up the whole. So, the pasts associated with other languages which have arguably played comparable roles (Pali, Tamil, Persian, etc.) are excluded or subordinated to a past constituted round Sanskrit that is renamed as the nation's past. Yet, the phrase 'Sanskrit is India' may also be read as a synecdoche in which Sanskrit is assigned the capacity to represent all of India. Indeed, the nationalizers of Sanskrit would like us to believe that the language is not just one part of a whole that is 'India', or even its most important part, but that

[1]Robert Alter, *Hebrew and Modernity* (Bloomington: Indiana University Press, 1994).

[2]Suniti Kumar Chatterjee, *India: A Polyglot Nation and its Linguistic Problems vis-à-vis National Integration* (Bombay, 1974), p. 32.

it is constitutive of *every* part that makes up the whole. As we shall see, the Sanskrit Commission took on that much-touted nationalist slogan 'unity in diversity' and insisted that it is Sanskrit that brought a 'remarkable unity' to India's 'bewildering diversity'. In the words of the commission, 'we can never insist too strongly on this signal fact that Sanskrit has been the Great Unifying Force of India, and that India with its nearly 400 millions of people [*sic*] is One Country, and not half or dozen or more countries, *only because of Sanskrit*.[3] In this view, Sanskrit transforms the many into One: it gives lie to the apparent heterogeneity of the nation by reminding modern Indians and the world at large that underneath all that 'bewildering diversity', India is really One.

Third and finally, this paper takes its cue from Sheldon Pollock's stimulating essay, 'The Language of the Gods in the World of Men', in which he rightly underscores the urgent need for a social history of Sanskrit. Such a social history, Pollock writes, ought to consider 'the ideological constraints that from an early period shaped its discourse'; chart 'the changing domains of usage and learning to hear the new speakers who find a voice in Sanskrit'; and above all, critically detail *'what it has meant in history to appropriate Sanskrit'.*[4] My paper considers only a very thin slice of the much larger discourse of power that has gathered around the language over the centuries, even while suggesting that a social history of Sanskrit along the lines proposed by Pollock has necessarily to bring in the present, and the efforts to nationalize the language in this century. This nationalization, I propose, has shaped our understanding of not just the pre-national history of the language, but of India's many pasts as well, in ways which we are just beginning to appreciate.[5] Further, recent attempts by Hindu nationalist groups to re-empower the language at the very least underscore the importance of learning more about what is going on with Sanskrit in independent

[3]*Report of the Sanskrit Commission*, 1956–7 (Delhi, 1958), pp. 80–1 (emphasis mine).

[4]Sheldon Pollock, 'The Language of the Gods in the World of Men: Reflections on Sanskrit in History' (unpublished manuscript, inaugural lecture, University of Chicago, 1990), emphasis mine. See also Sheldon Pollock, 'The Sanskrit Cosmopolis, 300–1300: Transculturation, Vernacularization, and the Question of Ideology', in Jan E.M. Houben (ed.), *The Ideology and Status of Sanskrit: Contributions to the History of the Sanskrit Language* (Leiden: J. Brillo, 1996), pp. 197–247.

[5]Carol Breckenridge and Peter van der Veer (eds), *Orientalism and the Post-colonial Predicament: Perspectives on South Asia* (New York: Oxford University Press, 1994).

India.[6] Yet, because the language has come to be so indelibly identified with India's antiquity and distant past, there are few serious studies of Sanskrit's intense, albeit troubled, participation in its modernity.[7] And so, this essay sets out to make a beginning in this direction.

SANSKRIT AND MODERNITY

In October 1956, amidst the turmoil of the states reorganization debates and the creation of linguistic states, the Government of India decided to appoint a commission to evaluate the state of Sanskrit in the nation. The ostensible reason for creating the Sanskrit Commission was pedagogical. Over the past decade, a number of government commissions investigating education and language issues—the University Education Commission (1948–9) chaired by S. Radhakrishnan, the Secondary School Education Commission (1952–3) under A. Lakshmanaswami Mudaliar, and the Official Language Commission (1955–6) chaired by B.G. Kher—had proclaimed their faith in the value of Sanskrit education for the Indian citizenry.[8] Sanskrit and its literature, it was pointed out, 'have served throughout these centuries not only as the reservoir of ideas, sentiments, and parables to be drawn upon freely by all for the embellishment of their literary output, but also as benchmarks of literacy excellence, as standards for social conduct, as exemplars of morality, and in short, as the repository of wit and wisdom of all the Indian peoples throughout the ages'.[9] Understandably, therefore, much concern was voiced by these commissions over a perceived deterioration in Sanskritic learning which, it was feared, would eventually lead to the extinction of the language, if the government did not step in add prevent a national disaster.

The government's response was to set up the Sanskrit Commission under the chairmanship of the renowned linguist, Suniti Kumar

[6]Sukumari Bhattacharji, 'New Education Policy and Sanskrit', *Economic and Political Weekly*, 25 (48–49), 1990, pp. 2641–2; Robert Goldman, 'The Communalization of Sanskrit and the Sanskritization of Communalism' (unpublished paper, 1993). Corstiaan J.G. van der Burg, 'The Place of Sanskrit in Neo-Hindu Ideology: From Religious Reform to National Awakening', in Houben (ed.), *The Ideology and Status of Sanskrit*, pp. 375–8.

[7]For some recent attempts to consider this issue, see especially essays by Victor A. van Bijlert, Corstiaan van der Burg, and Saroj Bhate, in Houben (ed.), *The Ideology and Status of Sanskrit*.

[8]*Report of the Sanskrit Commission*, pp. 3–4.

[9]*Report of the Official Language Commission* (New Delhi, 1957), p. 249.

Chatterjee, who was to be aided in his task by seven established
Sanskritists who included V. Raghavan of the University of Madras,
R.N. Dandekar from the University of Poona, and S.K. De of Jadavpur
University in Calcutta.[10] The official mandate of the Sanskrit
Commission was 'to undertake a survey of the existing facilities, for
Sanskrit education ...; to make proposals for promoting the study of
Sanskrit; [and] to examine the traditional system of Sanskrit Education
in order to find out what features from it could be usefully incorporated
into the modern system'.[11] It is clear, however, from the report submitted
by the commission a year later in November 1957, that it saw its task
as being more than just pedagogical, for at stake was the very survival
of the emergent nation. The commission was fiercely anxious about
'the growing fissiparous tendencies and linguistic parochialism which
are jeopardising the political unity of the country and are rocking the
very foundations of our freedom'.[12] A decade of linguistic jealousy

[10]Suniti Kumar Chatterjee (1890–1977), best known for his numerous publications in
comparative philology and historical linguistics of Indian languages, was Professor of Indian
Linguistics and Phonetics in the University of Calcutta (1922–52). He was elected to the West
Bengal Legislative Council in which he served until 1964 when he resigned to take up his
appointment as the National Professor of India in the Humanities. In addition to serving as
chair of the Sanskrit Commission in 1956–7, he was also a member of the Official Language
Commission appointed by the Government of India in 1955–6. His position on the official
language question varied over time. In 1943, he conceded that 'Hindi (Hindustani) alone has
the greatest claim to be [the] national language', although he also did not fail to insist that if
there were only Hindus in India, Sanskrit would continue to play its role as link language as it
had for thirty centuries (Suniti Kumar Chatterjee, *Languages and the Linguistic Problem* [London,
1943], p. 23). By 1956, he had become less enthusiastic about Hindi, and even appended 'a note
of dissent' to the *Report of the Official Language Commission* in which he expressed concern
over what he characterized as 'Hindi imperialism'; called for a retention of English; and suggested
that if there was need to have an Indian language as a symbol of Indian unity, 'we should not
forget the overwhelming claims of Sanskrit in this matter' (*Report of the Official Language
Commission*, pp. 271–314). In 1974, in a 'rethinking' of the language question, he proposed that
Sanskrit, English, and Hindi be all recognized as 'union languages', Chatterjee, *India*, pp. 62–6.
V. Raghavan (1908–79) has been much more consistent and open, at least in print, in his support
of Sanskrit as the official language, reluctantly conceding that if this could not come to pass,
only a sanskritized Hindi would be acceptable (V. Raghavan, *Sanskrit: Essays on the Value of the
Language and the Literature* [Madras, 1972], pp. 15–23). Raghavan, a widely-published Sanskrit
scholar, joined the Sanskrit faculty of the University of Madras in 1935, and became professor
and head of its Sanskrit department in 1955. In addition to serving in the Sanskrit Commission,
he went on to become member of the Central Sanskrit Board, and was Chairman of the Central
Sanskrit Institute, Tirupati. For biographical details on De and Dandekar, see N.R. Ray (ed.),
Dictionary of National Biography (Calcutta: South Asia Books, 1986), pp. 274–6, 320–1.

[11]*Report of the Sanskrit Commission*, p. 284.

[12]Ibid., p. 201.

and bitterness had marred the joys of independence; there had been much squabbling within the nation over state boundaries and territories; and Hindi, the proposed official language of India, had been found unacceptable by large numbers of its people. Everywhere, 'regionalism' and 'linguism' were on the rise.

The commission's solution to these problems was clear-cut: to put Indians on a good and steady diet of Sanskrit by making its study compulsory in schools, and by instituting it as the official language of the nation. Sanskrit was ideally suited for this role, for it was the 'Supreme Unifier' (p. 201) and the 'Great Unifying Force' (p. 81). 'The Indian people and the Indian civilization were born ... in the lap of Sanskrit' (p. 85). It is 'in our blood' (p. 81). It is 'the breath of our nostrils and the light of our eyes' (p. 87). Mixing its metaphors, the commission also variously described Sanskrit as 'the bedrock' of Indian existence, the 'main thread which runs through the entire fabric of the cultural life of an Indian' (p. 102), and the anchor that keeps the youth of India from losing their 'cultural moorings', (p. 51). 'If the binding force of Sanskrit [is] taken away, the people of India would cease to feel that they were parts of a single culture and a single nation' (p. 70). So, by restoring Sanskrit back to its citizens, the nation, too, would be restored, and its troubled waters calmed. For Sanskrit, it was declared, brings a 'symphony to our life' (p. 84).

The Sanskrit Commission was not the first to propose the candidacy of the language for the troubled role of independent India's lingua franca, or to offer it as panacea for the nation's many teething problems. The sanskritization of culture that is such a hallmark of India's modernity in the nineteenth and first half of the twentieth century inevitably also meant the (re)sanskritization of its languages. In the production of grammars, the standardization of dialects, the creation of new and 'modern' vocabularies for use in schools, courts, and offices, and in the attempts to write the histories of these languages, Sanskrit and its literature invariably provided the model (although, as has been demonstrated for many regions, not without contention from alternate standards offered by Persian, Tamil, and even English). Given the importance that Sanskrit had already assumed in the revamping of so many Indian languages, it is perhaps not surprising that in the later decades of the nineteenth century and sporadically in the early decades of the twentieth as well, it came to be also seen as a solution to what was increasingly being envisioned as a 'problem'. If India had to function as a nation, it had to have a 'national' language, for is this not what the historical experience of Europe suggested? In the writings of several leading intellectuals and in the pages of literary journals and news magazines such as *The Calcutta Review, Indian Mirror,* and *The Theosophist,* Sanskrit was a popular candidate, although it did have powerful rivals in Hindi-Hindustani and English.[13] Repeatedly identified as the 'Aryan language', Sanskrit held the key to the 'national regeneration' of (Hindu Aryan) India. So, in an 1879 essay entitled 'Should we call ourselves Aryas?', A. Mittra wrote:

Resolve solemnly to devote at least a couple of hours daily to the study of Sanskrit. Unite and strive for the general diffusion of Sanskrit learning. Let Aryan words and Aryan thoughts be far more familiar to your tongue and heart than English is at present ... can we who have not even a smattering of the Aryan tongue honestly claim the denomination of Arya? Is it not a painful, a shameful necessity that compels me, at the present moment, to advocate the cause of Aryan learning in a foreign tongue? Should not the Sanskrit rather than the English be the universal medium of communication in the Aryan land?[14]

In turn, this identification of Sanskrit as 'the universal medium of communication' echoed pronouncements in numerous colonial narratives from almost the beginning of British rule in India. For those colonials who supported the cause of Oriental learning and the opening of Sanskrit colleges, '[t]he acquisition of Sanskrit is indispensable not only for the study of the classical books composed' in that language but principally as the mother language of a great number of Indian dialects .... It is true and obvious that a true and radical reform of a nation in learning and morality (which is the object of a good

---

[13]Bruce McCully, *English Education and Origins of Indian Nationalism* (New York: Columbia University Press, 1940), pp. 254–7; Victor A. van Biljert, 'Sanskrit and Hindu National Identity in Nineteenth Century Bengal', in Houben (ed.), *The Ideology and Status of Sanskrit,* pp. 347–66; van der Burg, 'The Place of Sanskrit in Neo-Hindu Ideology'; K. Nambi Arooran, *Tamil Renaissance and Dravidian Nationalism, 1905–1944* (Madurai, 1980), pp. 186, 201. The dramatic increase in sanskrit and sanskritized Hindi books in many parts of north India offers further proof of this renewed interest in Sanskrit in the late colonial period. On this, see Christopher King, *One Language, Two Scripts: The Hindi Movement in Nineteenth Century North India* (New Delhi: Oxford University Press, 1994), pp. 37–47.

[14]Quoted in McCully, *English Education,* p. 257.

Government) will begin and proceed with the improvement of their own national language'. Sanskrit was routinely declared to be the 'root' of all other Indian languages, and 'the grand reservoir of [their] strength and beauty'.[15] Some, like Charles Wilkins and Monier Monier-Williams, even advised colonial administrators and missionaries that the absence of knowledge of any of the spoken languages of India could be compensated for by learning Sanskrit.[16] With it, they 'will be at home in every corner of our vast Indian territories ...' It was 'the best general language ... for those destined for an Indian life', and would stand them in good stead even if they 'were ignorant of the particular locality in which their lot may be cast ...'[17]

Not surprisingly, the Sanskrit Commission quoted with approval such references from the colonial archive which substantiated its own contention that Sanskrit was the only genuinely 'all-India' language that was known in every nook and corner of the nation. Additionally, it offered a list of famous nationalists (many of whom we would today identify as ideologically neo-Hindu) who had supported the cause of Sanskrit, and had even learnt the language, Dayananda Saraswati, Vivekananda, Aurobindo Ghosh, and Annie Besant being prominent

[15]Quoted in *Report of the Sanskrit Commission*, p. 18. For Europe's discovery of Sanskrit and enchantment with it, see Raymond Schwab, *The Oriental Renaissance: Europe's Discovery of India and the East, 1680–1880* (New York, 1974); Rosane Rocher, 'Sanskrit: Discovery by Europeans', in R.A. Asher, *et al.* (eds), *Encyclopedia of Language and Linguistic* (New York, 1994), pp. 3651–4.

[16]For the linguistic training of colonial officials and study of Sanskrit at the College at Fort William and in Haileybury, see Bernard S. Cohn, 'Recruitment and Training of British Civil Servants in India, 1600–1860', in Ralph Braibanti (ed.), *Asian Bureaucratic Systems Emergent from the British Imperial Tradition* (Durham: Duke University Press, 1966), pp. 111–28. Sanskrit was the only 'Oriental' language that students at Haileybury were required to pass, notwithstanding the increasing realization that it was as useful for anyone actually serving in India 'as a knowledge of ancient German would be to an English Commissioner of Police' (quoted in Cohn, 'Recruitment and Training', p. 124).

[17]Monier Monier-Williams, *The Study of Sanskrit in Relation to Missionary Work in India* (London: Williams and Norgate, 1861), pp. 41–6. In his later years, 'even Monier-Williams ... doubted its value as a compulsory subject' (Cohn, 'Recruitment and Training', p. 124). Nevertheless, nearly a century later, the Sanskrit Commission revived the recommendations of Monier-William and other colonial advocates of Sanskrit. It proposed that officers of the prestigious Indian Administrative Service should be taught Sanskrit, for a knowledge of the language 'would enable them to appreciate the deeper vein in the life and culture of the people under their charge, and at the same time bring in a touch of a great humanistic tradition in their mental make-up' (*Report of the Sanskrit Commission*, p. 203).

among those enumerated.[18] It had a more difficult time with Gandhi and Nehru, both of whom had passed over Sanskrit in favour of Hindustani as the national language. But even here, the commission reminded its interlocutors that Gandhi had declared that, if only to read the Bhagavad Gita, one ought to learn Sanskrit.[19] And Nehru, it was recalled, had confessed:

[18]*Report of the Sanskrit Commission*, p. 21. The commission was careful to point out that these nationalists had contributed to the 'cultural revival of the country and the growth of interest in Sanskrit classics with which such reawakening was intimately connected'. And yet it is important to remember that the admiration for Sanskrit thus expressed clearly produced a 'Hindi', 'Aryan', even a 'Brahmanical', revival, masquerading as 'Indian' regeneration. Dayananda abandoned his early dependence on Sanskrit in favour of Hindi for preaching and proselytizing by the early 1870s, but it continued to be crucial to the Arya Samaj's vision of Hindu/Aryan society in the 1880s and 1890s. In spite of some early controversy over its inclusion in the curriculum, Sanskrit continued to be an important part of Arya Samaj pedagogy well into this century, and from the outset, it was cast in opposition to Urdu/Arabic/Islam. (Kenneth Jones, *Arya Dharm: Hindu Consciousness in 19th-Century Punjab* [Berkeley: University of California Press, 1976], pp. 69–70, 90–1, 226). In the Madras Presidency, under the auspices of the Theosophical Society (whose clientele was mostly Brahman and upper caste), Sanskrit schools were opened in many big cities as well as smaller towns in the 1880s, and many local Theosophists sent their children to these before sending them on to the English-medium schools. Henry Olcatt even had plans for a grand 'national Sanskrit movement' that would assist in the teaching of the 'first principles of [the] national religion' (R. Suntharalingam, *Politics and Nationalist Awakening in South India, 1852–1891* [Tucson: University of Arizona Press, 1974], p. 303). For Vivekananda, as well, it was Sanskrit that gave 'prestige' and 'power' to the Hindu 'race'. While he conceded that the 'vernaculars' should be used for the general education of the masses, it was through Sanskrit that they would learn 'culture'. Without this, the masses would remain 'like savages'. He called upon the lower castes to stop fighting the higher castes in vain; instead, they could bring about a levelling of the caste system through learning the culture of the upper castes and 'raising [their] condition through a study of Sanskrit'. They could all become Brahman and Arya through appropriating Sanskrit, he suggested (*The Complete Works of Swami Vivekananda*, Vol. 3 [Calcutta, 1973], pp. 290–3). Of course, much more systematic work needs to be done on the revival of Sanskrit within the context of Indian nationalism, but for some recent beginnings in this direction, see van Biljert, 'Sanskrit and Hindu National Identity'; and van der Burg, 'The Place of Sanskrit in Neo-Hindu Ideology'.

[19]*Report of the Sanskrit Commission*, p. 22. Gandhi's position on Sanskrit was not without its share of contradictions. While in the north, he vehemently opposed the increased sanskritization of Hindi which distanced it from Hindustani/Urdu and alienated Muslims, in the south, he backed the cause of 'Hindi' as the national language precisely because, in his opinion, it contained a large number of Sanskrit words which would already be familiar to the speakers of south Indian languages. 'It is a matter of history that contact in the old days between the South and the North used to be maintained by means of Sanskrit' (Mohandas Gandhi, *Our Language Problem* [Karachi, 1942], pp. 18–19, 33–4). Elsewhere, he declared that the southern languages were 'daughters of Sanskrit': '... they have a large number of Sanskrit words in their vocabulary and when they are in difficulty, they go to Sanskrit as to

If I was asked what is the greatest treasure which India possesses and what is her finest heritage, I would answer unhesitatingly—it is the Sanskrit language and literature, and all that it contains. This is a magnificent inheritance, and so long as this endures and influences the life of our people, so long the basic genius of India will continue.[20]

Nehru, it was reported, had also said that he would 'personally like as many Indians as possible to know Sanskrit which is the very basis of our culture ...'[21]

Given that so many distinguished nationalists had expressed their faith in Sanskrit, it was disappointing to the Sanskrit Commission that in 1949, the Constituent Assembly had considered, and rejected proposals which would have instituted Sanskrit, rather than Hindi, as the official language of India. In 1956, the Official Language Commission

---

a mother—they seek her help and receive from her in the form of new words their requisite nourishment' (Mohandas Gandhi, *Evil Wrought by the English Medium* [Ahmedabad, 1958], p. 47). So much so that he claimed that he found it possible to understand the gist of what was being said in all four south Indian languages because of a shared Sanskrit vocabulary, and wrote that because of this, even though he was 67 years old, he felt that he could learn Kannada, for instance, in eight days (*Our Language Problem*, p. 18). Although he would have liked all Indians to know both the Urdu and Nagari scripts, in the end, he was in favour of the latter, for all Indian languages were in one capacity or another 'daughters of Sanskrit, by birth and adoption'. He even suggested that the Nagari script ought to be made compulsory for all Hindus (pp. 2–3, 46). In his autobiography, Gandhi recalls the difficulties he had in studying Sanskrit in high school, but nevertheless insists, 'every Hindu boy and girl should possess sound Sanskrit learning' (*The Story of My Experiments with Truth* [Boston, 1957], pp. 17–18).

[20]*Report of the Sanskrit Commission*, p. 72. That Nehru's enthusiasm for Sanskrit was shot through with skepticism about its capacity to function as a national language is apparent from the following statement in his reflections on the history of India: 'Speaking at the Oriental Conference held in 1937 at Trivandrum, over which he presided, Dr F.F. Thomas pointed out what a great unifying force Sanskrit had been in India and how widespread its use still was. He actually suggested that a simple form of Sanskrit, a kind of basic Sanskrit, should be encouraged as a common all-India language today!' (*The Discovery of India* [Delhi, 1993], p. 167).

[21]*Report of the Sanskrit Commission*, p. 99; see also Nehru, *Discovery of India*, pp. 164–70. R.N. Dandekar, a member of the Sanskrit Commission, elsewhere recalls that in 1961 Nehru declared in a speech at the University of Poona (where he was awarded an honorary degree of Doctor of Letters, and the citation was read out in Sanskrit) that 'One of my regrets in my life has been that I have had no occasion to learn Sanskrit.... I must confess that I was greatly moved and thrilled by the mellifluous rhythm of the Sanskrit language. Even the mere sound of that language gently couched and stirred the inner cord of my heart. I believe that history itself has established a kind of innate affinity between Sanskrit and the Indian soul' (quoted by Saroj Bhate, 'Position of Sanskrit in Public Education and Scientific Research in Modem India', in Houben (ed.), *The Ideology and Status of Sanskrit*, p. 400.

rejected a renewed plea on behalf of Sanskrit. Even if it was the pre-eminent language of Indian national culture, it was noted by that commission that Sanskrit was spoken by so few and any suggestion to make it the national medium of communication was mere 'escapism'. 'This escapism does not commend itself to us'.[22] Undeterred, a year later, the Sanskrit Commission offered Sanskrit, again, to the nation, this time as an 'additional official language':

While for all administrative and ordinary day-to-day purposes, some pan-Indian form of Hindi may be used, it appears inevitable that, in course of time, the prospective All-India Language—*Bharati Bhasa*—at least in its written form, which would be acceptable to all regions of India, especially in the higher reaches of education and literary activity, will be a form of simple and modernised Sanskrit.[23]

The commission's belief in the 'inevitability' of Sanskrit was premised on a specific reading of India's history. It insisted that in the distant past, when Sanskrit had been on the lips of every Indian, the 'nation' had been triumphant. If the nation had to rise from its ashes again, it had to be reintegrated with its Sanskritic soul and spirit from which it had been sundered under centuries of 'alien rule' by Persian, English, and the like, when 'the rolling current of Sanskrit had gradually thinned into a trickle or become cut up into stagnant-pools'.[24] To enable the nation's regeneration, Sanskrit had to once again become part of the everyday life of the citizen.

With such an agenda, the Sanskrit Commission went on to make a series of recommendations to the Government of India. If these recommendations were implemented, nothing less than a full-scale sanskritization of the nation and its citizenry would ensue. From the commission's point of view, operating as it did on the unshaken premise that there was no India outside and beyond the realm of Sanskrit, it was only restoring to the language what had been its to start with. However, not the least of the consequences of this project would be the dramatic, even revolutionary, transformation that Sanskrit itself would undergo. For, notwithstanding the claims made on its behalf by its modern advocates, Sanskrit had never played the kind of role in

[22]*Report of the Official Language Commission*, p. 39.
[23]*Report of the Sanskrit Commission*, p. 202.
[24]Ibid., pp. 143–4.

the nation's past that was now being envisaged for its present and future. For much of its long, complicated, and checkered career in the subcontinent, it had essentially functioned as a prestige language of high ritual, scholasticism, and elite culture. It was, as Sheldon Pollock has described it, a 'mandarin' language, a paradigmatic example of what he characterizes as a 'theodicy of privilege'. Through its nationalization, however, it stood to lose this aura of privilege and exclusivity that had been such a key to its power and mystique in pre-nationalist times. Formerly limited in provenance, if not normatively at least in everyday practice, to twice-born upper-caste men (and to a lesser extent, women) of specific social and ritual backgrounds, it was now enjoined that Sanskrit should be on the lips of every Indian, regardless of caste, class, religion, gender, occupation, or age. The vast underclasses of India were now invited to conduct all their activities through a language that had been largely denied to them in the past. Finally, this 'language of perfection', which had prided itself for so long in being *samskrta* ('refined'), was now to be dragged down into the mire of the everyday mundane world of *prakrta* ('natural') from which it had taken such pains to insulate itself over time. Where formerly much of its power stemmed from its restricted and contingent use in specific ritual, literary, and political tasks, it was now proposed that Sanskrit ought to be an essential part of the everyday life of the citizen.[25] Not surprisingly, the Sanskrit Commission confessed in its report that resistance to its proposed plans had been voiced not just by modernists who were skeptical about the ability of the language to express scientific and technological knowledge, but also by conservatives. These latter would rather that Sanskrit continue to play its traditional role in the national life of India, and remain on its 'high pedestal' and 'altar of honour'. Nevertheless, as far as the commission and others who supported Sanskrit's cause were concerned, it was too vital a 'living force' to be confined to 'its own ivory tower of isolation'.[26]

To a certain extent, the nationalization of Sanskrit proposed by the commission was already anticipated by the Orientalization of education

[25]Pollock, 'The Language of the Gods', and 'The Sanskrit Cosmopolis'; see also Madhav Deshpande, *Sociolinguistic Attitudes in India: An Historical Reconstruction* (Ann Arbor, 1979); George Cardona, 'On Attitudes towards Language in Ancient India', *Sino Platonic Papers*, 1990, 15, pp. 1–19.

[26]*Report of the Sanskrit Commission*, p. 219.

under colonial rule. Anglicist and vernacularist protests notwithstanding, through the nineteenth century, Sanskrit became increasingly available to all those who were interested in studying it, as it was introduced into the curricula of numerous high schools, colleges, and universities, sometimes even as a compulsory requirement. For a majority of students taking the entrance examinations to Bombay and Calcutta Universities, for instance, Sanskrit (in its guise as a 'classical language') was a mandatory second language, and in other institutions, it was allowed to be studied in lieu of the mother tongue. '... these Universities threw the portals of Sanskrit learning wide open to all pupils. In a sense, these Universities were primarily responsible for popularising the study of Sanskrit', the commission noted, in defending its own agenda.[27] Through the numerous 'national education' schemes proposed by the turn of this century, the 'portals of Sanskrit learning' continued to be widened to all those outside the circle of a privileged few. Indeed, the recurring concern for ensuring that the language was available to all those who sought it may be inferred from the various Sanskrit 'reorganization' committees set up by numerous provincial governments as well as princely states in the 1930s and 1940s.[28] From this perspective, the commission's recommendations in 1956 only continued a trend of democratization and demoticization of Sanskrit that had gained momentum over the past century or so.

All the same, by insisting, in the name of national 'regeneration', that Sanskrit ought to be foundational to every Indian citizen's linguistic repertoire, the commission sought inextricably to link membership in the nation with the mandatory learning of the language:

It is said that one of the fundamental aims of education should be 'to give a knowledge of the best and the noblest things that were said or done in the past'. If that be so, no system of education in India can afford to deny Sanskrit its rightful place without being untrue to itself. As a matter of fact, so far as Indian education is concerned, Sanskrit may not be counted merely as one of

[27]Ibid., p. 20. There are no detailed studies of the spread of Sanskrit education in the various provinces of colonial India, but for the Madras Presidency, see Nambi Arooran, *Tamil Renaissance*, pp. 70–110.

[28]*Report of the Sanskrit Commission*, pp. 285–6. See also Bhate, 'Position of Sanskrit in Public Education', pp. 383–91.

the numerous subjects of study; it must rather be regarded as constituting the foundation ...[29]

The real burden of the commission lay in making a case against all those who denied precisely this formulation, that Sanskrit was the foundation of the nation, and hence had to be made a mandatory subject of study in schools. It reluctantly exempted from the principle of compulsion those categories of citizens who were 'not within the atmosphere of Sanskrit'.[30] Yet, there is little doubt that its advocates hoped that the commission's report would convince all those Urdu-speaking Muslims, Tamil-speaking Dravidians, and English-speaking Anglo-Indians who had declared themselves to be 'outside the atmosphere of Sanskrit' that the language belonged to them as well. For, after all, were they not Indian? To be Indian, in the view of the commission, was to not deny Sanskrit's foundational value for the nation.

That the Sanskrit Commission would make this assertion is perhaps to be expected, given that a majority of its members were Sanskritists by profession, and Brahman by birth. Yet, this is not the only arena in which the call for Sanskrit as national language surfaced. A decade earlier, we can hear it in another context, at the meetings of the Constituent Assembly of India (1946–9), by men who were not necessarily Sanskritists or Brahman. And it is in this Assembly that Sanskrit's place in the future of the nation was first consolidated.

CONSTITUTING SANSKRIT

In September 1949, at the height of the Constituent Assembly's fraught debate over the future official language of India, one of its members from Assam, Kuladhar Chaliha, a former tea planter and lawyer, declared: 'We will become better Indians by adopting Sanskrit [as the national language], because Sanskrit and India are co-extensive'.[31] He was not alone in thus expressing his faith in the language. Twenty-seven other members made a similar proposal, among them B.R.

[29]*Report of the Sanskrit Commission*, p. 95. For the commission's reasons why Sanskrit should be made compulsory in schools, see pp. 93–107.

[30]*Report of the Sanskrit Commission*, p. 98–9.

[31]*Constituent Assembly Debates: Official Report*, Vol. 9 (New Delhi, 1949), p. 1402.

Ambedkar, T.T. Krishnamachari, G. Durgabai [Deshmukh], Pandit Lakshmikanta Maitra, and Naziruddin Ahmad.[32] A large number of those who supported the cause of Sanskrit were from Madras and West Bengal, for it was a useful weapon with which to counter the growing threat of 'Hindi imperialism'. At least one of its backers, Naziruddin Ahmad, was a member of the Muslim League from Bengal, and another, Ambedkar, Chairman of the Drafting Committee, was the leading spokesman for Dalit interests in the Assembly. Even for these maverick advocates, the raising of the standard of Sanskrit appears clearly to have been a last-ditch effort to salvage the linguistic mess in which the Constituent Assembly found itself after almost three years of deliberation over the future of India's languages. From the very beginning, chaos attended the Assembly's deliberations over the language provisions of the Constitution. As Granville Austin notes, almost every linguistic issue facing the Assembly—the language to be used in the conduct of its proceedings, the language in which the Constitution was to be framed, the script(s) for the official language(s) of the nation, the system of numerals to be adopted, and so on—was heavily contested, and bode ill for any reasonable consensus emerging in the short run. The Assembly's proceedings periodically broke down over several members' insistence that they would only speak in their 'mother tongue', much to the dismay of the majority who had no way of understanding what was being said. Members, especially from the south, frequently complained of non-comprehension when chaste Hindi speakers took the floor. And every now and then, we read about members engaging each other in heated debate even while pleading mutual incomprehension.[33]

Problems of communication and comprehension only exacerbated fundamental disagreements on the most important linguistic issue facing the Assembly, namely, the language to be named as the future official language of India. An early favourite, Hindustani, especially

[32]Granville Austin, 'Language and the Constitution—The Half-hearted Compromise', in *The Indian Constitution: Cornerstone of a Nation* (Oxford, 1966), p. 301.

[33]Granville Austin, 'Language and the Constitution', pp. 265–307. See also P. Kodanda Rao, *Language Issue in the Indian Constituent Assembly, 1946–50: Rational Support for English and Non-Rational Support for Hindi* (Bombay, 1969). Similar problems continued to plague the Indian parliament's activities in the next decade as well. On this, see Mahadev L. Apte, 'Language Controversies in the Indian Parliament (Lok Sabha): 1959–1960', in W. O'Barr and Jean O'Barr (eds), *Language and Politics* (Paris: Mouton, 1976), pp. 213–34.

popular because it had Gandhi's backing, became one of the numerous victims of the partition of India, an event that transpired even as the Assembly was in session. After August 1947, even those who had supported Hindustani hesitated to use that name, preferring the term 'broad Hindi'.[34] By early 1948, the Assembly was increasingly divided between all those who favoured a highly sanskritized Hindi, and those who did not. And amongst the latter, we hear some really passionate speeches on the value and worth of English which may well have been the language of colonialism, but was also, these members insisted, the language in which the Indian nation had been first wrought.[35] We also hear occasional voices from the fringes which declared that if antiquity, sophistication, and depth of literature were the criteria for choice of the official language, perhaps Bengali, Marathi, or Tamil, rather than the 'upstart' and 'rudimentary' Hindi, had a greater claim.[36]

In this Babeldom, it is perhaps not surprising that the cause of Sanskrit—unusual though it may appear at first sight—found a space. There were three, somewhat contrary, grounds on which its supporters built their case pragmatically, ideologically, and sentimentally. Pragmatically, as Naziruddin Ahmad shrewdly realized, the advantage Sanskrit had as the putative official language was that it would be equally disadvantageous for all citizens. 'I offer you a language which is the grandest and the greatest, and it is impartially difficult, equally difficult for all to learn'.[37] Since it was nobody's spoken language or 'mother tongue', no single community would have an unfair start in the race for jobs and privileges, as would be the case with Hindi.[38] At the same time, since so many of India's languages were already so infused with Sanskritic words, it was suggested that it would be easy for their

[34]Austin, 'Language and the Constitution', pp. 277–8.

[35]*Constituent Assembly Debates*, pp. 1331, 1358–9.

[36]Ibid., pp. 1333, 1375–6; see also Ludo Rocher, *Le Probleme Linguistique en Inde* (Brussels, 1967), pp. 9–35.

[37]*Constituent Assembly Debates*, p. 1334.

[38]So, B. Das, a non-Brahman member from Orissa, observed, 'This morning when Pandit Lakshmi Kanta Maitra was speaking, I was almost persuaded to accept Sanskrit as the official language of the State, so that everybody will start with an even keel in that mother of all languages. There will then be no rivalry between the sons and daughters of the leaders of U[nited] P[rovinces] and C[entral] P[rovinces] that are present here and the sons and daughters of leaders of Orissa or Madras. They will all learn Sanskrit.' *Constituent Assembly Debates*, p. 1396.

speakers readily to learn Sanskrit. Further, in contrast to Hindi, which was a mere 'provincial' language that could not be readily transformed into a 'national' language without a good deal of effort, it was argued that Sanskrit was already an all-India language. 'Wherever I have travelled, if I have not been able to make myself understood in any other language, I have been able to make myself understood in Sanskrit', one member recalled. Another pointed out that '[o]ur whole life is so interwoven with Sanskrit that you cannot get away from [it] ...'. In that case, why not make it the official language for everyone, he asked?[39]

Sanskrit's advocates were also quick to seize upon the comparable example of Israel and its recent efforts to revive Hebrew and install it as the official language of the Jewish state. In doing so, the Assembly was told, Jews were sending a signal to the world about the respect they had for their language, culture, civilization, and heritage. We Indians ought to do the same, for are not all our ancient glories contained in Sanskrit? 'Let the world know that we also know to respect the rich heritage of our spiritual culture.'[40] Like Bankimchandra and Vivekananda before him (and Max Mueller and others before them), Pandit Lakshmikanta Maitra, the chief spokesman for the Sanskrit cause in the Assembly and a Brahman member from West Bengal, insisted:

We should give our message to the West. The West is steeped in materialistic civilisation. The Message of the Gita, the Vedas, the Upanishads and the Tantras, the Charaka and Susrutha etc., will have to be disseminated to the West. It is thus and thus alone that we may be able to command the respect of the world; not by our political debates, nor by our scientific discoveries which, compared with their achievements, are nothing. The West looks to you to give them guidance in this war-torn world where morals are shattered and religious and spiritual life have gone to shambles ...[41]

Here, Maitra echoes what Partha Chatterjee has identified as the 'problematic' and 'thematic' of nationalist thought in India which asserted the autonomy of the nation from colonial domination even while continuing to use the knowledge procedures and modes of reasoning of post-Enlightenment thought based on timeless

[39]*Constituent Assembly Debates*, pp. 1354, 1402.
[40]Ibid., p. 1360.
[41]Ibid., p. 1359.

Manichean distinctions between 'West' and 'East'.[42] Especially in its 'moment of departure', nationalist discourse conceded that the West was indeed superior, but only in the realms of material culture and science; in the domain of spirituality, however, it was India that held the winning hand, and would indeed teach the West. So, true modernity for India 'would lie in combining the superior material culture of Western cultures with the spiritual greatness of the East'.[43] For its advocates in the Constituent Assembly, Sanskrit would guarantee such a modernity in which the nation's uniqueness would not be sacrificed in the rush towards material progress. Indeed, for Maitra, Sanskrit was to be the panacea for not just the nation's problems, but the world's as well. On the national front, 'I honestly believe that if we accept Sanskrit, all [our] troubles, all [our] jealousies, all [our] bitterness will vanish with all the psychological complex that has been created'. The Indian nation, thus spiritually rehabilitated through Sanskrit, would then be ready to guide the 'materialistic' West out of its moral and spiritual bankruptcy. Maitra's reasoning here is clearly couched in the vocabulary of patriarchal Orientalism. Indians ought to embrace Sanskrit because it was the language 'of their forefathers' and of 'their great *rishis* [sages].' It was also the language 'in which our culture is enshrined'. In his reading of the past, all of India's worth is reduced to its great spiritual truths, and these spiritual truths in turn are identified with Sanskrit. In the words of Kuladhar Chaliha, a fellow advocate, 'all that is good and all that is valuable and all that we fight for and we hold precious have come from Sanskrit literature'. So much so that if Indians did not embrace Sanskrit, Maitra continued, he could not fathom what other contribution they could make to the world. So, 'in the name of the great rishis' who gave Sanskrit to us, and 'in the name of that great culture and civilisation of which we are all proud', he called upon his fellow Indians 'to bury [their] hatchets' and 'cheerfully accept Sanskrit as the National and official language of free India'.[44]

The case for Sanskrit was built on sentimental grounds as well, and here, its advocates pulled out all the stops. They quoted profusely

[42]Partha Chatterjee, *Nationalist Thought and the Colonial World: A Derivative Discount?* (London, 1986), pp. 38–9.

[43]Ibid., p. 51.

[44]*Constituent Assembly Debates*, pp. 1359–60, 1402.

from the colonial and European archive—from William Jones, and Franz Bopp, and Max Mueller—and waxed eloquently about its mellifluousness, its sweetness, and its grandeur. Sanskrit is the 'mother' of all the languages of the world, even their 'revered grand mother'. 'When I am pleading for Sanskrit, let there be no derisive merriment anywhere in the House', warned Maitra. 'Let me ask every honorable Member of this House, irrespective of the province he comes from, "Does he disown his grandmother?"' To those who argued that Sanskrit was a 'dead' language, Maitra retorted: 'If Sanskrit is dead, may I say that Sanskrit is ruling us from her grave?'[45] Indeed, even those not in favour of Sanskrit agreed that it was the language par excellence, that its alphabet was 'the most perfect and scientific in the World'; that it was impossible to turn their backs on it for 'it is in our blood; it is the fountainhead of our mother tongues and the storehouse of our culture'. So, Purushottam Das Tandon, one of the more passionate advocates for Hindi as the official language declared, 'I bow to those who love Sanskrit. I am one of them. I love Sanskrit. I think every Indian born in this country should learn Sanskrit. Sanskrit preserves our ancient heritage for us ...[46]

Even in their wildest dreams, the most enthusiastic of Sanskrit's supporters could not have believed that their project had any chance of succeeding, taking on, as they had to, the powerful Hindi lobby in the Assembly, as well as numerous modernists and populists who accused the language of being 'difficult', 'archaic', inaccessible to the populace, and so on. However, even if they did not manage to institute Sanskrit as the official language, there were other ways in which they succeeded in bringing it through the back door into the nation's Constitution, and into its future.

First, and most crucially, the Constitution, even while identifying Hindi as the official language of India, clearly names Sanskrit as the primary source from which it should draw upon to enrich itself and develop its vocabulary.[47] Such a linking of Sanskrit to the official language is perhaps not surprising, for at least since the late eighteenth century, it had been identified by numerous colonial administrators

[45]Ibid., pp. 1354–5.
[46]Ibid., 1408, 1450.
[47]Ibid., p. 1489. See also Article 351 of the Constitution of India.

and missionaries as the 'fountainhead' and 'reservoir' of not just Hindi, but all the languages of 'Hindu' India.[48] Further, from the 1880s on, the supporters of Hindi had launched a sustained programme of sanskritizing Hindi, in their attempts to distance the language from its Persian-Urdu (read: 'Muslim') past.[49] By October 1948, the Hindi lobby in the Assembly had abandoned any pretence of working with a composite Hindustani, and singled out Sanskrit as the only language to which Hindi should turn for its improvement. In its view, 'the linguistic unity of India' as well as the 'highest dictates of nationalism' demanded that Sanskrit be made the sole source of new vocabulary for the new official language.[50] Indeed, Hindi enthusiasts shrewdly made a case for their language by insisting that Hindi had all the advantages of associating with Sanskrit, without the disadvantages of being Sanskrit. So, Hindi, it was declared, 'had descended from Vedic Sanskrit [which] contains our ancient culture ...'; it had the privilege of being 'the eldest and senior-most daughter' of the 'mother' of all Indian languages; and in its sanskritized form, it could be readily understood in the north as well as the south. In contrast to Sanskrit, however, it was spoken by a large majority of Indians, was easy to learn, comprehend, and write.[51] So, it was the language most appropriate for a democratic and modern, yet ancient and classical, nation.

Sanskrit also triumphed in the battle over scripts that was fought out on the floor of the Assembly. In the early days of the Assembly, there was some discussion of retaining both the 'Persian' and 'Devanagari' scripts for the official language. But by the time the Draft Constitution and its revised final version were produced in 1949, it was Devanagari that was clearly named as the sole script in which Hindi would be written and developed.[52] The triumph of (Deva)Nagari in this fashion

[48]Schwab, *Oriental Renaissance*.

[49]Christopher King, *One language, Two Scripts;* Krishna Kumar, 'Quest for Self-Identity: Cultural Consciousness and Education in the Hindi Region, 1880–1950', *Economic and Political Weekly*, 25 (25), 1990, pp. 1247–55; David Lelyveld, 'The Fate of Hindustani: Colonial Knowledge and the Project of a National Language', in Breckenridge and van der Veer (eds), *Orientalism and the Post-colonial Predicament*, pp. 189–214.

[50]Austin, 'Language and the Constitution', p. 283.

[51]*Constituent Assembly Debates*, pp. 1379, 1408. See also Raghu Vira, *India's National Language* (New Delhi, 1965).

[52]Austin, 'Language and the Constitution', p. 296. Article 343 (i) of the Constitution of India states clearly, 'The official language of the Union shall be Hindi in Devanagari script'.

had already been anticipated by the outcome of the various 'script wars' that had been fought in many parts of northern India since at least the last decades of the nineteenth century, between Urdu/Arabic/ Persian 'characters', and Nagari or Hindi 'characters'.[53] The horrors of partition only confirmed the reigning sentiment that the Arabic script, like its users, was 'alien' and 'foreign' to India. But above all, the selection of 'Devanagari' as the official script was ensured because it had been, in the view of many of its supporters, Sanskrit's script for centuries. As Alagu Rai Shastri unequivocally insisted: 'Our national language shall be Hindi and our script shall be Devanagari which we have got from the "Rigveda" and whose words have been borrowed from that great ocean of learning ...'[54]

There is more than a touch of (Orientalist) irony in the Constitution's naming of the script so unequivocally as 'Devanagari', for it is a term that appears to have gained in currency, over the more popular (and more ancient) 'Nagari', only in the colonial period, its earliest attestation possibly being 1776 (Walter Maurer, 'On the Name Devanagari', *Journal of American Orientalist Society*, 96 (1), 1976, p. 103). Note especially Maurer's observation, 'Though "Devanagiri" is but an extension of the much older name "Nagari" and is therefore synonymous with it, the two are not interchangeable. Thus what is Devanāgarī may be called Nāgarī, but not all that is Nagari may be termed "Devanagari"', (p. 104). Yet, it is the latter that has come to prevail. For a nationalist reading of the antiquity and widespread use of Devanagari, see V.S. Agarwala, 'The Devanāgarī Script', in *Indian Systems of Writing* (Delhi, 1966), pp. 12–16. Here, it may also be noted that supporters of Devanagari lost, by a narrow margin, the battle over numerals. The Constitution retains the use of international numerals, although the president does have the right to authorize the official use of Devanagari numerals as well, as per Article 343(2) (Austin, 'Language and the Constitution', pp. 294–5).

[53]King, *One Language, Two Scripts*. King has noted that supporters of Devanagari had to also contend with eliminating the popularity of numerous other versions of Nagari, especially Kaithi, a cursive variant of the script that had wide currency in many parts of eastern India, but which was deemed to be tainted because of its links with Hindustani or Urdu (ibid., pp. 65–9).

[54]*Constituent Assembly Debates*, pp. 1388–9; see also p. 1385. For the historical roots of such an identification, see King, *One Language, Two Scripts*. And yet, as the Sanskrit Commission noted a few years later, Devanagari had never been the only script of Sanskrit (which was typically written in a wide number of local scripts), and its identification as the authentic and sole script of Sanskrit came to be made by Europeans in the colonial period. The commission offered a number of very good reasons for this identification: the use of Devanagari by scholars in Banaras, a city that was seen as the authentic home of Sanskrit by Europeans; the educational practices of the three principal universities whose Sanskrit books and examinations were published in Devanagari; and above all, the printing of most Sanskrit works in the nineteenth century, in Europe as well as in India, in Devanagari, especially Max Mueller's edition of the *Rig Veda*. Beautifully anticipating Benedict Anderson's thesis on print-capitalism, the commission noted: 'Printing and the world-wide use of the printed book may, indeed, be said to have brought in the standardization of script for Sanskrit

Finally, although Sanskrit was named in the Draft Constitution as the primary language from which Hindi would draw to develop, surprisingly, it was *not*, at first, included in Schedule VIIA. This schedule identified thirteen other languages from which Hindi could borrow for its improvement, so that 'it may serve as a medium of expression for all the elements of the composite culture of India'.[55] Its advocates in the Assembly protested this oversight, and ensured that in the final version of the Constitution, Sanskrit was included in the Eighth Schedule (ES).[56] Since this schedule names the principal spoken languages of India that matter politically, economically, and demographically, by making it to this list, Sanskrit was assured, at the very least, a status similar to theirs. Of course, ironically, Sanskrit was now compelled to be on par with languages over which, in its own past, it had claimed superiority and lordship. Nevertheless its presence in the ES, even as it thus democratized and demoticized the language, rescued Sanskrit from the vaults of India's past and ensured a role for it in the nation's future.

NATIONALIZING SANSKRIT

Not least of the consequences of the empowerment of Sanskrit thus by the Constitution is that a space was opened up for the creation of government agencies such as the Sanskrit Commission and the Central Sanskrit Board, formed to ensure that the language would have a continuing significance in the lives and livelihood of modern Indians. In turn, the agendas of these agencies with regard to the place of Sanskrit in the nation's future derived from their imagination of its role in India's past. Here, there is little doubt that its advocates faced an uphill task in establishing their claim that Sanskrit had always been the one

---

works during the first half of the last century, and to have thereby bestowed upon Devanagari the status of the accepted all-India script for Sanskrit, and, to a large extent, even the national script of India'. The commission recommended to the government that 'while the knowledge of the Devanagari script should be made universal as the pan-Indian script, the employment of the local scripts as a potent aid in the dissemination of Sanskrit should be continued'. It was the commission's opinion that Sanskrit written in the same script as the mother tongue, rather than in Devanagari, could be learnt more easily, and would touch the heart of the speaker more quickly (*Report of the Sanskrit Commission*, pp. 194–7).

[55] Article 351 of the Constitution of India.

[56] *Constituent Assembly Debates*, pp. 1323, 1489.

and truly 'national' language of India from time immemorial. For, in the colonial archive, if the language had picked up several new (and influential) admirers, it had also received its share of brickbats. For every Jones who declared Sanskrit to be 'more perfect than the Greek, more copious than the Latin, and more exquisitely refined than either ...', there was a Macaulay or a Gilchrist who had characterized it as 'priestly', 'dead', 'mysterious', 'arcane', the select privilege of an exclusive few. By the middle decades of this century, many of these colonial charges found a renewed life in powerful arguments against the language launched from various quarters. So, the Dravidian movement identified Sanskrit as the weapon with which the Aryan Brahmanical north had conquered the Dravidian non-Brahman south; regionalists and populists declared that the 'mother tongues' had been marginalized by an enchantment with its classicism; modernists insisted that its baroqueness was an impediment to progress and scientization; and secularists were wary of its association with Hindu revivalism. So, the commission had to perforce rescue Sanskrit from the stigma of exclusivity, privilege, and arcaneness with which it had come to be burdened, and demonstrate that it was truly a language of and for all Indians, regardless of caste, class, religious, ethnic, regional, or linguistic affiliation. In other words, the language had to be discursively nationalized before it could be officially inserted into the mundane everyday world of the nation.

Not unexpectedly, the commission went about making its case through a selective (re)interpretation of India's textual, linguistic, and cultural history which had been put at its disposal by colonial and nationalist historiography. But the real innovation, of which it was justly proud, was that it supplemented its textual and historical survey with a detailed analysis of a questionnaire consisting of over ninety questions which was distributed to hundreds of individuals and institutions all over the country. The questionnaire (note its very first query: 'what special role has the Sanskritist to play in the national life of India today?') was in Sanskrit and English, and the commission was pleased to report that some 40 per cent of the replies were returned in Sanskrit.[57] In addition, members of the commission toured the country between January and May 1957, and interviewed '1,100 persons

[57]*Report of the Sanskrit Commission*, p. ii.

representing various shades of opinion', including leading Sanskrit scholars and pandits, political leaders, bureaucrats, educationalists, and even scientists. Highlights of the tour included visits to famous temples, listening to Vedic recitations, and watching an 'entertainment programme in Sanskrit' in Madras. The questionnaire, with the list of questions in English and Sanskrit (but not the answers), the 'log book' of the tour undertaken by its members, the list of individuals and institutions who sent replies, the list of institutions visited, the list of all those who gave oral testimony, all these were carefully appended to the published report for everyone to read.[58] In other words, the commission was anxious to establish that its findings had been arrived at not in a willy-nilly fashion, but by deploying the technologies of knowledge and methodologies of science available to the modern state. What better way to demonstrate the value and worth of Sanskrit to contemporary India than by showing that modern and scientific modes of survey and analysis substantiated such claims? Although a detailed socio-economic, professional, and ideological profile of the men and women interviewed may well reveal otherwise, the commission was particularly keen to stress the 'all-India' quality of its endeavours. No stone had been left unturned, no person worth asking had been left unasked. And the result? In his letter to the Minister of Education, Suniti Kumar Chatterjee wrote confidently: 'About the enthusiasm of the people of India as a whole for Sanskrit, we have received, in the course of our tour and our work, the most convincing evidence.'[59]

How convincing is the evidence presented about the nationwide popularity of the language? Given that it was set up in a decade marked by linguistic, regional, and ethnic tensions all over the nation, the commission was quick to characterize as 'untenable' the 'unfortunate propaganda' that Sanskrit was the language of a particular community:

That Sanskrit does not belong to any particular community is proved by Andhra and Kerala where the entire non-Brahman classes are imbued with Sanskrit ... In Kerala, even Izhavas, Thiyas, Moplas and Christians read Sanskrit. In Madhya Pradesh, we are told, a paper in Sanskrit was compulsory at the School Final Examination and even Muslims took it. In a Lucknow Intermediate College, there are Muslim girls studying Sanskrit; in Gujarat, Parsis study it;

[58]Ibid., pp. 285–439.
[59]Ibid., p. ii.

in Punjab, there are several Sikhs among Sanskrit students and teachers, and Sastris and research scholars in Sanskrit. The Director of Public Instruction of Madhya Pradesh, who is a Christian, told us that he advised the Anglo-Indian students also to read Sanskrit. It was necessary that, as future citizens of India, they gained an insight into the mind and the culture of the bulk of the Indian people. And this, he added, was possible only through the study of Sanskrit.[60]

This statement is typical of the simpler approach adopted by the commission to prove the universality of Sanskrit among all of India's religious communities, be they Christians in Kerala, Muslims in Lucknow, Parsis in Gujarat, or Sikhs in Punjab. Elsewhere, Buddhists and Jains are added to this list.[61] Indeed, the one community left unnamed are Hindus, for the commission laboured hard, at one level, to distance the language from the religion with which it had become exclusively identified over at least the past two centuries of Orientalist scholarship. 'It is definitely wrong to assume that Sanskrit represents only the religious literature of the Hindus', it was stated unequivocally.[62] Since Hinduism could not be officially privileged in the emergent national culture, and since Sanskrit had to function as the common medium of that national culture, it followed that the reputation of Sanskrit as the hegemonic scriptural language of Hinduism had to be disavowed.[63]

And yet, as in so much else in modern, 'secular' India, the undertone of unmarked Hinduism is visible in every other page of the commission's report, even as (Hindu) 'religion' is resignified as 'morality' or 'culture'. Texts and authors most frequently quoted to document Sanskrit's significance for modern Indians—the Upanishads, Valmiki, the Gita, Kalidasa—are invariably those that an Indian readership has learnt to

[60]Ibid., pp. 65–6.

[61]Ibid., p. 79.

[62]Ibid.

[63]Correspondingly, the commission was careful not to overtly blame Muslim rule for the decline of Sanskrit. Indeed, there is only one instance in its entire report in which Muslims, or some of their leaders at any rate, are represented as anti-Sanskrit: 'It is because some leaders among the Muslims of India, not attuned to the spirit of Sanskrit, or deliberately ignoring it, tried (partly through the inspiration of British imperialism) to channel the masses of Indian citizens professing Islam along a different line, seeking to throw off the inheritance of Sanskrit, that India had to suffer the pangs of a living amputation, bringing untold misery on millions of people ...' (*Report of the Sanskrit Commission*, pp. 81–2). These lines are particularly remarkable for the suggestion that the partition of India was a consequence of the neglect of Sanskrit.

associate with a Hindu sensibility. Statements like, 'educated Indians, whatever their chief vocation in life, are invariably drawn to the study of the *Gita* and the *Upanishads* and of the *Mahabharata* and the *Ramayana ...*', betray the working assumption of the commission that the 'Indian' is by definition 'Hindu'.[64] Indeed, it is telling that the only religious institutions that members of the commission visited on their all-India tour were Hindu temples and centres of Vedic and Vedantic learning. Their visits to these places convinced them that the government ought to regulate these institutions, so that their funds may be properly directed toward the encouragement of Sanskrit studies. Even though the commission conceded that a 'secular' state could not promote religious education, this did not mean that Vedic studies should not receive government support, for 'the *Vedas* form the bedrock of Sanskrit literature and Indian culture'.[65] It is worth noting that neither 'religion' nor 'Hinduism' are mentioned in this characterization of the Vedas. Because the Vedas are deemed to be the 'bedrock' of 'Indian culture', the Government had to take steps 'to preserve the oral tradition of Vedic recitals; young students should be encouraged to learn Vedic hymns by rote with correct intonation and accents according to the different schools; ... and special attention should be paid to the resuscitation and propagation of the traditions of the *Samaveda* and the *Atharvaveda*'. It was also recommended that the government's Five Year Plans should make provisions for the support of 'gifted exponents of the *Ramayana* and the *Mahabharata*', for 'epic and Puranic expositions could be effectively utilised for the purpose of cultural propaganda and the moral toning up of the masses'. All-India Radio should be encouraged to supplement its weekly Sanskrit broadcasts with daily recitations of moral sayings from the Gita and other classics, as well as celebrate special events such as Kalidasa Day. The government-run Films Division ought to produce documentary films based on the Sanskrit epics, clearly anticipating in this regard by at least three decades the broadcast of the Ramayana and the Mahabharata on national television.[66] So, the commission's disavowal of the exclusive association of Sanskrit with Hinduism notwithstanding, its own proposals for sanskritizing the nation only confirmed the Hinduness of Sanskrit, and of the nation.

[64]*Report of the Sanskrit Commission*, p. 102.
[65]Ibid., p. 209.
[66]Ibid., pp. 211–13; 225–6.

The other religious communities of India, let alone their texts (even those reportedly in Sanskrit), receive no attention whatsoever in this scheme of things.

Its advocates were also at pains to prove the truly national character of Sanskrit by denying its exclusive association with Brahmanical privilege and priestly orthodoxy. 'It has wrongly been averred that the study of Sanskrit is only sacerdotal ...'[67] To document their case in this regard, they turned to Tamil Nadu where over the past few decades, the Dravidian movement had tried to convince ('non-Brahman') Tamilians of Sanskrit's predatory role in their past, and of its irrelevance for their present and future.[68] But even here, the commission was able to interview 'several non-Brahmans in high position [sic] and active in public life, business etc., and ... found them all favourable to Sanskrit ... In Chidambaram, we were able to find a group of non-Brahman merchants of the town who appeared before us for interview as staunch supporters of Sanskrit education and culture'. Here, once again, as in Madhya Pradesh, Gujarat, and other places, the commission noted with satisfaction that in a Chidambaram high school, a Muslim student topped the Sanskrit class; that in Tanjavur, Christians, too, studied Sanskrit; and that in Madras, there were 'Harijans' who learnt the language.[69] 'As we moved among the people, in the temples and the streets, in public and private meetings, we found that, in Tamilnad[u],

[67]Ibid., p. 79.

[68]Nambi Arooran, *Tamil Renaissance*, pp. 70–110; Sumathi Ramaswamy, *Passions of the Tongue: Language Devotion in Tamil India, 1891–1970* (Berkeley: University of California Press,1997).

[69]For a revealing first-person impression of what it means for lower castes and 'Harijans' to study Sanskrit in independent India, the Sanskrit Commission's proud claims notwithstanding, see Kumud Pawde's poignant 'The Story of My Sanskrit', in Arjun Dangle (ed.), *A Corpse in the Well: Translations from Modern Marathi Dalit Autobiographies* (Bombay, 1992), pp. 24–34. Pawde writes movingly about the many trials she faced in her attempts to learn Sanskrit, overcoming which she became the first woman of a scheduled caste to secure a distinction in her Master's examinations in the language. Her caste status, however, prevented her from getting a job as a Sanskrit teacher for a long time in a nation that still linked Sanskritic learning with Brahmans and upper castes, although that same nation did not fail to appropriate her as an icon of its own progressive modernity. So she tells us she was introduced thus at a public meeting of Sanskrit scholars: 'Whereas our traditional books have forbidden the study of Sanskrit by women and Shudras, a woman from those very Shudras, from the lowest caste among them, will today, in Sanskrit, introduce these scholars. This is the beginning of a progressive way of thinking in independent India' (p. 26). I thank Robert Goldman for this reference.

the antipathy towards Sanskrit was confined to a section trying to make political capital out of it ....'. The report noted that so anxious were Tamilians about the fate of Sanskrit that Madras returned the largest number of replies to the commission's questionnaire.[70]

In turn, the commission was anxious to demonstrate that Sanskrit was not just a language of the Aryan north, but of the Dravidian south as well, the Dravidian movement's claims to the contrary notwithstanding:

Our Modern Indian languages, both Aryan and Dravidian, are in the same boat. They have been, all of them, under the aegis of Sanskrit. The Modern Aryan languages were all born in the lap of Sanskrit; and as for the Dravidian languages, ever since their earliest literary usage, they have been nurtured by Sanskrit ...[71]

The opening page of the report strategically quotes verses by two 'southerners', the Sanskrit playwright Dandin at the Pallava court, who had declared Sanskrit to be 'the Divine Speech set forth by the Great Sages'; and Senavaraiyar, the medieval commentator to the Tamil grammar, the *Tolkappiyam*, who wrote in Tamil that '... Sanskrit is common to all parts of the country'. Elsewhere, it quotes, another Tamil savant, Sivagnana Munivar, who had declared 'the nature of Tamil will not be clear to those who have not learnt Sanskrit'. When the great intellects of the south had wanted to express high and serious thoughts, they invariably turned to Sanskrit rather than to their own mother tongues, it was noted.[72] But it was not just with the great intellects of the south that Sanskrit mattered. 'For all common day-to-day activities, numerous Sanskrit words ... are freely used in South India in all strata of society', V. Raghavan declared in his inaugural speech to the 1948 All-India Oriental Conference. In another context, Chatterjee dismissed the efforts of the 'Pure Tamil' movement, and declared that 'at this late date, it would be impossible to make Tamil expressive of modern thoughts and ideas without borrowing from Sanskrit.'[73]

[70]*Report of the Sanskrit Commission*, p. 66. For the Madras government's less-than-enthusiastic reception of the Sanskrit Commission's proposals, see Government of Madras Order No. 1535 (Education), dated 6 August 1958.

[71]*Report of the Sanskrit Commission*, p. 85.

[72]Ibid.

[73]Raghavan, *Sanskrit*, p. 16; Suniti Kumar Chatterjee, *Samskrta Dig-Vijaya* (Calcutta: Sanskrit College, 1985), pp. 13–14.

Indeed, its advocates argued that rather than being the language of Brahmanical exclusivity in the south, Sanskrit had allowed southerners of all classes to communicate with other Indians. Without Sanskrit, south Indians would truly be cut off from the rest of India and not be able to participate in the nation. In turn, the south had for long been the 'veritable asylum' for 'Indian' culture and Sanskritic learning. The unspecified reason for this, of course, was the assumption that the north had been de-sanskritized (and hence de-Indianized) under Muslim rule.[74] So, when north Indians visited the south, it was Sanskrit that allowed them to communicate with their fellow Indians. So, Raghavan wrote confidently that 'if we take all the derived North Indian languages and the South Indian languages together into consideration, we find that the linguistic GCM [Greatest Common Measure] of India is Sanskrit'.[75]

Thus, the appropriateness of Sanskrit as national language lay in that it belonged to no one single region, caste, or religion, even while belonging to all of them. Like the mighty Ganga, the 'national' river of India, Sanskrit, too, was 'ageless, ever-flowing ... [absorbing] during its long space-time elements of value from all the regional cultures, [growing] into the greater, the larger, and the national tradition that it is'. Similarly, like the great banyan tree, Sanskrit, too, 'has also put forth its own shoots in the form of the earlier Prakrits and the later Apabhramsa which in course of time gave rise to the modern vernaculars'. Indeed, the very land 'from the snow-covered abode of Siva down to the wave-washed feet of Kumari' reverberates with the sounds of Sanskrit. Sanskrit's geography provided the template for the nation's geography, and the blueprint for its territorial unity.

Sanskrit has always projected a pan-Indian image, an image of India as one country ... Through its cosmology and the geographical account of the country and its boundaries, the seven great rivers, the seven great cities, the expression 'ā-setuhimācalam'—'from the Cape to the Himalayas'—and through the building up of a network of holy spots, holy waters and shrines and the institution of pilgrimage ... Sanskrit consolidated the territorial unity ... It developed the concept of one country, Bhāratavarsa, and love and veneration

---

[74]Raghavan, Sanskrit, p. 16; Report of the Sanskrit Commission, p. 66.
[75]Raghavan, Sanskrit, p. 16; see also Chatterjee, Samskrta Dig-Vijaya, pp. 11–12.

for the same as expressed in the saying, 'Mother and Motherland are greater than heaven'.[76]

So, Sanskrit was by definition the true national language of India, for the nation had always been its domain.

Yet, for all their concern with nationalizing Sanskrit by rooting it firmly within the nation's present territorial boundaries, its advocates also proudly pointed to its many extra-national affiliations, here echoing the claims of nationalist historiography of the previous decades about the existence of a 'Greater India' incorporating the Hindu 'colonies' of South-east and Central Asia:

The Middle East, Central Asia, China and Japan, and the whole of South-East Asia came under a sort of cultural empire inspired by Sanskrit language, its sciences and epics, its religion and philosophy and arts. Mathematics, Medicine and the Fables in Sanskrit were translated by Arabia to pass them on to Europe and to the modern scientific world. To Tibet, Central Asia, China and Japan, Sanskrit gave Buddhism in its Sanskrit schools. To Cambodia, Laos, Thailand, Burma and Indonesia and Ceylon, Hinduism and Buddhism, alphabet, script, literature, Ramayana and Mahabharata in sculpture and dance, temples and festivals were given by this language and its derivative the Pali. It is out of Pali and Sanskrit that Thailand is today building up its new technical and administrative vocabulary. Thus Sanskrit consolidated not only India but played an integrating role in the whole Orient.[77]

This is not the only instance in which we encounter the vocabulary of imperialism in relation to the spread of Sanskrit. A collection of essays by Suniti Kumar Chatterjee was posthumously published under the title, *Samskrita Dig-Vijaya* (The Universal Conquest of Sanskrit), and documented the progressive establishment of the 'empire of Sanskrit' first within India, and then elsewhere. Long before English underwrote Britain's 'civilizing' mission in its colonies, Sanskrit had 'civilized' many parts of the world—given them their literatures, their philosophy, their arts, and their scripts. Unlike the later-day colonial empires, however, Sanskrit's 'empire' was concerned with peace, happiness, and the quest for the Ultimate Reality.[78] It was asserted that 'Sanskrit has been, from

---

[76]Raghavan, *Sanskrit*, pp. 20, 32–41, 50–1.
[77]Ibid., pp. 32–3.
[78]Chatterjee, *Samskrita Dig-Vijaya*, pp. 8–9.

the most ancient times, a symbol and means of unity among the peoples of the world'. From Ireland to India, Sanskrit and its 'family' of Indo-European languages had 'embraced the vast stretch of the earth'. Indeed, it was the 'discovery' of this fact by William Jones that gave to Sanskrit 'a new importance and prestige in the world-context', and spurred, 'a new awakening of national consciousness' amongst the Indian intelligentsia.[79]

Here, it is quite clear that for its 'nationalist' admirers, the recognition that the West accorded to Sanskrit confirmed their own recognition of its greatness and prestige, and usefulness. Indeed, so enthusiastic was the commission about the admiration in the West for the language that it recommended to the government that Sanskrit should find a place not only in the Indian passport but also in the credentials that Indian ambassadors presented abroad to heads of states. For even if it was not as readily understood abroad as it is in India, it enjoys great prestige among Westerners who in any case think of India as 'Sanskrit India', the report noted. Some members of the commission even observed that it had been their experience that when Indians spoke in Sanskrit at international gatherings, their ideas 'had a much more respectful acceptance than would be accorded to a speech in any other Indian language'.[80] So, through Sanskrit, the emergent nation would secure the respect of the West, even while preserving its own authenticity and uniqueness.

However, if the admiration of the West for Sanskrit may ensure India's prestige and primacy in the hierarchy of modern nations, its advocates had to wrestle with the specific way in which that admiration had come packaged. For European scholars had domesticated Sanskrit by analogizing the language to 'classical' Greek and Latin. In the late nineteenth century, the analogy had proved useful to numerous Indian nationalists in asserting a parity between Indians and Europeans, even as they insisted that India was the 'parent' of the modern West. In the 1940s and 1950s, however, the same analogy was a source of embarrassment for supporters of Sanskrit, for these languages, especially Latin, were widely regarded as elite, literary tongues not spoken by the people. Recognizing that its comparability to classical

[79]Raghavan, *Sanskrit*, p. 143; *Report of the Sanskrit Commission*, p. 69.
[80]*Report of the Sanskrit Commission*, p. 89.

Greek and Latin may be important for establishing linguistic prestige, antiquity, and venerability, but was a liability in making a case for its everyday viability for the nation's populace, advocates of Sanskrit now dismissed the analogy as 'absurd'. So, it was argued that unlike Greek and Latin, Sanskrit was 'more than a mere classical language in India':

Greek and Latin did not and do not have the same sort of deep and all-inclusive influence which Sanskrit still has in Indian life. They are at the best academic, the concern of scholars. But Sanskrit is something more profound and more vital than that. Not only is it academic in the true sense of the term, but it is popular also ...[81]

The extent to which Sanskrit had been a popular spoken language in the past has for long been a matter of scholarly debate.[82] Both, the Constituent Assembly and the Official Language Commission had rejected the language on precisely these grounds, the latter even noting that 'only 500 odd persons returned themselves with Sanskrit as their mother tongue in the 1951 census'.[83] The Sanskrit Commission, however, operated on the principle that Sanskrit had once been the spoken language of the people of India, and indeed continues to be widely understood today. So Raghavan wrote: 'Thousands in every village, town and city sit to this day and listen to Valmiki and wipe off their tears as the exponent reads "*Ramo Rama Rama iti prājanām abhavan kathāh*". Is Homer expounded thus in the streets of Europe'?[84]

Its advocates also argued that it was especially scandalous to declare, following the Greek and Latin analogy, that Sanskrit was 'dead', a characterization which had picked up momentum by the middle of the nineteenth century in the course of the acrimonious debates between the Orientalists, Anglicists and vernacularists over the direction that colonial educational policy ought to take. The Sanskrit

[81]Ibid., p. 88.

[82]Hans H. Hock, 'Spoken Sanskrit in Uttar Pradesh: Profile of a Dying Prestige Language', in Edward C. Dimock and Braj B. Kachru (eds), *Dimensions of Sociolinguistics in South Asia* (New Delhi: Oxford University Press, 1992), pp. 247–60; A. Wezler, 'Do You Speak Sanskrit: On a Class of Sanskrit Texts Composed in the Late Middle Ages', in Houben (ed.), *The Ideology and Status of Sanskrit*, pp. 327–46.

[83]*Report of the Official Language Commission*, p. 39. From 1881 onwards, census reports show that several hundreds declared Sanskrit as the language of their home or as their 'parent tongue'. Colonial officials were invariably skeptical of such claims (see, for example, *Census of India, 1891: General Report* [London, 1893], p. 144).

[84]Raghavan, *Sanskrit*, p. 14.

Commission instead declared that Sanskrit 'is as much a live language as any mother tongue going about':

> Even at the present day, Sanskrit is very very living [*sic*], because a large number of people use Sanskrit in their conversation, when they come from different parts of the country, and composition in Sanskrit, in both prose, and verse, goes on almost unabated.... When Sanskrit is now being used even to express modern scientific or political ideas in essays or discourses on various modern subjects, it cannot be said to have closed the door to further development— it has still life in it. All these things would go to establish that Sanskrit is still a living force in Indian life.[85]

Given this conclusion that Sanskrit was still 'a living force in Indian life', the commission dismissed as absurd those detractors who claimed that 'Sanskrit can only help to make people reactionary in their attitude to life—make them shut their eyes to the actual conditions of life and merely hark back to an ideal past age'. On the contrary, the wealth of words in its repertoire would allow Indians to modernize and scientize without losing their nationality, and without giving up their pride in being Indian, for when Sanskrit is used to create new scientific and technological terminology, 'there is not the slightest feeling that the word is foreign or borrowed'.[86] And for those who doubted that Sanskrit contained words that would be adequate for modern science, Raghavan assured them that 'some of the sciences, in their origins in the West, had their roots in or were intimately connected with Sanskrit ...' So, why then, he asked, 'should there be any antagonism between science and Sanskrit?' On the contrary, Sanskrit would enable India to be authentically modern and scientific, to be *like* the West without *becoming* the West. The West had hitherto only recognized India's greatness in the spiritual and literary realms. But Sanskritic texts had made fundamental contributions towards the development of the physical sciences and mathematics as well. It was necessary to take stock of these, 'for the history of Chemistry or of Mathematics can be fully appreciated only by making a thorough study of the Indian contribution to these subjects [as embodied in Sanskrit] ....'[87]

---

[85]*Report of the Sanskrit Commission*, pp. 88–9; see also Raghavan, *Sanskrit*, p. 14.
[86]*Report of the Sanskrit Commission*, pp. 79, 197.
[87]Raghavan, *Sanskrit*, p. 12; *Report of the Sanskrit Commission*, pp. 86–7.

The impossibility of incompatibility between Sanskrit and science also finds frequent expression in the formulation that was widely circulated among many proponents of 'Hindu science', namely, that Sanskrit is the world's most 'scientific' language.[88] So, Raja Ramanna, one of India's leading nuclear physicists and chairman at one time of its Atomic Energy Commission, has published a short pamphlet entitled *Sanskrit and Science* in which he proposed that in its structure, Sanskrit mirrors the structures of mathematics, geometry, and logic. In the same vein, it is proposed that Panini's grammar 'is the first attempt in the history of the human mind to make a sort of 'chemical analysis' of a language on scientific lines'; Baudhayana's sutras from the sixth century BC already contain the formula that the world later associated with Pythagoras; and Brahmagupta had discovered in seventh century BC what a thousand years later would be rediscovered as the Pellian equation in Europe.[89] So, at this level, Sanskrit enthusiasts appear to be subverting the old Orientalist thematic that runs through nationalist thought as well, namely, that the West was the realm of science, and the East, the abode of the spirit. They argued instead that India, too, had contributed to the sciences, far before the West had, and that a renewed study of Sanskrit would allow both the West and modern Indians to become cognizant of this fact. Sanskrit thus confirmed the authenticity and antiquity of 'Indian' science, even as it provided the linguistic vehicle through which this science could be revived and receive respectability in the modern world.

All the same, the commission did note that 'every nation has some contribution to make to the sum-total of human civilisation', and that India's unique contribution lay in its special purchase on the meaning of Ultimate Reality which was made available through Sanskrit. 'Sanskrit is a language which through its sonority and mellifluousness has the power to lift us above ourselves ...'. Because of this power, Sanskrit was a 'potent aid to the formation of character and sense of exaltation'. So, in addition to the role that Sanskrit would play in

[88]For an important analysis of 'Hindu science' as a means through which Hindu/ nationalist intellectuals used the authority of science to revalidate their ancient scriptures, and reconfigured Hinduism as 'scientific', see Gyan Prakash, 'The Modern Nation's Return in the Archaic', *Critical Inquiry*, 23 (3), 1997, pp. 536–56.

[89]Raja Ramanna, *Sanskrit and Science* (Bombay, 1984).

ensuring pan-Indian cultural and political unity, the language would contribute to the moral, spiritual, and emotional (re)integration of the citizenry into a unified and harmonious whole. Like the ideal Sanskrit scholar, every citizen exposed to Sanskrit would be

actuated by the Principles of Dharma, and his actions towards all men, towards all living beings as a matter of fact, [would] take a colouring from the principles of *Ahimsa* or non-injury, of *Karuna* or Compassion, and of *Maitri* or Friendly Service. A certain amount of Gentleness of Spirit, of Humility, particularly in the matter of Unseen Forces of Life, of a desire to give to the others their proper due, and an attitude of Tolerance with regard to other people's faith and belief, and above all a certain moral approach and earnestness [would] be noticeable ...[90]

In the view of the commission, the Sanskrit pandit was the paradigmatic Indian, the model that every citizen ought to emulate.

So impressed was the commission with the 'dignity' and 'solemnity' that Sanskrit inevitably bestowed upon all that it touched that it recommended to the government that the language be used widely for all formal state functions. Sanskrit ought to be used for oath-taking by members of parliament and state legislatures, of electoral colleges as well as other official bodies; the swearing-in ceremonies of the president, governors, ministers, judges, and so on should be conducted in Sanskrit; the sessions of states legislatures and the parliament, as well as government-sponsored national and international conferences, ought to begin with the recitation of the Rig Vedic hymn (X. 191.2–4) which celebrates concord and unanimity, and should conclude with the recitation of another Vedic hymn.[91] Here, it is hard not to conclude that the commission's statements about the 'dignity' and 'stateliness' of the language were a throwback to older notions about the magical power of Sanskrit words, even as they represent a secular adaptation to the needs of the modern state.

Since the language was filled with so much prestige and dignity, when Indians imbibed its spirit, they, too, would acquire the self-respect, intellectual self-assurance, and self-confidence that they so badly needed to function in today's world:

[90]*Report of the Sanskrit Commission*, pp. 83–4.
[91]Ibid., p. 191–2.

Time and often, it has been seen that Indian youth abroad seem to be carried away by the rushing stream of modern life, whether in England or France or Germany or America, and they seem to accept everything on its face-value, if they do not have the sense of balance and the ballast which are furnished by an acquaintance with their own cultural moorings which can be supplied only by Sanskrit and its literature ...[92]

The commission therefore recommended that from early childhood, every Indian ought to be taught essential lessons of morality and social conduct through Sanskrit, for the 'importance of Sanskrit as a great stabilizing force in life—as a moral anchor—cannot be emphasized too strongly ...' Its verses

breathe a high moral tone and display a precious note of what might be called High and Serious Enlightenment. Persons who are attuned to this spirit through an acquaintance from early childhood with verses of this type, these Subhasitas ... and who have been nurtured in the atmosphere of the Ramayana and the Mahabharata, including the Gita, and also of the Upanishads, have a balanced and cultured outlook upon life both of their own country and of other countries which would be rare to find in those who have been denied all this ... the message of Sanskrit read or chanted is that of sursum corda, 'lift up your hearts'.[93]

Given this, it is not surprising, Raghavan declared, that even 'from the Śmaśāna [graveyard] of destroyed values in the West, thinking men are casting their hope-seeking looks eastward, and stretching their hands into Sanskrit's granary for grains of sustaining wisdom...'.[94] Like Lakshmikanta Maitra and his colleagues in the Constituent Assembly, Raghavan and his colleagues in the Sanskrit Commission proposed that with the help of Sanskrit, the nation would first regenerate itself, politically, spiritually, and morally. Thus regenerated, India would then rescue and revive all those other unfortunate nations and cultures of the world that had lost their spiritual mooring and their moral anchor.

The Sanskrit Commission's agenda thus was an old nationalist agenda, with an important postcolonial twist. Much of what we hear from its advocates about Sanskrit in the 1950s echoes what many a

[92]Ibid., p. 90.
[93]Ibid., p. 84.
[94]Raghavan, Sanskrit, p. 13.

(Hindu) nationalist had claimed for Hinduism in late colonial India. In what Partha Chatterjee has identified as its 'moment of departure', the national project picked up Hinduism as the means through which to define a distinctive and sovereign cultural identity for the emergent nation, as well as to assert the superiority of India over the materialist West. A revitalized Hinduism would ensure that its citizens would continue to remain Indian even while learning the ways of the West. In what we may characterize as the 'moment of departure' for nationalist thought in independent India, the project remains the same, more or less, but the means of implementing it undergo a radical transformation, on the surface at any rate, as language, primarily, and culture and morality, secondarily, are favoured over religion. This is not surprising, for the commission functioned under the mantle of a Constitution that had only recently declared the nation to be 'secular', and submitted its report in a political climate in which memories of partition were still vivid, and the anti-Hindu polemics of the Dravidian movement gathering momentum. The spiritual, cultural, and moral work of regeneration with which Hinduism had been entrusted in an earlier period, was now thrust upon language, and upon one language in particular, Sanskrit. In that process, the overt connections of the language with Hinduism were severed, even as the content and message of that religion were selectively dredged up to provide the moral and emotional moorings for a nation that was adrift but could hopefully be anchored down by Sanskrit.

Sanskritizing the Nation

In 1974, twenty or so years after he had chaired the Sanskrit Commission, Suniti Kumar Chatterjee quoted with approval two Russian scholars who had recently declared that it was hard, even impossible, to imagine India without Sanskrit, and went on to remind Indians, once again, that '*Sanskrit is India*, The progressive Unification of the Indian Peoples into a single Nation can correctly be described as the Sanskritization of India'.[95] So the question remains: to what extent have advocates of Sanskrit succeeded, in the name of national 'regeneration' and 'unification', in sanskritizing India? Important enough as this question

[95]Chatterjee, *India*, p. 32 (emphasis in original).

is, it has drawn little scholarly scrutiny, even as the recent extension of support to Sanskrit by Hindu nationalism only reminds us of the urgency of attending to this issue.[96]

As the Sanskrit Commission itself noted with satisfaction, there are many signs of the symbolic importance accorded to Sanskrit in independent India. The Constitution recognizes the nation by its Sanskrit name, Bharata, and the Upanishadic saying, *Satyam eva jayate*, 'truth alone triumphs', has been adopted as the national motto. The national anthem of India, we are told, is 90 per cent Sanskrit and 10 per cent Sanskritic and 'hence is understood all over India'. The Government of India has officially adopted *Sri* and *Srimati* replacing the English Mr and Mrs as honorific forms of address. Various state bodies and agencies—parliament, All India Radio, the Life Insurance Corporation, and so on—have all adopted mottoes drawn from Sanskrit literature, and even the Indian Navy has taken as its guiding principle the Vedic prayer, *sam no varunah*.[97]

At the institutional level, in 1959, the Government of India appointed the Central Sanskrit Board, made up of Sanskritists and educationalists, as an advisory body that would coordinate state efforts in the development and promotion of Sanskrit. In 1970, this board was replaced by the more high-powered Kendriya Sanskrit Parishad consisting of representatives from various state governments, central government agencies and ministries, as well as universities. In addition to these agencies, a special branch of the Ministry of Education and Social Welfare, called the Sanskrit Division, also deals with government policy on Sanskrit. These agencies have taken as their mandate the implementation of the proposals made by the Sanskrit Commission in 1956, hence the centrality I have accorded in this essay to its report. The schemes undertaken over the next few decades have included cataloguing of rare manuscripts and publishing of numerous textbooks and journals in Sanskrit; offering grants-in-aid to voluntary

---

[96]In terms that eerily resonate the assertions of the Sanskrit Commission, the Vishva Hindu Parishad declared in a pamphlet published in 1991 that 'to treat the glorious Sanskrit language at par with Arabic, Persian or Urdu is madness' for 'our spirituality is our life-blood, it is the life of our national life. And Sanskrit is the sole reservoir which conserves for us this spirituality, because at the very sound of Sanskrit, the nation receives a kind of glory, power and right'. Accordingly, 'the preservation of Sanskrit' is enjoined to be 'a divine task' (quoted in Bhattacharji, 'New Education Policy', pp. 2641–2).

[97]*Report of the Sanskrit Commission*, p. 71.

organizations as well as traditional centres of Sanskritic learning; and the improvement of Sanskrit pedagogy in schools and universities. Following the recommendations of the Sanskrit Commission and the central government, numerous state governments as well as the union territory of Delhi did make the study of Sanskrit mandatory in schools, and in some universities as well. Additionally, various All-India seminars, Sanskrit elocution contests, Vedic conventions, and so on have been periodically held under government sponsorship. Pension schemes have also been instituted for indigent Sanskrit scholars and scholarships awarded to students. The funds for these ventures have been provided through the various Five Year Plans which allocated Rs 5 lakhs in 1956, Rs 75 lakhs in 1961, and Rs 2.75 crores in 1969. Not surprisingly, given that the government promised financial remuneration to those institutions undertaking the spread of the language, a dramatic increase in voluntary Sanskrit organizations (from 5, in 1958–9 to 500 in 1970–1) has been noted. These associations conduct private examinations, publish manuals and guides for quick and easy learning of the language, commemorate the birth and death anniversaries of important Sanskrit literary figures, and arrange public lectures. Older centres of Sanskritic learning have also been revamped, and new institutions such as Kendriya Sanskrit Vidyapeetha at Tirupati and the Shri Lal Bahadur Shastri Kendriya Sanskrit Vidyapeetha in New Delhi, were opened in the 1960s, with plans to open other state-supported centres over the next few years.[98]

So, the lamentations of its supporters over the decline in state patronage for Sanskrit during the past few centuries appear therefore to have been answered at last, with the central government itself stepping in as a new and powerful patron. Indeed, as the Sanskrit Commission noted, Sanskrit reaped an important dividend with the reorganization of states on linguistic principles in the 1950s. From then on, the development of India's regional languages became the responsibility of various state governments, whereas Sanskrit, because it was 'state-less' and because it was declared to be key to the maintenance of the nation's integrity, came directly under the patronage of the centre, and stood therefore to benefit from this, materially as well as

[98]Ibid., pp. 221–4; *Sanskrit in India* (New Delhi, 1972); Hock, 'Spoken Sanskrit'; Bhate, 'Position of Sanskrit in Public Education', pp. 391–400.

ideologically. Its supporters still continue to complain that government patronage notwithstanding, the language continues to decline for want of support; that efforts to transform it into an everyday spoken language have all but failed; and that even centres of Sanskritic learning frequently fall back on English, Hindi, or the regional languages to teach Sanskrit.[99] Nonetheless, not least because of the intervention of the Sanskrit Commission and other such organizations, Sanskrit has been assured a visibility in modern India that has been denied to other languages, such as Persian, that have played analogous roles in India's past.

But if Sanskrit has arguably profited from being appropriated by the nation, what gains has the nation made by associating itself with the language? Why indeed have India's nationalizers, or at least some of them, found Sanskrit to be so useful in imagining the nation? As I have suggested, Sanskrit (re)emerges as the 'great unifier' at a time that I have characterized, following Partha Chatterjee, as the moment of departure for the nation on its postcolonial journey. It inherits the task that had been assigned to Hinduism three-quarters of a century ago, a task that had only rendered that religion was suspect and illegitimate for any kind of unifying role in independent India. Sanskrit steps into—or is made to occupy—the breach vacated by Hinduism, for like the latter, it too had been identified by more than two centuries of colonial-Orientalist scholarship as the 'essence' of India; it, too, could enable the emergent nation in being like the West without becoming the West. But unlike Hinduism, it had not become directly implicated in the divisive communal politics of the pre-partition years. The Sanskrit Commission indeed made sure, as we have seen, to disavow all intimacies between Sanskrit and religiosity, and between Sanskrit and Hinduism, instead offering the language to the nation as the repository of its 'culture' and 'morality'.

On another level, it is clear that as long as the troubled question of an acceptable official language of the union stands unresolved, Sanskrit will continue to surface as a candidate, if only because, as members of the Constituent Assembly were quick to point out, it is nobody's 'mother tongue', and every Indian is equally disadvantaged with respect to it. So, ironically, this language of high privilege and exclusivity can be put to work as the great leveller of the nation, to ensure that all citizens had

[99]Hock, 'Spoken Sanskrit'; Bhate, 'Position of Sanskrit in Public Education', pp. 394–5.

an equal start in the race for jobs and benefits. Such a reasoning certainly unsettles the assumption that the nation is about the forging of a 'deep horizontal comradeship', and the subordination of particular interests to the general, the individual to the collective. India's linguistic crisis which turns around the resistance to Hindi as the common link language, reminds us that nationalism is not just about every member of the nation agreeing to put their best foot forward and working towards a common goal, as it is also about ensuring that no one citizen or group of citizens has a head start. So, Naziruddin Ahmad was able to stand up in the Constituent Assembly and declare: 'I offer you a language which is the grandest and the greatest, and it is impartially difficult, equally difficult for all to learn'. Sanskrit, on the face of it, the most hierarchical of all languages, would potentially guarantee, in its new incarnation as 'national language', the (linguistic) equality of the nation's citizens.

And yet, as the first part of Ahmad's statement also clearly reveals, Sanskrit's hold on the collective imagination of so many Indians cannot be satisfactorily explained by resorting to this kind of pragmatic, even cynical, reasoning alone. The Sanskrit standard continues to be raised, again and again, because it allows the nation to mask its modernity, its 'astonishing youth', its newness. As Sudipta Kaviraj rightly points out:

The nation, India ... is a thing without a past. It is radically modern. It can only look for subterfuges of antiquity. It fears to face and admit its own terrible modernity, because to admit modernity is to make itself vulnerable. As a proposal for modern living, on a scale quite unprecedented ..., in a society still knowing only one legitimizing criterion—tradition—it must seek to find past disguises for these wholly modern proposals.[100]

By attaching itself to Sanskrit, the nation can make up for an absence of antiquity by borrowing from Sanskrit's antiquity, it can gloss over its lark of continuity by hiding behind Sanskrit's apparent depth; it can reaffirm its own unity and authenticity by pointing to Sanskrit's claims to unity and authenticity. But, as this essay has sought to demonstrate, the nation's attempt to create an aura of antiquity,

---

[100]Sudipta Kaviraj, 'The Imaginary Institution of India', in Partha Chatterjee and Gyanendra Pandey (eds), *Subaltern Studies VII: Writings on South Asian History and Society* (Delhi: Oxford University Press, 1995), p. 13.

autonomy, and authenticity for itself by appropriating Sanskrit involves, at the very least, a dramatic recasting of Sanskrit, and its re-presentation to the nation, no longer as the sacred language of one of its communities but as the language of 'culture' and 'morality' for all its constituents; as not just the repository of ancient 'wit' and 'wisdom' but as the very guarantor of an authentic modern science; and, above all, as not just a mandarin language of high privilege and learning but as an everyday language of even the humblest of its citizens. Such a recasting and re-presentation which underpins what I have referred to as the 'nationalization' of Sanskrit, has not been without its share of contradictions and ironies. Not the least of these, and here I paraphrase Sheldon Pollock, is that this language of the gods and of pristine perfection can assure itself of a place in the modern nation only by mixing it up, so to speak, in the mundane world of mere humans.

Postscript

Quaint, even absurd, though the claims of the Sanskrit Commission may appear, in its own report and no doubt in my rendering of these, they clearly are but reflections of the troubling dilemmas of imagining the nation in colonial and postcolonial contexts. The advocates of Sanskrit in the Constituent Assembly and in the Sanskrit Commission, as indeed most Indian nationalists, functioned with the Herderian assumption, inherited from their colonial masters and predecessors, that to be a nation meant the possession of a 'national' language that would serve one and all, and that would be the repository of the national essence even as it knitted the community into a unified whole. In forging language policies around such an assumption, nations like India with linguistic pasts that did not approximate those of the West, nevertheless committed themselves to a linguistic trajectory that would bring them in line with Europe's modernity. From this point of view, the Sanskrit Commission's advocacy of Sanskrit seems both subversive and tragic. Subversive because in seeking to revamp an ancient mandarin language that was nobody's 'mother tongue' and institute it as the official language of a modern nation, the commission at least dared to pursue an alternate imagination which did not replicate the historical experience of the West. Tragic, because, in the end, its advocates made their case by deploying the logic of (Western) nationalism and modernity and by recasting Sanskrit in the image of other national tongues. In the nationalization of Sanskrit, as with so much else in the colonial and postcolonial world, difference struggles with and ultimately loses out to sameness.

SELECT REFERENCES

Agarwala, V.S., 1966. 'The Devanagari Script,' in *Indian Systems of Writing.* Delhi.

Alter, Robert, 1994. *Hebrew and Modernity.* Bloomington: Indiana University Press.

Austin, Granville, 1966. 'Language and the Constitution—The Half-hearted Compromise', in *The Indian Constitution: Cornerstone of a Nation.* Oxford: Clarendon Press, pp. 265–307.

Bhate, Saroj, 1996. Position of Sanskrit in Public Education and Scientific Research in Modern India, in Jan E.M. Houben (ed.), *The Ideology and Status of Sanskrit.* Leiden: J. Brilo, pp. 378–400.

Bhattacharji, Sukumari, 1990. New Education Policy and Sanskrit, *Economic and Political Weekly,* 25(48–49): 2641–2.

Biljert, Victor A. van, 1996. Sanskrit and Hindu National Identity in Nineteenth Century Bengal, in Jan E.M. Houben (ed.), *The Ideology and Status of Sanskrit.* Leiden: J. Brilo, 1996. pp. 347–66.

Breckenridge, Carol and Peter van der Veer (eds), 1994. *Orientalism and the Post-colonial Predicament: Perspectives in South Asia.* New York: Oxford University Press.

Burg, J.G. Corstiaan van der, 1996. 'The Place of Sanskrit in Neo-Hindu Ideology: From Religious Reform to National Awakening', in Jan E.M. Houben (ed.), *The Ideology and Status of Sanskrit.* Leiden: J. Brilo, 1996. pp. 375–8.

Cardona, George, 1990. 'On Attitudes towards Language in Ancient India', *Sino-Platonic Papers,* 15: 1–19.

Census of India, 1891: *General Report.* London: 1893, p. 1440.

Chatterjee, Partha, 1986. *Nationalist Thought and the Colonial World: A Derivative Discourse?* London: Zed Books.

Chatterji, Suniti Kumar, 1943. *Languages and the Linguistic Problem.* London: Geoffrey Cumberlege Oxford University Press.

———, 1974, *India: A Polyglot Nation and Its Linguistic Problems vis-a-vis National Integration.* Bombay: Mahatma Gandhi Memorial Research Centre, Hindustan Prachar Sabha.

_____, 1985. *Samskrta Dig-Vijaya.* Calcutta: Sanskrit College.

Cohn, Bernard S., 1966. 'Recruitment and Training of British Civil Servants in India 1600–1860', in Ralph Braibanti (ed.), *Asian Bureaucratic Systems Emergent from the British Imperial Tradition*, Durham: Duke University Press.

Constituent Assembly Debates: Official Report, Vol. 9, 1949. New Delhi: Government of India.

Deshpande, Madhav, 1979. *Sociolinguistic Attitudes in India: An Historical Reconstruction.* Ann Arbor: Karoma Publications.

Gandhi, Mohandas K., 1942. *Our Language Problem.* Karachi: A.T. Hingorani.

_____, 1957. *The Story of My Experiments with Truth.* Boston: Beacon Press.

_____, 1958. *Evil Wrought by the English Medium.* Ahmedabad: Navjivan.

Goldman, Robert, 1993. 'The Communalization of Sanskrit and the Sanskritization of Communalism' (unpublished manuscript).

Hock, Hans Heinrich, 1992. 'Spoken Sanskrit in Uttar Pradesh: Profile of a Dying Prestige Language', in Edward C. Dimock and Braj B. Kachru (eds), *Dimensions of Sociolinguistic in South Asia.* New Delhi: Oxford and IBH, pp. 247–60.

Houben, Jan E.M. (ed.), 1996. *The Ideology and Status of Sanskrit: Contributions to the History of the Sanskrit Language.* Leiden: J. Brilo.

Jones, Kenneth, 1976. *Arya Dharm: Hindu Consciousness in 19th-Century Punjab*, Berkeley: University of California Press.

Kaviraj, Sudipta, 1993. 'The Imaginary Institution of India', in Partha Chatterjee and Gyanendra Pandey (eds), *Subaltern Studies VII: Writings on South Asian History and Society.* New Delhi: Oxford University Press, pp. 1–39.

_____, forthcoming. *Unhappy Consciousness.* New Delhi: Oxford University Press.

King, Christopher, 1994. *One Language, Two Scripts: The Hindi Movement in Nineteenth Century North India.* New Delhi: Oxford University Press.

Kodanda Rao, P., 1969. *Language Issue in the Indian Constituent Assembly, 1946–50. Rational Support for English and Non-Rational Support for Hindi.* Bombay: International Book House.

Kumar, Krishna, 'Quest for Self-Identity: Cultural Consciousness and Education in the Hindi Region, 1880–1950', *EPW*, 25(2), 1990, pp. 1247–55.

Maurer, Walter, 1976. 'On the Name Devanagari', *Journal of American Orientalist Society*, 96(1): 101–4.

McCully, Bruce, 1940. *English Education and Origins of Indian Nationalism.* New York: Columbia University Press.

Monier-Williams, Monier, 1861. *The Study of Sanskrit in Relation to Missionary Work in India.* London: Williams and Norgate.

Nambi Arooran, K.A., 1980. *Tamil Renaissance and Dravidian Nationalism, 1905–1944.* Madurai: Koodal Publishers.

Nehru, Jawaharlal, 1993 [1946]. *The Discovery of India*. Delhi: Oxofrd University Press.

Pawde, Kumud, 1992. 'The Story of My Sanskrit', in Arjun Dangle (ed.), *A Corpse in the Well: Translations from Modern Marathi Dalit Autobiographies*. Bombay: Disha Books, pp. 24–34.

Pollock, Sheldon, 1990. 'The Language of the Gods in the World of Men: Reflections on Sanskrit in History' (unpublished manuscript).

Prakash, Gyan, 'The Modern Nations Return in the Archaic', *Critical Inquriry*, 93(3), 1997, pp. 536–6.

Raghavan, V., 1972. *Sanskrit: Essays on the Value of the Language and the Literature*. Madras: Sanskrit Education Society.

Ramanna, Raja, 1984. *Sanskrit and Science*. Bombay: Bharatiya Vidya Bhawan.

Ramaswamy, Sumathi, 1997. *Passions of the Tongue: Language Devotion in Tamil India, 1891–1970*. Berkeley: University of California Press.

Report of the Official Language Commission, 1957. New Delhi: Government of India.

Report of the Sanskrit Commission, 1956–57, 1958. Delhi: Government of India.

Rocher, Ludo, 1967. *Le probleme linguistique en Inde*. Brusells: Academic Royale des Sciences d' Outre-Mer.

Rocher, Rosane, 1994. 'Sanskrit: Discovery by Europeans', in R.A. Asher *et al.* (eds), *Encyclopedia of Language and Linguistics*. London: Pergamon, pp. 3651–4.

Sanskrit in India, 1972. New Delhi: Rashtriya Sanskrit Sansthan.

Ray, N.R. (ed.), 1986. *Dictionary of National Biography*. Calcutta: South Asia Books.

Schwab, Raymond, 1974. *The Oriental Renaissance: Europe's Discovery of India and the East, 1680–1880*. New York: Columbia University Press.

Suntharalingam, R., 1974. *Politics and Nationalist Awakening in South India, 1852–1891*. Tucson: University of Arizona Press.

Vira, Raghu, 1965. *India's National Language*. New Delhi: International Academy of Indian Culture.

Wezler, A., 1996. 'Do You Speak Sanskrit: On a Class of Sanskrit Text Composed in the Late Middle Ages', in Jan E.M. Houben (ed.), *Ideology and Status of Sanskrit: Contributions to the History of the Sanskrit Language*. Leiden: J. Brillo.

3

Factors in the Linguistic Reorganization of Indian States*

Joseph E. Schwartzberg†

INTRODUCTION

In 1920, the Indian National Congress, meeting in Nagpur, resolved to reorganize its own party structure according to linguistic provinces and called on the government to reorganize the administration of the provinces of British India along similar lines.[1] At the time, not quite a third of the population of the provinces under direct British rule spoke languages different from those of the most numerous linguistic group within their respective areas, and slightly more than half the total area of British India (including Burma and the frontier agencies) comprised districts in which a clear majority of the population spoke languages other than those of the plurality groups.[2] Although language

*Originally published as 'Factors in the Linguistic Reorganization of Indian States', in Paul Wallace (ed.), *Region and Nation in India* (New Delhi: Oxford & IBH Publishing Company Pvt. Ltd., 1985), pp. 155–82.

†The author is indebted to Gregory Chu and Carol Gersmehl for assistance in the preparation of the maps and graph accompanying this article.

[1]Government of India, *States Reorganization Commission Report*, New Delhi's Mgr. of Publications, 1955 (Henceforth, *SRC*), p. 13.

[2]All population figures, including linguistic data, presented in this paper are derived from the decennial Indian censuses of the period 1921–71, unless otherwise stated. The 1921 linguistic data available to the author in readily usable form were at the national and provincial levels only; hence, for certain calculations involving aggregations of district-level data for 1920, it was necessary to make estimates by recasting the 1931 data into the administration framework

data from the 1981 census are not yet available, a projection of 1971 figures to the present would indicate that only about one-sixth of India's population now belong to linguistic minorities within their respective states and union territories. But more striking, perhaps, as a measure of the administrative changes that India has experienced in response to demands for linguistic reorganization is the fact that districts in which the numerically predominant language differs from that of the state or union territory in which the district is located account for only 9.6 per cent of the total area of the republic and for a mere 2.7 per cent of its population.[3] It would, thus, appear that the process of reshaping India's political map to accord with the linguistic distribution of its inhabitants has virtually run its course. We may, therefore, have reached a vantage point in history from which we can look back over the greater part of this century and attempt a dispassionate summary and assessment of the manner in which linguistic reorganization occurred, the pace at which that often stormy process proceeded, the factors considered in specific reorganization decisions (including decisions *not* to implement suggested changes), and the scope, if any, for additional changes in the future. This brief essay, along with its accompanying maps and graphs, attempts to satisfy those objectives. It will also consider the implications of the present distribution of linguistic groups, by political regions, in respect to the future unity and well-being of the Indian nation.

But before we can proceed, it is necessary to state a number of caveats with respect to our statistical data lest the reader accord them a greater degree of scientific validity than they warrant. To begin with, we must note that no two Indian censuses have been wholly in agreement with one another in regard to the inclusiveness of specific languages. This inconsistency is of particular importance with respect to Hindi, Urdu, and other allegedly mutually comprehensible tongues, including—at times—Hindustani, Bihari, Rajasthani, Punjabi, Pahari, and literally scores of other 'mother tongues' or dialects grouped under one or more of those designations, depending on the specific census year. The varying

---

of the earlier period, which was scarcely different from that for 1931. The area figures cited for 1920 were measured by the author on his own maps (based on figure 3.1).

[3] For the present day, estimates for both area and population are extrapolations of district-level data of the 1971 Census.

practices from one census to another will be clarified in footnotes relating to appropriate portions of the subsequent text.

Apart from the arbitrariness and regional inconsistency of the census treatment of many mother tongues, one must recognize that the census returns are vitiated by a certain degree of intentional falsification, either by the respondents or by the enumerators, to advance the cause of one or another linguistic group. The returns for Urdu are particularly suspect in many districts (with a tendency toward under-enumeration since independence); but, as we have consistently grouped Urdu with Hindi, our analysis is not thereby significantly affected. Similarly, in the areas now comprising Punjab and Haryana a bias on the part of Sikhs and Hindus in favour of returning Punjabi and Hindi respectively is generally acknowledged. Other sources of biased data undoubtedly exist; but in regard to language, we do not feel that they are likely to have a marked bearing on our findings.[4]

A question that must be addressed if the following analysis is to make sense is just what constitutes a linguistic minority. While admitting the sociological fact that minority status is to some degree a matter of external perception and self-identification, we are hardly in a position to determine which groups think of themselves and of others with whom they interact as belonging to minorities. We are, therefore, forced to fall back on the available statistics in making our determinations. The statistics reporting 'mother tongues' spoken may relate either to 'languages' or 'dialects.' For purposes of this essay, no group speaking a particular dialect of a specified language will be considered as a minority group with respect to a majority speaking another dialect or group of dialects of the same language. Mutual comprehensibility (known or presumed) is the criterion for specifying that two mother tongues (for example, Awadhi and Bhojpuri) are different dialects of the same language, while, conversely, mutual incomprehensibility (for example, Ao Naga and Sema Naga) is the test for stipulating that they are, in fact, different languages. The Constitutional distinction between Hindi and Urdu, both of which are recognized as 'official languages,' and so enumerated by all post-independence censuses does not affect our

---

[4]A discussion of how to recognize and deal with biased enumerations appears in Joseph E. Schwartzberg, 'Sources and Types of Census Error,' in *The Census in British India, New Perspectives* (New Delhi: Manohar, 1981), pp. 41–60.

general rule. While most speakers of Urdu are undoubtebly part of an *ethnic* minority, the principal basis for their minority status is religious rather than linguistic, and we have treated Hindi-Urdu as a single language.

Rajasthani, Pahari, and Punjabi pose different problems. While most speakers of those tongues, in their various dialects, are probably able to understand the Hindi of the regions close to their respective territories more or less well, they will probably experience considerable difficulty with the Hindi of more distant regions. But, as 'mutual comprehensibility' is, in the final analysis, a matter of degree, we have chosen to regard the former group of languages, as does the census itself until 1961 (following Grierson), as distinct from Hindi.[5] This decision accords well with political and social realities, we believe, and allows us to present a reasonably standardized set of maps up to 1961. The census decision in 1971 to lump all speakers of Rajasthani and Pahari with those speaking Hindi is one for which we cannot make realistic adjustments. Consequently, comparisons of our 1971 maps and data with those for earlier censuses will, in that regard, be somewhat vitiated.

The linguistic minorities we shall be dealing with in this paper are those that exist at the provincial level in the pre-independence period, for which time our analysis relates to British India only, and at the state or union territory level for the period since the adoption of the Indian Constitution in January 1950. Persons whose *primary* language is one other than that accounting for a plurality—if not an absolute majority—of the population of their state or union territory are here taken as members of a linguistic minority, even though locally (that is, at the district or lower level of analysis) they may be in the majority. The question of non-Hindi-speaking states as minority regions within the Republic of India is one on which we shall not focus, though we shall refer to it briefly in our concluding remarks. As census data are normally reported only down to the district level, our regional analysis can penetrate no deeper than that, despite the fact that there are a number of regions in which a finer breakdown (by *tahsil, taluk,* or subdivision) would be quite useful.

[5]Despite the census decision to retain the separateness of Pahari—or more precisely a variety of Pahari languages and dialects, the actual practice for the large area of Himalayan UP at certain censuses was to enumerate Pahari speakers as speakers of Hindi.

THE COURSE OF LINGUISTIC REORGANIZATION

Although, as stated at the outset, Congress officially endorsed the establishment of linguistic provinces in 1920, the idea had been mooted by both the British and the Congress on a variety of occasions since 1903, when Sir Herbert Risley, then Home Secretary in the Government of India, first raised the issue in connection with the proposed partition of the sprawling polyglot Bengal Presidency.[6] As matters turned out, Curzon's partition of 1905 could scarcely have done greater violence to the principle of linguistic homogeneity. But, in rectifying that political blunder in 1912, Bengal was recreated as an essentially unilingual province, thereafter divested of the large multilingual area of Bihar and Orissa, though not including several million Bengali speakers in the restored province of Assam.[7] Officially, this was the first British concession to the linguistic principle; however, that was but one among many considerations bearing on the final decision taken. The 1905 partition, arguably, was what first aroused Congress' sensitivity to the language issue in respect to the territorial organization of British India, and it was in the context of the protest over partition that the first Congress linguistic province was established in Bihar in 1908. Other such Congress provinces were set up in Sind and Andhra in 1917. The following year, not surprisingly, the authors of the Montagu-Chelmsford report 'examined the suggestion for the formation, within the existing provinces, of sub-provinces on a linguistic and racial [sic] basis, with a view to providing suitable units for experiment in responsible government', but, while admitting 'that the business of government would be simplified if administrative units were both smaller and more homogeneous', they concluded that action to

[6]*SRC*, p. 10. For further historical details, see chapter II, 'Rationale for Reorganisation,' and chapter III, 'Time for Reorganization,' pp. 10–24. A fuller, very judicious account is provided in Ram Gopal, *Linguistic Affairs of India* (Bombay: Asia Publishing House, 1996), chapter V, 'The Principle of Linguistic Homogeneity', and chapter VI, 'Linguistic States,' pp. 63–113. Much of the subsequent discussion is based on these two sources.

[7]Detailed maps of all territorial changes referred to in this paper, maps of the distribution of specific languages, and statistical data relating to the effect of political changes on the distribution of language groups are provided in Joseph E. Schwartzberg (ed.), *A Historical Atlas of South Asia* (Chicago: University of Chicago Press, 1978), pp. 66, 76–8, and 100–2. The accompanying text is on pp. 217, 224–5, and 234–6.

establish such units was, at the time, impractical and would have to follow the administrative reforms they were about to propose.[8]

Between its initial 1920 declaration and the outbreak of World War II, the Indian National Congress called repeatedly for the reorganization of India on linguistic lines. The British too paid lip service, from time to time, to the theoretical desirability of linguistic provinces, provided that they could be made economically viable and established with the general agreement of the populations concerned. It was not until April 1936, however, that two new linguistic provinces, Sind and Orissa, were finally established. No other such reforms were to occur prior to the granting of independence.

Figures 3.1 and 3.2 provide some indication of the dimensions of the problem of linguistic heterogeneity at the provincial level for the period from 1920 to 1936. Though the data for these two maps are drawn from the 1931 census, which is more detailed and easier to use than that of 1921, the picture that would have been portrayed had the 1921 data also been mapped varies so little from that of 1931, that an additional pair of maps for the earlier year would appear redundant.[9] Among the major provinces of India, those that appeared most egregiously to be in need of linguistic reorganization were Madras and Bombay in which approximately three-fifths of the total

[8]*SRC*, p. 11; the second quoted passage is from the *Report on Indian Constitutional Reforms*, 1918, paragraph 246. See also Ram Gopal, *Linguistic Affairs*, pp. 65–6.

[9]In 1921, Western and Eastern Hindi were enumerated separately, with Hindustani and Urdu grouped under the former (without individual enumeration). Eastern Hindi was actually tabulated, however, only in the Central Provinces and Berar and in the Central India Agency, its speakers (including all but 4,000 speakers of Bihari) being grouped in other provinces with those of Western Hindi. Rajasthani, Punjabi, Lahnda (Western Punjabi) and Central, Eastern, and Western Pahari were all separately tabulated, but the vast majority of speakers of the former (i.e., those of the United Provinces) were counted along with those speaking Western Hindi.

In 1931, the distinction between Western and Eastern Hindi was maintained but the areal coverage of the latter group was extended to Assam, Bengal, and several other provinces and princely states where it was not especially important. Bihari was now separately enumerated in Bihar and Orissa and adjoining princely states; but neither it nor Eastern Hindi was tabulated in the United Provinces, resulting in inflation of the figures for Western Hindi. Urdu too was again included with Western Hindi throughout India. The treatment of speakers of Rajasthani, Punjabi, and Lahnda, as well as of Central, Eastern, and Western Pahari remained the same as in the 1921 census. In order to maximize comparability from one map to another throughout this paper we have combined figures for Western and Eastern Hindi, Urdu, and Bihari wherever they are separately given.

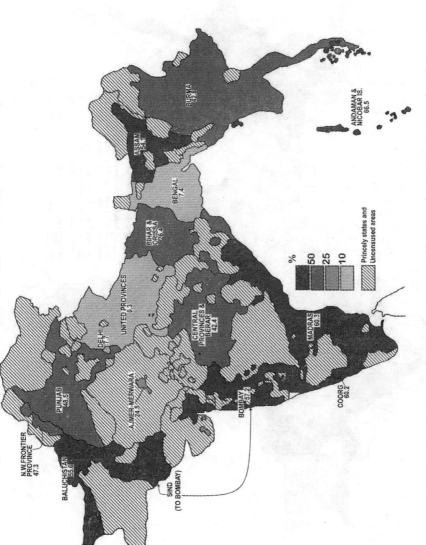

Figure 3.1: Linguistic Minorities as Percentage of Provincial Population in British India, 1931

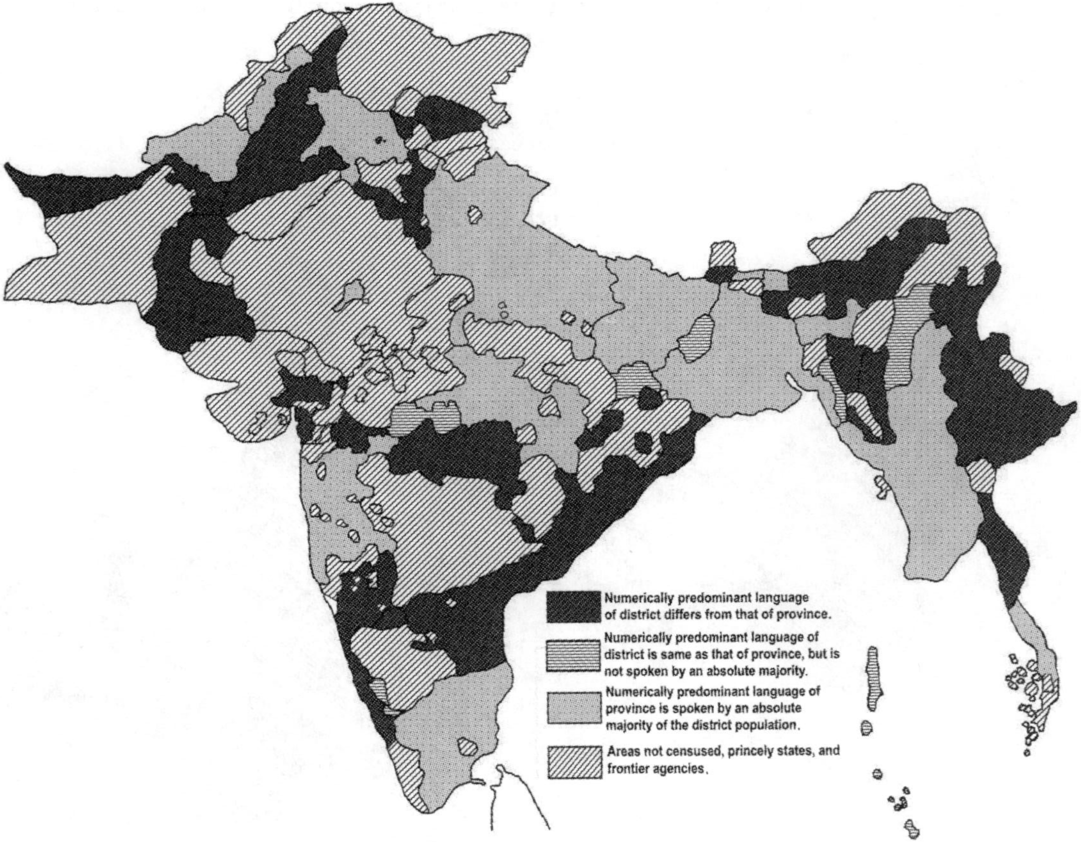

Figure 3.2: Linguistic Minority Districts of British India, 1931

Numerically predominant language of district differs from that of province.

Numerically predominant language of district is same as that of province, but is not spoken by an absolute majority.

Numerically predominant language of province is spoken by an absolute majority of the district population.

Areas not censused, princely states, and frontier agencies.

population spoke minority languages. Non-Tamils in Madras included 17.7 million speakers of Telugu, and 4.0, 3.7, and 1.7 millions speaking Oriya, Malayalam, and Kannada respectively. Among the non-Marathi speakers of Bombay were 3.4, 3.1, and 2.6 millions, whose respective mother tongues were Gujarati, Sindhi, and Kannada. Minor provinces (those governed by chief commissioners) with particularly pronounced minority problems were Assam, where Bengalis, not Assamese, were the most numerous group; Baluchistan, where Pushtu speakers outnumbered speakers of Baluchi; and the statistically insignificant areas of Coorg and the Andaman and Nicobar Islands.

In the remaining jurisdictions, the 5.4 million Marathi speakers posed a special problem in the Central Provinces and Berar, as did the 5.1 million Oriyas in Bihar and Orissa. Elsewhere, the 6.5 million Lahnda speakers and several million Hindi speakers in Punjab provided little cause for concern, presumably because their local dialects graded smoothly into the dominant Punjabi vernacular and because whatever linguistic cleavages existed in the region were overshadowed by more salient communal divisions. And in Burma, more than two-fifths of the population that spoke languages other than Burmese were spread among so many different largely isolated tribal groups that no serious thought had to be given to administrative reform on their behalf. Finally (ignoring the minor jurisdictions of Delhi and Ajmer-Merwara), we come to Bengal and the Hindi-speaking United Provinces, which in 1931 were the only two essentially unilingual provinces of India. Of those two, the latter—now the state of Uttar Pradesh—has been, since its creation, the most linguistically homogeneous region of the subcontinent.

Figure 3.2 indicates in dark grey, the extensive tracts over which the above-noted minorities and smaller unspecified groups were predominant at the district level, as well as a small number of additional, largely tribal districts, shown in medium grey, in which all minorities combined comprised over half the total population even though no single group was as numerous as the principal linguistic group of the province. Combined, these two sets of districts accounted, as noted in the introduction, for roughly half the total area of British India.

Among the six hundred or so princely states of India were some (example, Hyderabad) that were as linguistically diversified as the provinces shown in the darkest pattern of Figure 3.1. Nevertheless, on all of our maps of the pre-independence period, we have shown the areas of the princely states by a diagonal lined pattern, because the British, who had come by the twentieth century to regard the princely territories as virtually inviolate, never seriously considered them as subject to administrative reorganization on either linguistic or other grounds. But, given the complex interdigitation of the territories of the states with those under direct British rule, attempts at achieving the political unification of certain major linguistic groups within the latter areas would have only resulted in the creation of bizarrely shaped, discontiguous, and difficult-to-administer provinces. On the other hand, such extensive multilingual and culturally, physically, and economically diversified provinces as Madras and Bombay were also quite difficult to administer in ways that were responsive to the needs of all the people, particularly those most distant from the provincial capitals.

Figure 3.3 provides some intimation of the differential difficulty faced by various provinces in dealing, as of 1931, with the concerns of their major minority language groups. The implicit assumption of this map is that, *ceteris paribus*, the further a group is situated from the seat of administration, the greater will be the costs of responding to its needs and the greater will be its perception that those needs are not being adequately addressed. The median distance (in miles) of each group from its respective provincial capital is indicated on the map along a line connecting the capital with the so-called population 'centroid' of the group.[10] The greatly varying distances on Figure 3.3 explain, perhaps better than any other single factor, why Orissa and Sind were the first and only linguistic provinces to be established in the period between 1912 and the granting of Indian independence.

The failure of the British to accede to the demands of those who wanted to create a province of Andhra out of the Telugu-majority districts of Madras province calls for comment, especially in light of the fact that the 17.7 million Telugu speakers of Madras (as of 1931)

[10]The population centroid is the point of intersection of east-west and north-south median lines, each dividing a given population into two equal groups. It is similar to, though not identical with the population's centre of gravity, but much easier to determine. The centroids shown on figure 3.3 were determined by the author by plotting the 1931 data on the linguistic groups in question on district maps and, where necessary, prorating the population by area in districts along the likely median lines to fix those lines with the precision necessary for the present analysis. It is doubtful that any of the points so determined is as much as fifteen or twenty miles from its precise mathematical position.

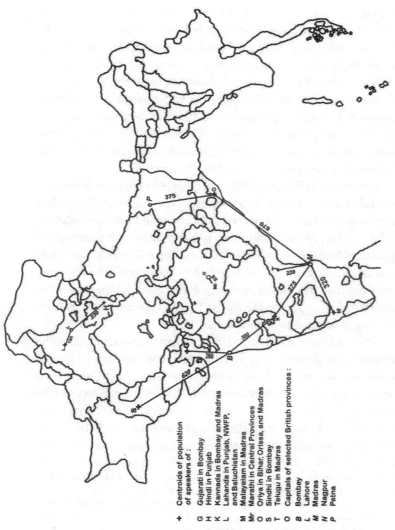

Figure 3.3: Distances of Population Centroids of Selected Linguistic Minorities from Capitals of the Provinces of British India in which They are Situated, 1931*

+ Centroids of population of speakers of :

G Gujarati in Bombay
H Hindi in Punjab
K Kannada in Bombay and Madras
L Lahanda in Punjab, NWFP, and Baluchistan
M Malayalam in Madras
Mr Marathi in Central Provinces
O Oriya in Bihar, Orissa, and Madras
S Sindhi in Bombay
T Telugu in Madras

O Capitals of selected British provinces :

B Bombay
L Lahore
M Madras
N Nagpur
P Patna

*Note: *All distances are given in miles.*

far outnumbered the 7.4 and 3.2 million Oriya and Sindhi speakers who then lived in territories subsequently assigned to Orissa and Sind respectively. Part of the problem in regard to the distribution of the Telugu population, in addition to their relative proximity to the city of Madras and consequent ease of governance, was the fact that Telugus are an important minority in almost all of the Tamil-majority districts.[11] Thus, the separation of Andhra from Madras would have left roughly 2.5 million Telugu speakers in the remaining portion of the province, in a position much more disadvantaged politically than were all Telugu speakers in the undivided province. By and large, then, these Telugu speakers opposed the suggested partition.[12] No comparable issue arose in respect to Orissa or Sind.

Apart from the Telugu population, other large linguistic minorities who failed to be granted their own provinces were—in descending order of population—the speakers of Lahnda in Punjab, of Marathi in the Central Provinces and Berar, of Kannada in both Bombay and Madras, of Malayalam in Madras, and of Gujarati in Bombay. While none of these groups was as populous as the Oriyas, all were more numerous than the Sindhis. But, for none of these did the burdens of administration appear to the British to be so onerous as to warrant the costs of political reorganization.

While we have emphasized how distance contributed to the administrative difficulties of governing the areas that were in 1936 to become Orissa and Sind, we must also point out some additional considerations that were surely relevant. The cultural gap between the dominant populations of the two new provinces and the populations from which they were separated was greater than that between the other major minorities just cited and the dominant groups to which

[11]This will be particularly evident from plate 29 of Roland J.L. Breton's *Atlas Géographique des Langues et des Ethnies de l'Inde et du Subcontinent* (Québec: Les Presses de l'Université Laval, 1976). Careful study of this important work, whose fifty plates of black-and-white maps and graphs are supplemented by nearly six hundred pages of text, will throw much light on a great variety of problems relating to the linguistic geography of South Asia throughout the twentieth century.

[12]I am indebted to Robert E. Frykenberg for calling this fact to my attention. According to Frykenberg, the anti-Brahmanism of the Telugu peasant castes of what was to become Andhra was not shared by the Telugu peasants of Tamil-majority areas, because of the identification of the Brahmans as those who had the greatest stake in maintaining the unity of Madras province.

they were politically joined. This was especially true in regard to the predominantly Muslim population of Sind. It is hardly surprising, in the communally charged political atmosphere of the 1930s, that Muslims in other parts of India should have strongly supported Sind's separation from the Hindu-majority province of Bombay; and it was widely believed that Britain's acquiescence in the establishment of Sind—which the Hindus of that area strongly opposed—was, in part at least, a sop to the Indian Muslim community.[13] Whether the largely tribal nature of portions of what was to become Orissa weighed heavily in the British decision to create that province is questionable; I have read nothing to suggest that it was. A final comparative observation: whereas Sind's excision from Bombay was a relatively simple act of political surgery, the establishment of Orissa from discontiguous areas of three provinces (Bihar and Orissa, Madras, and Central Provinces and Berar), was a much more complicated undertaking, entailing, among other things, the partition of several long-established British districts.

Figures 3.4 and 3.5 show the linguistic situation in the provinces of British India as of 1941 in terms comparable to those applicable for Figures 3.1 and 3.2. Although no language returns were tabulated for those provinces in the greatly curtailed wartime census, we can derive a reasonably accurate representation of the distribution and relative strength of linguistic minorities by prorating the district proportions of various linguistic groups, as reported in the 1931 census, among the district populations reported in 1941. Although two new provinces were created in the interim, the areas of only a very small number of districts were significantly affected. In the case of those changed in order to create Orissa—the establishment of which was already anticipated when the 1931 census was published—detailed subdistrict breakdowns are available and fairly good estimates for 1941 can therefore be made. In short, the pictures presented by Figures 3.4 and 3.5 can be regarded as reasonably reliable and representative of the situation that obtained in India from 1937, when Burma was split off to become a separate crown colony, to 1947, the year of the independence and partition of the subcontinent.

The only striking differences between the 1931 and the 1941 maps are in respect to the areas affected by the establishment of Sind and

[13]Ram Gopal, *Linguistic Affairs*, p. 69.

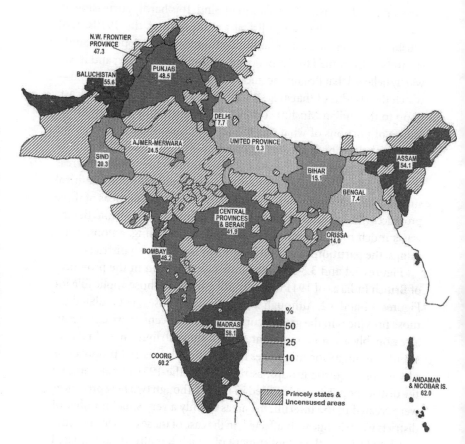

Figure 3.4: Linguistic Minorities as Percentage of Provincial Population in British India, 1941*

Note: *All percentages are estimates. 1931 figures are used where there is no significant change in area of province. 1931 district data are recast within new boundaries where significant changes have occurred.

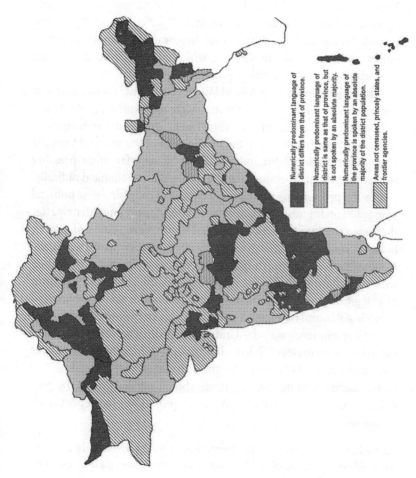

Figure 3.5: Linguistic Minority Districts of British India, 1941

■ Numerically predominant language of
district differs from that of province.

▨ Numerically predominant language of
district is same as that of province, but
is not spoken by an absolute majority.

▢ Numerically predominant language of
the province is spoken by an absolute
majority of the district population.

▧ Areas not censused, princely states, and
frontier agencies.

Orissa. In the former of those two provinces, linguistic minorities came in 1941 to one-fifth of the population and in the latter to only one-seventh, a proportion slightly lower than in the remaining area of Bihar. The reduction in the minority proportion of the total populations of Madras and of the Central Provinces and Berar was not especially significant; but in Bombay it fell from 57.2 per cent to 48.2 per cent. Of note on Figure 3.5 is the fact that there was not a single district in either Sind or Orissa in 1941 in which all linguistic minorities comprised a majority of the population.

The resignation during World War II of all Congress ministries in the provinces of British India in which they ruled resulted in a temporary cessation of any significant demand for linguistic reorganization. In any event, the prosecution of the war and then the preparation of India for independence became far more pressing concerns. With independence in 1947, the situation changed radically. Led by the proponents of Andhra, a chorus of calls for a new political map based on linguistic principles was raised almost immediately after the new government was installed. The responsibilities of power, however, caused Congress to reconsider its former stance on that issue. Now, the tasks of putting the new nation into working order, of dealing with the millions of refugees, of coping with the conflict in Kashmir, of integrating and consolidating into governable units the myriad princely states, and framing a constitution became the most urgent items on the government's agenda. 'Unity' and 'security' were the slogans of the day. Nevertheless, Nehru did appoint a Linguistic Provinces Commission in 1948 to consider the question of reorganization. The commission's findings were considerably at variance with the pre-independence position of Congress. Paragraph 125 of its report reads as follows:

Linguistic homogeneity in the formation of new provinces is certainly attainable within certain limits but only at the cost of creating a fresh minority problem. More than half the Malayalam and Kannada speaking people are living in Indian States, and only a little less than half of Telugu and Marathi speaking people are living either in Indian States or in Union Provinces from which they cannot be transferred to new linguistic provinces either for want of geographical contiguity or want of their consent to be so transferred. These must remain, at least for many years to come, outside the sphere of a linguistic province. Even in the limited areas of the Union, which can be made homogeneous linguistically, border districts on each side and the capital cities of Bombay and Madras will remain bilingual or multilingual. And, nowhere will it be possible to form a linguistic province of more than 70 to 80 per cent of the people speaking the same language, thus leaving in each province a minority of at least 20 per cent of people speaking other languages.[14]

A population speaking a common language but comprising only 70 to 80 per cent of a province's population, reasoned the commission, could not be called a 'linguistic group,' but only a 'big majority.'[15] As we shall presently see, the conclusions of the commission were statistically invalid and history has shown, I believe, that its fundamental fears as to the likely impact of reorganization on the development of a sense of Indian nationhood were ill-founded.

Figures 3.6 and 3.7 show the distribution and relative strength of linguistic minorities as of the 1951 census and may be taken as representative of the situation obtaining in India from the time of the adoption of the Constitution in January 1950 until the establishment of the state of Andhra in October 1953. These two maps differ markedly from their counterparts for 1931 and 1941 insofar as they lack the large diagonally ruled areas by which the princely states were represented in the earlier periods. Only Jammu and Kashmir, to which the 1951 census did not extend; the North-East Frontier Tracts (later NEFA) of Assam, also uncensused; and Sikkim, which was not yet fully integrated into the Indian union, are shown in a lined pattern on the maps for 1951.

Our treatment of language in the areas of Punjab, PEPSU (Patiala and East Punjab States Union), Himachal Pradesh, Bilaspur, and Delhi calls for some comment. Although languages were, by and large, enumerated for other states of India according to the actual responses of those interviewed, in the areas just named that was not the case. Rather, 'As a result of the controversy over the language question, the figures for Hindi, Urdu, Punjabi, Pahari, and their various dilects [sic] have been put together at the time of sorting under the heading "Hindi-Punjabi-Urdu-Pahari"....'[16] While this linguistic merger by fiat may have satisfied the responsible authorities and denied proponents of a separate unilingual Punjabi-speaking state the statistical ammunition

---

[14]Cited in Ram Gopal, *Linguistic Affairs*, p. 76.

[15]Ibid., p. 77.

[16]Census of India, *Languages—1951 Census,* Paper No. 1, 1954, Part III, 'State Tables,' Section 15, 'Punjab, PEPSU, Himachal Pradesh, Bilaspur and Delhi', p. 1.

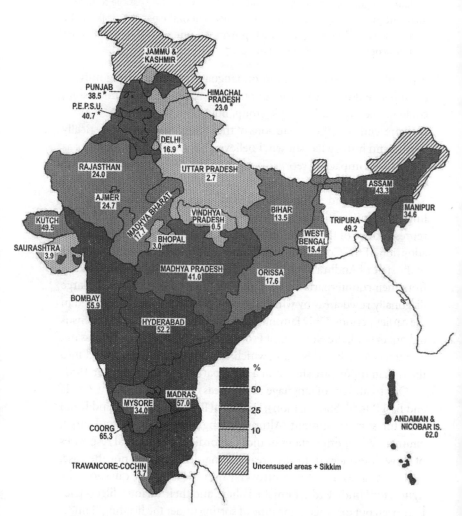

Figure 3.6: Linguistic Minorities as Percentage of State Population in India, 1951*

Note: *1951 data not tabulated; figure is based on recasting of 1961 data.

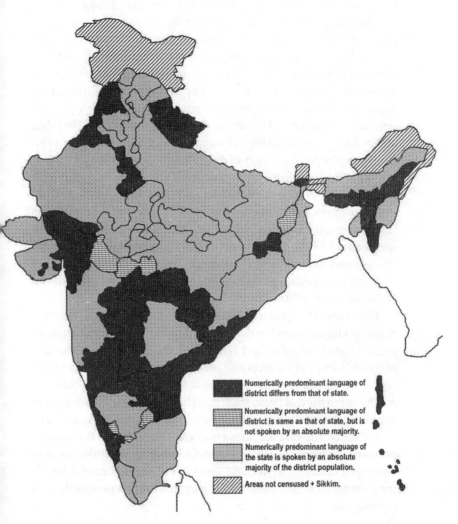

Figure 3.7: Linguistic Minority Districts of India, 1951

with which to further their cause, the populations concerned—or, at least, their more vocal spokesmen—were less than happy with the expedient employed by the census and, in the absence of official figures, could, within limits, concoct whatever figures they wished in respect to their respective numerical strengths. But, irrespective of what they may have publicly proclaimed, both groups probably had a fairly good idea of their proportions to the total population of each district of the region and it seems appropriate, therefore, to map the best possible estimates for the time. This we have done by recasting the 1961 data within the boundaries of the states and districts that existed as of 1951. Given the general consistency of district boundaries between 1951 and 1961 (but for the creation of two new districts in Himalayan Punjab and Himachal Pradesh), this was an easy statistical operation. Thus, we derive minority totals equivalent to 38.5 per cent of the population (mainly Punjabi speakers) in Punjab, 40.7 per cent (mainly Hindi speakers) in PEPSU, 23.0 per cent (mainly Hindi speakers) in Himachal Pradesh and Bilaspur, and 16.9 per cent in Delhi. The sizable area of the Punjabi-speaking, predominantly Sikh minority in the northwest of Punjab, as constituted in 1951, stands out on the map.

Elsewhere, the formerly patchy tracts of Gujarati and Kannada minorities that appeared on the 1941 map appear in 1951 as substantially greater areas in Bombay and Hyderabad; the Marathi minority area of the old Central Provinces and Berar is expanded by the emergence of the adjoining area of the same language in Marathwada, the northwestern third of Hyderabad; new Hindi and Pahari minority areas appear in Rajasthan and Uttar Pradesh; the old Assamese minority area of the North-East becomes a majority area, while the Bengali area of Assam, reduced in size by territorial losses to East Pakistan, now becomes a minority region; and a number of small, scattered, largely tribal minority areas appear on the map in what had previously been princely states.[17]

[17]In the 1951 census, the distinction between Western and Eastern Hindi was eliminated; but Urdu and Hindustani were now, in most areas, enumerated separately from the former. Only a few thousand individuals returned! Bihari as their mother tongue; while Chhattisgarhi claimed nearly a million speakers. 'Rajasthani,' formerly the language of millions, was recorded for only 645,000 persons, with a commensurate growth in the numbers declaring Marwari, Mewari, Jaipuri (Dhundhari) and many other regional vernaculars. In place of the three Pahari groups of previous censuses, Kumauni, Garhwali, Nepali, and many other mother tongues were separately enumerated. Punjabi was retained as a separate language

The proportion of the 1951 population that we have classified as belonging to linguistic minorities in India as a whole was 29.5 per cent, only marginally less than our 31.7 per cent estimate for 1921, just after Congress' initial espousal of the idea of linguistic provinces. And, as in 1921, the greatest concentrations of minority population were in the peninsular portion of the country, where three large states, Madras, Bombay, and Hyderabad all had more than half their populations in minority groups. Rather sizeable and important minorities were also to be found in the northeast and northwest. Among the major states of India (the so-called class A and class B states of the 1950 Constitution), only in Uttar Pradesh were linguistic minorities (exclusive of those claiming Urdu as a mother tongue) of negligible importance.[18] Surely, the situation in 1951 was one which offered exceedingly broad scope for improvement in the political map of India.

Notwithstanding the negative findings of the Linguistic Provinces Commission of 1948, demands for the establishment of linguistic states were not stilled. In 1953, following the dramatic fast unto death of Potti Sriramalu in support of the long frustrated demand for a Telugu-speaking Andhra state, Congress was forced to change its position. Andhra was carved out of Madras in October of that year; and, in response to the mounting flood of additional demands, a States Reorganization Commission was established in December to reconsider the entire issue.

Some measure of the intensity of sentiment in regard to the linguistic reorganization of India can be derived from the fact that between the time of its formation and the issuance of its report in October 1955, the new commission received some 152,250 documents in support of or in opposition to specific changes, of which, it was estimated, perhaps

---

over most of India; but in the key region of the northwest (Punjab, PEPSU, Delhi, Himachal Pradesh and Bilaspore) Hindi, Urdu, Punjabi, and Pahari were grouped together. Hence, to make the 1951 data of figures 3.6 and 3.7 most comparable to those for other census years, we have combined various Rajasthani and Pahari mother tongues to make their respective speakers comparable to the groups so designated for previous censuses. Finally, we have retained Urdu, Hindustani, and Chhattisgarhi with Hindi, as in previous maps, and, for the sake of consistency, have maintained their equivalence in maps for 1961 and 1972.

[18]The principal reason for the increase from 0.3 per cent to 2.7 per cent in the proportion of linguistic minorities in UP was that Pahari speakers, who were dominant over most of the Himalayan districts, were counted separately from Hindi speakers in 1951, but not so in 1931. In 1961 the distinction was retained; but in 1971 it was again suppressed.

as many as 2,000 were 'well-considered memoranda.'[19] Within the scope of this paper, it is not possible to consider the details of the recommendations of the commission. In any event, they were not binding and never fully implemented. Suffice it to say that in 1956, largely in response to those recommendations, and in some respects going beyond them, the Seventh Amendment to the Indian Constitution sweepingly reordered the nation's political map. Though linguistic considerations were not the sole basis for the changes made, they surely outweighed all other arguments.

Among the principal outcomes of the 1956 reorganization was the elimination of the categories of states as class A, B, and C. The small class C states either became 'union territories' or were merged with larger, more viable units speaking the same language; and class B states, former large princely states or states unions, headed by *rajpramukhs*, were put on a par with the class A states, which were formed from the old major British provinces. Thus, with the clearing away of the institution of the *rajpramukh*, in effect a relic of the *ancien régime*, there was no longer any legal impediment to territorial reorganization in areas previously under princely rule and they could either be enlarged, as was Mysore, or totally eliminated as was the large but linguistically heterogeneous state of Hyderabad. The one former princely state that continued to enjoy a special constitutional status was Jammu and Kashmir, because of the exceptional circumstances attending its accession to the Indian union (on which we shall not here elaborate). Hence, the States Reorganization Commission never considered any alterations of its boundaries.[20] To the best of my knowledge, the central government continues to regard these boundaries as inviolate.

In regard to linguistic reorganization, the principal changes of 1956 were as follows: (1) Andhra, restyled Andhra Pradesh, was enlarged by the annexation of the Telugu-speaking Telangana region of Hyderabad; (2) Mysore, as noted, was also enlarged by absorption of the Kannada-speaking areas of Hyderabad, Madras, and Bombay; (3) Bombay became a bilingual state, the largest in the union, by the addition to the core region of the old presidency of two Marathi-speaking areas, the Marathwada region of Hyderabad and the Berar region of the Central Provinces and Berar, and by the Gujarati-speaking states of Saurashtra

[19]*SRC*, p. ii.
[20]*SRC*, p. 203.

and Cutch; (4) the Central Provinces, renamed Madhya Pradesh, though diminished in the south by the loss of the associated area of Berar, was substantially enlarged by its merger with three other Hindi-speaking states, Madhya Bharat, Vindhya Pradesh, and Bhopal; (5) Punjab was enlarged by a merger with PEPSU to form a second bilingual state, in which the Hindi majority and Punjabi minority dominated in the south and north respectively; and (6) Travancore-Cochin was enlarged by the absorption of a portion of the Malabar coast of Madras to form the Malayalam-speaking state of Kerala. Elsewhere, there were border adjustments and minor mergers, too numerous to mention, almost all of which led to a significantly greater degree of linguistic homogeneity. While a large proportion of the changes affected involved the transfer of entire districts or groups of districts from one state to another, the number of instances in which districts were partitioned was sufficient to establish a precedent for further such actions.

Following states reorganization, for the first time in India's modern history there was not a single state or province in the country in which all linguistic minorities combined comprised more than half of the total population. Even in Bombay, where Gujaratis accounted for a third of the population, where immigrants from other areas to the cosmopolitan metropolis of Bombay and other cities were particularly numerous, and where tribal groups were also significant, the combined minority total was only 49 per cent.[21] Other states with combined minorities of over 40 per cent (see Figure 3.8) were, in descending order, Jammu and Kashmir (mainly Punjabi), Rajasthan (mainly Hindi and not a problem), Punjab (overwhelmingly Punjabi), and Assam (Bengali plus tribal languages), while in Mysore a diversity of language groups collectively comprised more than a third of the population. In all other states the total of minority populations was significantly below the national average of approximately 22 per cent.

Two territorial changes further altered the political map between 1956, the date of states reorganization, and the taking of the subsequent census in 1961. The establishment of the Naga Hills-Tuensang area in 1957, was the first of a series of concessions by the central government to the political aspirations of tribal peoples in the far northeast of India. Though the linguistic differences of the highland Nagas from the lowland Assamese were substantial, Nagaland, as the area became

[21]Schwartzberg, *Historical Atlas*, p. 101, map X.B.2.c.

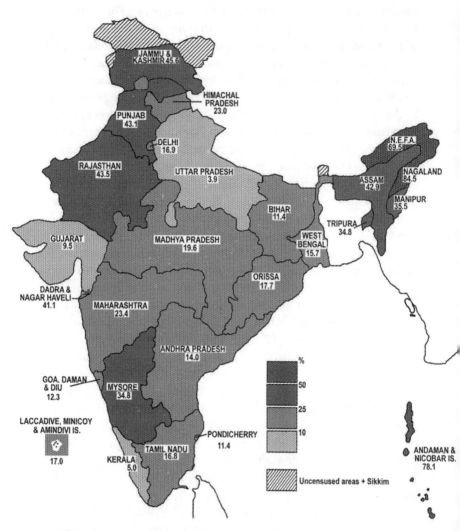

Figure 3.8: Linguistic Minorities as Percentage of State/Union Territory Population in India, 1961

known on achieving statehood in 1963, could hardly be considered a linguistic state; for, not only did the many culturally related Naga tribes speak a host of mutually incomprehensible languages, but they also overlapped considerably into the union territory of Manipur, the North-East Frontier Agency (established in 1954), and the republic of Burma.

The second change, the partitioning of Bombay into its larger Marathi-speaking and a smaller Gujarati-speaking area, which became Maharashtra and Gujarat, respectively, created two more essentially linguistic states. Of the two, the former, in which the city of Bombay was still more than half non-Marathi, retained something of its polyglot nature, with minorities comprising nearly a fourth of the total population. Gujarat, however, where Gujarati speakers were now more than nine-tenths of the total population, became one of India's most linguistically homogeneous states. These changes are indicated on Figures 3.8 and 3.9, which are based on language data of the census of 1961.[22]

Not counting the special case of Jammu and Kashmir and ignoring the inconsequential differences between Rajasthani and Hindi in Rajasthan, Punjab was, in 1961, India's only essentially bilingual state. While, objectively, the differences between the Punjabi and the Hindi spoken in that area were probably no greater than those between the various Rajasthani and Hindi dialects of Rajasthan, the aforementioned communal identifications of the two languages in Punjab, with a resurgent Sikhism and with Hinduism, respectively, tended to magnify the significance of whatever distinctions there were. Further, Punjabi was now being increasingly written in Gurumukhi, the Sikh liturgical script, rather than in the previously widely used Perso-Arabic or

[22]The 1961 treatment of language is the most detailed and systematic of any Indian census. Nevertheless, it poses a number of difficulties. Bihari here re-emerges as a language separate from Hindi, with 16.4 million speakers; but the spatial distribution of those speakers made little sense, since most speakers of the three principal Bihari vernaculars (Bhójpuri, Magahi, and Maithili) continued to return Hindi as their mother tongue. The various Rajasthani vernaculars, on the other hand, declined noticeably in relation to Hindi, while retaining their predominance over most of Rajasthan. Chhattisgarhi, while still a widely claimed mother tongue in eastern Madhya Pradesh, is again grouped by the census with Hindi. Punjabi is now separate throughout India. And, Pahari continues to encompass a congeries of dialects grouped under more than half a dozen principal tongues. For the maps in this paper we have combined Bihari, Urdu, and Hindustani (now of negligible importance) with Hindi; retained Rajasthani, with its numerous local variants as a separate language (in which regard we differ from the author's decision in the 1961 language maps of *A Historical Atlas of South Asia*); and combined all Pahari vernaculars other than Nepali.

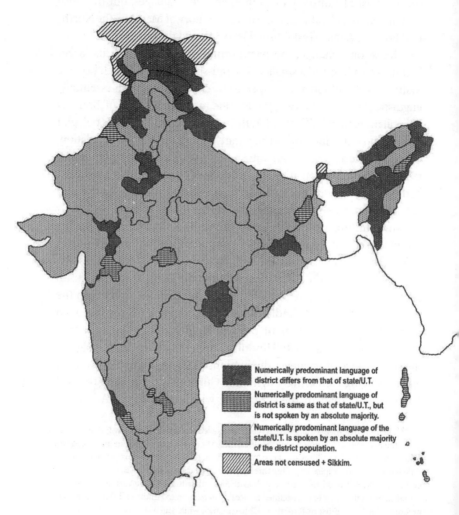

| | Numerically predominant language of district differs from that of state/U.T. |
| Numerically predominant language of district is same as that of state/U.T., but is not spoken by an absolute majority. |
| Numerically predominant language of the state/U.T. is spoken by an absolute majority of the district population. |
| Areas not censused + Sikkim. |

Figure 3.9: Linguistic Minority Districts of India, 1961

Devanagari, the national script employed for Hindi. In the face of an ever-mounting Sikh demand for a 'Punjabi Suba,' the government finally acceded. In 1966 Punjab too was partitioned. The overwhelmingly Hindu mountainous regions, in which both Hindi and various West Pahari languages were most commonly spoken were transferred to Himachal Pradesh, which was then raised in status from union territory to state; and, on the larger plains area, the mainly Hindi-speaking districts (minus Hoshiarpur, which had a near fifty-fifty language split) were carved off to form the new state of Haryana. Between Haryana and the truncated Punjab, the city of Chandigarh was established as a new union territory to serve as a capital for both its neighbouring states.

All subsequent changes in the political map of India have taken place in the North-East. Most of these related to tribal concerns. Among those concerns linguistic distinctiveness was but one aspect of a wide-ranging cultural cleavage between the indigenous, mainly highland populations, and the mainly lowland Assamese and Bengalis. After the previously noted creation of a Naga state, the next new tribal territory to be established was Meghalaya. Instituted in 1970 as an 'autonomous hill state' in the area in which the Khasi and Garo tribes were predominant, it attained full state status in January 1972. At the same time, the North-East Frontier Agency and the Mizo Hills districts of Assam, respectively, became the union territories of Arunachal Pradesh and Mizoram, while Manipur and Tripura, both union territories since 1956, were proclaimed full-fledged states. The most recent alteration of the map, India's annexation of Sikkim in 1975, had nothing to do with the internal linguistic politics of India. Nevertheless, the fact that the dominant linguistic group within Sikkim had, because of prolonged immigration, become Nepali, a Hindu group rather different from the older Buddhist Lepcha ruling community, was obviously not without significance.

Figures 3.10 and 3.11 indicate the situation in regard to linguistic minorities as of 1972.[23] We have projected the census date of 1971 to

---

[23]The 1971 census presents a set of language tables that is substantially simpler than any previous enumeration since 1881. Bihari, Rajasthani, and Pahari are all grouped with Hindi, and we are not provided with separate figures for any of them or for their constituent vernaculars. Urdu, as one of India's official languages, continues to be separately enumerated, though in our maps it is combined, again, with Hindi. Dogri, however, which previously was enumerated as a dialect of Punjabi, now appears as a separate language.

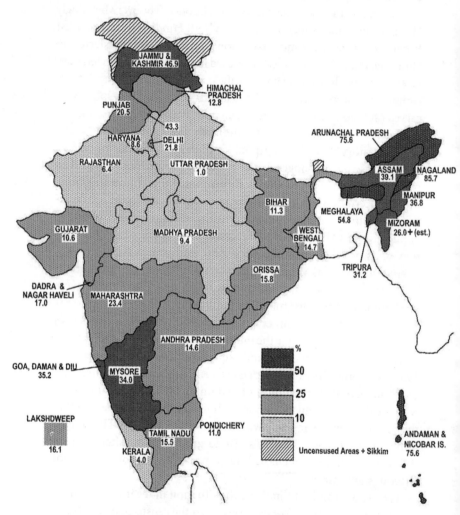

Figure 3.10: Linguistic Minorities as Percentage of State/Union Territory
Population in India, 1972

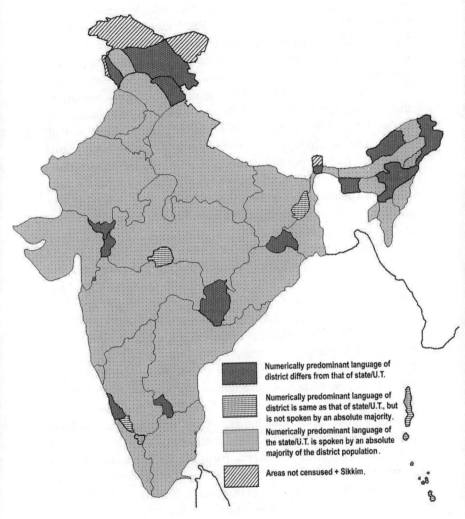

Numerically predominant language of district differs from that of state/U.T.

Numerically predominant language of district is same as that of state/U.T., but is not spoken by an absolute majority.

Numerically predominant language of the state/U.T. is spoken by an absolute majority of the district population.

Areas not censused + Sikkim.

Figure 3.11: Linguistic Minority Districts of India, 1972

that year so as to take account on our maps of the few subsequent changes noted above, though, obviously, the differences between 1971 and 1972 can hardly be regarded as consequential. We now see a map (Figure 3.10) in which only the North-East remains a region with very heavy concentrations of linguistic minorities at the state or union territorial level, in some instances more than 50 per cent (86 per cent in Nagaland). Additionally, Jammu and Kashmir and Mysore (subsequently renamed Karnataka) retain the heavy concentrations that were noted in the census of 1961 as does Goa, which India annexed in December of that year. At the district level (Figure 3.11), almost all of the areas in which the combined linguistic minorities constitute more than half the population are predominantly tribal. And, apart from the North-East, Jammu and Kashmir, and Himachal Pradesh, every such district occupies an interstitial boundary position between the areas dominated by two or, in a few instances, three of the major, official languages of India.

Figure 3.12 indicates the extent to which the linguistic reorganization of provinces in pre-independence British India and of states and union territories in the post-independence period has reduced the proportion of the total population living as linguistic minorities in their respective areas. The top half of the graph covers the period from 1920, the year of the initial Congress resolution in support of linguistic provinces, to the census year 1941. Because World War II and preparations for independence precluded any further change, there was no point in carrying the graph further. The amount of change registered in this entire period was modest, coming almost entirely in the year 1936, when Orissa and Sind provinces were created. The minor change shown for 1937 resulted from the separation of Burma from India. The entire period witnessed a decline from 31.7 per cent to 28.3 per cent. The lower half of the graph covers the period from 1950, by which time the absorption of princely states and the adoption of a constitution again made linguistic reorganization a realistic policy option, to 1972, the year of the last internal territorial changes. The period registered a decline in the linguistic minority population from 29.5 per cent to only 16.5 per cent (some 96 million persons at the 1971 census).

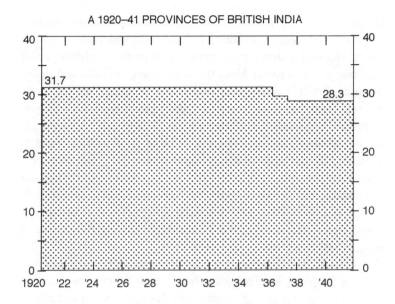

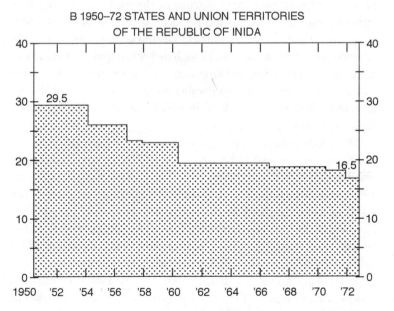

Figure 3.12: Proportion of Indian Population in Linguistic Minorities

FACTORS CONSIDERED

The factors that weighed most heavily in the minds of decision makers in the linguistic reorganization of India varied considerably from the pre- to the post-independence period, and within the latter period from one year to another. Since the British were not beholden to any electorate for their power, they operated in a political context quite different from that of the ruling Congress party after 1947. Further, as they issued no manifestos calling for administrative reform, they could not be called on, as was Congress, to be as good as their word in conceding the demands of major linguistic groups. Congress, on the other hand, inherited a situation in 1947 in which rapid change was unavoidable and, in its response to such change, it had to demonstrate considerable flexibility. In the following paragraphs, we shall consider a number of factors that were considered during the course of reorganization over the period since 1920.

Foremost, perhaps, among the factors to be taken into account, is that any proposed linguistic state had to have a population and an economic base large enough to make it viable. In the pre-independence period one could argue that the requisite threshold was around four million persons, which was the population of Sind in 1936, when, despite prior British declarations as to its unviability, that area finally attained provincial status. But, as we have seen, population alone was not a sufficient criterion for being accorded such status; for there were a number of other areas considerably more populous and at least as economically developed as Sind in which aspirations for provincial status were never recognized.

Since independence, the importance of the population factor obviously changed with the passage of time. While a number of rather small and/or not very populous class C states were recognized by the 1950 Constitution, these were entirely eliminated or relegated to the status of union territory by the States Reorganization Act of 1956, after which the least populous state (except for Jammu and Kashmir, whose status was inviolate) was Assam, with a 1961 population of 11.9 million inhabitants. In 1963, however, when Nagaland (whose population in 1961 was less than 400,000) became a state, the situation was radically altered; and in the subsequent eleven years a number of additional, mainly tribal or largely tribal states were established in the

North-East with populations of from, roughly, 0.5 to 1.6 million (1971). One could have argued, however, that the political expediency of giving in to local sentiment in the North-East entailed strategic and other considerations quite different from those in which previous linguistically based decisions had been made. Elsewhere, it was not until 1966, when Punjab was partitioned, that Haryana came into being with a population (just over 10 million in 1971) that was smaller than Assam's; and five years later the situation changed again when Himachal Pradesh (3.5 million) was elevated from a union territory to a state.

The degree of linguistic homogeneity within proposed linguistic provinces or states was certainly a factor to be weighed in any reorganization decision. What the British would have regarded as the maximum allowable proportion of minorities is impossible to judge from the lone examples of Orissa and Sind (14.0 per cent and 20.3 per cent, respectively); but, despite the concern on this matter, expressed in the quoted passage of the 1948 *Report of the Linguistic Provinces Commission*, the Republic of India was, in 1956 and subsequently, obviously willing to tolerate the existence of rather sizable minorities, so long as there was a clearly dominant group throughout all or virtually all of the territory of a proposed new linguistic state. Thus, leaving aside the two intentionally bilingual states of Bombay and Punjab, as they were constituted in 1956, the linguistic minorities in the then expanded state of Mysore came to some 35 per cent of the total population. Of course, the fact that Mysore's area was, in a sense, determined by decisions made in regard to all four of its neighbouring states precluded any possibility of bringing its minority proportion much below that figure. But the acceptability of even higher limits, at least in the tribal states of the North-East, is made evident by the 1972 figures for both Nagaland and Meghalaya.

Related to the preceding consideration was the question of how many persons of a given linguistic group would have to be left out of a proposed province or state if it were to include only those areas where that group was in a majority. As we have seen, this factor appears to have been important to many Telugu-speakers in the Tamil-majority areas of pre-independence Madras and may have been an important reason why an Andhra province was never achieved under the aegis of the British. Similarly, the large number of Gujaratis in Bombay and other Deccani cities who would have been isolated from the main body of Gujarati speakers if Maharashtra state had come into existence in 1956 was certainly a factor in the decision to retain a bilingual state of Bombay. Ultimately, however, in the two cases cited and others where similar concerns may have been expressed, the issue was decided on the majoritarian principle.

The saliency of the differences between the languages of adjoining areas is obviously important, though difficult to quantify. We have noted that the objective differences between the Hindi and Punjabi spoken in Punjab prior to its partition in 1966 may have been no greater or even less than those between the dialects of Hindi and Rajasthani then spoken in Rajasthan. But, because of the communal nexus of the linguistic question, the former differences loomed as important, at least to the Sikhs, while the latter did not appear to be a matter for major concern; consequently, the fact that we recorded 43.5 per cent of Rajasthan's population as belonging to minority language groups (mainly Hindi-Urdu) is not indicative of a serious desire for linguistic reorganization. On the other hand, the sudden emergence in 1961 of millions of speakers of Maithili, Magahi, and Bhojpuri, all grouped by the census as dialects of Bihari, in districts that were previously almost solidly Hindi-speaking, suggests that the perception of linguistic differences is a barometric phenomenon and that, even in areas where no problems are thought to exist, their emergence is possible. Recognition of this prospect is what may have laid behind the decision in the 1971 census to consolidate the returns for Hindi, Rajasthani, Bihari, and Pahari and to suppress totally the enumeration of dialects in these and other mother tongues. (Urdu, however, as one of the official 'languages' of India, had to continue to be enumerated separately, from Hindi.)

Apart from purely linguistic considerations, other ethnic factors did, from time to time, enter into decisions in regard to the creation of new provinces and states. The dominantly Muslim make-up of the population of Sind, the attainment of a Sikh majority in the post-1966 truncated area of Punjab, and the racial and cultural distinctiveness of the tribal states of North-Eastern India are cases in point. Caste too seems to have played a role. Telugu-speaking cultivating castes in predominantly Tamil districts of Madras opposed the establishment of Andhra as did both Tamil and Telugu-speaking Brahmans in Telugu-majority districts, the former because of concerns about Tamil chauvinism, the latter because of fear in regard to mounting anti-Brahmanism. Undoubtedly, 'other cases of similar caste concerns could be adduced. All such considerations, however, appear to have been ad hoc and expedient; so generalizations are difficult.

Arguments in respect to the economic and social backwardness of various areas were not infrequently advanced as justification either for opposing the establishment of specific new units (for example, Sind prior to 1936) or for merging certain units with others, sometimes irrespective of the linguistic problems that such mergers would create. Thus, the *SRC* recommended the absorption of all class C states, except for Delhi and Manipur, into their principal neighbouring states.[24] That recommendation, however, was never fully implemented. But the arguments occasionally ran the other way. In a note appended to the *SRC*, S. Fazl Ali argued that precisely because of its backwardness—among other reasons—Himachal Pradesh should be protected from a merger with Punjab, whose more enterprising population, he suggested, would exploit the mountain region in ways that would not be in the best interests of the local people.[25] And we may note in passing that, even in well-established linguistic states, separatist movements of relatively backward, historically distinct regions, such as Telangana and Berar, in Andhra Pradesh and Maharashtra respectively, have posed serious and occasionally bloody threats to the government.

Perhaps the principal areas in which economic and social backwardness has inhibited serious consideration of the establishment of new linguistically distinctive states or union territories are those of predominantly tribal population to the south of the Gangetic Plain. While some of these areas are linguistically quite mixed (for example, most of the Chhota Nagpur) others are relatively homogeneous (for example, the hilly Santal tracts of the Santal Parganas, the Gond tracts of Bastar, and the Bhil tracts of the southern Aravallis). Only a few of the scattered predominantly tribal areas are large or populous enough to be represented on Figure 3.11; but if that figure were drawn on the basis of subdistrict data (by subdivision, tahsil, or taluk) the tribal

[24]*SRC*, pp. 203–4 and 67–202, *passim*.
[25]*SRC*, pp. 238–243.

areas would loom much larger and occupy several sizable territories astride district and state boundaries.

The differences between these tribal areas just noted and those of northeast India are substantial. In the North-East, the cultural cleavage between the tribal and the dominant plains population tends to be much deeper than in other parts of India, where most of the tribals were Hinduized in varying degrees (including those who since converted to Christianity) and many have given up their tribal languages. The proportion of Christian converts among the tribals of the North-East is much higher than elsewhere, as are the local rates of literacy, which are among India's highest. Thus, the concessions granted to the highly politicized, well-educated tribal elites of the North-East—though possibly made primarily on the basis of political considerations that have little to do with their social advancement—do not automatically establish precedents for more backward tribal regions elsewhere. In any event, the once vociferous demand for a tribal state, Jharkhand, in Chhota Nagpur, has received little outside support and appears, for the time being, to be moribund.

Several purely geographic factors came into play in the reorganization of Indian provinces and states. In Figure 3.3 we directed attention to one that appears to have figured prominently in the decisions to establish Sind and Orissa provinces within British India, namely, the distance of certain linguistic groups, the Sindhis and Oriyas, from the capitals of the provinces to which they were attached and the commensurate difficulty in administering their territories effectively. Because these were the only two such difficult cases and because of improvements in transportation and communication after 1936, this distance factor was probably not again of major significance. Other concerns that were relatively important in the pre-independence period, but of little consequence after 1950—by which date the integration of the princely states was completed—were the discontiguity of several population groups in the provinces of British India and the peculiar shapes that proposed new linguistic provinces might have on account of the haphazard interpenetration of British and princely territories.

Finally, we may note that there were a number of local circumstances that led to clear deviations from the linguistic principal in the rearrangement of boundaries, particularly in the post-independence period. In Kolar district of Mysore state (now Karnataka) for example,

Telugu speakers outnumbered Kannada speakers in 1951 by 54 per cent to 21 per cent of the total population. But, because the gold mines of that district were developed by Mysore government capital, were powered by hydroelectricity from Mysore, and were economically more oriented toward Mysore than toward Andhra, the States Reorganization Commission's recommendation that the district be maintained in Mysore was followed.[26] A rather different situation led to an alteration in a part of the West Bengal-Bihar boundary. Because the creation of East Pakistan led to the separation of the three districts of Darjeeling, Jalpaiguri, and Cooch Behar from the rest of West Bengal, a small part of Hindi-speaking Purnea district was transferred from Bihar to create a corridor between the two portions of West Bengal. Other special circumstances had to do with the efficient management of irrigation systems, the orientation of commerce, and the like. Space does not permit a full accounting of such local details; but the two cases cited should suggest the complexity of the issues confronting the administration of India, especially during the period leading up to the great reorganization of 1956.

The general approach of the States Reorganization Commission was succinctly stated in their own report:

The problems of reorganization vary from region to region. It has to be kept in mind that the inter-play for centuries of historical, linguistic, geographical, economic and other factors has produced peculiar patterns in different regions. Each case, therefore, has its own background.

Besides, the problems of reorganization are so complex that it would be unrealistic to determine any case by a single test alone.... We have, accordingly, examined each case on its own merits and in its own context and arrived at conclusions after taking into consideration the totality of circumstances and on an overall assessment of the solutions proposed.'[27]

SCOPE FOR FUTURE CHANGE

As noted, the linguistic minorities in India at the state level totalled roughly 96 million persons (16.5 per cent) as of the 1971 census. While one might suppose from that figure that there was then still

[26]SRC, p. 93.
[27]SRC, p. 66.

considerable scope for further political reorganization, that is not really the case; for, as Figure 3.11 shows, the number of districts in which linguistic minorities account for more than half the population is now quite small, collectively they account for fewer than 26 million persons (4.7 per cent). And, if one excludes from the group the six districts, including Bombay, in which the principal language group, though less than an absolute majority was the same as the principal group in the state (for example, Marathi in both Bombay and Maharashtra), we are left with districts containing fewer than fifteen million persons (2.7 per cent). While this small remaining area and population offers the greatest scope for change, under certain foreseeable circumstances, others might also be considered.

Allowing for population growth in India since 1971 and for a slight acceleration in the rate of interstate migration, the present linguistic minority population—again at the state level—is probably close to 125 million and would include several rather distinct cohorts. Of these, the largest, probably more than a third of the total, are interstate migrants and their still incompletely assimilated second- and later-generation descendants. The 1971 census enumerated nearly 19 million persons residing in states in which they were not born (with allowances for changes in state boundaries) of whom 11 million were residents of urban areas, with particularly heavy concentrations in the larger, more cosmopolitan cities.[28] Of the nearly 7.6 million migrants resident in rural areas (2.9 million males and 4.7 million females), we can assume that most travelled only short distances, mainly as a result of marriage, between two places situated in close proximity to a state border. While not all of the urban group moved into states with majority languages other than their own (consider a move from Bihar to Uttar Pradesh), most undoubtedly did; but a smaller fraction, possibly less than half of the rural group, would have become part of a linguistic minority by virtue of migration. Of course, interstate migration to such rural jobs as plantation work, mining, and the like would often involve a move to a new language area. There is virtually nothing that can be done administratively to reduce the size of this minority. Assimilation will, of course, have an effect; but, in the near future, it is questionable

[28]C.K. Mehrotra, *Birth Place Migration in India*, Census of India, 1971, Special Monograph No. 1 (New Delhi: Office of the Registrar General, India, 1974), p. 26.

whether assimilation will reduce minorities faster than new migration swells their ranks.

A second large and very varied subset of minorities would include groups who are the descendants of migrants who settled in particular regions many generations, if not centuries ago. Among such groups would be the Muslim speakers of Urdu outside the Hindi-majority states, who numbered as many as 12.4 million according to the 1971 census; various Telugu-speaking cultivating castes who are found in appreciable numbers in virtually all districts of Tamil Nadu and many of Karnataka; Marwari and other trading castes over many parts of India; Lambadi and other so-called 'gypsy' castes of Rajasthani origin, who are probably more than a million strong in the Deccan; and perhaps as many as 200,000 Anglo-Indians scattered throughout India. This set of minorities, like the one previously discussed, cannot be diminished significantly by further states reorganization and it has already shown its marked resistance to assimilation. Its size, therefore, will remain large for the foreseeable future.

Probably third in size among the groups of linguistic minorities, and possibly second—depending on the extent of census bias in the direction of under-enumeration—are India's tribals. Although the 1971 census enumerated 38 million persons as members of scheduled tribes, the number reported as speaking any one of the scores of tribal languages was less than 19 million.[29] Of the tribal languages, five accounted for more than a million each. Santali, 3.8 million; Bhili/Bhilodi, 3.4; Gondi, 1.7; Kurukh/Oraon, 1.2; and Mundari/Munda, 1.1. Six others exceeded 300,000, a figure which is noteworthy because it corresponds to the approximate number of Lushais/Mizos, the dominant group in Mizoram, the smallest tribal union territory. (Not included among the six other tribal groups, however, were the Mizos themselves or the half million Khasis, who also constitute a locally dominant group in the state of Meghalaya.) Thus, if India were willing to accede at some future date to the wishes of increasingly politicized tribal groups of appreciable size, by establishing for them states or

[29]Calculated by the author from data in Census of India 1971, Series I, Part II-c (i), *Social and Cultural Tables* (Delhi: Controller of Publications, 1977). Union Table C-V-B, 'Speakers of languages ... other than those specified in Schedule VIII to the Constitution of India', pp. 68–86. The total for *all* non-Schedule VIII (i.e., non-official) languages in 1971 was 25.4 million.

union territories of their own, along the model of the autonomous tribal regions of the Soviet Union, the proportion of minorities in the population could be significantly reduced. It is quite likely too that many tribals who have given up their tribal language, but who still live in or adjacent to tracts in which those languages predominate would wish to be a part of any contemplated tribal units. Setting up such units, however, would be difficult. The question of their viability would surely arise; but even greater obstacles would stem from the fact that the tribal areas south of the Gangetic plain are, for the most part, small, scattered, situated on rather poor land, and deficient in transport and other infrastructure.[30] Further, in many localities various tribal groups are intermixed, while in others, immigrant non-tribal Hindus have acquired possession of much of what little good land there is. In combination, these problems might often prove to be insuperable obstacles in the way of satisfying future tribal territorial aspirations.

Yet another subset of minorities are the handful of sizable, non-tribal linguistic groups who occupy compact areas in which the establishment of new linguistic states might be feasible. These would include more than a million Tulu speakers in and near South Kanara district on the coast of Karnataka and more than a million speakers of Dogri, the largest group in the Jammu region of Jammu and Kashmir. Although Dogri was, until 1961, classified as a dialect of Punjabi, it is unlikely that the Sikh majority of Punjab would wish to have the predominantly Hindu area of Jammu annexed to Punjab on linguistic grounds, because to do so would then again make them a communal minority in their own state. It seems not unlikely that that is the reason why the census authorities upgraded Dogri to the status of a language in its own right. If the Government of India—possibly after the conclusion of a lasting accord on Jammu and Kashmir with Pakistan—were ever to partition that state on linguistic grounds, it seems quite likely that it would also consider a previously mooted suggestion for a new union territory of Ladakh, which is culturally and linguistically quite different from the rest of the state (and more than 50 per cent Buddhist). Ladakh, however, is very thinly settled, with barely more than 100,000

---

[30]Areas of India, at the subdistrict level (subdivisions, tahsils, and taluks) that are more than 50 per cent tribal in population, though not necessarily with more than 50 per cent speaking tribal languages, are indicated in Schwartzberg (ed.), *A Historical Atlas of South Asia*, plate XIII. C. 3, p. 143.

population; if it were to be combined with the adjoining linguistically similar districts of Kinnaur and Lahul and Spiti in Himachal Pradesh (also largely Buddhist), its population would be nearly doubled and its viability enhanced.

Several other territorial mergers that would reduce the proportion of India's population and area in linguistic minorities suggest themselves. The most important, potentially, would be a merger of the overwhelmingly Bengali district of Cachar in Assam with the adjacent, preponderantly Bengali-speaking state of Tripura. That would result in ridding Assam of more than a million Bengalis, whose large numbers in the state are presently a major source of grievance to the Assamese-speaking majority. It would also make Tripura into a more viable economic unit. Similarly, most of the Darjeeling district of West Bengal could be merged with Sikkim as in both areas the principal language spoken is now Nepali. (A small part of Darjeeling would have to be retained by West Bengal to maintain a road and rail link to its other two northern districts.) Finally, Goa might be slightly expanded to both the north and south by adding on adjacent taluks of Karnataka and Maharashtra that have a Konkani-speaking majority. (It is not possible to ascertain from the published data if, in fact, there are any such taluks, though it seems likely. The 1971 Census indicates that there are 600,000 and 300,000 Konkani speakers in Karnataka and Maharashtra respectively, in addition to the 600,000 in Goa, but data by taluks are not available.)[31]

Finally, there are the minorities speaking major languages of India situated along the state borders in districts or smaller administrative units, that, despite reorganization, have remained—like Kolar district in Karnataka—with a particular state despite the fact that the largest part of their population speaks a language of a neighbouring state. Because of the unavailability of data below the district level, it is very difficult to estimate how numerous these border-area minorities might be; but several million would appear to be a reasonable guess. The Telugu-speakers of Kolar alone were 1.25 million in 1971; and, a strong case could now be made for transferring much, if not all, of that district to Andhra Pradesh.

[31]The Konkani language is not to be confused with the Konkani dialect of Marathi, which was not separately enumerated at the 1971 census.

If all the possible changes suggested above were actually implemented—a most unlikely prospect—the present proportion of India's population in linguistic minorities, 16.5 per cent, would probably be reduced by not more than 3 or 4 per cent, because any territorial shift one might recommend would not only shift some portion of the population from minority to majority status, but, at the same time, shift those formerly in the majority (at the state level) into a minority status and would leave certain third and lower ranking linguistic minority groups virtually unaffected. Thus, to take the case of the aforementioned polyglot district of Kolar, in which all linguistic minorities (non-Kannada speakers) totaled 76 per cent of the 1971 population, its transfer to Andhra Pradesh, because of its small Telugu majority, would reduce the minority proportion to only 45 per cent.

To the best of the author's knowledge, there is at the present time no strong demand anywhere in India for further reorganization of the political map on essentially linguistic grounds and no serious thought on the government's part of making further changes. Demands for new territorial units, however, often emerge when formerly backward groups with a sense of ethnic distinctiveness—whether based on linguistic or other criteria—become politicized and press for administrative recognition of their distinctiveness. The process of politicization is often a consequence of the education of a new elite (for example, the Christian leadership of the tribal Nagas, Khasis, and Mizos, in that order of their emergence), and/or of the perception of relative social and economic deprivation. It is, therefore, very difficult to foretell what the future holds for as ethnically heterogeneous a country as India. It certainly appeared, judging from the returns in the 1961 census, that there was an emergence of a sense of separateness of Maithili, Magahi, and Bhojpuri speakers in Bihar from the great mass of Hindi speakers of north-central India and it would not have surprised the author if strident demands by one or more of those groups for their own linguistic states had followed in the subsequent decades. But that has not yet happened, at least not to any significant degree.

There is, however, one other important consideration that might drastically affect the political map of India and bring about a surfacing of calls for new states of the type just suggested. One must remember that India is a vast country, with a population now (1983 estimate) on the order of 725 million.[32] Discounting the nine union territories, with a combined population of not more than 10 million, India's twenty-two states have an average population of 32.5 million, while the most populous state, Uttar Pradesh passed the hundred million mark before the taking of the 1981 census. Thus, Indian states, on average, are more populous than all but twenty-two countries in the world (not counting India itself), while UP alone is more populous than all but China, the USSR, the USA, Indonesia, Brazil, and Japan. Some observers feel that states of this size are too large and too populous to administer effectively and that, as the role of government expands, smaller states will better be able to respond to the diverse local needs of the people. The most carefully thought-through proposal (complete with map) that I have seen for a radical reorganization of India with these considerations in mind is that of Professor Rasheeduddin Khan, who advocated the establishment of a federal system based on fifty-nine 'socio-cultural sub-regions.' In his words, a stage in India's political development:

... has now arrived in which we have to go from large, administratively unwieldy, politically troublesome and economically unequal though linguistically homogeneous States to a more rational reorganisation based on the principles of techno-economic viability, socio-cultural homogeneity, and administrative and political manageability. This would restore a balance between the federating States and the Centre and would made planned growth more feasible.[33]

While it is not my place to endorse this or any other proposal for the further territorial reorganization of India and while I find certain specifics of the proposed scheme questionable, I believe that it and other such thoughtful proposals that might be advanced are worthy of serious attention.

[32]Extrapolated from a figure of 714 million given by Population Reference Bureau, *World Population Data Sheet, 1982* (Washington, D.C.: PRB, 1982).

[33]Rasheeduddin Khan, 'Federal Nation-building in India: The Regional Dimension', in S. Manzoor Alam and G. Ram Reddy (eds), *Socio-Economic Development, Problems in South and Southeast Asia*, Papers and Proceedings of the International Seminar on Inter-Regional Cooperation in South and Southeast Asia, held at Osmania University, Hyderabad, January 1975 (Bombay: Popular Prakashan, 1978), pp. 194–215, quotation from p. 205.

CONCLUSIONS: IMPLICATIONS OF PAST AND POSSIBLE FUTURE CHANGES

The sensibilities of many linguistic and other ethnic groups in India, as in many other parts of the world, are potent and easily aroused. In the evolution of the Indian polity during the period since 1920 and, more particularly, in the period since the achievement of independence, language questions have been an important item on the political agenda of both the central government and, the governments of India's constituent provinces or states. Making territorial changes in favour of particular linguistic groups aspiring to have or to expand, a province or state of their own and, at the same time, protecting the rights of minorities speaking other languages has called repeatedly for the exercise of careful diplomacy and the making of exceedingly difficult and complex decisions. Many such decisions have had to be made in a political context fraught with the potential for massive violence. Yet, on the whole, one would have to acclaim the remarkable success to date of the nation's decision makers in keeping violence within manageable limits, in effecting workable territorial arrangements, in forestalling threats of secession by powerful linguistic groups, and in safeguarding the rights of linguistic minorities. The flexibility of the government's response to demands for change and its general willingness at least to consider all points of view has stood the nation in good stead and distinguished it from other ethnically diverse Third World countries who could find no alternative to force in dealing with the frustrated demands of their minorities.

In the author's judgement the changes that India has made to date in its political map have preserved the essential unity of the nation, rather than contributing, as many predicted, to a process of Balkanization. In creating a system of essentially linguistic states, India has provided a local political milieu that is conducive to the flowering of many linguistically-rooted cultures and thereby evolved a system which greatly enriches the cultural life of the nation as a whole. Further changes along purely linguistic lines are not likely to be great. Whether or not the states that have evolved to this point, however, represent the most efficient territorial vehicles for the future economic progress of the nation is debatable. Although no major changes now appear on the political horizon, it seems not unlikely that on economic and administrative grounds further alterations of the system will become a pressing issue.

4

Elite Interests, Popular Passions, and Social Power in the Language Politics of India*

Paul R. Brass

THE POLITICS OF LANGUAGE MOVEMENTS

Language movements and the politics of language are inherently and necessarily associated with the modern state and modern politics.[1] Before the rise of nationalism and language movements, rulers might make choices concerning the use of particular languages for official purposes, but any disagreements on the matter would not have involved a mass public. At the same time, *contra* Gellner, there is no necessary and inherent association between language and ethnicity.[2] Nor does every modern state require, for administrative or other purposes, a single official language. It is, nevertheless, the case that most

---

*This is a substantially revised essay originally published in *Ethnic and Racial Studies*, 27 (3), May 2004, pp. 353–75. As will be indicated in the footnotes, many of the revisions have been made as a result of an e-mail exchange with E. Annamalai concerning the original essay, for which I am grateful.

[1] Abram De Swaan, *Words of the World: The Global Language System* (Cambridge: Polity Press, 2001) p. 64; Dominique Arel, 'Language Categories in Censuses: Backward-or Forward-Looking', in David I. Kertzer and Dominique Arel (eds), *Census and Identity: The Politics of Race, Ethnicity and Language in National Censuses* (Cambridge: Cambridge University Press, 2002), p. 92.

[2] D.A. Washbrook, 'Ethnicity and Racialism in Colonial Indian Society', in R. Ross (ed.), *Racism and Colonialism* (The Hague: Martinus Nijhoff, 1982), p. 173.

modern states choose to have a single language for official purposes. It is also the case, in South Asia and elsewhere, that every choice regarding a single or multiple languages for official and/or educational purposes has consequences for the equalization or not of life chances, and for the empowerment or disempowerment of speakers of different languages.[3]

Further, language is not necessarily the primary form of ethnic affiliation or, to be more precise, it is not necessarily the central affiliation, symbol, or basis for the expression of political demands by, or on behalf of, particular social categories in multicultural, multilingual, or multireligious societies. On the contrary, as I argued in my *Language, Religion, and Politics in North India* thirty years ago, the politics of nationalism may be defined rather as the struggle—impossible ever to achieve completely—of establishing multi-symbol congruence within a constructed community.[4] The nation-constructing process in multicultural societies always begins with a single central symbol, which may be either language, or religion, or color, or any other cultural or ethnic marker, whichever serves simultaneously to separate one group from another and is at the same time politically convenient.

That is to say that in such societies, especially where there is considerable bilingualism, either at the elite level or at the mass level, the ethnic symbol that comes into play depends primarily on the categories recognized by the state and by elite conflicts for political power within those state-recognized categories. Thus, before independence in India, the British provided political opportunities to religiously defined groups—Hindus, Muslims, and Sikhs in particular. In consequence, language politics and language movements, in north India above all, took second place—though they developed simultaneously alongside

---

[3]E.J. Hobsbawm, *Nations and Nationalism Since 1780: Programme, Myth, Reality* (Cambridge: Cambridge University Press, 1990), p. 110. For South Asia, however, Ghosh has argued, in an article, on the rise of literary Bengali in nineteenth-century Bengal, that such consequences nevertheless left room for 'different sections of the Bengali middle classes to voice their distinctive concerns.' While this is an important argument on a neglected aspect of research on language politics in India, it does not appear to me to contradict the fact, as she writes, that a 'linguistic elite' arose in Bengal, as elsewhere in India at different times, whose members thereby maintained or acquired 'greater access to the power structure than other speech or dialect communities.' Anindita Ghosh, 'Revisiting the "Bengal Renaissance": Literary Bengali and Low-life Print in Colonial India', *EPW*, 19 October 2002, online at epw.org.in.

[4]Paul R. Brass, *Language, Religion, and Politics in North India* (Cambridge: Cambridge University Press, 1974).

politicized religious movements. In the post-independence period, however, when it became taboo for groups to express their demands for political recognition on the basis of religion, language movements flourished and, in several cases, displaced religious identification for political purposes. While it is true that the displacement of religious identification by language was merely a political ruse in the case, for example, of the Sikhs in Punjab, at the same time, for Hindus in Punjab, it involved a real generational change in the primary spoken language from Punjabi to Hindi.

Yet, a further example of the subordination of language to religious communal identification concerns the historic recognition of one form of Hindi, known as *khari boli*, as the regional standard language of northern India, and ultimately as the official language of the country, which has involved, as well, the absorption of a multiplicity of local languages, dialects, mother tongues, whatever one wants to call them. It is in part a consequence of elite competition from 'the then under-privileged Hindu majority'[5] with the Urdu-speaking and Urdu-writing privileged classes of northern India, whose tongue and script, it was said, were foreign and Muslim, that Hindi devotees have succeeded in this process of absorption and displacement of all other alternatives in that part of the country. At the same time, in the nineteenth century, a similar process of absorption and displacement of local dialects and languages by standardized Urdu was promoted by Muslim religious elites in the famous Deoband school, located in western Uttar Pradesh (UP), and its affiliated institutions spread widely across north India and beyond to other parts of the subcontinent.[6] But, the political conflict that led to Muslim separatism did not arise from this institution and its associated political-cultural organization, the Jami'at-I 'Ulama'-yi Hind, which remained staunchly pro-Congress throughout the twentieth century and opposed Muslim political separatism and the Pakistan movement. The latter movement, rather, found its support in another Muslim educational institution, the Aligarh Muslim University, also located in western UP. Though its curriculum included Muslim and Urdu studies, the elites who founded it, as well as its students, came

[5]Christopher Shackle and Rupert Snell, *Hindi and Urdu since 1800: A Common Reader* (London: School of Oriental and African Studies, 1990), p. 7.

[6]Barbara D. Metcalf, *Islamic Revival in British India: Deoband, 1860–1900* (Princeton, N.J.: Princeton University Press, 1982), p. 209.

from entirely different backgrounds from those who founded and attended Deoband. They came primarily from upper-class Muslim families of landlords and government servants, in search of government jobs, for whom the defence of Urdu against the claims of Hindi served the purpose of maintaining their privileged access to those jobs.[7]

The Hindi-Urdu conflict in north India was tinged with Hindu-Muslim difference from the beginning, and gradually and increasingly became saturated with Hindu-Muslim competition and animosity that ultimately led to the political divergence which culminated in the Muslim separatist movement, the partition of India, and the creation of Pakistan. The religious basis of the Hindi movement was clear enough by the end of the nineteenth century and the beginning of the twentieth. It was centred in the Hindu holy city of Banaras, where both the Hindi Sahitya Sammelan, the pre-eminent organization for the Hindi movement, and the Banaras Hindu University (BHU) were located. A central figure in both movements was Madan Mohan Malaviya, who was actually a native of the city of Allahabad, but who took the lead in the establishment of the BHU in Banaras and was its vice-chancellor for twenty years, from 1919 to 1939. The curriculum he wished to see established there was to emphasize Sanskrit and classical Hindu religious, legal, and philosophical texts as well as the native languages of India, with Hindi as the medium of instruction. However, owing to the insistence of the British rulers, English became the primary medium of instruction. Malaviya himself, however, had greater success earlier, in his campaign to promote the adoption of the Hindi language as a language of state administration and primary education in the NWP (now Uttar Pradesh), coequal with Urdu; the campaign achieved its goal in 1900. He was also deeply involved in Hindu movements of religious purification. The Hindi language that men like Malaviya wished to promote was also to be purified through the displacement of Persian-Arabic vocabulary by direct and indirect borrowings from Sanskrit and the Persian-Arabic script by the Devanagari.[8]

[7]Ibid., pp. 327–8. For an analysis of the multiple pressures that the Urdu-speaking elite, particularly the landlords among them, faced at the end of the nineteenth century, see Francis Robinson, *Separatism Among Indian Muslims: The Politics of the United Provinces' Muslims, 1860–1923* (Delhi: Vikas, 1975), esp. pp. 33–4.

[8]Marzia Casolari, 'Role of Benares in Constructing Political Hindu Identity', *EPW*, 13 April 2002.

But, there has been a profound difference in identity choices between the northern Hindi-Urdu speaking provinces—now states— of India, on the one hand, and the southern states especially. In the former, where the primary line of elite competition was between privileged Muslim and rising Hindu elites, religion was the primary symbol of political identity—and remains so today—and displaced potential language/dialect conflicts that were overridden by a politico-religious identity. The extent of displacement or subordination of such subsidiary languages and dialects to Hindi may be discerned even now, in the 1991 census, where, under the heading of Hindi, forty-eight 'languages and mother tongues' are subsumed, along with an unspecified number of 'others'.[9] While some of these languages and mother tongues are spurious, merely alternative, local names of various mutually intelligible dialects, others are well known, widely spread, long recognized (especially since the great linguist, George Grierson identified them in his massive, multi-volume *Linguistic Survey of India*, published at the turn of the twentieth century), and numerically quite large. For example, Bhojpuri, the largest, with 23,102,050 speakers had a larger number of speakers, according to the 1991 census, than seven of the eighteen scheduled languages,[10] including languages such as Assamese, which is the official language of the state of Assam. It has nearly the same number of speakers as Punjabi, which is also an official state language, of Punjab. There are several other mother tongues subsumed under Hindi, which outnumber some of the scheduled languages.

In the south, on the other hand, where upper-caste Hindu elites were dominant—particularly the Brahman castes identified with the historic Sanskritic culture of Indian civilization—rising middle castes challenged their dominance through the medium and vehicle of the vernacular languages alone. In the north, Muslims and their form of Hindi-Urdu were characterized as foreign; in the south, it was Brahmanic, Sanskritic culture that was so defined.

The politics of language in India display another feature that contradicts any attempt to claim an overriding primacy of language

---

[9]Census of India, *Census Data Online* 1991, *censusindia.net/cendat/datable2.htm*, accessed 5 March 2003.

[10]That is, those listed on the Eighth Schedule of the Constitution of India, which guarantees their use for certain official purposes. The figure for the number of Bhojpuri-speakers comes from Census of India 1991a, p. 77.

loyalty and identification against other languages when life chances are involved. This feature operates primarily at the elite level in the non-Hindi-speaking areas of the country, where highly educated persons choose English as their language of communication outside home and family—and sometimes even there as well—to enhance their job opportunities in higher administration, global corporations, international institutions, and colleges and universities abroad. This kind of choice in favour of English, of course, is nowadays hardly confined to Indian regional language speakers, but is frequently made at both elite and intermediate social levels throughout the world.[11]

BILINGUALISM AND ELITE LANGUAGE CHOICE

But there is one characteristic of elite language choice in India that is not shared with the rest of the world, which arises from the simultaneous existence of two alternative official languages for the country as a whole, while the vast majority of the people speak either only their regional language or some combination of a local 'mother tongue' and the regional language. That presents a situation of a double displacement, separating elite and mass levels of language use and life opportunities. Educated Hindi-speakers, especially if they know enough English as well, can compete successfully with non-Hindi-region English language speakers for the highest posts in the central government (though not in the foreign and global corporations and institutions unless they have easy fluency in English), leaving the higher-level provincial government jobs in the Hindi-speaking states to less educated Hindi-speakers, and the middle-and lowest-level jobs to those who have had either limited advanced educational opportunities or none at all. With regard to the latter, it is important to recognize that effective literacy in most of the Hindi-speaking region

[11]A fact explicitly and commonly recognized and accepted in India. See, for example, a commentary on the opportunities provided to English-educated Indians for jobs in 'business process outsourcing ... call centres. Anonymous, 'BPO Boom and Teaching of English', *EPW*, 21 June 2003, pp. 2444–5. These jobs require near-perfect command of spoken, unaccented English, though, as an India specialist, I always know, from the ineradicable accent of the technician, when my calls to Dell computer for technical support land in Bangalore, where the technicians are surprised when I ask if they are in fact in Bangalore.

is probably still below 50 per cent (even though the official figures for 1991 declared 52.2 per cent total literacy).[12] Those people who are illiterate in Hindi are usually also bilingual in their mother tongue and Hindi, but lack even the limited opportunities available to the intermediate and lower social categories in the non-Hindi-speaking states where literacy rates are much higher. It is, of course, also true that the vast majority of women in India are illiterate[13] though women who have higher education in English, chiefly, and Hindi, to some extent, have opportunities available to them that are quite lacking for most men, who have only an intermediate, lower level, or no education.[14]

Thus, a first take, as it were, on the relationship between possible language choices and life chances in India presents us with three broad levels: (1) higher-level elite speakers of English, with English-knowing

[12]Swaan also takes note of this; Swaan, *Words of the World*, pp. 62–3, 73. The official literacy figures, of course, are much higher for males (64.1 per cent) than for females (39.3 per cent), according to the 1991 census. The regional variation ranged in 1991 from a low of 38.5 per cent in benighted Bihar to a high of 89.8 per cent in Kerala (Census of India). Since this article was originally published, the 2001 census tables on literacy have become available, which give the following figures: 64.8 per cent total literacy, 75.3 per cent for males, 53.7 per cent for females. Total literacy for Bihar in 2001 was given as 47.0 per cent, still at the bottom, with the additional distinction of being the only state in the country in which literacy rates remained below 50 per cent. Kerala remained at the top with 90.9 per cent total literacy. It remains likely that the effective literacy rates in most parts of the country are considerably below the official figures.

[13]This statement probably remains true despite the fact that the 2001 census gives a literacy figure for females for the country as a whole as 53.7 per cent. In four large states (Rajasthan, Uttar Pradesh, Bihar, and Jharkhand) and in one small union territory (Dadra & Nagar Haveli), even the official literacy figures for women remain below 50 per cent, with Bihar, of course, well to the bottom again with a 33.1 per cent official literacy rate for women.

[14]Khare has argued that, in effect, the predominance of English has meant the linguistic disempowerment of 'the overwhelming majority of India's population'; Santhosh Kumar Khare, 'Truth about Language in India', *EPW*, 14 December 2002, online at epw.org.in. While I think that the disempowerment is relative, leaving intermediate levels of opportunities for many who have varying degrees of command of the languages of power, I also agree that the majority of the people of the country remain disempowered by the coexistence of social and linguistic hierarchies with widespread illiteracy. Further, even among the literate, it has been argued that there is a dramatic cultural and social divide between persons educated in English-medium schools and those educated in Hindi-medium schools in the Hindi-speaking areas of north India, in which the life chances of the English-educated and those who do not know English well are significantly different. See, on this point, the excellent article by David Faust and Richa Nagar, 'Politics of Development in Postcolonial India: English Medium Education and Social Fracturing', *EPW*, 28 May 2001, pp. 2, 879–83.

Hindi-speakers (Hindi bilinguals) having an added advantage in the central government and in the national capital, where Hindi is the dominant language, in postings in the Hindi-speaking region and in the states adjacent to the Hindi-speaking region as well as in those states, such as Andhra, where variants of Hindi-Urdu are known to a large segment of the population;[15] (2) intermediate level elite speakers of Hindi only, or a regional language; (3) lower-level non-elite, poorly educated or even illiterate speakers of a regional language, and/or a local 'mother tongue'.[16] At the upper levels, however, as Swaan has noted, those who are bilingual play critical mediating roles.[17] This was the case in the colonial period; it is also the case today. Bilinguals are also likely to rise to the highest political and administrative positions available at each level: central, regional, or local. They are also likely as well to want to preserve the status of the languages in which they are fluent, to promote those which offer possibilities of advancement for themselves, and to be uninterested in advancing universal literacy in the country. So, in India, English has been supported for advanced education most strongly in the non-Hindi-speaking states in order to equalize the life chances of the regional elites against the elites from the Hindi-speaking regions.

Among the non-Hindi-speaking states, Tamil Nadu has gone the furthest in virtually banning the Hindi language from the curriculum and offering instruction in only two languages at the primary and secondary levels: Tamil (or other 'mother tongues' spoken in the state) and English. As a consequence of both relatively high literacy rates in the state and one of the highest levels of bilingualism and trilingualism in English in the country (above 14 per cent),[18] elites

[15]My formulation here has been influenced and altered substantially by comments from E. Annamalai on the earlier version of this article;

[16]Swaan also (sub)divides the elites at the highest union level into three categories: users of English only, speakers of Hindi only, and those who use both Hindi and English, each set of whom have 'divergent interests'; among these three groups, those who have command of both Hindi and English have the strongest possible communicative position and, therefore, the most favourable life chances. Swaan, *Words of the World*, pp. 77–8.

[17]Ibid., pp. 67–8 and elsewhere.

[18]Census of India, 1999b, *Census of India, 1991*, Series 1-*India*, Part IV (B) (i) (b)-C Series, *Bilingualism and Trilingualism*, Table C-8, *India, States and Union Territories*, by M. Vijayanunni (Delhi: Controller of Publications, 1999) p. 11.

from Tamil Nadu have retained a very strong competitive advantage for access to jobs in the central government, global corporations, and, increasingly, in international educational institutions. It remains true, however, again as Swaan has pointed out, that, even in Tamil Nadu, English, 'the former colonial language,' has not become 'a language of mass instruction.'[19] The vast majority of Tamil speakers in Tamil Nadu are monolingual.

Further, English remains a principal second language for bilinguals in virtually every state in the Indian union. Not only that, the number of speakers of English as second or third language listed in the 1991 Indian census figures is 90,042,487, outnumbering the number of speakers of Hindi as second or third language (70,744,505) by approximately 20 million.[20] However, the figure for English bilinguals and trilinguals includes those with Hindi as the first language. After deducting their number from the total, we get a figure of 60,184,313 non-Hindi-speakers who know English and a figure of 29,858,174 Hindi-speakers who know English, providing perhaps a clearer picture of the actual competitive situation between persons from the Hindi-speaking and the non-Hindi-speaking areas. I say perhaps because these figures, which rely entirely on respondent statements, do not specify the degree of knowledge of English (or Hindi) required for the status of bilingual or trilingual. Nor can they be easily correlated with literacy since language figures are provided by number of speakers in the country as a whole and literacy figures are provided only by the state.[21] Nevertheless, I am confident in saying that, insofar as the elite positions available to Indians at the national and international level are concerned, the competitive advantage for English-knowing bilinguals and trilinguals is certain and, therefore, that non-Hindi-speakers in that category have a competitive advantage at the topmost levels in comparison with the smaller numbers of English-knowing bilinguals and trilinguals from the Hindi-speaking pool. At the highest

[19]Swaan, *Words of the World*, pp. 67–8.

[20]*Census of India, 1996*, pp. 11–12.

[21]As Probal Dasgupta has remarked, 'the crucial correlation between literacy and bilingualism is missing'; Probal Dasgupta, 'Introduction', in E. Annamalai (ed.), *Managing Multilingualism in India: Political and Linguistic Manifestations* (New Delhi: Sage, 2001), p. 13.

Table 4.1: Per cent of (Scheduled Language) Speakers, with English
and/or Hindi as Second or Third Language*

Language	English or Hindi (per cent)	English only (per cent)	Hindi only (per cent)
Sindhi	70.10	19.45	50.65
Punjabi	59.97	23.72	36.25
Konkani	59.90	34.85	25.04
Manipuri	50.58	26.27	24.31
Nepali	43.66	8.20	35.46
Malayalam	43.41	24.35	19.07
Marathi	37.89	12.10	25.79
Gujarati	34.51	10.60	23.91
Assamese	31.15	14.22	16.93
Urdu	28.47	7.86	20.61
Oriya	24.03	12.66	11.37
Kannada	20.95	11.98	8.97
Telugu	19.11	11.10	8.01
Bengali	15.67	9.04	6.64
Tamil	15.61	14.05	1.56
Hindi	8.85	8.85	NA

Correlation coefficient for columns 3 and 4 = .32.

Note: *Excluding Kashmiri, for which census data are incomplete, and Sanskrit, whose numbers are very low and somewhat spurious.

level, therefore, we can say with assurance that English bilinguals—those at least who have as well a higher education—maintain what Swaan calls a 'mediation monopoly' for 'an educated minority' in the country,[22] who constitute, in effect, the ruling elite of India or, in Gaetano Mosca's terminology, the ruling class from which the ruling elites are drawn. It is from this class also that 'a modernised techno-managerial elite' has been produced, whose members fill nearly all the highest positions in the Indian Administrative Service and the

[22]Swaan, *Words of the World*, pp. 67–8. See also his Q-value figures for English and Hindi at pp. 74–5, which appear to give a competitive advantage in general to English over Hindi, but the index numbers are difficult to comprehend and replicate, and contain some inaccuracies. Further, Swaan says at one point that, 'as second languages, Hindi and English are now on a par,' while also stating that 'the Q-value of English in the Indian constellation is about half that of Hindi', p. 78. Each of these figures reflect different aspects of the competition between Hindi and English as the preferred language for enhancing one's life chances. My stress above is that English remains the pre-eminent language of prestige and opportunity in India and that non-Hindi-speakers have achieved a competitive advantage against Hindi-speakers in the number of persons who can use English.

managerial positions in the global corporations and international institutions operating in India.[23]

Table 4.1 illustrates further aspects of the bilingual choices'[24] made by the speakers of scheduled languages in India. The table lists in rank order, in the second column, the proportion of persons bilingual in at least one of the two official languages, English or Hindi, in fifteen scheduled languages, excluding Hindi, as well as Kashmiri (where data could not be collected for the 1991 census), and Sanskrit (which is more a cultural symbol than language of communication). The first thing to note is that two of the five highest-ranked languages, namely, Sindhi and Nepali, are not official languages in any state and, therefore, do not have a competitive advantage for state public sector employment in any state in India. Therefore, in order to compete for public sector posts at both the state and central government level, it is crucial that speakers of these languages have competence in at least one of the official languages of India or of the Hindi-speaking states in which they reside. In the case of Sindhi-speakers, their distribution over several states in India, especially (but not only) in the Hindi-speaking regions, where many of them are occupied in business and trade, requires proficiency in Hindi.

Second, although Konkani written in the Devanagari script is the official language of Goa and Manipuri is the official language of Manipur, English is widely used in these and many other of the smaller states. It has been argued that one possible reason for this is the 'limited job market' within such states.[25] However, it cannot be ascertained without further research whether *the proportion* of jobs available in such states in relation to the population of job-seekers in each state is, in fact, significantly different. Further, with regard to Konkani, its speakers are distributed across several states in western India where other regional languages are dominant and where, therefore, English

[23]Faust and Nagar, *Politics of Development*, p. 2, 878, referring also to Rajni Kothari, *Growing Amnesia: An Essay on Poverty and Human Consciousness* (New Delhi: Penguin, 1993).

[24]Dasgupta, 'Introduction' to Annamalai, p. 11. The term 'choice' assumes conscious decision on the part of students or their parents. This is not the right word for everyday code switching, but it is more suitable when discussing Hindi and English bilingualism since 'nearly half the bilinguals for whom Hindi is the second language learn it in school' and 'nearly all the Indians who use English as a second language learn it that way', p. 14.

[25]This point was made to me in a personal communication from E. Annamalai.

proficiency would give them the greatest competitive advantage, which would explain their preference for that language over Hindi.

An additional noteworthy aspect of the figures is the high proportion of bilinguals in one or the other of the official languages in states adjacent to or close to the Hindi-speaking region, where Hindi has spread widely. These languages, which are official languages in such states, are, in rank order, Punjabi, Marathi, Gujarati, and Assamese. The anomaly in the rank is Malayalam, a deep southern state, second only to Punjabi in bilingual speakers of at least one of the two official languages.

A further feature of the figures concerns Urdu, which comes next, after Assamese, in the rank order of languages, but even so is certainly too low since virtually all Urdu-speakers outside of the state of Andhra Pradesh—and probably even there as well—are, in effect, Hindi-speakers, though the census does not take note of that and merely records what respondents state.

Finally, it is also noteworthy that all the southern languages, except Malayalam, and the two eastern languages, Oriya and Bengali, rank at the bottom in knowledge of one or more of the two official languages. This ranking constitutes, in reverse order, a more or less deliberate rejection of Hindi as a cultural language and a preference for English only, for practical purposes, with Tamil leading this group, Bengali second, the other two large south Indian languages, Telugu and Kannada, coming next, and finally Oriya.

Columns 3 and 4 reveal the distinctive second language choices, between Hindi and English, made by speakers of the scheduled languages. That they are distinctive is indicated by the correlation coefficient between the per cent choosing English and the per cent choosing Hindi as second language, which is positive at .32, but with a low significance level (.250). Hindi is the preferred second language choice for speakers of Sindhi, Punjabi, Nepali, Marathi, Gujarati, Urdu, and Assamese (only slightly). English is the preferred second language choice for Konkani, Manipuri (slightly), Malayalam, Tamil, Oriya, Kannada, Telugu, Bengali, and Tamil speakers, confirming once again the division between the northern and western languages, on the one hand, and the southern and eastern languages, on the other hand, with the northern and western language speakers preferring Hindi, and the southern and eastern, English. As for the more marginal languages, with no state recognizing their language as official, their speakers opt either for Hindi primarily or for both (that is, with numbers of persons choosing Hindi or English in similar proportions). Finally, Hindi speakers rank close to the bottom in choice of English as a second language, for the obvious reason that they retain a competitive advantage through Hindi alone, though, as just stated, proficient English speakers continue to have the edge at the top.

ELITES AND LANGUAGE MOVEMENTS

In their initial and developing stages, language movements are everywhere vehicles for the pursuit of economic advancement, social status, and political power by specific elites. The dialect/language chosen, as well as its form and style, constitute political as well as 'linguistic acts', in which the type of linguistic act chosen arises from different 'social conditions'.[26] In other words, different elites in different social and political circumstances may choose a borrowing strategy or a purification strategy, depending on the political and economic goals they choose and whether or not they wish to identify with or distance themselves from another group.

In multilingual societies such as India, which also encompass a multiplicity of 'mother tongues', bilingualism, as we have just seen, is widespread, but it is of two types. At the mass level, as already noted, most people, in addition to their own mother tongue, speak—with varying degrees of fluency—broader languages of communication, bazaar Hindi-Urdu in northern India or, nowadays, the Hindi regional standard language. At the elite level, bilingualism—which may also be trilingualism—includes knowledge of both a regional standard native language and a broader language of interregional and/or international communication. In India, again as said above, that language is, of course, English and/or for well-educated Hindi-speakers, Hinglish—that

[26]E. Annamalai, 'The Linguistic and Social Dimensions of Purism', in Bjorn H. Jernudd and Michael J. Shapiro (eds), *The Politics of Language Purism* (Berlin: Mouton de Gruyter, 1989), p. 226.

wonderful language that combines English and Hindi noun and verb forms in a single sentence. It is important to note that elite bilingualism arises, in the first instance, and has always arisen, among those persons who already occupy an elite position in their society. Everywhere in India in the colonial period, such elites maintained and enhanced their status by acquiring English, just as they had earlier acquired Persian. Moreover, at the same time that they acquired the language of rule under the British, they sought also to standardize and modernize their own languages to make them fit vehicles for literature and for creating a speech community.[27] By doing so, these elites also placed themselves in what Swaan characterizes as a mediating position, in which they could communicate effectively with the rulers, acquire positions of influence and power in government administration, and build a constituency among their own language speakers on whose behalf they might then make a claim to speak and, thereby, to enhance further their own political influence.

In such multilingual environments, a dual movement takes place. On the one hand, elites promoting a particular dialect to the status of a regional standard seek to enlarge, or even create, a new speech community through the medium of a regional or national standard language that simultaneously displaces some, and encompasses other dialects. On the other hand, elite competition may then develop, which takes the striking form of establishing and maintaining barriers of communication between groups differently defined,[28] who may in fact speak more or less the same language. We think of these two processes as language standardization and language purification. Once again, the Hindi-Urdu controversy provides an example of both: standardization of Hindi to encompass as many as possible of the dialects and mother tongues of northern and western India, combined with linguistic purification through sanskritization, and insistence on the use of the Devanagari script to impose a symbolic barrier to communication between Hindus and Muslims, which does not exist in fact. However,

---

[27]Chatterjee makes this argument concerning the Bengali elite in the nineteenth century. Partha Chatterjee, *The Nation and its Fragments: Colonial and Postcolonial Histories* (Princeton, N.J.: Princeton University Press, 1993), pp. 6–7.

[28]Brass, *Language, Religion, and Politics*, p. 423; Annamalai, 'The Linguistic and Social Dimensions of Purism', p. 229.

Table 4.2: Ratio of Urdu Speakers to the Muslim Population by State, 1991

State	Per cent of Urdu-speakers to Muslim population	Muslim Population (Rank)	Percentage of Muslims to total population (Rank)	Percentage of Urdu-speakers to total population	Number of Urdu-speakers
Andhra Pradesh	93.83	5,923,954 (7)	8.91 (8)	8.36	5,560,154
Orissa	86.89	577,775 (14)	1.83 (14)	1.59	502,102
Karnataka	85.40	5,234,023 (8)	11.64 (6)	9.94	4,480,038
Maharashtra	74.77	7,628,755 (4)	9.67 (7)	7.23	5,734,468
Bihar	66.78	12,787,985 (3)	14.81 (5)	9.89	8,542,463
UP	51.82	24,109,684 (1)	17.33 (4)	8.98	12,492,927
Madhya Pradesh	37.30	3,282,800 (11)	4.96 (12)	1.85	1,227,672
Haryana	34.27	763,775 (13)	4.64 (13)	1.59	261,820
Tamil Nadu	34.00	3,052,717 (12)	5.47 (11)	1.86	1,036,660
Rajasthan	26.97	3,525,339 (10)	8.01 (10)	2.16	953,497
Gujarat	15.12	3,606,920 (9)	8.73 (9)	1.32	547,737
West Bengal	11.22	16,075,836 (2)	23.61 (2)	2.65	1,455,649
Punjab	5.93	239,401 (15)	1.18 (15)	0.07	13,416
Kerala	0.17	6,788,364 (5)	23.33 (3)	0.04	12,625
Assam	.00	6,373,204 (6)	28.43 (1)	0.02	3,900
Total	42.74	101,596,057	12.12	5.18	42,825,128

Source: Compiled from Census of India, 1991, Series-1: India, Paper 1 of 1995: Religion, by M. VIjayanunni and Series 1—India: Part IV B(i)(a)-C Series: Language, Table C-7, India, States and Union Territories, by M. Vijayanunni, Statement 9.

that process has culminated in north India, especially in the state of UP, in a drastic decline in the prevalence of the Urdu written and spoken forms of the traditional north Indian language of wider communication.[29] This has meant that most Muslims who go to government schools in northern India do not learn and cannot read the Persian-Arabic script. But, this process of including Muslim children in the newly formed Hindi speech community has not done away with the symbolic, politico-religious barrier between Hindus and Muslims in north India, which has intensified in the last two decades more than ever, taking the form of increasingly vicious Hindu-Muslim riots and anti-Muslim pogroms.[30]

It is another anomaly, moreover, that, according to the 1991 census, identification of Muslims with the Urdu language is higher in many states where Urdu has not traditionally been the language of Muslims than it is in states where that has traditionally been the case (see Table 4.2). Thus, the correspondence between the number of Urdu speakers and the Muslim population is closer in the states of Andhra Pradesh,

---

[29]See Ather Farouqui, 'The Emerging Dilemma of the Urdu Press in India; A Viewpoint', *South Asia*, 18(1), 1995, pp. 91–103; Danial Latifi, 'Urdu in UP', *Nation and the World*, 16 August 1999, pp. 44–6; Jagdish C. Pant, 'Urdu as Mother Tongue Medium at Primary Level', unpublished paper presented at the conference organized by the Zakir Hussain Study Circle at Vigyan Bhawan, New Delhi, 8–11 February 2002.

[30]Nor is this kind of symbolic linguistic divergence peculiar to northern India. It has been mirrored in the artificial divergence between Croatian and Serbian, which appear to stand in nearly precisely the same relationship as Hindi and Urdu. Both cases constitute striking examples of linguistic change or purification or 're-standardization' for the purpose, on the one hand, of establishing standardized speech forms congruent with politically defined communities, while setting up barriers of communication between such communities. Once again, language plays here a secondary role in communal/ethnic identification.

Arel, who holds the opposite view to that presented here concerning the primacy of language identification in nationalist movements, nevertheless provides further examples of its secondary character. The prevalence of Irish nationalism in the face of language loss, which he mentions, is well enough known. Less well known, to me at least, is the case of the Masurians, said to have spoken 'a dialectical variety of the Polish spoken in Warsaw', who 'staunchly clung to a Prussian/German identity, claiming that their mother tongue did *not politically matter*'. While Arel argues that 'this did not prevent Polish nationalists from claiming that the Masurians were *theirs* (emphasis in original), it would seem clearly to indicate the opposite point to the one he makes, namely, that language is often clearly subordinate to other ethnonational identities. Arel, 'Language Categories in Censuses', in *The Politics of Language Purism*, p. 92.

Orissa, Karnataka, and Maharashtra than it is in the northern states of Bihar, UP, Madhya Pradesh, and Haryana. In Andhra, a form of Urdu has been the language of Muslims and, in the Bombay metropolis of Maharashtra, there are many Urdu-speakers who have migrated from the north, but Oriya has traditionally been the language of Muslims in Orissa, and Kannada the language of Muslims in Karnataka.[31] The point here, though, is simply that, once again, language and ethnic or religious identifications vary according to many factors, among which 'mother tongue' is only one. In India, those other factors are social and economic opportunities provided by different language choices, government discrimination or acceptance, and intensity of communal religious conflict (which can either strengthen or weaken linguistic identification).

Yet a further example of the subordination of linguistic/ vernacular/mother tongue identifications to alternative languages, for both political reasons and for the enhancement of life chances, comes from one of the most hotly and dangerously contested regions of the world, the Indian state of Jammu and Kashmir. Here the spoken, everyday language of the majority of the people is Kashmiri. However, 'Urdu and English are the languages of teaching and official use in Kashmir'.[32] Further, whereas the 1981 census figures list Kashmiri and Dogri as the two most widely spoken languages in the state (comprising 52.29 per cent and 24.39 per cent of the population, respectively), the three-language formula for language instruction in the primary and secondary schools of the state includes only Urdu,

---

[31]There is no evident reason, however, why there should be a greater degree of Urdu-consciousness among Muslims in Orissa and Karnataka where it has been presumed that Muslims, like their Hindu brethren, speak mostly Oriya or Kannada, respectively. Khalidi, however, has cited interviewees in Bangalore, who claim that urban Muslims in Karnataka 'find it difficult to cope with the Kannada language'; Omar Khalidi, *Khaki and Ethnic Violence in India* (New Delhi: Three Essays, 2003), pp. 83–4. A full understanding of the differences among the several states in this respect will require an examination of the relations between Hindus and Muslims in them, of the educational policies pursued with regard to provisions for the use of Urdu in the schools, and of political, social, and religious movements and institutions, which have sought to promote Urdu-consciousness in the several states.

[32]Madhu Kishwar, 'Religion at the Service of Nationalism: An Analysis of Sangh Parivar Politics', in *Religion at the Service of Nationalism and Other Essays* (Delhi: Oxford University Press, 1998), p. 279.

Hindi, and English.[33] In this case, Urdu serves a dual purpose as the marker of Muslim identity while being, for practical purposes of communication outside of Kashmir, identical to Hindi. Some of the regional nationalist and separatist leaders and movements in Kashmir have adopted the slogan of 'Kashmiriyat,' arguing for unity between Muslims and Hindus on the basis of the Kashmiri language and the distinctive culture of the region. However, it would appear that education in the mother tongues of the people in Kashmir has been subordinated to both Hindi-Urdu and English, thereby enabling educated Kashmiris to compete from a potentially more favourable position than regional elites in some of the other non-Hindi-speaking states for access to high status jobs outside their state.

Equally interesting and notable is the situation that Ramaswamy describes in the multilingual south Indian province of Madras in the 1920s and 1930s.[34] At a time when Hindu-Muslim political differences over representation and language identifications had become consolidated in north India, Muslims in the Madras province were divided between Tamil-speaking Muslims, on the one hand, who aligned with a backward caste movement that was challenging the dominance of both 'Hinduism and Brahmanism' in economic, social and political life, and the Urdu-speaking elite, on the other hand, dominant among Muslims in the province. Yet a further twist in this situation was the support given by the latter to Hindustani, that is, to the idea that Hindi and Urdu were basically the same language written in two different scripts. This state of affairs sounds rather complicated, but the principal point is that language identifications depend both upon perceived life chances offered by particular language choices and, equally important and connected

---

[33]The reports of the Commissioner for Linguistic Minorities (of which the 1994–5 report cited here is the latest available), which used to be published by the Home Ministry of the Government of India and were largely ignored by most state governments, are now published (after a lapse of several years) under the aegis of the Ministry of Social Justice & Empowerment. This switch is a fine example of newspeak, for, if any ministry has power in India, it is Home, whereas the 'Empowerment' ministry surely is at or near the bottom of the list of powerful ministries. Government of India (GoI), *The Thirty-Fifth Report of the Commissioner for Linguistic Minorities (CLM) in India (For The Period July, 1994 to June 1995)*, 1995.

[34]Sumathi Ramaswamy, *Passions of the Tongue: Language Devotion in Tamil India, 1891–1970* (Berkeley: University of California Press, 1997), p. 175.

to the question of life chances, upon patterns of elite political competition for power.

POPULAR PASSIONS AND ELITE INTERESTS IN THE POLITICS OF LANGUAGE: MOTHER'S MILK, BOTTLED MILK, AND LINGUISTIC NARCISSISM

In any discussion of the political and economic interests that underlie all language movements and that, as I have argued, often lead people to discard their language for another, even to disown their own language in order to separate themselves clearly from another group who speak the same language, someone always asks the question: how then do you explain the attachment that most people feel towards their language, the passion that it arouses, and the willingness of some people to die in defence of their language in language movements? My initial response to this set of questions is that it is not at all clear to me that most people are so attached to their language, that their attachment is passionate, and that it may move some amongst them to die in its cause. It appears to me rather that such attachments, passions, and commitments also arise only under specific conditions, that they are often a mask behind which lie other interests, and that the passionate attachment is not to the language but to the self.[35]

It is perhaps difficult for an English speaker to empathize with such claimed feelings of passion for one's own language, for it is increasingly rare for us to be in situations where we cannot somehow manage to be understood and to get what we want. When we cannot, our feelings are likely to be a sense of frustration, of deficiency, of isolation, but not a feeling of love for our own language. If the situation is prolonged,

[35]There are exceptions, of course. As E. Annamalai has pointed out in a personal communication, the self-immolation of Tamils (or, in other circumstances, the actions of suicide bombers) certainly cannot be explained in terms of self-interest or self-love. But, however dramatic and however much attention is paid to such actions, they are acts of very small numbers of people. Further, the motives for such actions are not easily discerned. There must be a multiplicity of motives involved in such acts: desire for revenge (in the case of suicide bombers), self-glorification, religious belief, clinical depression, desperation about one's life chances. However, I find it difficult to believe that many persons sacrifice their lives for love of their language instead of fighting, moving, joining with others to protest. Perhaps some do, but then how to differentiate such a presumed motive from mental derangement?

then, of course, one must strive to learn another tongue, which so many millions of immigrants to America have done successfully during the past two centuries. In either case, whether temporary or permanent, it is one's sense of self that is at stake, one's self-respect, one's sense of importance, the loss of the sense of centrality of one's person in a world of communication.

When a person says, 'I love my language,' what is meant is, 'I love myself,' a statement that cannot be uttered aloud in society. One may argue in a rational or emotional way about whether French or Bengali is the most beautiful and expressive language in the world, German or Arabic the most unpleasantly guttural, English the most versatile and comprehensive, Yiddish the funniest, etc.[36] But this is an aesthetic question, not a question of passionate attachment, no matter how passionate one may get over the matter. Rather, the more passionate one gets about such a matter, the more there are grounds for suspicion that the terms used to describe one's own language and that of another reflect narcissism with regard to oneself and one's group and repulsion with regard to the other. In a word, this love of one's language is a form of displacement of narcissism of the self onto the language, and of derision and disregard onto the language of the other.[37]

What is involved here is metaphorical displacement as well, through the use of the language of the body and of the mother and of the mother's body, to stand in for the self and the group. Moreover, it smacks of a kind of infantilism as well. While it is common enough for such metaphorical imagery to be used in many cultures, it appears to me to be impossible to judge the authenticity of the feelings expressed

[36]For example, 'Any number of attributes like sweet, green, fertile, virgin etc. were used to describe Tamil to assert its sweetness, liveliness, vitality, purity and other qualities'. E. Annamalai, 'Movements for Linguistic Purism: The Case of Tamil', in E. Annamalai (ed.), Language Movements in India (Manasagangotri, Mysore: Central Institute of Indian Languages, 1979), pp. 39–40.

[37]Thus, when one says one hates another language, 'it means you hate the people speaking it.' There are also more subtle ways of expressing this feeling about another language and its speakers, as in the case against Hindi for its lack of 'richness,' which amounts to a statement that its speakers are culturally deficient. The quotes come from a rather rare Tamilian source of sentiment in favour of Hindi as the official language of India, M. Bhaktavatsalam, former chief minister of Tamil Nadu; M. Bhaktavatsalam, The Absurdity of Anti-Hindi Policy (Madras: Udayar, 1978), p. 16.

through such imagery. What can it possibly mean when an adult, such as one Crystal cites, whose language is dying out, says that he feels that he has 'drunk the milk of a strange woman,' that he 'grew up alongside another person,' that he feels like this because he does 'not speak [his] mother's language'?[38] How is it possible that he cannot speak to his mother in her language? What kind of love for his mother can it be that has terminated effective and affective communication with her?

But then it is probably more often the case that one defends one's mother tongue when one cannot speak at all or well a language of wider communication when one's own language is dying out or is useless for improving one's life chances. In such a situation, the use of the mother tongue metaphor must mean that one has lost one's mother's protection and that the speaker feels like a child, isolated in a world of adults who speak another language. There are only two adult responses to such a situation: learn to speak the other language or join a movement to protect and promote one's own and, thereby, protect and promote one's social, economic, and political standing and interests.

Many such movements have been founded, using the infantile and narcissistic metaphors of mother tongue and mother's milk. This 'talk of mother-tongue and mother's milk,' is, as Pollock notes, the talk 'of language and blood,'[39] of separation and difference, of self-glorification and other-disparagement. Like the languages of blood, race, and religious identification, it is a language of political mobilization and separation. In the case of the Tamil language movement of the past century and more, the Tamil language became the central symbol of Tamil regional nationalism, overriding all other 'alternative selves, contrary allegiances, and prior commitments.' Thus, in complete contrast to the north Indian case of Hindi and Urdu, where religio-political identification overrode language identification by absorbing a multiplicity of language/ dialects/mother tongues, the Tamil movement was religiously inclusive, absorbing Hindus, Muslims, and Christians, as long as they acknowledged Tamil as their mother tongue.[40] The disparaged other

[38]David Crystal, *Language Death* (Cambridge: Cambridge University Press, 2000) p. 24.
[39]Sheldon Pollock, 'Cosmopolitan and Vernacular in History', *Public Culture*, 12(3), 2000, p. 596.
[40]Ramaswamy, *Passions of the Tongue*, p. 252.

was the Brahman, dubbed as foreign, Aryan rather than Dravidian in origin. That the Tamil movement has not led to riotous violence against and killing of Brahmans probably reflects more the fact that, though privileged, Tamil Brahmans were relatively small in number, more easily displaced from political power than the Muslims of north India, and were not associated with powerful countermovements such as led to Muslim separatism in north India, the partition of the country in 1947, and a consequent wellspring of resentment against Muslims that has persisted to the present day.

Moreover, consistent with my argument above, this identification of one's language with one's mother, which has gone in the Tamil case to the utmost extreme of creation of a new mother goddess of the Tamil language in the pantheon of deities, this identification has to be instilled. It is not innate, it is not acquired from suckling at the mother's breast or at the milk bottle—to recall the exchange between Joshua Fishman and Ernest Gellner in Seattle over a quarter century ago.[41] All linguistic claims to the contrary concerning mutual comprehensibility or its absence, linguists cannot definitively mark the boundaries between languages and dialects, at least in a way that will put an end to politically arbitrary decisions on the matter. On the contrary, it is not mutual comprehensibility that has led to the absorption of fifteen or twenty, or forty-eight north Indian languages/dialects by Hindi,[42] but the movement, begun in the nineteenth century, to establish the supremacy of the Hindi language through standardization of the Khari/Boli variant. This movement led also to the demotion of various regional and local languages/dialects to inferior status, a process intensified and partly inspired by Hindu-Muslim difference and the opposing movement to maintain the previous supremacy of Urdu. Nor is it mutual incomprehensibility that led to 'the sudden emergence in 1961 of

[41]This exchange, sharp but civil, was quite prolonged, intense, and, at least to me, unforgettable. It took place at a conference held June 11–13, 1976 at the University of Washington. The final papers from this conference were published in Peter F. Sugar (ed.), *Ethnic Diversity and Conflict in Eastern Europe* (Santa Barbara: ABC-Clio, 1980).

[42]The figures vary from census to census depending upon the types of 'groupings' adopted and the definitions thereof. The figure of 48, for example, comes from *Census of India 1999a*, p. 3, where there is a list of 48 mother tongues included in Hindi, plus a further subgrouping of 'Others,' numbering 4, 642, 964 persons.

millions of speakers of Maithili, Magahi, and Bhojpuri, all grouped by the census as dialects of Bihari, in districts that were previously almost solidly Hindi-speaking,' as Schwartzberg has put it.[43] But the point is they were not 'almost solidly Hindi-speaking.' True, knowledge of standardized Hindi had certainly increased somewhat in these areas. But, it was a political decision that led to the re-emergence of these languages, recognized a half-century earlier by Grierson in his great *Linguistic Survey of India*. These languages have since then once again disappeared from or been marginalized in the Indian censuses, or listed as merely mother tongues included in Hindi, because they have failed to develop sustained political movements on their behalf.

Similar recognition and derecognition, classification and reclassification of the languages of India has taken place in other states in India and in the Indian census as a whole.[44] Thus, the 1971 census listed 1,652 mother tongues from Abhalaik to Zunwar (each of which had only one claimed speaker), in four language families and thirty or thirty-two language 'groups.' The 1991 census, however, simplified matters with a new classification of Indian languages into eighteen 'scheduled' languages—those recognized on the Eighth Schedule (ES) of the Constitution[45]—and ninety-six named non-scheduled languages plus one category of 'other languages' not named. Even this reduced list contains some remarkable names, such as 'Kisan,' which means peasant in Hindi, listed in the 1971 census under 'mother tongue with unspecified family affiliation,' along with English for some reason. The number of speakers of 'Kisan' has increased, according to the census volumes, from 50,378 to 162,088.[46]

I should like to say at this point that I do not want to be misunderstood. I believe that the only fair and honest census of languages is one that accepts what the respondent says and notes it down. My point is simply

---

[43]Joseph E. Schwartzberg, 'Factors in the Linguistic Reorganisation of Indian States', in Paul Wallace (ed.), *Region and Nation in India* (New Delhi: Oxford University Press, 1985), p. 170.

[44]Ibid., pp. 180–1.

[45]The number of languages was expanded by an act of parliament in 2003 to include five others, increasing the total number to 22, including Maithili, on which see below.

[46]Ranked 83rd out of 216 recognized mother tongues. Census of India 1999a *Census of India, 1991*, Series 1-*India*, Part IV 13 (i) (a)—C Series, *Language*, Table C-7, *India, States and Union Territories*, by M. Vijayanunni (Delhi: Controller of Publications, 1999), Statement 1, p. 225.

this: the decisions concerning grouping, classification, recognition, are ultimately political decisions, not scientific, linguistic ones. Nor are they based on the greatness of a language's literary tradition, its subtlety or richness or expressiveness. Nor can they be maintained by self-love or mother-love in the absence of a political movement on their behalf. Nor will it improve the life chances of speakers of what Crystal calls 'endangered languages' to set out to preserve them.

SELF-RESPECT, SELF-INTEREST, COMMUNITY, AND LANGUAGE[47]

At the same time, where there exists a substantial base of elite support for the recognition of a language or where other symbolic elements exist that are shared by both the speakers of a marginal or minority language and the dominant language speakers and interests in a country, language movements may garner recognition on the basis of self-interest, community interest, symbolic status or some combination of these factors even in the absence of any significant component of a transfer of the urge for self-respect onto a language movement. Three examples will suggest the possibilities here. The first, already mentioned, is the case of Sanskrit, which is granted separate recognition in the ES of the Constitution of India and in all censuses. The number of persons claiming Sanskrit as their language is less than 50,000, but the number who actually use it as a language of communication is certainly much less. Nor is there any territorially based community of Sanskrit language speakers with political influence. However, Sanskrit is a potent symbol of the distinctive culture and history of the predominant religious grouping in India, standing for Hindu civilization as a whole.[48] Its status, therefore, is virtually unchallengeable and goes virtually unchallenged. It represents no partial interest, has no separate political base, and offends no one, though efforts to 'Sanskritize' the Hindi language by substituting words of Sanskrit origin for the

[47]This section has been added to the original version of the article as a consequence of an email discussion with E. Annamalai.

[48]Put in another way, Sanskrit has a predominant function in India 'of expressing Hinduism.' See Rajeshwari V. Pandharipande, 'Minority Matters: Issues in Minority Languages in India', *International Journal on Multicultural Societies*, 4 (2), 2002, pp. 213–34.

prevailing words that have Arabic or Persian roots are resented, and even ridiculed by many.

A second example[49] comes from the movement by Sindhi speakers in India in the 1950s for inclusion of the Sindhi language in the ES of the Constitution. This was a movement, mostly of Hindus,[50] displaced from their home territory in what became Pakistan in 1947. Those displaced, who moved to India, contained a very high proportion of traders, businessmen, and highly educated persons. As Table 4.1 has shown, they soon acquired proficiency in either Hindi or English (or both) and actually shifted to the use of Hindi as the home language in preference to Sindhi. There was little question of self-respect or loss of it, though there was then and persists now a high degree of resentment among many Sindhis over the creation of Pakistan and their displacement from their home region. How then to interpret the bases for the movement and its success? Here, the answer would be that a combination of community interest, self-interest, and 'language symbolism' were involved, none of which threatened the perceived national interest, but rather could be seen as in the national interest. It would obviously be beneficial for the entire Sindhi community to have the community recognized as a separate group within the Indian state, but as one part of the broader Hindu community. There would be no 'collective good(s)' problem here. What was good for the community was good for the group. Recognition of the community *by means of its language* enhanced the status of the community as a whole and, by that very fact, of every individual member of it. Finally, recognition of the language involved no cost to the Government of India while providing some advantage. Sindhis, having now no territory to call their own, could not threaten the unity of India. Further, recognition of the Sindhi language as a language of India by the central government would also imply a rejection, in principle, of the very idea of the partition of India and the separation of the province of Sindh from India.[51]

[49]Suggested to me in a personal communication from E. Annamalai.

[50]And Sahajdhari Sikhs.

[51]This case is the mirror image, the precise opposite of the rejection of the Punjabi language by Punjabi-speaking Hindus, in the Punjab province in the censuses of 1950 and 1960, when the majority of Punjabi speakers declared that Hindi was their mother tongue, not Punjabi. They disowned their own language for reasons of political and community interest to separate themselves from the Sikhs and their demands for a separate province and took

The third example comes from the quite recent recognition of the Maithili language in the ES of the Constitution.[52] This recognition came thirty years *after* the failure of an elite-dominated movement for recognition of the separate status of both the language and the Maithili region.[53] In this case again, there was no question of self-respect, no particular benefit for the vast majority of the people of the region claimed as Maithili speakers, and only marginal material benefit for elite language speakers, but considerable symbolic importance for the latter. Most important, there was *no* political movement before the granting of recognition to the Maithili language in the ES. The benefit, rather, was for the political party that promoted it, namely, the BJP in power at the time in the central government (but not in the state of Bihar), whose leaders sought to establish and consolidate a political base in the Maithili-speaking region among the upper castes who claimed Maithili as their mother tongue[54] and who would be gratified by such recognition after so many long years of disregard by all political parties. This recognition also came at a time when, contrary to the situation thirty years earlier, the leaders of the country had lost their fear of 'Balkanization' of India and, instead of resisting movements for recognition of linguistic and other regional groups demanding separate states of their own, were now prepared to use such demands for carving up the larger states—and even districts—of India into smaller units for the sake of political advantage.[55]

---

to Hindi instead, whereas the Sindhi speakers, though they also switched to Hindi (and English), demanded recognition of the very language they were discarding or relegating to mere symbolic status.

[52]By the Constitution (Ninety-second Amendment) Act, 2003.

[53]On which, see *LRP*, chapter II, and specifically on the earlier failure to gain recognition in the ES, pp. 105–6.

[54]Support for this argument may be found in the excellent M.A. thesis of Anshuman Pandey, 'Avenging Maithili: The Eighth Schedule and Electoral Politics in Bihar, 1999–2004', Jackson School of International Studies, University of Washington, June 2006.

[55]The recognition of Maithili also indicates that immediate political advantage nowadays may override the fears of proponents of Hindi that the status of Hindi as one of the two official languages of the country may be threatened by the separate recognition of languages such as Maithili, which are classified as 'dialects' of Hindi, rather than as separate languages. The consequence of such recognition would be a reduction of the numbers of Hindi speakers in the decennial censuses. This point is made in Pandey, 'Avenging Maithili'. Among the so-called Hindi 'dialects' still not recognized as separate languages in the ES is Bhojpuri, which, if numbers alone were a criterion, had a better claim than Maithili to such recognition. The

These examples, however, constitute types of deviation from the more general pattern of movements for language recognition in the modern world, that is, during the colonial and post-colonial periods of the last two centuries especially. The more general pattern is outlined in the next section.

VERNACULAR EMPOWERMENT, AND DISEMPOWERMENT

I want to conclude by outlining a preliminary schemata of the movement, in the competition between elite and non-elite groups and languages, from powerlessness to power, from being disempowered to being empowered, and the threat of a reverse movement as well. The movement will follow a different course depending upon where the group is placed at any chosen starting point. For the powerless, the movement is as follows:

lower-level elite (writers, teachers, lower-rung bureaucrats) promotion of the vernacular, inculcating > linguistic narcissism, creating > a movement for self-respect, and > group recognition, > identifying the language of the dominant as alien, enslaving, and (sometimes) corrupt, leading to > language purification, and > official recognition of the vernacular, displacement of the alien, enslaving language, and empowerment of the formerly powerless

The movement in the other direction may be encapsulated as follows:

dominant elite defence of the language of rule as the most fit instrument for communication and modernity and as the repository of the glories of the people's high culture > disparagement of the vernaculars as unfit and uncouth > acceptance of the vernaculars as fit only for primary and secondary education, good enough for the masses, for whom education in the elite language will remain unattainable > continued use of the elite language at the highest official levels, against all competitors > and retention of the power of the upper class, upper caste users in government and/or in the global network of intellectual and corporate power

These schemata, of course, are only that, and numerous variations in detail occur in practice, most especially, as in the north Indian case,

---

1991 census found more than 23 million Bhojpuri speakers and 10.5 million Magahi speakers compared to 7.7 million Maithili speakers.

where there have been competing vernaculars as well as competing elite languages. Moreover, the competitive movements may, as in the Indian case, result in compromises. But the compromises also need to be evaluated with regard to the relations of power that are sanctified through them. For now, I can do no more than provide some examples of how the processes outlined have developed in India, how they have come in conflict, and how they have been resolved.

Examples

The origins of the Hindi-Urdu controversy in north India lay in the initial encouragement in the 1860s of two alternative media of education in the primary and secondary schools, Hindi and Urdu, which then produced 'vernacular elites' educated primarily 'in Hindi or Urdu and looking to government service for their livelihoods'.[56] The dominant elites in UP were Urdu-speaking and Urdu-writing,[57] their position was gradually challenged by the new Hindi-speaking, Devanagari-writing elites, culminating in the achievement in 1900 of official recognition for the latter, along with Urdu, in the courts and primary and secondary schools. It is important to note that the situation in north India was entirely different from that in other regions such as Bengal, Tamil Nadu, and Maharashtra, where the issue was primarily one of standardizing a single vernacular language, Bengali or Marathi.[58] Moreover, in these regions, particularly Tamil Nadu, a second issue was the separation between high and low versions of the language, that is, the issue of diglossia. Forms of diglossia have arisen in all major language regions of India, but Tamil is generally used as

[56]Christopher King, 'Images of Virtue and Vice: The Hindi-Urdu Controversy in Two Nineteenth-century Plays', in *Religious Controversy in British India; Dialogues in South Asian Languages* (Albany: State University of New York Press, 1992), p. 124.

[57]It should be stressed that these elites, though predominantly Muslim, comprised also high caste Hindus in government employment, especially from the Kayastha caste. Brass, *Language, Religion, and Politics*, chapter III; Robinson, *Separatism Among Indian Muslims*, pp. 33–4.

[58]On the rise of vernacular education and vernacular elites in the Marathi-speaking areas in the 19th century, see Naregal, which is, however, somewhat deficient in providing detailed facts and figures on linguistic change, spread, education, literacy, and the like. Veena Naregal, *Language Politics, Elites, and the Public Sphere* (New Delhi: Permanent Black, 2001).

the classic example in South Asia.[59] Diglossia also, of course, is an issue that involves elite-mass differentiations.

In all cases, however, the inculcation of linguistic narcissism is prominent, as well as the identification of the vernacular language with the mother. In the north, in addition, disparagement of the competing vernacular and, of the other 'mother' as well, is intense. Thus, in the examples given by King from nineteenth century Hindi plays, Persian is described as the mother of Urdu, whose women are prostitutes.[60] India itself has become identified, among Hindu revivalists in the northern, Hindi-speaking region with the mother, Bharat Mata,[61] who has been elevated to the status of a Hindu deity, which has been 'taken out in procession and worshipped by hundreds of thousands of people' in militant Hindu-sponsored movements of popular mobilization.[62] In fact, there is a mother trinity comprising 'Mother India, Mother Ganga and Mother Cow'.[63]

And, in Tamil Nadu, the Tamil language is represented by the newly created goddess, Tamilttay, figure of womanly virtue, 'benevolent mother and pure virgin'[64] whose body is threatened with violation by those opposed to the Tamil language, who do not share the devotion that has been and continues to be required for its preservation and advancement[65] especially against Hindi.[66] The threat of violation of its women, a trope that also appears continuously in the northern Hindu-Muslim discourse of animosity, is a threat to the community, to dishonour the group as a whole, the Hindu, community or the Tamil speech community.[67] Ramaswamy also notes, like Pollock, that the

[59]See Francis Britto, which discusses, and applies to the Tamil language in south India, Ferguson's theory, and its 'extension' by Fishman. Britto, *Diglossia: A Study of the Theory with Application to Tamil* (Washington D.C.: Georgetown University Press, 1986).

[60]From Pandit Gauri Datta's Play (c. 1883–1900) in King, 'Images of Virtue and Vice', in *Religious Controversy in British India*, p. 132.

[61]Peter van der Veer, '"God must be Liberated": A Hindu Liberation Movement in Ayodhya', *Modern Asian Studies*, 31(2), 1987, p. 293.

[62]Yogendra K. Malik, and Dhirendra K. Vajpeyi, 'The Rise of Hindu Militancy: India's Secular Democracy at Risk,' *Asian Survey*, 39(3), 1989, p. 315.

[63]Gautam Navlakha, 'A Show of "Hindu Power"', *EPW*, 1 April 1989, p. 658.

[64]Ramaswamy, *Passions of the Tongue*, p. 80.

[65]Ibid., p. 84.

[66]K. Perumal Udayar, 'Introduction', in M. Bhaktavatsalam, *The Absurdity of Anti-Hindi Policy*, p. 4.

[67]Ramaswamy, *Passions of the Tongue*, p. 112.

language of 'motherhood' in the Tamil devotional movement is also the language of 'shared blood'.[68] What transpires in this Tamil narrative of linguistic devotion is, as Ramaswamy has described it, a situation in which the 'self merges into the imagined self of Tamil, whose life experiences are subordinated to the superior cause of the language',[69] that is, to the group.

The dishonouring of the mother and the group implies a threat to the purity of the group, to its very being and identity, which requires, therefore, purification,[70] that is to say, removal of the impurities that have arisen as a consequence of previous and present contacts with alien, enslaving others: Muslims or Brahmans, the Urdu language or Sanskrit or English. In its mildest form, in language movements of purification, it is a matter of removing words identified with an alien language and disallowing further borrowings.[71] In its most extreme form, it may involve removal of the other persons through violence, justified as retaliatory against the alleged depredations of the other. It may also require self-sacrifice in defence of the language, the religion, the community. What is involved in all cases, limited or extreme, is a search for dignity and self-respect for oneself through identification with the group and the community and the elevation of its symbols of identity. That demand for self-respect, however, does not in all cases call for 'respectful acceptance'[72] of other groups. Indeed, it commonly works in quite the opposite way, as the Indian examples—and many others in other parts of the world—have amply demonstrated.[73]

[68]Ibid., p. 63.

[69]Ibid., pp. 182–3.

[70]Annamalai, 'The Linguistic and Social Dimensions of Purism', in *The Politics of Language Purism*, p. 230.

[71]For the changing historical relationship in this respect between Tamil and Sanskrit, and their principal users and adherents (non-Brahmans and Brahmans), see Annamalai 'Movement for Linguistic Purism', in *Language Movements in India*, pp. 38–40.

[72]Joshna A. Fishman, 'Social Theory and Ethnography: Neglected Perspectives on Language and Ethnicity in Eastern Europe', in Sugar (ed.), *Ethnic Diversity and Conflict in Eastern Europe*, p. 95.

[73]Indeed, Shapiro has argued that language purification movements carry the odor of moral as well as linguistic differentiation, dividing the morally/linguistically pure from their impure, even evil opposites. Michael J. Shapiro, 'A Political Approach to Language Purism', in Jernudd and Shapiro (eds), *The Politics of Language Purism*, pp. 22–3.

The most one can say is that there are benign and malignant forms of the search for self-respect through group identity, but that all such movements have the potential for disparagement of and violence towards the other. It is, therefore, necessary to acknowledge that such movements may be required in order to change 'relations of power, authority and control between Self and the Other'.[74] Once the power relations have been altered, however, the dichotomization that has been created may yet persist in the form of scapegoating when the rising group finds that its aspirations are still blocked. Such is the case in contemporary India where Muslim privileges were ended a half century ago, where Hindi is the official language of the country, but where India itself and its leaders have little respect in the world of nations. Suffering from widespread feelings of *ressentiment* against the West, whose level of economic growth and well-being they have not been able to approach, militant Hindus find the source of their problems in the Muslims, whom they continue to describe as 'pampered', to discriminate against their language and script, and to produce anti-Muslim riots and pogroms in numerous cities and towns, especially in the northern and western parts of the country.[75]

Insofar as India as a whole is concerned, however, language is not now at the centre of the group conflict and violence that are endemic. On the contrary, from the point of view of 'national integration', the resolution of the language issues has been a success story in several respects. First, the country has been divided into federal units in most of which there is a single dominant, official language of education and administration. Second, a viable compromise has been reached between advocates of Hindi and those who opposed its adoption as official language of the country through the simultaneous retention of English as an additional official language. Third, partly as a result,

---

[74]Bjord H. Jernudd, 'The Texture of Language Purism: An Introduction', in Jernudd and Shapiro (eds), *The Politics of Language Purism*, p. 1.

[75]Paul R. Brass, *The Production of Hindu-Muslim Violence in Contemporary India* (Seattle: University of Washington Press, 2003). The position of India in the world of nations has, however, been undergoing some change in very recent years, as its economy appears to be booming, some of its entrepreneurs are operating effectively in the global economy, and the United States appears to be courting India. But this raises other questions that are not relevant to the main arguments in this essay.

competition among the upper-tier elites for power and economic advantage has been equalized in the country as a whole.

From the point of view of empowerment and disempowerment, however, the inter-linguistic balance that prevails in India rests upon a base of mass illiteracy in most languages and a consequent demarcation of opportunities for power, as well as dignity and economic advancement, into the three broad tiers outlined earlier: the upper elite tier of the bilinguals, who are proficient in English,; the intermediate tier of educated speakers of a dominant regional language only; and the lower tier of poorly educated or illiterate monolinguals or bilinguals in regional and/or local languages/dialects/mother tongues. A worthwhile task for future research on language and power in contemporary India would be to collect systematic data on the relationship between linguistic capabilities and employment in selected sectors of the Indian polity and economy, on the one hand, and linguistic capabilities and advancement in politics, on the other hand.

References

Annamalai, E., 1979. 'Movement for Linguistic Purism: The Case of Tamil,' in E. Annamalai (ed.), *Language Movements in India*. Manasagangotri, Mysore: Central Institute of Indian Languages.

———, 1989 'The Linguistic and Social Dimensions of Purism,' in Bjorn H. Jernudd and Michael J. Shapiro (eds), *The Politics of Language Purism*. Berlin: Mouton de Gruyter.

Anonymous, 2003. 'BPO Boom and Teaching of English,' *Economic and Political Weekly* [hereafter *EPW*], June 21, pp. 2444–5.

Arel, Dominique, 2002. 'Language Categories in Censuses: Backward—or Forward-Looking?' in David I. Kertzer and Dominique Arel (eds), *Census and Identity: The Politics of Race, Ethnicity, and Language in National Censuses*. Cambridge: Cambridge University Press, 2002.

Bhaktavatsalam, M., 1978. *The Absurdity of Anti-Hindi Policy*. Madras: Udayar.

Brass, Paul R., 1974. *Language, Religion, and Politics in North India*. Cambridge: Cambridge University Press.

———, 2003. *The Production of Hindu-Muslim Violence in Contemporary India*. Seattle: University of Washington Press.

Britto, Francis, 1986. *Diglossia: A Study of the Theory with Application to Tamil*. Washington, D.C.: Georgetown University Press.

Casolari, Marzia, 2002. 'Role of Benares in Constructing Political Hindu Identity,' *EPW*, April 13.

Census of India, *Census Data Online* 1991 *censusindia.net/cendat/ datatable2.htm*, accessed 5 March 2003.

_____, 1999a. *Census of India, 1991*, Series 1—*India*, Part IV B (i)(a)—C Series, *Language*, Table C—7, *India, States and Union Territories*, by M. Vijayanunni, Delhi: Controller of Publications, Statement 1.

_____, 1999b. *Census of India, 1991*, Series 1—*India*, Part IV B (i)(b)—C Series, *Bilingualism and Trilingualism*, Table C-8, *India, States and Union Territories*, by M. Vijayanunni, Delhi: Controller of Publications, Statement 1.

_____, 2001. *Census of India 2001*, Number of Literates and Literacy Rate by Sex, *Census Data Online* 2001 *censusindia.net*, accessed 23 August 2006.

Chatterjee, Partha, 1993. *The Nation and Its Fragments: Colonial and Postcolonial Histories*. Princeton, N.J.: Princeton University Press.

Crystal, David, 2000. *Language Death*. Cambridge: Cambridge University Press.

Dasgupta, Probal, 2001. 'Introduction' to E. Annamalai, *Managing Multilinguism in India: Political and Linguistic Manifestations*. New Delhi: Sage.

Farouqui, Ather, 1995. 'The Emerging Dilemma of the Urdu Press in India: A Viewpoint,' *South Asia*, 18(1), pp. 91–103.

Fishman, Joshua A., 1980. 'Social Theory and Ethnography: Neglected Perspectives on Language and Ethnicity in Eastern Europe,' in Peter Sugar (ed.), *Ethnic Diversity and Conflict in Eastern Europe*. Santa Barbara, CA: ABC-Clio.

Faust, David and Richa Nagar, 2001. 'Politics of Development in Postcolonial India: English-Medium Education and Social Fracturing,' *EPW*, May 28, pp. 2879–83.

Ghosh, Anindita, 2002. 'Revisiting the 'Bengal Renaissance': Literary Bengali and Low-Life Print in Colonial India,' *EPW*, 19 October, online at epw.org.in.

Government of India (GoI), 1995. *The Thirty-Fifth Report of the Commissioner for Linguistic Minorities [CLM] in India (For the period July 1994 to June 1995)*.

Hobsbawm, E.J., 1990. *Nations and Nationalism Since 1780: Programme, Myth, Reality*. Cambridge: Cambridge University Press, 1990.

Jernudd, Bjord H., 1989. 'The Texture of Language Purism: An Introduction,' in Bjord H. Jernudd and Michael J. Shapiro (eds), *The Politics of Language Purism*. Berlin: Mouton de Gruyter.

Khalidi, Omar, 2003. *Khaki and Ethnic Violence in India*. New Delhi: Three Essays.

Khare, Santosh Kumar, 2002. 'Truth about Language in India,' *EPW*, December 14, online at epw.org.in.

King, Christopher, 1992. 'Images of Virtue and Vice: The Hindi-Urdu Controversy in Two Nineteenth-century Hindi Plays,' in Kenneth W. Jones (ed.), *Religious Controversy in British India: Dialogues in South Asian Languages*. Albany: State University of New York Press.

Kishwar, Madhu, 1998. 'Religion at the Service of Nationalism: An Analysis of Sangh Parivar Politics,' in Madhu Kishwar, *Religion at the Service of Nationalism and Other Essays*. Delhi: Oxford University Press, pp. 248–78.

Latifi, Danial, 1999. 'Urdu in UP,' *Nation and the World*, 16 August 1999, pp. 44–46.

Malik, Yogendra K. and Dhirendra K. Vajpeyi, 1989. 'The Rise of Hindu Militancy: India's Secular Democracy at Risk,' *Asian Survey*, 39(3), pp. 308-25.

Metcalf, Barbara D., 1982. *Islamic Revival in British India: Deoband, 1860–1900*. Princeton, N.J.: Princeton University Press, 1982.

Naregal, Veena, 2001. *Language Politics, Elites, and the Public Sphere*. New Delhi: Permanent Black.

Navlakha, Gautam, 1989. 'A Show of Hindu Power', *EPW*, 1 April 1989, p. 658.

Pandey, Anshuman, 2006. 'Avenging Maithili: The Eighth Schedule and Electoral Politics in Bihar, 1999–2004', Master's Thesis, Jackson School of International Studies, University of Washington.

Pandharipande, Rajeshwari V., 2002. 'Minority Matters: Issues in Minority Languages in India', *International Journal on Multicultural Societies*, 4(2), pp. 213–34.

Pant, Jagdish C., 2002. 'Urdu as Mother Tongue Medium at Primary Level', unpublished paper presented at the conference organized by the Dr Zakir Hussain Study Circle at Vigyan Bhawan, New Delhi, 8–11 February 2002.

Pollock, Sheldon, 2000. 'Cosmopolitan and Vernacular in History,' *Public Culture*, 12(3), pp. 591–625.

Ramaswamy, Sumathi, 1997. *Passions of the Tongue: Language Devotion in Tamil India, 1891–1970*. Berkeley: University of California Press.

Robinson, Francis, 1975. *Separatism Among Indian Muslims: The Politics of the United Provinces' Muslims, 1860–1923*. Delhi: Vikas.

Schwartzberg, Joseph E., 1985. 'Factors in the Linguistic Reorganization of Indian States,' in Paul Wallace (ed.), *Region and Nation in India*. New Delhi: Oxford, pp. 155-82.

Shackle, Christopher and Rupert Snell, 1990. *Hindi and Urdu since 1800: A Common Reader*. London: School of Oriental and African Studies.

Shapiro, Michael J., 1989. 'A Political Approach to Language Purism,' in Bjorn

H. Jernudd and Michael J. Shapiro (eds), *The Politics of Language Purism.* Berlin: Mouton de Gruyter, pp. 21–29.

Sugar, Peter F. (ed.), 1980. *Ethnic Diversity and Conflict in Eastern Europe.* Santa Barbara: ABC-Clio.

Swaan, Abram De, 2001. *Words of the World: The Global Language System.* Cambridge: Polity.

Udayar, K. Perumal, 1978. 'Introduction,' in S. Bhaktavatsalam, *The Absurdity of Anti-Hindi Policy,* Madras, K. Perumal Udayar, pp. 3–8.

van der Veer, Peter, 1987. '"God must be Liberated!": A Hindu Liberation Movement in Ayodhya,' *Modern Asian Studies,* 31(2), pp. 283-301.

Washbrook D.A., 1982. 'Ethnicity and Racialism in Colonial Indian Society,' in R. Ross (ed.), *Racism and Colonialism.* The Hague: Martinus Nijhoff, pp. 143–81.

PART II
LANGUAGE, REGION, AND STATE

5

The Political Saliency of Language in Bihar and Uttar Pradesh*

Selma K. Sonntag

What makes language a potentially explosive political issue? Recently it has been a salient political issue in various economically and politically diverse states, as shown by language riots in Bangalore (India) in the autumn of 1994 over Urdu language broadcasts, wrangling over the status of Russian in the newly independent Baltic states of the former Soviet Union, and the secessionist referendum in Quebec in the autumn of 1995. In contrast, in the USA, although the language issue has been raised by numerous politicians, including presidential candidate Robert Dole in 1995,[1] it remains on the back-burner. In India also the issue was of such relative unimportance during the 1970s that Paul Brass could write of that period, '[s]everal studies of various aspects of India's language problems were published, arriving at a consensus that the major linguistic issues were resolved'.[2]

Theoretical explanations are as varied as the cases themselves. Analyses range from the earlier Marxist and liberal theses that

---

*Originally published as 'The Political Saliency of Language in Bihar and Uttar Pradesh', *Journal of Commonwealth and Comparative Politics*, 34 (2), July 1996, pp. 1–18.

[1]David S. Broder, 'Dole Climbs Aboard the Drive to Make English "Official"', *The Washington Post National Weekly Edition* (Washington, DC), 11–17 September 1995, p. 13.

[2]Paul R. Brass, *Ethnicity and Nationalism* (New Delhi: Sage, 1991), p. 119.

modernization mitigates conflict based on ascriptive identities to the more recent contention that modernization breeds such conflict.[3] Parsonian 'grand theory' approaches to explaining the political saliency of linguistic (or religious or ethnic) identity, that is, viewing larger impersonal social forces such as modernization as the cause, frequently lead to the prescription of the state as mediator or regulator of language conflict.[4] Neo-Marxist structuralists, on the other hand, recognize the state's vested interest in reproducing structural inequalities that exacerbate linguistic (or ethnic or religious) differentiation, but they often fail to grasp the fluidity of structural relations caused by the dialectics of subalternity.[5]

In rejecting macro-causal approaches which reduce the political arena to a neutral forum for mediating social forces or to a tool of a particular group (be it linguistic, ethnic, religious, or class-based), I assume that politics itself is the arena of contestation. I hypothesize that the nature of this contest affects the degree of saliency of language issues.[6] In adopting the comparative approach, I need to 'find cases that are as similar as possible, in as many aspects as possible, and then find a crucial difference that can explain what one wants to explain'.[7] The cases presented here, based partly on field research in 1993-4, are the two north Indian states of Bihar and Uttar Pradesh (UP). While differences exist in the details, in general terms, Bihar and UP are relatively similar in historical, cultural, linguistic and economic

[3]See Selma K. Sonntag, 'Political Science and Contact Linguistics', in H. Goebl, P.H. Nelde, Z. Stary, and W. Wolck ((eds), *Contact Linguistics: An International Handbook of Contemporary Research* (Berlin: Walter de Gruyter, 1996); Saul Newman, 'Does Modernization Breed Ethnic Political Conflict?', *World Politics*, 43, 1991, pp. 451–78.

[4]William R. Beer, 'Toward a Theory of Linguistic Mobilization', in W. Beer and J. Jacob (eds), *Language Policy and National Unity* (Totowa, NJ: Rowman & Allanheld, 1985), pp. 217–35.

[5]India has been fertile ground for subaltern studies which attempt to alter the dominant historical discourse by injecting the (largely unwritten) history of the subordinate masses. See Ranajit Guha (ed.), *Subaltern Studies* (Delhi: Oxford University Press, 1982–9).

[6]'Salient' is defined in dictionaries as 'prominent' or 'conspicuous'. In the analysis offered here, a high degree of saliency means that language issues figure regularly and prominently on the political agenda. The latter includes policy activity (for example, legislation), government pronouncements, direct political action (demonstrations, strikes, riots), electoral propaganda and media coverage.

[7]Adam Przeworski, *et al.*, 'The Role of Theory in Comparative Politics: A Symposium', *World Politics*, 48 (1), 1995, p. 17.

aspects.[8] The two states differ, however, in terms of recent politics. What this analysis of the differences in politics in the two states reveals is that when political competition is fierce, characterized by rivalry between established and emerging elites, then language issues attain a high degree of saliency. Such fierce competition generally occurs when the political leadership of the state does not have an independent basis of power, when it is vying for power as opposed to consolidating its existing power base, and when it is unable to rely on the support of non-party intermediary groups.

Although some of the political variables identified above may be particular to the case studies examined here, they provide a listing of potential variables that may hold explanatory value in other cases—for example, the Quiet Revolution in Quebec suggests the emergence of a competing elite while, in contrast, the recent dearth of interest in the language issue in the US may be linked to its raising by a political party that is consolidating its power rather than vying for it. As Peter Evans has recently pointed out, 'a compelling interpretation of a particular case is only interesting if it points to ways of understanding other cases as well'.[9] Let me now proceed with what I hope is a compelling interpretation of the political saliency of language issues in two north Indian states.

The degree of political saliency of language issues differs between Bihar and UP, and this is what I propose to explain by analysing recent politics. While language issues have not been prominent since 1980 in Bihar, the same is not true for UP. Tension and controversy over these issues continued in UP throughout the 1980s and into the 1990s. Although often seemingly crowded out by the issues of religion and caste, language remains salient in UP. The language issues are frequently linked with these other 'burning' issues, but it is the contrast between saliency of language issues in Bihar and UP that is so apparent rather

[8]Although it may be argued that partition affected UP more severely than Bihar, both states form part of the same historical-cultural Hindi heartland. Some suggest that Bihar is more linguistic, or at least dialectally diverse than UP, given that Maithili, Bhojpuri, Magadhi, and so on are spoken as mother tongues, but, as Ashis Banerjee notes, UP also has great dialectal variation. And while Bihar may be poorer than UP, both states are among the most economically backward in India. Ashis Banerjee, 'Is U.P. Viable', *Seminar*, 432, 1995, p. 39.

[9]Peter Evans, *et al.*, 'The Role of Theory in Comparative Politics: A Symposium', p. 4.

than between religious and caste issues, rendering the former especially
relevant for comparison. The contrast between Bihar and UP is evident
in regard to the Hindi versus Urdu controversy (that is, the controversy
over granting Urdu second official language status) and the Hindi versus
English controversy (the *angrezi hatao,* or remove English, movement).
These are the two language issues that I shall examine in this article.

THE URDU CONTROVERSY

1980 is a useful starting point for an analysis of recent controversies
over: Urdu in Bihar and UP because in that year the Congress(I) party
manifesto for the 1980 general election promised to grant second official
language status to Urdu in these two states. This was a symbolic electoral
appeal to Muslims: official language status could be granted by a
legislative act without necessarily affecting the linguistic behaviour of
either Urdu or non-Urdu speakers.[10] Indeed, with hindsight, many
Muslim Urdu-supporters in UP, where the issue was and remains very
contentious, argue that such symbolism is the wrong approach. They
argue that a more concrete approach of using Urdu as a medium of
instruction in schools, for example, would have yielded more benefits
for Urdu speakers and less political controversy. This concrete approach
was outlined in the Gujral Report on Urdu that had been commissioned
by the Congress(I) government in the early 1970s, then shelved, then
'leapfrogged' over by the Congress(I) 1980 manifesto promise.[11]

Upon winning the 1980 general election and subsequent state
elections, the Congress(I) in Bihar and UP acted upon this manifesto
promise in quite different ways. In Bihar, within forty-eight hours of

[10]See AS, 'Language Muddle', *Economic and Political Weekly,* 15(8), 20 September 1980,
pp. 1580–1. This is similar to the (lack of) impact of the 1986 amendment to the California
state constitution making English the official language of the state.

[11]'I.K. Gujral on the Story of His Report on Urdu, Seminar, April, 1987', *Muslim India,*
54, June 1987, p. 257. The preference for a more concrete and less symbolic Urdu policy was
expressed by Urdu supporters in personal interviews in Nov. 1993 in Lucknow and Jan.
1994 in New Delhi; see also *Muslim India,* September 1984, p. 430. I.K. Gujral made the
same argument himself in 1984; 'Controversy will Hamper Promotion of Urdu', *Indian Express*
(New Delhi), 5 April 1984. Paul R. Brass also notes this argument at the end of his discussion
of 'The Status of the Urdu Language'. In this discussion Brass tends to assume that Bihar
and UP are similar if not identical in their treatment of Urdu in the 1980s, a position with
which I disagree. Paul R. Brass, *The Politics of India since Independence* (New York: Cambridge
University Press, 1990), pp. 156–9.

the new Congress(I) government in June 1980, a cabinet decision had been taken to make Urdu official, with an ordinance to this effect issued in November and legislation passed in December.[12] In contrast, in UP, Chief Minister V.P. Singh, after failing to act on repeated promises, finally issued an ordinance in 1982 granting Urdu status as the 'second language' (but not second 'official' language) for limited purposes. The V.P. Singh government never attempted to convert the ordinance into legislation.

What was the difference between Bihar and UP in 1980 in regard to Urdu-language policy and what was the impact of this difference, on language politics in each state? Ironically, the answer is very similar to Brass's in explaining the reverse circumstances in the 1960s when 'the Urdu issue and communal politics in Bihar took such a bitter violent turn in comparison to UP.': Brass pointed to 'differences in political leadership and coalition patterns in the two states' in his explanation.[13]

The 1980 difference in political leadership on the Urdu issue in the two states can be traced at least partially to differences in the bases of power of the new Congress (I) chief ministers. The Bihar Chief Minister (the chief executive of the state government), Jagannath Mishra, as a Maithili Brahmin, already had the backing of the most politically active region and caste group in the state and of Maithili speakers.[14] Maithili, recognised by the national Sahitya Academy, is the one other language

---

[12]AS, 'Language Muddle'; 'Urdu Made Second Official Language', *The Indian Nation* (Patna), 20 November 1980, p. 1.

[13]Paul R. Brass, *Language, Religion and Politics in North India* (London: Cambridge University Press, 1974), p. 269.

[14]Interview with members of *Chetna Samiti*, a Maithili-language organisation, Patna, 8 October 1993. Brass (*Language, Religion and Politics*, pp. 51–2, 93) notes that although north Bihar (which includes Mithilanchal, an administrative term that is increasingly used to designate ancient Mithila) is more economically and socially backward than the rest of the state, it has a higher voter turnout; AS ('Language Muddle', 1980) notes the 'political power of (the Maithili) regional elite'.

The question of whether Maithili is a language specific to Maithili Brahmins or is spoken by all castes in Mithilanchal is still widely debated in Bihar, with a large dose of politics influencing one's assessment. For example, Ghulam Sarwar, Speaker of the Assembly, and a Janata Dal Muslim representing a district in Mithilanchal, claimed that his non-Brahmin constituents speak Hindi or a non-Maithili dialect (interview with Ghulam Sarwar, Patna, 9 October 1993). This is the position taken as well by his boss, Lallu Prasad Yadav, as will be discussed further in this article. The Director of the A.N. Sinha Institute of Social Studies, a think-tank closely linked with the current Janata Dal state government, himself a non-Brahmin Maithili speaker, claims that Maithili is the common dialect throughout the region (conversation with M.N. Karna, Patna, 13 October 1993).

in Bihar, in addition to Urdu, that has a strong claim for official sanction. Although there were some Maithili protests against Mishra's legislation regarding Urdu in 1980, it was easily contained. Mishra appealed to Maithili speakers not to protest the Urdu decision, while he dedicated new hospital units and other pork-barrel favours in the Maithili region where the first ten districts to be covered by the new legislation were located.[15]

With his home base secure, Jagannath Mishra could attempt to extend his appeal. During his tenure as chief minister during the emergency (1975–7), Mishra had implemented rural policies that endeared him to dalits while alienating farmers.[16] Since significant portions of the latter formed the support base for the opposition, in power in the late 1970s between Mishra's two stints as chief minister, Mishra could target Muslims to shore up his power base without further reinforcing the solidarity of his opposition. Indeed, the opposition, when in power in the late 1960s, had tried to act upon making Urdu official, only to be internally torn apart by language riots because of dissension by its Jana Sangh coalition partner.[17] In contrast to 1967, in 1980, 'opponents of the government [including most of the BJP] did not outright oppose granting status to Urdu. Even opposition benches at moments congratulated the government for the decision'.[18] Five to ten people died in protesting the Urdu policy in 1980 compared to over 150 in 1967.[19] A bandh (strike) organised by a transitory student group in mid-

[15]*The Indian Nation* (Patna), 12 December 1980, p. 3; 4 December 1980, p. 4; 13 December 1980; 22 December 1980, p. 4; AS, 'Language Muddle'.

[16]Francine R. Frankel, 'Caste, Land and Dominance in Bihar', in F. Frankel and M.S.A. Rao (eds), *Dominance and State Power in Modern India,* Vol. 1 (Delhi: Oxford University Press, 1989), p. 105. See also P.N. Ojha (gen. ed.), *History of Indian National Congress in Bihar, 1885–1895* (Patna: K.P. Jayaswal Research Institute, 1985), pp. 802–13.

[17]Brass, *Language, Religion and Politics,* pp. 260–72. It was the role of the Jana Sangh in the non-Congress coalition governments in the late 1960s in Bihar and UP that Brass contrasts in explaining the differing effect of coalition patterns on the Urdu issue in each state.

[18]'Smooth Passage for Urdu Bill', *The Indian Nation* (Patna), 20 December 1980, p. 1. When asked what was the biggest difference between 1967 and 1980 in regard to the Urdu issue, Ghulam Sarwar (who was very involved in 1967; see Brass, *Language, Religion and Politics,* pp. 243–4) immediately pointed to the obstructionist position taken by the Jana Sangh in 1967 compared with the virtual inactivity of the BJP (the successor to the Jana Sangh) on the issue in 1980 (interview with Ghulam Sarwar, Patna, 9 October 1993).

[19]*The Indian Nation* (Patna), 18/19/20 December 1980, p. 1; 'Bihar CPM Backs Stir on Farmers' Dues', *Hindustan Times* (New Delhi), 6 January 1981, p. 5. For numbers dead in 1967, see Brass, *Language, Religion and Politics,* p. 261.

December 1980 was as much, if not more, in protest against a police lathi charge (baton charge) during an earlier demonstration as it was against the Urdu policy itself.[20] The opposition leader, Karpuri Thakur, opposed the bandh and 'deprecated the tendency to communalise the language issue'.[21] However, apparently in response to the mostly student-led agitations, Chief Minister Jagannath Mishra did slow down implementation of the legislation.[22]

Thus, with relatively little fallout, Jagannath Mishra was able to expand his base of support. Although considered a 'Sanjay man',[23] Mishra's political mentor was his elder brother, L.N. Mishra.[24] With his brother's decease, Mishra was careful to cultivate his own independent basis of power. While it is unclear whether his decision to make Urdu official was made independently of the centre, it is clear that once made he milked it to his maximum advantage.[25] Mishra had a reputation

[20]*The Indian Nation* (Patna), 10 December 1980, p. 1; 12 December 1980, p. 1.

[21]*The Indian Nation* (Patna), 13 December 1980.

[22]'Urdu Bill Okayed', *The Indian Nation* (Patna), 20 December 1980, p. 4. I am grateful to the audience at a talk I gave at the Centre of Linguistics and English, School of Language, Jawaharlal Nehru University, New Delhi, 21 January 1994, for reminding me of the importance of this.

[23]Atul Kohli, *Democracy and Discontent* (New York: Cambridge University Press, 1991), p. 215.

[24]Upendra Mishra, *Caste and Politics in India* (New Delhi: Uppal Publishing House, 1986), p. 249.

[25]According to *The Indian Nation* (Patna), 25 December 1980, Home Minister Zail Singh claimed that Bihar had not consulted the centre before declaring Urdu the second official language in 1980. On the other hand, Khaliq Anjum, General Secretary of the *Anjuman Taraqqi Urdu (Hind)*, told me in an interview (New Delhi, 25 January 1994) that in 1980 a high-ranking Muslim in the Home Ministry informed Anjum that Mrs Gandhi wanted to declare Urdu the second official language in one of the two states promised in the Congress(I) 1980 manifesto, that is, either Bihar or UP, and asked Anjum's opinion on which of these two. Anjum responded that Bihar would be the better choice because the issue would be too controversial and would be perceived in communal terms in UP. So, according to Anjum, Mrs Gandhi ordered Jagannath Mishra to declare second official language status for Urdu. That Jagannath Mishra was able personally to reap the benefits of the decision is apparent in the extent to which Urdu organisations feted him and continue to do so, as well as, more anecdotally, the extent to which advocates of the Urdu cause whom I interviewed imparted admirable qualities to Mishra and credited him for the decision. Even an adversary such as Ghulam Sarwar admitted in an interview (Patna, 9 October 1993) that Jagannath Mishra deserved credit. When, in 1989, Bihar Chief Minister S.N. Sinha tried to gain political mileage out of extending the 1980 Urdu legislation to all districts in Bihar, political infighting within Congress(I) broke out between him and Jagannath Mishra over who rightly deserved credit. See 'Cong(I) Men Use Urdu to Knife Each Other', *Indian Express* (New Delhi), 5 October 1989; 'Bihar Cong-I Joins Urdu Bandwagon', *The Statesman* (Calcutta), 30 September 1989.

for challenging Congress(I) bigwigs; by 1983, Indira Gandhi had sacked him, and Rajiv Gandhi's dislike of him was well known.[26] Today he is himself a Congress(I) bigwig, inducted into Prime Minister Rao's cabinet. He remains quite popular in Bihar and is perceived by the current Chief Minister, Lalu Prasad Yadav, as his biggest rival.[27]

In contrast, V.P. Singh in Uttar Pradesh was dependent for his support base in 1980 on Mrs Gandhi and Sanjay Gandhi.[28] Indeed, he was 'shunted off' to Lucknow by Mrs Gandhi to be chief minister 'knowing full well that the Government of UP would in effect be run from New Delhi by Indira Gandhi, Sanjay and their myriad minions and that he would be left with responsibility without power'.[29] V.P. Singh's need was to please his patron and not to rock the boat by reaching out for clients such as Muslims. His position within the Congress(I) party was not as secure as Jagannath Mishra's. In contrast to the latter, this was V.P. Singh's first stint as Chief Minister. He had given promises throughout the beginning of his tenure as Chief Minister that he would make 1981 the year he acted upon the Congress(I) party manifesto in regard to Urdu. Finally, on 29 December 1981, he announced his intention to make Urdu official but could not get his ministers, nor apparently the prime minister, to agree to his issuing an ordinance to this effect by 31 December. Instead, his government announced its intentions to delete the word 'official', rendering Urdu UP's second language (an ordinance to this effect was finally promulgated in April 1982).[30] Despite the watering down, violent protests and riots against

[26]'Jagannath Mishra: Solving Other's Problems', *India Today,* 15 February 1994. p. 35; Harry W. Blair, 'Local Support Bases and the Ninth General Election in Bihar and Maharashtra', in Harold A. Gould and Sumit Ganguly (eds), *India Votes* (San Francisco: Westview Press, 1993), p. 51.

[27]Interview with Nil Ratan, political scientist at A.N. Sinha Institute of Social Studies, Patna, 27 September 1993.

[28]'Cover Story: The Aftermath: All Eyes on Mrs Gandhi', *India Today,* V. 13 (1–15 July 1980), p. 57.

[29]G.S. Bhargava, 'Vishwanath Pratap Singh: A Thumbnail Sketch', in G.S. Bhargava (ed.), *Perestroika in India: V.P. Singh's Prime Ministership* (New Delhi: Gian Publishing House, 1990), p. 33.

[30]'Second Language Status for Urdu by December 31: UP CM', *Indian Express* (New Delhi), 30 December 1981; 'UP Ordinance on Urdu Withheld', *Indian Express* (New Delhi), 1 January 1982; 'UP Ordinance on Urdu', *Indian Express* (New Delhi), 10 April 1982. V.P. Singh had claimed privately that the PM and the centre had been preventing him from acting on his promises regarding Urdu all along (interview with Ram Lall, Lucknow, 28 November 1993).

the ordinance ensued with police reacting with lathi charges and open firing.[31] Protests and lathi charges continued throughout January, the former organised by a transitory student organisation, as in the case of Bihar, although the role of the BJP-affiliated ABVP student union seems to have been more conspicuous.[32]

In contrast to Bihar, in Uttar Pradesh not only did the opposition agitate against the ordinance, but there was also dissension within the governing Congress(I) party over the issue, a problem that would grow during the 1980s. The main anti-Urdu voice within the UP Congress(I), and indeed within the cabinet of ministers, was that of Vasudev Singh. In the early 1980s, Vasudev Singh was also the president of the UP Hindi Sahitya Sammelan, a permanent, influential organisation (compared with the quickly organised anti-Urdu student groups) that strongly backed the anti-Urdu antagonists.[33] Nominally a non-political organization, the sammelan is supposed to limit itself to promoting Hindi; however, in UP, this promotion is defined as defeating Urdu as well.

With the breakdown of the Congress(I) party organizational structure at all levels under Indira Gandhi, the role of non-party intermediary groups, such as the Hindi Sahitya Sammelan, must be examined in seeking an explanation for the differences in Bihar and UP in the 1980s in regard to the Urdu issue. Although the Bihar branch of the Hindi Sahitya Sammelan was active in opposing the 1967 attempt to make Urdu official in Bihar,[34] it did not appear in media accounts as a significant factor in 1980. On the other hand, the Bihar branch of the Anjuman Taraqqi-e-Urdu played a very active role in 1980. In both Bihar and UP in 1980, the Anjuman Taraqqi-e-Urdu was the most important formally constituted, non-transitory, non-governmental interest group working for the Urdu cause. Yet the difference between the Bihar chapter and the UP chapter could not be more striking.

[31]'9 Varanasi Students Hurt in Firing', *Hindustan Times* (New Delhi), 14 January 1982; 'Three Varanasi Students Hurt in Police Firing', *Patriot* (New Delhi), 14 January 1982.

[32]'Road Blockade Plan against Urdu in UP', *Indian Express* (New Delhi), 25 January 1982; 'Urdu: Policy Mess By V.P. Singh Govt', *Patriot* (New Delhi), 29 January 1982; 'Anti-Urdu Rally by Bihar BVP', *Patriot* (New Delhi), 13 March 1981.

[33]'Urdu: Policy Mess by V.P. Singh Govt', *Patriot* (New Delhi), 29 January 1982; 'Urdu Imbroglio in Uttar Pradesh', *M.P. Chronicle* (Bhopal), 4 February 1982; 'Fighting on Status of Urdu', *Free Press Journal* (Bombay), 7 May 1982.

[34]Brass, *Language, Religion and Politics*, p. 262.

The Anjuman Taraqqi-e-Urdu in Bihar, although split by factions, was very active; this is particularly true of the pro-Congress(I) faction under Professor Abdul Moghni, which, according to Moghni, currently has approximately 600,000 members.[35] Moghni privately claims to have given an ultimatum to Congress(I) in 1980: if action was not taken on Urdu immediately after winning the election, then the Anjuman would undertake a direct action campaign. In the meantime, Moghni would publicly support Congress(I) and Jagannath Mishra in the elections, although the Anjuman itself could not publicly endorse any party or candidate according to its by-laws.[36] Publicly Moghni has written: 'The Anjuman conducted a successful democratic movement for the recognition of Urdu as the second official language of Bihar ... The Jagannath Mishra ministry conceded this demand, in 1980'.[37] Jagannath Mishra would not acknowledge Moghni's ultimatum and in fact denied knowing about it.[38] Nevertheless, it is true that a close relationship existed between the two men and it is quite likely that the Anjuman functioned as an intermediary group in mobilizing voters and pressurizing the new Bihar government to act on its electoral promise.[39]

In UP, the Anjuman was and still is a private fiefdom of a particular family, the head of which, Hayat Ullah Ansari, was a prominent Congress(I) MP. His influence in Congress(I) is apparent from his claim

[35]This suggests, especially when compared to the Anjuman in UP, that a breakdown into factions does not necessarily render an organization incompetent, but may actually lead to healthy competition. The other main faction of the Bihar Anjuman is controlled by Ghulam Sarwar; indeed Sarwar was the leader of the Anjuman when Brass was doing his study (*Language, Religion and Politics*, p. 243). The split between the two occurred in 1978 over an internal election controversy. Today, the Ghulam Sarwar faction is the weaker of the two (interviews with Dr Rab, A.N. Sinha Institute of Social Studies, Patna, 15 October 1993; Khaliq Anjum, *Anjuman Taraqqi Urdu (Hind)*, New Delhi, 25 January 1994). For membership numbers, see 'Working and Performance of Anjuman Taraqqi-e-Urdu Bihar', Monograph (Patna: Anjuman Taraqqi-e-Urdu, Bihar, 22 May 1990). Professor Moghni kindly provided me with an English translation of this monograph written in Urdu.

[36]Interview with Abdul Moghni, Patna, 29 September 1993.

[37]'Working and Performance of Anjuman Taraqqi-e-Urdu Bihar', Monograph.

[38]Interview with Jagannath Mishra, Patna, 17 October 1993.

[39]*The Indian Nation* (Patna), 3 December 1980, p. 4. Harry Blair notes that the 1980 election results in Bihar appear to confirm the return of Muslims to the Congress(I) fold, whereas this does not appear to be the case for UP Muslims, at least not to the same extent ('The 1980 Election in Bihar: Disintegration or Emerging Party Stability?', unpublished MS, Bucknell University, July 1983, 16); see also Paul R. Brass, *Caste, Faction and Party in Indian Politics*, Vol. 2 (Delhi: Chanakya, 1985), pp. 200, 312.

that 'I never asked, even Mrs Gandhi, for a [legislative] seat for my wife', that is, as though it was his for the asking.[40] In UP, the Anjuman is less of a pressure group than an extension of the Congress(I) itself, or at least an extension of a particular Congress(I) MP. Ansari's wife was president of the UP Anjuman in 1980 (and still is). Mrs Ansari, as wife of an established Congress(I) MP and as president of an organisation that according to many sources is barely active despite receiving more financial aid than the Anjuman in Bihar,[41] could not perhaps take an independent role in pressurizing the V.P. Singh state government as Moghni had done in Bihar (Moghni has never sought any political office).

Thus, in contrast to Jagannath Mishra, V.P. Singh was hindered rather than aided by intermediary groups in any attempt to make Urdu official. Furthermore, again in contrast to Mishra, V.P. Singh confronted intense opposition within his own party at both the state and centre levels to implementing the party manifesto promise. This was at least partly due to V.P. Singh's weaker independent power base than Jagannath Mishra's, despite both being chief ministers.

The situation in UP did not resolve itself with the replacement of V.P. Singh by Shripathi Mishra as chief minister. The ordinance regarding Urdu as second language was repromulgated, leading to a lawsuit being brought by the UP Hindi Sahitya Sammelan.[42] In their 6 April 1984 decision, the two judges of the Lucknow Bench of the Allahabad High Court deciding the case gave concurring opinions, in essence striking down repromulgation but not necessarily the content of the ordinance. This led to different interpretations of the judges' decision on content: some legal experts claim that the 1984 court decision cast doubts upon the legality of any attempt to make Urdu the second official language of UP, while others claim the decision was limited to striking down the repromulgation.[43] It is important to note, however, that there had been

---

[40]Interview with Hayat Ullah Ansari, Lucknow, 23 November 1993.

[41]*Pioneer* (Lucknow), 23 January 1989; interviews with Abdul Moghni, Patna, 29 September 1993. Khaliq Anjum, New Delhi, 25 January 1994; Abdus Salam Siddiqui, Lucknow, 21 November 1993; Syed Shahabuddin, New Delhi, 14 January 1994.

[42]'Urdu Ordinance Challenged', *National Herald*, 18 January 1984; 'Official Status to Urdu Challenged', *Northern India Patrika* (hereafter *NIP*) (Lucknow), 18 January 1984.

[43]'Urdu Ordinance Verdict', *Pioneer* (Lucknow), 14 April 1984; *NIP* (Lucknow), 13 April 1984; *Muslim India* (May 1984), p. 239; interviews with Zafaryab Jilani and Abdul Mannan (both of whom represented the Urdu Academy in the suit), Lucknow, 21 November 1993.

no attempt to make Urdu the second *official* language of the state, only to make it the 'second language' of UP; the latter confers much less legality than the former. The judges' decision therefore appeared to speculate what might be the legality *if* Urdu were to be made official (in the future).

The UP government tried to cover itself during the lawsuit against attacks on its repromulgation authority (as well as trying to appeal to Muslims in the expected forthcoming elections) by immediately proposing legislation granting second-language status to Urdu (again, with no attempt to introduce 'official' status).[44] The abruptness with which the Chief Minister, Shripati Mishra, announced the cabinet decision to propose the legislation and with which the bill was admitted in the state assembly (22 March 1984), became apparent when one cabinet member, the pro-Hindi Vasudev Singh, broke collective responsibility and criticised the decision. With the ranks of the ruling party divided on the issue and the High Court's ambiguous decision, the bill was left to die and the ordinance lapsed.[45]

Although some Congress(I) officials asked for Vasudev Singh to be disciplined for shirking collective responsibility, '[t]he party leadership ... decided to gloss over the faux pas of Mr Vasudev Singh,

Although the court decision explicitly stated that 'promotion of Urdu language would not be violative of Article 351 (Directive for Development of Hindi) of the Constitution', it did state that giving Urdu full-fledged status as an official language would involve 'insurmountable difficulties'. The court, however, only explicitly ruled that the ordinance was ultra vires because of Article 213 of the Constitution, that is, the circumstances permitting repromulgation of the ordinance were not satisfied in this case; the court did not 'quash' the ordinance because it said that an ordinance was not even necessary to accomplish what this ordinance stipulated, but instead could be done through government orders. See 'U.P. Govt. Will Stick to Urdu Policy: CM', *The Hindu* (Madras), 9 April 1984.

[44]'No Action Mooted against Vasudev', *Indian Express* (New Delhi), 25 March 1984; 'Urdu Bill Creates Crisis in House', *NIP* (Lucknow), 23 March 1984; *Muslim India* (May 1984), 287. A few months earlier (December 1983), on the eve of a by-election, Chief Minister Shripati Mishra had similarly proposed submitting a bill mirroring the ordinance in the next session of the Assembly. 'UP's Quandary over Urdu', *Deccan Herald* (Bangalore), 31 December 1983; 'Row over Urdu in UP Cong-I', *Patriot* (New Delhi), 15 December 1983; 'UP to Accord Urdu High Status', *Indian Express* (New Delhi), 5 December 1983.

[45]'Shripati stands by Decision on Urdu', *Indian Express* (New Delhi), 8 April 1984; 'UP Allow Ordinance on Urdu to Lapse', *Indian Express* (New Delhi), 9 May 1984. The UP government initiated an appeal to the Supreme Court, primarily because of the implication of the High Court's decision for virtually all ordinances. However, it did not follow through completely on the appeal process. 'UP Govt to Move SC on Urdu Issue', *Indian Express* (New Delhi), 10 April 1984; interview with Zafaryab Jilani, Lucknow, 21 November 1993.

which has no precedent'.[46] Instead he was again a cabinet minister in the reconstituted UP Congress(I) government, under Chief Minister N.D. Tiwari, in preparation for the forthcoming elections. That the Congress(I) in the December 1984 general elections, and subsequent state assembly elections, attempted to ride the 'Hindu wave' helps explain the lack of disciplinary action against Vasudev Singh.[47]

Vasudev Singh went on in May 1985 allegedly to suggest at a Hindi function that the faces of Urdu supporters should be blackened and then they should be paraded in public on a donkey.[48] Although this led to frenzied activity among some sections of the Urdu community (for example, establishment of the Rabta Committee and protests and hunger strikes), the more prominent political members of the state government's Urdu Academy fell in line with the government and again no action was taken against Vasudev Singh.[49]

What all this suggests is that the Urdu issue was continuously in the news in the 1980s in UP and that the Congress(I) repeatedly tried to use the issue to mobilize electoral support only to have it frequently backfire, whereas in Bihar the legislation to make Urdu official was gradually and quietly extended through government notifications to more and more districts until, by 1989, the whole state was covered.[50]

In 1989, in UP, Chief Minister N.D. Tiwari, already being criticized by Rajiv Gandhi's advisers in Delhi as being too ambitious and popular and thus a potential threat to Rajiv, sought to calm the political waters by going along with Rajiv's advisers' strategy of 'delivering' the Muslim vote to Rajiv by promising legislation to make Urdu official.[51] There was also the calculation that bringing such a bill to the floor would

[46]'No Action Mooted against Vasudev'.

[47]See Nirmal Mukarji and Ashis Banerjee, 'Neo-nationalism', *Seminar*, 313, September 1985, p. 27.

[48]NIP (Lucknow), 16 July 1985.

[49]Interview with Ram Lall (Chair of Rabta Committee in 1985), Lucknow, 28 November 1993.

[50]For example, six more districts were added in 1986; *Muslim India*, May 1986, p. 239. For expansion to whole of the state in 1989, see 'Urdu Gets Official status in All Bihar Districts', *The Telegraph* (Calcutta), 20 August 1989. Note, however, that criticisms of implementation continue to occur; see *Hindustan Times* (Patna), 1 August 1993. Note also that in Bihar, the 1980 legislation did grant official status to Urdu, whereas in UP the fight was over second-language status with no mention of official status.

[51]*Times of India* (Lucknow), 16 September 1989; 'Urdu Bill at PM's Behest', *The Tribune* (Chandigarh), 8 October 1989.

expose cracks in the Janata Dal-BJP electoral alliance.[52] The legislation was introduced in late September 1989, and apparently many Congress(I) members were 'taken aback' by the fact that this new bill introduced for the first time the term 'official' in regard to the Urdu status.[53] Then all hell broke loose in Badaun: a procession in support of the legislation and against an anti-Urdu petition filed to local authorities was taken out by students from one local college, then confronted by students from another college, and riots ensued which left at least 26 dead (official count). The bill was nevertheless passed, with the help of deft manoeuvres in the state assembly, the Chief Minister's strong position in state politics, and probably the fact that by this time Vasudev Singh was deceased.[54]

In the meantime, the Hindi Sahitya Sammelan had again filed suit, this time against the 1989 legislation making Urdu official. In the summer of 1993, the two judges hearing the case rendered a split decision and asked for a third judge to break the deadlock. The UP Attorney General sought to challenge the addition of a new judge at this stage, thus hoping to lead to an acquittal of the case.[55] As of early 1994 that is where the issue stood, with the legislation never being implemented in UP, although the new government elected in November 1993 made some conciliatory statements on the issue to its Muslim supporters.[56]

[52]'Uttar Pradesh: Using Urdu to Catch Votes', *Deccan Herald* (Bangalore), 25 September 1989. 'Urdu Bill to Sabotage Opposition Unity', *The Statesman* (New Delhi), 1 October 1989.

[53]'Urdu Bill to Sabotage Opposition Unity', *The Statesman* (New Delhi), 1 October 1989; 'Intriguing Aspect in Urdu Bill', *The Hindu* (Madras), 7 October 1989.

[54]'Urdu Bill Passed Amid Uproar', *Indian Express* (New Delhi), 30 September 1989.

[55]Interviews with Zafaryab Jilani and Abdul Mannan, Lucknow, 21 November 1993.

[56]Because of the ambiguous status of the 1989 legislation, it is not surprising that there is much confusion in many secondary sources on the status of Urdu in UP, especially when compared with Bihar. For example, Arvind Das states that '[r]ecently, after much agitation on the issue and in order to mollify the Muslim electorate, Urdu has been accorded the status of secondary official language in Bihar and Uttar Pradesh', implying the same timeframe for making legislation official in both states; Arvind Das, *India Invented* (Delhi: Manohar, 1992), p. 126. Brass claims that neither Bihar nor UP passed formal legislation making Urdu official, but rather both relied on ordinances, with the UP ordinance lapsing; Brass, *The Politics of India since Independence*. Christopher King claims that Urdu became the second official language in UP in 1989, a questionable claim given the legal suit thwarting implementation of the legislation; Christopher King, *One Language, Two Scripts* (Bombay: Oxford University Press, 1994), p. xi.

THE *ANGREZI HATAO* MOVEMENT

The Urdu controversy remained an albatross for the Congress(I) party in UP throughout the 1980s compared with Bihar, where it was quickly and quietly resolved. Ironically the resolution, if only symbolic, of the Urdu controversy in Bihar may have facilitated the political consolidation of an emerging elite, represented by the current Chief Minister, Lallu Prasad Yadav, that is displacing the established elite represented by the Congress(I). With Urdu legislation already in place by previous Congress(I) state governments, Lallu Prasad Yadav wooed away Muslim voters from the Congress(I) by 'seizing the moment' when he arrested Advani while the latter was on his *rath yatra* (chariot journey) in 1990.[57] As the current Bihar Chief Minister, Lallu Prasad Yadav has also been able to follow through on his promise that Yadavs will not massacre Muslims (as they did in Bhagalpur in 1989) and thereby 'deliver' on the security issue.[58]

In contrast, in UP, the competitive political struggle between established elites, represented primarily by Congress since independence, and emerging elites, represented by the 'bullock capitalists' among the backward castes (whether manifested in Lok Dal, Janata Dal, or Samajwadi parties), is less resolved than in Bihar.[59] As noted by a prominent Indian news magazine soon after the November 1993 UP

[57]Interview with Uttam Sengupta, Patna, 15 October 1993. *Rath yatra* refers to the political mobilization of Hindu nationalists by Advani as he journeyed through north India in a van decorated like the chariot of the Hindu god, Rama.

[58]Interview with Zafaryab Jilani, Lucknow, 21 November 1993.

[59]The term 'bullock capitalists' is used by Lloyd I. Rudolph and Susanne Hoeber Rudolph, *In Pursuit of Lakshmi* (Chicago: Chicago University Press, 1987). Marxists (for example, Achin Vanaik use the term 'kulak farmers'; Vanaik, *The Painful Transition* (New York: Verso, 1990). D.L. Sheth uses he term '*mofussils*' ('No English Please, We're Indian', *The Illustrated Weekly of India*, 19 August 1990, 34–7). Brass prefers 'middle (proprietary) castes' (see Brass, *Caste, Faction and Party*, p. 202, note 6). Harry Blair discusses the overlap between progressive farmers and backward castes in Bihar ('Structural Change, the Agricultural Sector, and Politics in Bihar', in J.R. Wood (ed.), *State Politics in Contemporary India* (Boulder: Westview Press, 1984), p. 67.

For a general treatment of the competitive struggle between established and emerging elites as manifested in language politics in India (as well as in the US, Belgium, and the former Soviet Union), see Selma K. Sonntag, 'Elite Competition and Official Language, Movements', in J. Tollefson (ed.), *Power and Inequality in Language Education* (New York; Cambridge University Press, 1995), pp. 91–111.

state election results: 'Bihar, where Lallu Prasad Yadav of the Janata Dal has built up a coalition of backward classes, Muslims and Dalits, provides the model for the new phase of political consolidation in UP.'[60] Yet, despite the victory of a Yadav, Mulayam Singh Yadav, in this November 1993 UP state election, his government 'fell before he had completed the task of consolidating a Muslim-Backward-Dalit coalition under his leadership'.[61] This means that emotive, symbolic issues, such as language, that can be used as tools of popular mobilization, are not as critical currently in Bihar as in UP—for example, Lallu Prasad Yadav can even talk of making English compulsory rather than projecting English as the bastion of the established elite that needs to be stormed.

Indeed, it was over the angrezi hatao (remove English) issue, the old socialist slogan proposed by Rammanohar Lohia,[62] and not over the Urdu issue, that Mulayam Singh Yadav, during his first tenure as the UP Chief Minister, stirred the embers of linguistic conflict. The issue is as full of class content today as it was during Lohia's advocacy in the 1960s. Today it also has a significant caste content.

The real issue in the current debate is ... not about the language *per se*. The discourse is not in terms of pedagogy; it is a political discourse.... [T]he debate reflects a conflict over power in society between two elite groups; the nationally entrenched English-educated elite and the new but ascendant elite sans the trappings of an English education.... The differences between the two are indexed in terms of their urban-rural and caste backgrounds.[63]

As Badri Raina puts it,

Social groups and formations that began to register a political and economic presence in the sixties (and emerged into leaderships—with the franchise of

[60]Sukumar Muralidharan, 'BJP the Loser', *Frontline,* 17 December 1993, p. 6. See also Ajit Roy, 'New Thrust of Caste Mobilisation', *Economic and Political Weekly,* 4 December 1993, p. 2641. The incorporation of dalits in Lallu Prasad Yadav's coalition is less explicit than in the 1993–5 SP-BSP coalition in UP (see Kalyan Chaudhuri, 'The Dalit Card', *Frontline,* 28 January 1994, pp. 42–3), but nevertheless is present, shown by his frequent, often highly personalized, campaigns, such as literally scrubbing dalits clean. See also *Hindustan Times* (New Delhi), 1 February 1994, p. 5.

[61]Gillian Wright, 'The Decline of Congress: The Rise of Mulayam', *Seminar,* 432, August 1995, p. 23.

[62]For background on Lohia, see Girish Mishra and B.K. Pandey, *Rammanohar Lohia: The Man and his Ism* (New Delhi: Eastern Books, 1992). For Lohia's own pronouncements on English, see Rammanohar Lohia, *Language* (Hyderabad: Navakind, 1966).

[63]Sheth, 'No English Please, We're Indian', p. 35.

1989) seem to retain in potent measure critical and conceptual links with [Mahatma] Gandhi and Lohia. Such leaderships which speak for a new resurgent rural elite are beginning to critique, from all accounts along a secular politics, the linkages between a dominant English-knowing urban middle class and developmental hypotheses which have, over the last four decades, fattened the metropolitan sectors at the expense of the vast countryside. In that critique, once again, the English language and English education are perceived to be key determinants of a comprehensive historical oppression. Thus, in the strategic states of Uttar Pradesh and Bihar. Hindi protagonism seems to re-emerge not as a communal or entirely provincial phenomenon, but essentially as a second anti-colonial movement.[64]

However, the backward-caste, 'mofussil' ascending elite (as D.L. Sheth, refers to the likes of Mulayam Singh Yadav) is far from united on policy implications. The policy gap, and differences in the diagnosis of the problem itself, can best be gleaned from, again, a comparison of Bihar and Uttar Pradesh. Both states had Yadav chief ministers in the early 1990s, both of whom claimed political lineage from Lohia and had in essence the same constituency base make-up, the bulk of which is backward castes. The backward castes desire 'to move into the professional and administrative areas of society where substantial power and prestige resides to round off their gains in the political and economic areas'.[65] This desire is fraught with all sorts of linguistic implications that attaining political and economic gains did not necessarily entail,[66] and 'English has become a barrier to their social and physical mobility'.[67] But Mulayam Singh Yadav in UP and Lallu Prasad Yadav in Bihar have increasingly diverged on the issue. The former has been a champion of 'angrezi hatao' while the latter stirred

[64]Badri Raina, 'A Note on Language, and the Politics of English in India', in S. Joshi (ed.), *Rethinking English* (New Delhi: Trianka. 1991), pp. 293–25.

[65]Mukarji and Banerjee, 'Neo-nationalism', p. 25.

[66]Critical to economic gains were land reform, the green revolution, and general agricultural transformation toward capitalism. On the latter, see Blair, 'Structural Change, the Agricultural Sector, and Politics in Bihar'. For political gains, D.L. Sheth points to the 'logic of numbers' in the democratisation process at the state level; however, Sheth notes that this logic of numbers will not work in wresting national power from the 'neo-colonial Nehruvian elite' because here power is legitimised through defining the terms of political discourse and the political agenda rather than simply majority rule. Prestige and social status are critical in this type of legitimation. Sheth, 'No English Please, We're Indian'.

[67]Ibid., p. 35.

up a controversy in the summer of 1993 by suggesting that English be reintroduced as a compulsory subject in state schools.

Each justifies his policy preference in pedagogical and social terms. There are potential political explanations as well. Mulayam Singh Yadav is (and was during his first stint as Chief Minister) much more politically embattled than Lallu Prasad Yadav. The former, in his election bid in November 1993, was competing against the English-speaking elite represented not only by the Congress(I) (which was barely a political force in UP in this election) but also against the Janata Dal in the likes of V.P. Singh (who, it turned out, was politically inconsequential in the election, although this was not predictable until quite late in the campaign). When asked two months prior to the election what his problem was with V.P. Singh, Mulayam Singh Yadav responded by noting three shortcomings of Janata Dal leaders: their collusion with the BJP 'when it suited them'; their lack of support for the angrezi hatao language policy; and their lack of support for reversing the anti-copying policy.[68] In contrast, Lallu Prasad Yadav *is* the Janata Dal in Bihar (and increasingly nationwide); he is not using the English language issue to defeat electoral competitors but rather to consolidate his own support base among aspiring backward-caste youths who see English as their ticket for upward mobility, as well as, possibly, reaching out beyond his local base to non-Hindi states in a bid for national recognition. Opposition within his own party allowed Lallu Prasad Yadav to back off his recommendation of reintroducing English in schools, thus enabling him to enlarge his personal appeal without committing himself to a policy ideologically distasteful to his party.[69] The Chief Minister 'indirectly admitted [to newsmen] that he had given way to the popular opinion in the Lower House over the issue because he did not think it to be the right time to assert his stand in the House'.[70]

Mulayam Singh Yadav's most threatening competitor was the BJP

[68]"We Will Defeat the BJP": Interview with Mulayam Singh Yadav', *Frontline*, 24 September 1993, p. 119. Reversing the anti-copying policy is also indicative of Mulayam Singh Yadav's support for his backward-caste constituency: as upwardly mobile backward-caste youths move into university for the first time, they find themselves at an educational disadvantage vis-a-vis the forward-caste youths, for whom attaining university education is not a new phenomenon among their castes; the backward-caste youths can overcome this disadvantage by 'copying' (cheating).

[69]'Govt Revokes Decision on English', *Hindustan Times* (Patna), 16 July 1993, p. 1.

[70]'CM Strong Votary of English', *Hindustan Times* (Patna), 19 July 1993, p. 1.

(the Bharatiya Janata Party), representing the revivalist *Hindutva* which claims Sanskritised Hindi as its symbol.[71] In promoting this symbol, there are elements within the BJP who make common cause with Mulayam Singh Yadav's *angrezi hatao* stance, although this has not been condoned by BJP leaders such as L.K. Advani.[72] Indeed, although the first Mulayam Singh Yadav administration took numerous decisions enforcing the exclusive use of Hindi in the UP government, the subsequent BJP Kalyan Singh government reinforced these decisions, leading to the Secretary of Language in UP claiming that both are equally ardent in their pro-Hindi stands.[73] In getting mileage out of the language issue vis-a-vis his main opponent, the BJP, Mulayam Singh Yadav needs to move away from the *angrezi hatao* slogan to a potentially more radical position of 're-appropriating' Hindi (read Hindustani) as the language of the masses and of the state, that is, away from sanskritised Hindi appropriated by revivalist Hindus since the 1930s, currently represented by the BJP.[74]

The BJP in Bihar as well has kept an iron in the language fire. Language 'activists' among the BJP are busy organizing among the Maithili speakers,[75] reinforcing BJP's upper-caste image which is

[71] Krishna Kumar, 'Foul Contract', *Seminar*, 377, January 1991, pp. 43–6.

[72] On L.K. Advani's stand, see 'Laloo's Retreat' (editorial), *Hindustan Times* (Patna), 17 July 1993, p. 7. One of the biggest advocates of angrezi hatao is V.P. Vaidik, editor *of Bhasha*, the Hindi news agency of Press Trust of India; see his *Angrezi hatao: Kyo our Kaise?* (Delhi: Prabhat Prakashan, 1991), who is also a BJP sympathizer (interview with Krishna Kumar, Delhi, 19 January 1994). V.P. Vaidik (interview, New Delhi, 15 January 1994) told me he had been in contact with Mulayam Singh Yadav after the latter had been reinstated as Chief Minister in early December 1993 in regard to a tentative plan for another angrezi hatao conference along the lines of the 1991 Indore conference. Mulayam Singh Yadav's subsequent troubles because of resistance to his extension of reservations to backward castes may have put a damper on his collusion with V.P. Vaidik on angrezi hatao since, in Vaidik's philosophy, · if English were removed then there would be no need for reservations for backward castes or dalits since English, not caste stigma, is the major barrier to upward mobility. As another indication of BJP support for angrezi hatao, the BJP Delhi city government, elected in November 1993, attempted to drop the study of English from the initial primary grades of schools under its jurisdiction and proposed making Hindi the sole official language of the city government ('Hindi Replaces English in New Delhi', United Press International, 15 February 1995).

[73] Interview with S.N. Jha, Lucknow, 8 November 1993.

[74] Krishna Kumar, 'Quest for Self-Identity', *Economic and Political Weekly*, 9 June 1990, pp. 1247–55; interview with Krishna Kumar, Delhi, 19 January 1994.

[75] Interview with Anil Kumar Jha (BJP Maithili language activist), Patna, 11 October 1993.

particularly strong in Bihar[76]—and thereby biting into Jagannath Mishra's Congress(I) base in Mithilanchal,[77] already under siege by the recent language tactics of Lallu Prasad Yadav. In 1992 the Lallu Prasad Yadav government removed Maithili from the list of examination languages of the Bihar state public service commission. As many acknowledge, this was clearly part of Lallu's anti-Brahmin, pro-backward castes/dalits strategy, since Maithili is associated with Maithili Brahmins.[78] Indeed, Lallu Prasad Yadav apparently justified removal on grounds that Maithili belongs to members of a particular caste and hence only that caste has benefited.[79] He may also be attempting to show the established Bihar political elite from this region, including Jagannath Mishra, who is in control.[80] First he deals this linguistic blow to Maithili speakers, though most of those who identify themselves as such do not support him anyway, and then he 'rebuilds' Mithilanchal as his own constituency through allocating other favours to the region.[81]

Although there was some protest against Lallu Prasad Yadav's move against Maithili, particularly by the BJP, it was muted at best. As argued throughout this article, language issues are no longer contentious in Bihar. Maithili speakers were unable to mount resistance.[82] The BJP

[76]Interview with Uttam Sengupta, Patna, 15 October 1993.

[77]Amalendu, 'The Great Language Divide: Politicising the Issue', *Hindustan Times, Sunday Special* (Patna), 15 March 1992, p. 7: 'Already encouraged by a swing of the Brahmin voters towards the party, the BJP think-tank is now engaged to give more political teeth to the issue by marginalising others, particularly the Congress whose main vote bank has been the Brahmins over the years'.

[78]Amalendu, 'The Great Language Divide'; interview with Ghulam Sarwar, Patna, 9 October 1993.

[79]*Hindustan Times* (Patna), 13 March 1992, p. 4.

[80]Conversation with Nil Ratan, A.N. Sinha Institute of Social Studies, Patna, 27 September 1993. In an interview with Jagannath Mishra (Patna, 17 October 1993), Mishra claimed that Lallu Prasad Yadav had removed Maithili from the public service exam because Maithili speakers support Congress(I). Mishra's assistant, also present during the interview, noted the association of the Maithili language with Brahmins, hence Lallu Prasad Yadav's decision to consolidate anti-Brahmin appeal.

[81]Conversation with Nil Ratan, A.N. Sinha Institute of Social Studies, Patna, 27 September 1993.

[82]'Bihar Headed for Linguistic Conflict', *Hindustan Times* (Patna), 29 February 1992, p. 1. On the BJP opposition, see 'Maithili's Deletion to Be Opposed', *Hindustan Times* (Patna), 28 February 1992, p. 2. Jagannath Mishra also opposed the government's decision to drop Maithili, calling it unconstitutional and creating caste hatred; *Hindustan Times* (Patna), 2 March 1992, p. 3. The *Chetna Samiti* has filed a suit against the government's move, but not much has come of this.

could not sustain the agitation because non-Brahmins did not associate with the cause.[83] One BJP activist suggested that it was not a priority issue for his party at that time.[84]

CONCLUSION

One prediction to be drawn from the above analysis is that if Mulayam Singh Yadav were to consolidate power, language issues (including the angrezi hatao issue) will lose their saliency in UP, as has been the case in Bihar. Mulayam Singh Yadav's recent (late 1995) alliance of his Samajwadi party with Janata Dal suggests he may now be more receptive to the idea of Lallu Prasad Yadav as a model. On the other hand, the short-lived replacement of his chief ministership with that of the dalit leader, Mayawati, suggests that any consolidation of a backward caste–dalit–Muslim alliance is still a long way off in UP, especially given Mayawati's alienation of Muslims and her alliance with the BJP.[85]

It may indeed be difficult to predict north Indian politics from the analysis of the politics of language given above. However, as stated at the beginning of this article, the dependent variable is the saliency of language issues, and the level of political competition is the independent explanatory variable. Given that Lallu Prasad Yadav was re-elected chief minister for another term in the spring of 1995, I would predict that language issues remain non-contentious in Bihar, even if Lallu Prasad Yadav were to move forward again on his reinstatement of English in the school curriculum. On the other hand, I would predict that the Urdu issue and the angrezi hatao issue remain salient in UP. As the emerging elites in UP compete with the established elites, in a more drawn-out competition than that which occurred in Bihar, it may be that they discover the need for a much more radical politics of language in order to use language issues as a strategic tool, a 'revolution' as Raina suggests and as Kumar implies.

The future of the politics of language in UP will be instructive for other cases. UP will matter for the rest of India,[86] not because it is at

---

[83]Conversation with Arun Jha, Patna, 15 October 1993.

[84]Interview with Anil Kumar Jha, Patna, 11 October 1993.

[85]"'I Have Fought Wordy Wars": Interview with Dr Masood Ahamed', *Frontline*, 29 July 1994, pp. 13–14.

[86]See *Seminar*, 432, August 1995.

the vanguard or a bellwether, but because the prolonged competitive struggle between emerging and established elites seems likely to keep on the agenda emotive, symbolic issues such as language. The above analysis of both the Bihar and UP cases suggests that when language issues *do* become politically salient, it is not necessarily an indication of mismanagement by the state, as suggested by Parsonian liberals, or of the capturing of the state by a particular vested interest, as suggested by the neo-Marxists, but may instead be indicative of political competition. As D.L. Sheth describes, the linguistic manifestation of the competition between the Nehruvian national elites and an emerging backward-caste elite, 'the intra-elite conflict illustrated by the language debate is an outgrowth of the democratic process of polities'.[87]

---

[87]D.L. Sheth, 'The Great Language Debate: Politics of Metropolitan versus Vernacular India', in Upendra Baxi and Bhikhu Parekh (eds), *Crisis and Change in Contemporary India* (New Delhi: Sage, 1995), p. 194.

6

Language and Politics in Jammu and Kashmir

Issues and Perspectives*

K. Warikoo

Language is the most powerful means of communication, vehicle of expression of cultural values and aspirations, and instrument of conserving culture. As such, language is an important means to acquire and preserve the identity of a particular group or community. Language and culture are interrelated because the language regions possess certain homogeneity of culture and are characterized by common traits in history, folklore, and literature. Among various cultural symbols—religion, race, language, traditions, and customs, etc.—that differentiate an ethnic group from the other, language is the most potent cultural marker providing for group identity. Its spatial spread over a fixed territory makes language more important than religion as a basis of ethnic identity formation.

In the emerging world order, when the rise of ethnonationalism is posing a major challenge to the nation-state, political assertion of language or religious identities has assumed importance. However, events in Pakistan, which was established in 1947 as an Islamic state on the basis of religious factors, have demonstrated the inherent conflict between language and religious identities. It was the language variable

*Originally published as 'Language and Politics in Jammu and Kashmir: Issues and Perspectives', in P.N. Pushp and K. Warikoo (eds), *Jammu, Kashmir and Ladakh: Linguistic Predicament*, New Delhi: Har-Anand Publications under the auspices of Himalayan Research and Cultural Foundation, 1996, pp. 183–221.

that led to the break-up of Pakistan in 1971 and the creation of a new independent nation—Bangladesh. The Bengali language proved to be more powerful an ethnic factor than common Muslim identity. Similarly, political manifestation of language rivalry has now gained primacy in the ongoing ethnic conflicts between Sindhis, Punjabis, Saraikis, Baluchis, and Urdu speakers in Pakistan, even though all of them belong to the Muslim *Ummah*. Ironically, it is religion rather than language that has been the key motivating and mobilizing factor in the present secessionist movement in Kashmir. Yet there have been frequent though vague references by the political and intellectual elite to propose various solutions to the problems on the basis of '*Kashmiriat*'. Since language and particularly mother tongue forms the core of this much publicized concept of Kashmiriat, this study has been undertaken to analyse the complex dynamics of language and politics in the multilingual state of Jammu and Kashmir. Often described as a three-storeyed edifice composed of three geographical divisions of Jammu, Kashmir, Ladakh and Baltistan, bound together by bonds of history and geography and linked together by a common destiny, Jammu and Kashmir state presents a classic case of linguistic and ethnoreligious diversity.

LANGUAGE DEMOGRAPHY

An in-depth and objective study of the language situation in Jammu and Kashmir calls for an understanding of the language demography of the state, which would indicate the spatial distribution of various linguistic groups and communities. This in turn reflects the variegated ethnocultural mosaic of the state. The language and cultural areas are not only correlated but are generally specific to a particular area. For the purpose of this study, J&K Census Reports of 1941, 1961, 1971 and 1981 have been relied upon,[1] (no census was carried out in the state in

[1] *Census of India, 1941, Vol. XXII, Jammu and Kashmir,* Parts I and II, by R.G. Wreford, Jammu, 1943, pp. 302–35; *Census of India, 1971, Jammu and Kashmir,* Part IIC (Cultural & Migration Tables), by M.H. Kamili, Srinagar, 1975, pp. 207–267; *Census of India, 1971, Jammu and Kashmir,* Series 8 (Part II-CCII)—Social and Cultural Tables by J.N. Zutshi, pp. 101–133; *Census of India, Jammu and Kashmir,* Paper 1 of 1987 (Households and household population by language), by A.H. Khan, New Delhi, 1987.

Table 6.1: Jammu and Kashmir Major Linguistic
Population Groups, 1941

Total population of J&K, (1941 Census) = 40,21,616

Language	J&K State	Kashmir Province	Jammu Province	Frontier Districts Ladakh* Gilgit, Gilgit Agency, Astor, etc.	
Kashmiri	15,49,460[i]	13,69,537	1,78,390	1174	323
Punjabi (Dogri)	10,75,273[ii]	73,473[iii]	10,00,018	453	1329
Rajasthani (Gojri)[iv]	2,83,741	92,392	1,87,980	Nil	3369
Western Pahari[v]	5,31,319	1,70,432[vi]	3,60,870[vii]	5	12
Hindustani[viii] (Hindi & Urdu)	1,78,528	10,631	1,67,368	22	507
Lahanda (Pothwari)	82,993	8	82,975[ix]	5	5
Balti	1,34,012	352	184	1,33,163	313
Ladakhi	46,953	230	299	46,420	4
Shina (Dardi)	84,604	7,888[x]	114	13,562	63,040[xi]
Burushaski[xii]	33,132	3	Nil	244	32,885
Tibetan	503	26	145	317	15

Notes: *Before independence, Skardo/Baltistan (now in Pak-occupied Kashmir/Northern Areas) was a Tehsil of Ladakh District.

i. In the 1941 Census, persons speaking Kishtwari (11,170), Siraji (17,617), Rambani (1,202), Poguli (5,812), and Banjwahi (747), totalling 36,548 persons, have been included under the head Kashmiri.

ii. Dogri has been taken as a dialect under Punjabi, thereby enumerating 4,13,754 Punjabi-speaking persons mainly in Mirpur together with 6,59,995 Dogri speakers.

iii. Out of this figure, 48,163 persons are from Muzaffarabad (now in POK).

iv. Gojri, the language of Gujars, has been included with Rajasthani.

v. Pahari, which is enumerated separately, is closely connected with Gujari and is spoken in much the same areas.

vi. Includes 1,55,595 persons in Muzaffarabad (now in POK).

vii. Includes 2,36,713 persons in Poonch, Haveli, Mendhar.

viii. Hindi and Urdu have been combined and enumerated as Hindustani.

ix. Nearly all (82,887 persons) are concentrated in Mirpur.

x. Includes 7,785 persons in Baramulla (Gurez area).

xi. Shina language is spoken chiefly in Gilgit area.

xii. It is mainly spoken in Hunza, Nagar, and Yasin.

Table 6.2: Jammu and Kashmir Major Linguistic Population Groups, 1961

Total Population of J & K, (1961 Census) = 35,60,976

Language	J&K State	Kashmir Province	Jammu Province	Ladakh District
Kashmiri	18,96,149	17,17,259	1,78,281 (mainly in Doda)	609
Dogri	8,69,199	1,784	8,67,201	214
Gojri	2,09,327	64,493	1,44,834	Nil
Ladakhi	49,950	79	42	49,829
Punjabi	1,09,174	32,866	76,308	Nil
Balti	33,458	514	38	32,905 (mainly in Kargil)
Hindi	22,323	2,494	19,868	61
Urdu	12,445	3,504	8,941	Nil
Dardi Shina	7,854	7,605 (Mainly in Guruez area of Baramulla)	30	219
Tibetan	2,076	Nil	148	1,899

Table 6.3: Jammu and Kashmir Major Linguistic Population Groups, 1971

Total Population of J&K, (1971 Census) = 46,16,632

Language	J&K State	Kashmir Division	Jammu Division	Ladakh Division
Kashmiri	24,53,430	21,75,588	2,77,070	772
Dogri	11,39,259	8,161	11,30,845	253
Hindi* (Gojri)	6,95,375	1,80,837	5,14,177	361
Ladakhi	59,823	1,446	1,562	56,815
Punjabi	1,59,098	46,316	1,12,258	524
Lahanda (Pothwari)	22,003	109	21,894 (Mainly in Rajouri)	Nil
Urdu	12,740	4,521	8,209	10
Balti	40,135	822	280	39,033 (Mainly in Kargil)
Shina	10,274	9,276 (Mainly in Gurez area of Baramulla)	251	747
Tibetan	3,803	867	Nil	2,936

Note: *Gojri, the language of Gujars, has been included with Hindi.

Table 6.4: Jammu and Kashmir Major Linguistic
Population Groups, 1981

Total Population of J&K, (1981 Census) = 59,87,389

Language	J&K State	Kashmir Division	Jammu Division	Ladakh Division
Kashmiri	31,33,146	28,06,441 (Mainly in Doda District)	3,28,229	1,476
Dogri	14,54,441	2,943	14,51,329	169
Hindi* (Gojri)	10,12,808	2,55,310 (Mainly in Baramulla and Kupwara Districts)	7,67,344 (Mainly in Doda, Poonch and Rajouri Districts)	155
Ladakhi	71,852	471	1,190	70,191
Punjabi	1,63,049	41,181	1,12,668	200
Lahanda (Pothwari)	13,184	21	13,163	Nil
Urdu	47,701	811	Nil	46,890 (Mainly in Kargil)
Shina (Dardi)	15,017	12,159 (Mainly in Gurez area of Baramulla)	Nil	2,858 (Mainly in Da Hanu)
Tibetan	4,178	796 (Mainly in Srinagar)	Nil	3,382 (Mainly in Leh Tehsil

Note: *Gojri, the language of the Gujars has been included with Hindi.

1951 and 1991). The population of various linguistic groups as detailed in each of these censuses, is given in Tables 6.1 to 6.4.

The people of Jammu and Kashmir, whether Kashmiris, Dogras, Gujars-Bakarwals, Ladakhis, Baltis, Dards, etc., have, in all the censuses, unambiguously identified their indigenous languages as their 'mother tongues' thereby consolidating their respective ethnolinguistic and cultural identities. This is particularly important in view of the fact that the Muslims of the state have thus acted in a manner quite different from that of Muslims in most of the Indian states.

It is also in stark contrast to the experience in Punjab, where Hindus, though speaking Punjabi at home, earlier claimed Hindi as their mother tongue during the census operations. Similarly, the Muslims in various Indian states such as Karnataka, Andhra Pradesh, Kerala, etc., who registered local languages as their mother tongues in the 1951 census, opted for Urdu in 1961 and afterwards, thereby leading to a dramatic rise in the number of Urdu-speaking persons in India.[2] Same is the case with the Muslims of Uttar Pradesh, who registered their language as Hindustani in 1951 Census, but have been claiming Urdu as their mother tongue subsequently.[3] This demonstrates the urge of the Muslims in other Indian states to identify themselves with Urdu rather than with Hindustani (the basic substratum of Hindi and Urdu, it does not have any communal and politicized connotation) or the indigenous mother tongues, in a bid to consolidate themselves as a distinct collective group linked together by common bond of religion and Urdu which they believe to be representing their Muslim cultural identity. Clearly these Muslims have moved away from regional towards the ethnoreligious identity.[4]

It is precisely for avoiding any such communal polarization between Hindus and Muslims on the issue of Hindi and Urdu languages, that the Jammu and Kashmir state census authorities decided, in 1941, to club Hindi and Urdu together and use Hindustani. This, however, resulted in inflating the number of persons claiming Hindi and Urdu speakers to 1,78,528 (mostly in Jammu province). R.G. Wreford, the then Census Commissioner admits it in his report, saying that 'The figures for Hindustani are inflated as the result of the Urdu-Hindi controversy. Propaganda was carried on during the Census by the adherents of both parties to the dispute with the result that many Hindus gave Hindi as their mother tongue and many Muslims gave Urdu quite contrary to the facts in the great majority of cases. The dispute is largely political and so to keep politics out of the Census, it was decided to lump Hindi and Urdu together as Hindustani.'[5]

In the 1961, 1971, and 1981 censuses, usage of the term 'Hindustani' has been discarded in favour of separate enumeration for Hindi- and Urdu-speaking persons. The 1961 census, which has treated Hindi and Gojri language separately (unlike the 1971 and 1981 censuses, where

[2]Ashish Bose, 'Some Aspects of the Linguistic Demography of India', in *Language and Society in India: Proceedings of a Seminar* (Simla: IIAS, 1969), pp. 37–51.

[3]Ibid. See also Paul R. Brass, *Language, Religion and Politics in North India* (Cambridge: Cambridge University Press, 1974), pp. 119–274.

[4]L. Khubchandani, 'Language Policy for a Plural Society', in Satish Saberwal (ed.), *Towards a Cultural Policy* (Delhi: Indian Institute of Advanced Studies 1971), p. 101.

[5]*Census of India, 1941: Jammu and Kashmir*, Parts I and II, Jammu, 1943. p. 39.

Gojri is included into Hindi) should be taken as the authentic base for calculating the number of persons claiming Hindi as their mother tongue. Yet there is no denying the fact that though respective mother tongues are spoken universally by various ethnic groups in their households or among themselves, the people of the state are generally bilingual or even trilingual in some cases. Thus if a Kashmiri uses his mother tongue within his group, he uses Urdu, Hindi, or Hindustani in his conversation with people from Jammu Province, Ladakh division, and from the rest of India. Similarly, a Dogra would use Dogri within his group, Punjabi with his counterparts from Punjab and Delhi, and Hindi or Hindustani with others. Ladakhis would use Ladakhi among themselves and Hindi, Urdu, or Hindustani with others. English has also become popular, owing to its common usage in administrative offices, trade, industry, and educational institutions.

The prevalence of Urdu as a link language is not only due to its being the official language, but also due to its popularization through the publication of books, newspapers and periodicals in large numbers. Besides, the close socio-economic contacts between the people of the state and rest of India, plus the impact of tourism, modernization, and educational development have contributed to the use of Urdu and Hindi in the state, in addition to the mother tongues.

The census report of 1941 for Jammu and Kashmir, provides an insight into the language situation in the state before independence, that is, before a large chunk of the state in Mirpur, Muzaffarabad, and Frontier Districts (Baltistan, Astore, Gilgit, etc.) was occupied by Pakistan in 1947–8. This area is now known as Pak-occupied Kashmir/ Northern Areas. The 1941 census has listed Kashmiri, Dogri, Punjabi, Rajasthani, Western Pahari, Balti, Ladakhi, Shina/Dardi, and Burushaski as the main languages, spoken in the state. The 1941 census has followed the general scheme of classification, whereby Dogri and Gojri have been included as dialects under Punjabi and Rajasthani respectively, which is likely to create confusion to the non-discerning reader. However, the census has provided a solution by indicating the actual number of Dogri and Punjabi speakers as 6,59,995 and 4,13,754 respectively.[6] Whereas the Dogri speakers were concentrated in Jammu, Udhampur, Kathua, and Chenani Jagir districts, most of the Punjabi

[6]Ibid., p. 331.

speakers were settled mainly in Mirpur and also in Muzaffarabad (48,163 persons).[7] Similarly out of 82,993 Lahanda speakers (including those speaking Pothawri dialect), 82,887 persons were concentrated in Mirpur district.[8]

Gojri, the language of Gujars and Bakarwals (now declared as scheduled tribes), was included as a dialect under Rajasthani because of its close affinities with that language. But, Pahari which is closely connected with Gojri and continues to be spoken in much the same areas, was enumerated separately. Thus we have 2,83,741 Gojri speakers and 5,31,319 Western Pahari speakers (including those speaking Bhadrawahi, Gaddi, Padari, Sarori dialects).[9] Reasi, Jammu, Poonch, Haveli, Mandhar, Baramulla, Anantnag, and Muzaffarabad districts were shown as the main concentration points of Gojri and Western Pahari speakers, thereby testifying to their widespread distribution throughout the state. The subsequent census reports of 1961, 1971, and 1981 have removed this anomaly of enumerating Gojri and Pahari separately. However, the census reports of 1971 and 1981 have followed a new anomalous practice of including Gojri (Rajasthani), Bhadrawahi, and Padari with Hindi. This has not only inflated the numbers of those claiming Hindi as their mother tongue but also camouflaged the actual strength of Gojri speakers, thereby causing disenchantment among this tribal community.

As most of these Hindi albeit Gojri speakers have been shown as concentrated in Baramulla, Kupwara, Poonch, Rajuri, and Doda districts, their Gujar identity becomes obvious. The 1961 census, which does not mix up Hindi with Gojri, puts the number of Gojri speakers at 2,09,327 and that of Hindi speakers at 22,323.[10] Urdu is placed next with only 12,445 persons claiming it to be their mother tongue.

Tables 6.1 to 6.4 make it amply clear that Kashmiri commands the largest number of speakers, with Dogri at second and Gojri at third positions respectively. The number of Punjabi speakers in the 1961,1971, and 1981 census reports, actually reflects the number of

[7]Ibid., p. 307.

[8]Ibid., p. 309.

[9]Ibid., pp. 307–8.

[10]Census of India, 1971, Jammu and Kashmir, Part II C (Cultural & Migration Tables), by M.H. Kamili, Srinagar, 1965, pp. 207–67.

Sikhs who have maintained their language and culture, and who are concentrated mainly in Srinagar, Budgam, Tral, Baramulla (all in Kashmir Province), Udhampur and Jammu. In case of Ladakh, several ethnolinguistic identities emerge on the basis of mother tongue and area of settlement. Ladakhis (people of Buddhist-dominated Ladakh district and Zanskar) have claimed Ladakhi, popularly known as Bhoti, as their mother tongue. Interestingly, the Tibetan language has been consistently identified as distinct language/mother tongue in all the census reports under review, and it is spoken by the small group of Tibetan refugees settled in Srinagar and Leh. As against this, the Shia Muslims of Kargil have claimed Balti, another dialect of the Tibetan language. The Baltis of Kargil are separated by the Line of Actual Control (LAC) from their ethnolinguistic brothers in Baltistan area of 'Northern Areas' in Pak-occupied Kashmir, who also speak the same Balti dialect. There are some Dardic speaking pockets in Gurez area of Baramulla in Kashmir, Dras, and Da Hanu in Ladakh. The people of Hunza, Nagar, and Yasin in the 'Northern Areas' of Pak-occupied Kashmir, speak the Burushaski language. The state of Jammu and Kashmir thus presents a classic case of linguistic and ethnoreligious diversity.

Neglect of Mother Tongues

It is established that Kashmiri ranks first among the mother tongues of the state, commanding the largest number of speakers, with Dogri in second and Gojri in third position, followed by Punjabi, Bodhi, Balti, Shina/Dardi in succession. Whereas Kashmiri and Dogri have been included in the Eighth schedule of the Constitution of India, the demands of similar treatment for Gojri and Bhoti are yet to be conceded. Conscious of the ethnolinguistic heterogeneity of the state, the 'New Kashmir' Programme adopted by the Jammu and Kashmir National Conference under the stewardship of Sheikh Abdulla, as early as 1944, had envisaged the declaration of Kashmiri, Dogri, Balti, Dardi, Punjabi, Hindi, and Urdu as the national languages of the state.[11] Urdu was to be the 'lingua franca' of the state. It was also laid down that:[12]

---

[11] *New Kashmir,* Foreword by S.M. Abdullah, New Delhi, p. 21.
[12] Ibid.

The State shall foster and encourage the growth and development of these languages, by every possible means, including the following:-
(1) The establishment of State Language Academy, where scholars and grammarians shall work to develop the languages,
   (a) by perfecting and providing scripts,
   (b) by enriching them through foreign translations,
   (c) by studying their history,
   (d) by producing dictionaries and textbooks.
(2) The founding of State scholarships for these languages.
(3) The fostering of local press and publications in local languages.

The Constitution of Jammu and Kashmir has recognized Urdu as the official language of the state, treating Kashmiri, Dogri, Balti, Dardi, Punjabi, Pahari, and Ladakhi as regional languages. But the state Constitution has not taken cognizance of the need 'to protect the right of minorities to conserve their distinctive language, script or culture; to provide adequate facilities for instruction in the mother tongue, to the children of linguistic minorities', as has been explicitly provided in the Constitution of India in Articles 29, 30, and 350.

What was laid down in the original manifesto of the National Conference, has been fulfilled only to the extent of setting up of the Jammu and Kashmir Academy of Art, Culture, and Languages. Circumstantial evidence indicates that there has been an organized effort by the state political-bureaucratic elite to stifle the growth of Kashmiri language and other local mother tongues. It becomes obvious from the following facts:

1. Teaching of Kashmiri has not been introduced at the secondary school and college levels in the state. Not only that, no textbooks in Kashmiri are available even though a set of such books was prepared by experts. The Post Graduate Department of Kashmiri was created as a superstructure without any ground support at the primary and secondary levels. This is despite the general desire among Kashmiri masses to have Kashmiri as a medium of instruction particularly at the primary and middle levels of education. This gets amply reflected in a survey, in which 83 per cent of the respondents showed their preference for use of Kashmiri as a medium of instruction at primary levels and 48 per cent preferred the same at middle level of education, whereas

49 per cent wanted to have English at high or higher secondary levels.[13]

2. Notwithstanding the publication of hundreds of newspapers and periodicals mostly in Urdu and some in English, hardly any newspaper or periodical is published in any local language in the state. The journal *Sheeraza,* which is brought out by the Jammu and Kashmir Cultural Academy in Kashmiri, Dogri, Gojri, and Bhoti languages, has a limited circulation among the literary circles. Local masses have to rely exclusively on Urdu and English newspapers/periodicals published locally or coming from Punjab or Delhi, though the people of the Valley would like to have Kashmiri newspapers. A sociolinguistic survey in Kashmir revealed that 47 per cent of the respondents reported their preference for local newspapers in the Kashmiri language.[14] Jammu and Kashmir is perhaps the only Indian state where local language press and publications are virtually absent.

3. Usage of Urdu has received official patronage, it being the medium of instruction in primary and secondary levels. Persi-Arabic script has been adopted for the Kashmiri language. The functional role of Kashmiri in the domain of written communication has been reduced to a minimum, as all personal letters, official correspondence, etc., are written in Urdu, English, or Hindi languages.[15] The Sharda script, though indigenous to Kashmir, has been totally ignored. Not only that, the treasure of ancient MSS in the Sharda script is decaying in various libraries/archives in Jammu and Kashmir state and needs immediate retrieval. Sharda script was used for preparing horoscopes, though its usage is now restricted to a few practising Brahmins. With the result, this ancient tradition has gone into oblivion. Similarly, the demands of the ethnoreligious minority of Kashmiri Hindus, presently living in forced exile, for adopting Devanagari as an alternate script for the Kashmiri language have been ignored. With the result, this sizable minority of Kashmir has not only been deprived of

---

[13]For further details see Omkar N. Kaul and Ruth Laila Schmidt, *Kashmiri: A Socio-Linguistic Survey* (Patiala: Indian Institute of Language Studies, 1983), pp. 53–4.

[14]See Ibid., pp. 66–7.

[15]Ibid., p. 63.

access to the rich fund of Kashmiri language and literature, their right to preserve and promote their ancient cultural heritage has also been denied. This is in clear contravention of Articles 29, 30, and 350 of Indian Constitution. On the other hand, the state government has adopted Persi-Arabic script as an alternate script for Dogri and Punjabi, thereby, in addition, displaying their motivated double standards. That Devanagari script has been in prevalence for Kashmiri is obvious from the publication of several Kashmiri books/journals in this script. Not only that, Maharaja Hari Singh of Jammu and Kashmir while conceding the demands of both the Hindu and Muslim communities, issued orders in late 1940 allowing the usage of both Persian and Devanagari scripts in schools, even while the common medium of instruction would be simple Urdu.[16] Students were given the option of choosing either of the two scripts for reading and writing.[17]

4. During the past two decades or so, there have been organized efforts by the Islamic fundamentalist social, cultural, and political organizations, often receiving assistance from foreign Muslim countries, to saturate the Kashmiri language and culture with aggressive revivalistic overtones. It is not a mere coincidence that all the names of various militant organisations in Kashmir, titles of office-bearers, their slogans and literature are in the highly Persianized-Arabicized form. Similarly, names of hundreds of villages and towns in Kashmir were changed from ancient indigenous Sanskritic names to Persian/Islamic names by the state government. To quote a Kashmiri writer, 'Language was subverted through substitution of Pan-Islamic morphology and taxonomy for the Kashmiri one. Perfectly Islamic person names like Ghulam Mohammed, Ghulam Hassan, Abdul Aziz, Ghulam Rasool which were abundantly common in Kashmir were substituted by double decker names which were indistinguishable from Pakistani and Afghan names'.[18] In this manner linguistic and cultural subversion was carried out to 'subsume the Kashmiri identity of Kashmir by

---

[16]Shanti Veer Kaul, 'Memory-Counter Memory', *Trumpet*, New Delhi, 1 September 1995, p. 6.

[17]Ibid.

[18]Ibid.

a Pan-Islamic identity' after 'tampering with the racial and historical memory of an ethnic sub-nationality through a Pan-Islamic ideal'.[19] Kashmir was thus projected as 'an un-annexed Islamic enclave' which should secede from the secular and democratic India.

5. Films Division of the Government of India, which used to dub films in thirteen Indian languages, including Kashmiri, for exhibition among the local masses, stopped doing so at the instance of the state administration. They were instead asked to do it in simple Urdu.

6. That the state bureaucracy even foiled the attempts by Progress Publishers, Moscow, to start translation and publication of Russian classics in Kashmir, is established by the following information provided to this author by Raisa Tugasheva who was actively associated with this programme.

It was in 1972 that the Progress Publishers, Moscow (successor to Foreign Language Publishing House which published in 13 languages) decided to start publication of Kashmiri translations of Russian literature. Some Urdu-knowing scholars were recruited for the task. Ms Raisa Tugasheva (who had worked as Urdu announcer at Tashkent Radio for twenty years) was made Head and Editor-in-Chief of the Kashmiri Section of Progress Publishers. Besides two Assistant editors and one Kashmiri Muslim student at Moscow were associated with the Project. At the first instance, a few books of Russian literature were taken up and later translated into Kashmiri. One assistant editor Lena was sent to Kashmir for further study. When a delegation of Progress Publishers visited Kashmir to survey the potential and prospects of circulation of these books, their proposal met with a hostile State government response. It was found that the State administrative machinery was against the publication and circulation of the Kashmir translations of Russian books. With the result the whole project was quietly wound up.

7. Central government grants provided to the State Education Department from time to time for development of Kashmiri language and literature have either been spent on other heads or allowed to lapse. Similarly the 100 per cent financial assistance provided by the central government for translation of the Constitution of India into Kashmiri was not availed of. Instead

[19]Ibid.

these funds were deviated for the promotion of Urdu which was misleadingly projected as the regional language of the state.

8. It was as late as November 2000 that the Jammu and Kashmir government took a historic decision to introduce Kashmiri and other mother tongues in all the government and private schools in the state. But, this decision has been implemented only half-heartedly, and private schools in particular have not executed the decision. Several literary and cultural organizations in the state have, therefore, been pressing for the introduction of Kashmiri language in all schools as a compulsory subject from Class I to Class VIII.

9. Dogri which is spoken in the Jammu region and the adjoining areas of Himachal Pradesh and Punjab, has been recognised as one of the regional languages in the VI Schedule of the state's Constitution. The Sahitya Academy started giving its awards for Dogri in 1970. When in mid-1992 the central government was taking steps to include Nepali, Konkani, and Manipuri in the ES, the Dogri Sangharsh Morcha started a movement in Jammu, pressing for acceptance of their demand for the inclusion of Dogri in the ES of the Constitution of India. Though the matter was raised in parliament, nothing happened. The people of Jammu pointed to the rich literary heritage of Dogri, its wide prevalence in Jammu and Kashmir, Himachal Pradesh, and Punjab and also the usage of the easy Devanagari script for this language, and the contribution of the people of Jammu to maintain national integrity, as sufficient grounds for inclusion of Dogri in the ES.[20] However, it was the BJP-led government at the centre which accepted their demand, and Dogri was included in the ES, vide 92nd Constitution Amendment Act, 2003 published in the *Gazette of India* on 8 January 2004.

10. In Ladakh too, Urdu was imposed as a medium of instruction, though the majority of people there speak and write Ladakhi (Bodhi), a dialect of Tibetan and which has a script of its own. It was during the latter years of Dogra rule that Urdu was introduced

[20]For further details see text of Memorandum dated 6 July 1992, by Dograi Sangharsh Morcha in Appendix B.

as the official language throughout the state including Ladakh. Even at that time, Ladakhi Buddhists had resented the 'infliction of Urdu' as a medium of instruction in primary schools. The report of the Kashmir Raj Bodhi Maha Sabha, Srinagar (1935) provides an insight into the sharp reaction evoked by this practice among the local people. It states:[21]

The infliction of Urdu—to them a completely foreign tongue—on the Ladakh Buddhists as a medium of instruction in the primary stage is a pedagogical atrocity which accounts, in large measure, for their aversion to going to school. Nowhere in the world are boys in the primary stage taught through the medium of a foreign tongue. And so, the Buddhist boy whose mother tongue is Tibetan must struggle with the complicacies of the Urdu script and acquire a knowledge of this alien tongue in order to learn the rudiments of Arithmetic, Geography, and what not.... This deplorable and irrational practice is being upheld in face of the fact that printed text books for all Primary school subjects do exist in Tibetan and have been utilized with good results by the Moravian Mission at Leh.

Ironically, even after the end of Dogra Raj, Urdu continues to be the medium of instruction. Though Ladakhi and Arabic have also been introduced in government schools along with English, private Islamic schools teach Urdu and Arabic only. This educational policy has led to the building up of segmented religious identities as against a secular one, thereby polarizing the traditional and tolerant Ladakhi society on communal lines.

11. Instead of recognizing Gojri, the mother tongue of over eight lakh Gujars, the Constitution of Jammu and Kashmir included Pahari as one of the regional languages in its VI schedule. This anomalous situation is a result of the impression that Gojri is part of Pahari, though it is actually more akin to Rajasthani. And, the census of 1941 has included Gojri under Rajasthani, whereas the subsequent censuses of 1961, 1971, and 1981 have not mentioned Pahari at all. This is one of the contributory factors that have led to the Gojri-Pahari controversy, which has been explained in the following pages. The Gujars of Jammu and Kashmir have been demanding their identification and enumeration by the census authorities

[21] *The Triennial Report of Kashmir Raj Bodhi Maha Sabha*, Srinagar, 1935, p. 11.

on the basis of their tribal rather than linguistic identity, so as to avoid an overlap with the Paharis and the consequent underestimation of their population.

12. Balti, a dialect of the Tibetan language, used to be written in the Tibetan script before the advent of Islam in Baltistan in the sixteenth century. Numerous rock inscriptions which still exist in Baltistan (in Pak-occupied Kashmir), are a living testimony to this fact. Following the conversion of Baltis to Islam, the indigenous Tibetan script for the Balti language was discarded 'as profane'.[22] Instead, the Persian script was introduced even though it did not 'suit the language due to certain phonological difference'.[23] But after Baltistan was occupied by Pakistan in 1948, Urdu has prevailed in the area. As a result, the indigenous Balti language has been further weakened owing to the heavy influence of Persian and Urdu. The same is true of Baltis living in the Indian state of Jammu and Kashmir. The Baltis in Pakistan are deeply disturbed over the loss of their inherited culture, particularly during the past two decades because of the 'onslaught of religious fanaticism'.[24] This change is ascribed to the Islamic Revolution in Iran, following which *maulvis,* flush with money, entered the area and banned singing, dancing, and all forms of traditional cultural activities.[25] Interestingly, the Shia Muslims in the Kargil area of Ladakh, who also speak the Balti language and share their culture with the Baltis of Baltistan, have been subjected to similar change. They have been allowed to be swayed under the pernicious influence of mullahs and *mujtahid*s, most of whom receive theological training and support from Iran.

These mujtahids, have stripped the festivals and ceremonies in Kargil of their traditional music and fanfare. The traditional musicians—Doms—who used to play drums and windpipe instruments on all festive occasions, have been rendered jobless. This situation has resulted in the destruction of rich folk, linguistic, literary, and cultural heritage of the Baltis. The only saving grace is that most of the Balti folk

[22]'The Lost Word,' *The Herald,* Karachi, September 1994, p. 80.
[23]See interview by Sayed Abbas Kazmi in *The Herald.*
[24]See Zaighan Khan, 'The Lost Horizon,' *The Herald,* Karachi, September 1994, pp. 78–80.
[25]Ibid.

literature is still preserved in the oral unwritten tradition. Besides, there is an organized effort inside Pak-occupied Baltistan by Balti intellectuals led by Syed Abbas Kazmi to revive the Balti heritage including its Tibetan script. The Baltistan Research Center, Skardo, is doing a commendable job in this regard. Similar efforts need to be initiated by Jammu and Kashmir Cultural Academy inside the Kargil area.

Foregoing discussion of the state of affairs of mother tongues in the state of Jammu and Kashmir throws up important political issues. It becomes clear that despite the local urge to preserve and promote their mother tongues, whether it is Kashmiri, Dogri, Gojri, Bhoti, or Balti, the same have been denied their due place. This has been done as part of the calculated policy of the Islamist bureaucracy and political leadership to subvert the indigenous linguistic and ethnocultural identities which inherit a composite cultural heritage. Thus a supranational Islamic identity has been sought to be imposed in different regions of the state, which essentially are different language and culture areas. Simultaneously a whispering campaign was launched in Kashmir, alleging the central government's apathy towards the Kashmiri language, which is, however, belied by facts. Apart from inclusion of Kashmiri in the ES, the Sahitya Academy has been giving awards for Kashmiri Writers from 1956 though it started doing so for Dogri only in 1970. What is needed now is to remove the existing imbalances and introduce Sahitya Academy awards for Gojri, Bhoti, and Balti, besides officially recognizing Devanagari as an alternate script for Kashmiri.

Conclusion

The language geography of the state has changed after 1947, when a large chunk of the state was occupied by Pakistan, what is now known as Pak-occupied Kashmir and Northern Areas. The new ground situation is that all the Kashmiri, Dogri, Gojri, and Ladakhi speaking areas fall within the Indian side of Jammu and Kashmir. As against this, the Burushaski- and Dardi- speaking areas fall within the Northern Areas now under the occupation of Pakistan. Yet, some small pockets of Dardi-speaking people—Buddhist Brukpas in Da Hanu area of Ladakh, people of Dras (Ladakh) and Gurez (Baramulla)—lie within the Indian part of Jammu and Kashmir. Similarly, all the Pothwari-(Lahanda) speaking areas in Poonch, Mirpur, etc., remain within Pak-occupied Kashmir. As regards the Baltis, they are divided between those living in Kargil in Indian Ladakh and across the LAC in Baltistan (Northern Areas). From within the Kashmiri-speaking community, the entire Kashmiri Hindu minority of over 400,000 people has been forced out of the valley in 1989–90 by the Islamist militants. Thus, this significant and indigenous minority community has been deprived of its ancient habitat and language culture area in the Kashmir valley. Given the precarious condition of these displaced persons living in forced exile in various parts of India and struggling for survival, their language and culture have become the worst casualty of their ethnic-religious cleansing. The question of resettlement of this displaced minority in their ancient birthland in a manner that ensures their ethnolinguistic and territorial homogeneity and adequate constitutional/administrative safeguards for protection of their human rights is directly linked to the permanent solution of the Kashmir imbroglio.

A study of the language demography of Jammu and Kashmir establishes the fact that the Lahanda-(Pothwari) speaking area falls almost entirely across the LAC in Pak-occupied Kashmir. That the LAC on the western side coincides with the specific language-culture area, provides a natural permanence to the LAC on ethnolinguistic lines in this sector. This should provide a key to finding a lasting solution to the vexed Kashmir problem between India and Pakistan. However, this is not true of the Balti-speaking area, which remains divided by the LAC between Kargil area of Jammu and Kashmir in India and Baltistan region of Pak-occupied Kashmir. That there is a renewed urge among the Baltis to revive their ancient Balti language and heritage only demonstrates their cultural roots in Ladakh.

Regarding the evolution and affinities of various mother tongues in Jammu and Kashmir, it is established that most of the languages are rooted in or have close affinities with the Indo-Aryan languages. Whereas Dogri is closely related to Punjabi, Gojri is akin to Rajasthani. Grierson's theory of Kashmiri belonging to the Dardic branch of languages has been disputed by the insider view emanating from Kashmir and elsewhere. Most of the linguistic researches conducted in Kashmir during the past forty years,[26] have established that Kashmiri bears close resemblance to Sanskritic languages, thereby testifying to the close civilizational contacts and ties between Kashmir and India since ancient times. Grierson who has misleadingly adopted the religious distinction between 'Hindu Kashmiri' and 'Muslim Kashmiri' has actually followed the colonial approach towards non-European societies. Ironically, Grierson's theory has been used as pretext by an American geographer, J.E. Schwartzberg, who has advocated the merger of Kashmir valley with the Dardic-speaking areas of Pak-occupied Kashmir on the basis of linguistic and cultural affinity.[27] Grierson's theory has since been disputed. Besides, the fact remains that the people of Kashmir valley are not only linguistically different from those living across the Line of Control in Pak-occupied Kashmir, but also have different cultural moorings and social ethos. Though Ladakhi and Balti belong to the Tibeto-Burman group of languages, the presence of a Sanskritic impact among the Garkuns of Ladakh is a living example of the extent of Indian cultural presence in this remote area. Given the importance of the subject, it is incumbent upon the linguists and anthropologists in India to unravel the mysteries of evolution and affinities of various mother tongues of Jammu and Kashmir, in the broader context of race movement and civilizational evolution in north and northwestern India.

Kashmiri is the main language spoken in the state, its spatial distribution being limited to the central valley of Kashmir and some parts of Doda. Though Kashmiri has no 'functional role as a written language' now, it is 'overwhelmingly the language of personal and in-group communication. It is the medium of dreams, mental arithmetic and reflection, of communication within the family, with friends and in market places, in places of worship, etc.'[28] According to a survey,

[26]See for further details, T.N. Ganjoo, 'Origin and Development of Kashmiri Language', University of Kashmir (Ph.D. Thesis). T.N. Ganjoo, 'Linguistic Sociology of Ancient Kashmir', *Studies of Kashmir Council of Research*, Vol. 2, November 1977, pp. 24–33. T.N. Ganjoo, 'Kashri Zaban-i-mutalaq akh nov soch' ('New Perspective on Kashmiri Language') (in Kashmiri), *Anhaar*, Department of Kashmiri, University of Kashmir, 1 (l), 1977, pp. 7–35. B.N. Kalla, 'Kashri Zaban-i-manz Vedic zaban hand ansar ('Elements of Vedic Language in Kashmiri') (in Kashmiri), *Anhaar*, 1 (l), 1977, pp. 49–62.

[27]See J.E. Schwartzberg's *Proposal for a Peaceful Resolution of the Indo–Pakistani Dispute over Kashmir.*

[28]N. Kaul and Schmidt, *Kashmiri: A Sociolinguistic Survey,* p. 67.

the Kashmiris view their language as 'an integral part of their identity' and want it to be accorded its due role in the fields of education, mass-media and administration.[29] The neglect of mother tongues by the state is the most salient language issue in Jammu and Kashmir, and the earlier it is remedied, the better. However, the only silver lining is that both Kashmiri Hindus and Muslims have identified Kashmiri as their mother tongue.

Though Pahari has not been enumerated as a separate language in the Jammu and Kashmir state census reports of 1961, 1971, and 1981, of late there have been demands for grant of some concessions to 'Paharis' in the state. The Pahari versus Gujar issue is a potential source of ethnic conflict as both the Pahari and Gujar interests are in conflict with each other. Both the Pahari and Gujar identities overlap in certain aspects particularly their hill settlement pattern and some common language features. Granting of scheduled tribe status on 19th April 1991 by the central government, entitles the Gujars—the third largest community in the State—to preferential treatment in government services, educational, professional and technical education, etc. Gujars also claim proportionate representation in the state assembly. The non-Gujar Muslims of the state have been peeved at the conferment of scheduled tribe status and its benefits to the Gujars. They have now demanded similar concession and the privileges associated with it for the 'Paharis' of Rajouri, Poonch, Kupwara, and Baramulla districts, that is, where the Gujars are in sizable numbers. The central government decision to meet the demand of Gujars has also evoked some reaction from the local press.[30] The new 'Pahari' demand is being backed by the valley-dominated political and bureaucratic Muslim elite, which even succeeded in persuading the state Governor to take a few steps in this direction. On 17 May 1992, the non-Gujar 'Pahari Board' was set up, with eight Kashmiri Muslims, eight Rajput Muslims, two Syeds, and four non-Muslims as its members. On 18 December 1993, the state Governor, General K.V. Krishna Rao issued a statement urging the central government to declare the Paharis as scheduled tribes.

Obviously, the Jammu and Kashmir state administration is trying to construct new identities such as 'Paharis' in a bid to undermine the

[29]Ibid., pp. 64–5, 68.
[30]See *Greater Kashmir*, Srinagar, 18 August 1993; *Kashmir Times*, Jammu, 26 January 1994.

Gujars and their ethnolinguistic identity in the areas where they are dominant. That is why the demands of 'Paharis' of Rajouri, Poonch, Kupwara, and Baramulla, (where Gujars are concentrated) are raised, whereas the backward and neglected hill people of Ramban, Kishtwar, Padar, and Bhadarwah, who speak distinct dialects of Rambani, Kishtwari, Padari, and Bhadarwahi, have been excluded from the purview of the so called 'Pahari'. This is a subtle move to deprive the Gujars of their numerical advantage and fully marginalise them in the political, administrative, and other institutional structures of the state.

The existing spatial distribution of Gujar speakers does provide some sort of linguistic territorial homogeneity, which, however, needs to be further consolidated to help in the preservation and promotion of Gojri language and ethnocultural heritage and fulfilling their socio-economic and political aspirations within the state. Gojri has been included as one of the regional language in the VI schedule of the state's Constitution. It is also taught up to Class IV primary school as an optional subjects in the schools in Poonch and Rajouri districts of the state. The Sahitya Academy needs to institute awards for Gojri writers. Of late the Gujars of Jammu and Kashmir have stepped up their mobilization campaign for getting Gojri included in the ES of the Indian Constitution, as there are about ten million Gojri speakers in Jammu and Kashmir, Himachal Pradesh, Uttarakhand, Uttar Pradesh, Haryana, and Rajasthan.

That the Gujars are concentrated in specific border belts surrounding the main Kashmiri speaking area, which mostly fall within the Indian side of LAC, is yet another aspect of political importance. It is not only a physical obstacle in the way of attaining the goals of the ongoing secessionist movement based on Pan-Islamic-Kashmiri identities, it also demonstrates that, barring some possible minor adjustments here and there, the present LAC provides the best possible solution to the Kashmir problem.

As already stated, all the census reports have made a clear distinction between the Ladakhi (Bhoti) and Tibetan-speaking persons in Ladakh, the former being indigenous Ladakhis and the latter being Tibetan refugee settlers. Interestingly, various political activist groups such as Himalayan Committee for Action on Tibet, Himalayan Buddhist Cultural Association, Tibet Sangharsh Samiti, etc., which have been spearheading in India the campaign for Tibet's independence and have opened their branches in various Himalayan states of India, have been demanding the inclusion of the Bhoti language in the ES of the Indian Constitution. At the same time, there have been sustained efforts by the Tibetan scholars at Dharamshala or abroad towards preparing a unified system of the Tibetan language so that the same script, dialect, etc., is applied to all the Bhoti/Tibetan-speaking peoples whether in Indian Himalayas or elsewhere. This raises the question of Tibetanization of society, culture, and politics of the Indian Himalayas particularly in Ladakh, Himachal Pradesh, Sikkim, Arunachal Pradesh, Kalimpong, Darjeeling, etc. It has been noticed that Tibetan refugees living in these areas never use the local dialect and seek to exercise their cultural hegemony over the local Buddhist inhabitants. Owing to divergent modes of economic activity being followed by the Tibetan refugees and the indigenous Buddhists in this Himalayan region, the former being engaged in marketing and industrial activities and the latter being involved in primary agrarian economy, there have been social conflicts between these two culturally similar groups with the locals viewing the Tibetan refugees as exploiters. Such a conflict has been experienced in Ladakh, Himachal Pradesh, Arunachal Pradesh, etc. It becomes imperative for the concerned government and non-government agencies to ensure that the indigenous Bhoti/Ladakhi and even Balti ethnolinguistic heritage is preserved and promoted. The Bhoti language is spoken by about one million people in Ladakh, Zanskar, Lahaul, Spiti, Sikkim, Arunachal Pradesh, parts of Uttarakhand, besides among a large section of people in Nepal.

Central Institutes of Buddhist Studies at Leh and Sarnath, Institute of Tibetology in Gangtok, Tawang, numerous universities such as Delhi University, Punjab University, Chandigarh, Patiala University, Shanti Niketan, Allahabad, Nalanda, and Magadh offer courses in the Bhoti language. That old classical tenets, Buddhist scriptures, etc., are all available in the Bhoti language, make it all the more necessary for keeping the Bhoti language alive. Leh Hill Autonomous Council decided to make Bhoti language teaching from primary up to secondary level compulsory in Ladakh. And, textbooks on history, social studies, etc., in the Bhoti language have already been prepared by Ladakhi scholars like Lama Paldan, Geshes K. Wongdu and Jamyang Gyaltsen. Bhoti is even taught in the Moravian Mission school and other private schools at Leh. Bhoti is also taught at about fifty primary schools affiliated to various *gonpas* (monasteries) which are run by the Central Institute of Buddhist Studies at Choglamsar, Ladakh. However, the inclusion of Bhoti in the ES is a step that requires sufficient mobilization and political decision at the central level.

The state government's policy towards local mother tongues including Kashmiri, reflects the political dynamics of Muslim majoritarianism, in which supra-national religious ethnicity has been artificially superimposed over linguistic ethnicity. This has been done with the object of bringing Kashmiri Muslims closer to the Muslim *Ummah* in the subcontinent, and particularly with the adjoining Islamic state of Pakistan. This task has been carried forward by numerous Islamic political, social, and cultural institutions particularly the Jamat-i-Islami, Ahl-e-Hadis, Anjuman Tableegh-i-Islam, etc., and the madrasas or even public schools run by these organizations, all of which have been preaching and promoting Islamic worldview in political and social and cultural affairs. With the result a firm ideological base has been prepared to mould the political and cultural views of Kashmiri Muslims on religious lines rather than on an ethnolinguistic/ cultural basis, thereby negating the indigenous secular and composite cultural heritage. The same thing has happened in Pak-occupied Kashmir (including Northern Areas), where Urdu—the national language of Pakistan—has been imposed and popularized, and local mother tongues—Pothwari, Khowar, Burushaski, Dardi/Shina, and Balti remain neglected. Whereas adoption of such a policy by the Islamic Republic of Pakistan is understandable, it is quite ironical and unthinkable as to how such a state of affairs has been allowed in Jammu and Kashmir, part of the secular and democratic Republic of India which has otherwise provided specific constitutional safeguards for promotion of mother tongues and protection of rights of linguistic and cultural minorities.

It is surprising that the neglect of Kashmiri has never been a theme of unrest and anti-Indian movement in Kashmir. It is mainly because the Kashmiri Muslims have been swayed by their intellectual elite and political leaders of all hues (whether in power or out of it), most of whom have been educated at the Aligarh Muslim University, thereby imbibing the spirit of the Aligarh movement which regards Urdu as the symbol of Muslim cultural identity. This policy is derived from the Muslim League strategy adopted so successfully by M.A. Jinnah, 'for political mobilization of the Muslim Community around the symbols of Muslim identification—Islam, Urdu and the new slogan of Pakistan'.[31] That explains why primacy has been given to Islam instead of language, thereby consolidating the religious divide between Kashmiri Muslims and Hindus, who otherwise inherit the same language, habitat, and way of the life. The true spirit of Kashmiriat can be restored only after giving rightful place to the indigenous Kashmiri language and culture. Besides, steps need to be taken to promote other mother tongues of the state—Dogri, Gojri, Bhoti (Ladakhi), and Balti. The Sahitya Academy should give awards for literary works in Gojri and Bhoti as is done by it for Maithili and Rajasthani which are not listed in the ES. Devanagari should be recognized as an alternate script for the Kashmiri language which will meet the long-standing demand of the sizable ethnoreligious minority of Kashmiri Hindus. The Linguistic Survey of India and the Census Commissioner of India need to review Grierson's classification and evolve a suitable enumeration code and proper classification marks for various languages and mother tongues prevalent in Jammu and Kashmir, so that the linguistic and cultural aspirations of numerous ethnolinguistic groups in the state are duly reflected and protected.

[31]Paul R. Brass, *Language, Religion and Politics in Northern India* (Delhi, 1974), p. 180.

7

The Great Language Debate
Politics of Metropolitan versus Vernacular India*[1]

D.L. Sheth

The use of a regional language as the language of administration in a state and as the medium of instruction in schools is by now an established policy. It has been followed (although not uniformly) in almost all the states of the Indian union. About three years ago Mulayam Singh Yadav, the Chief Minister of Uttar Pradesh, chose to reaffirm this policy. And that precipitated a fierce attack from the powerful English language press in India. My interest in this event is not confined to commenting on the role that the English press played in countering the implementation of an established policy in an Indian state. Using that as a vantage point, I shall focus on the wider debate that this event generated, after forty-four years of independence, on

*Originally published as 'The Great Language Debate: Politics of Metropolitan versus Vernacular India', in Upendra Baxi and Bhikhu Parekh (eds), *Crisis and Change in Contemporary India* (New Delhi: Sage Publications, 1995), pp. 187–215.

[1]The term vernacular is used in two senses: linguistic and cultural. In the former sense vernacular refers to all non-English Indian languages as a diffused countervailing reality confronting the pre-eminence of English in India. As such these languages comprise the constitutionally recognized Indian languages such as Bengali, Gujarati, Marathi, Tamil, etc., which in common parlance are referred as the 'regional' languages. In this context Hindi is also referred to as vernacular, although it is competing with English at the national level and is aspiring to become and being recognized as the lingua franca of India. Other Indian languages and the so-called dialects which have yet not acquired legal-constitutional recognition (such as Konkani, Dogri, Tulu, etc.) also comprise the vernacular languages.

the future of English language in India. More than articulating the issues involved in the policy as such, the debate brought to the surface the changed relationships among social groups in politics and the divergence of perspectives between the contending groups—the proponents and opponents of English—on language policy as a means of nation building. The purpose of this essay, therefore, is to situate the language debate in the politics of social change and to show how the clue to the language issue may lie in viewing democratization rather than the continuing political hegemony of an elite class as the means of nation building for India.

The viciousness with which the press attacked Mulayam Singh Yadav was not surprising; the English language press has always reserved a special treatment for such rustic interlopers in our metropolitan world as a Raj Narain or a Tau. And for the English-language media, a Yadav, whether a Mulayam Singh or a Lallu Prasad, is a chip of the same vernacular block. What was remarkable, however, was the unity of opinion in support of the English language expressed by all shades of commentators, irrespective of their radically different ideological backgrounds. One is hard put to recall any such event in the recent past of our fractured public discourse. Even such issues as sati, violation of human rights, threats to our environment and to the livelihood of the poor through so-called development projects, or even something like Bhopal have failed to achieve such a unanimity of opinion and commonality of attitude in the press as was reflected on the issue of the importance of English language. One, of course, heard the odd dissenting voice, but the main thrust of importance of the writings in the English language press was and has remained, till today, in support

---

The term vernacular when used in the larger cultural context refers to a cultural identity in politics, of people and social-political elites who are identified as such for their non-use of English in the national political discourse. The use of non-English Indian languages by the 'vernaculars' (people, elites, etc.) may be due to conscious preference or the inability to use English as their first language. In the pan-Indian discourse the non-use of English is uniformly associated with lack of sophistication, parochialism and cultural underdevelopment. And therefore all articulation and activity in Indian languages is seen as devoid of a genuine national perspective and modernist content. This has given rise to a counter-cultural identity in politics of people and elites not using English as the first language; they are variously described as regional, provincial, mofussil, indigenous, or vernacular.

of the continued pre-eminence of English over all other Indian languages, especially Hindi, in modern India's life.

Admittedly, the closing of ranks by the English language press was not a reaction to an imagined threat. Mulayam Singh Yadav did more than merely revive an old policy for implementation in the state of which he was Chief Minister. He declared his intention to give teeth to the policy which was only hissing till then, not biting any one. The mode of implementation he chose was radically different from the one that had been followed in his own state or, for that matter, in any other Indian state. In the process, he touched some raw nerves.

Yadav was not content with making pious pronouncements about 'promoting' Hindi in a manner that did not threaten the prevalent role of English language in the education system and generally in our public life—this is how the policy has been 'implemented' in the states so far. His mode of implementation involved replacement of English, *wherever* it was used, by Hindi—both as a language of education and administration in his state and as a language of communication between his state and other states in India and the union government. In interstate communications he insisted on translations directly from one state language to another, without the mediation of English. The implications of such a step are not far to seek.

Even thirty-odd years after the creation of linguistic states, the language policy followed so far in several Indian states has not been able to establish the regional language as a universal medium of education and administration in a state. This half-hearted and partial implementation of the regional language policy has allowed the market principle of demand and supply to prevail over policy which, in effect, has given rise to a dual system of schooling in every state. One school system caters to those who can afford private schooling, the so-called 'public schools', in which English is the medium of instruction from the first standard. Even the nursery schools belonging to this system use English as the first language. In these schools children are discouraged to use the language they speak at home even as a peer group language. However sound may be the pedagogical principle of using the mother tongue as the medium of teaching and learning in theory, it is contemptuously rejected by this system. As is the case in other realms of Indian society, such a principle is applied in practice only for the masses. The latter are served, if that is the word, by the other system, in which the mother tongue or a regional language is the medium of instruction. This system comprises almost all the government and the municipal schools in a state. The vast majority of parents have no alternative but to send their children to these schools.

Yadav's dispensation, had it been actually implemented, would have put an end to such a dual system of schooling, at least in the state of Uttar Pradesh. But that is not all. Beyond making specific policy announcements about using Hindi—which also happens to be the regional language of Uttar Pradesh—as a medium of education and administration in the state, Yadav made bold to air his views on the wider issue of what role and status the English language should have in India after over four decades of independence. He even went further and referred to the self-serving interests of the class which supports the continued dominance of English in our public life and proceeded to elaborate on its lifestyles and motives. Coming as it did from a 'mofussil' elite, this was too much to take for a class which operates with the self-consciousness of being the 'Builders of Modern India'. In its support for English, or for that matter its stand on any other issue, this class of self-proclaimed nation-builders cannot admit of any motive other than that of protecting the 'national interest', both present and future. Its support for English, it is convinced, is for promoting the noble causes of development and national integration. Those who fail to share this altruistic logic lack, in its view, a 'national perspective' and are victims of such dreaded and atavistic ideologies as regionalism, traditionalism, and obscurantism.

Despite his bold stand later on the issue of secularism, a cause which a large section of the English language press loudly espouses, Mulayam Singh Yadav could not retrieve his lost ground with the press and generally with the metropolitan elite. In fact, this was one of the major factors that eventually brought his career as the Chief Minister of Uttar Pradesh to an end.

Yadav will have to fight his own political battles. But the debate on the language policy triggered off by him has brought to the surface issues that had remained dormant in the earlier debates of the sixties. Unlike in the past, the debate now is not about educational problems involved in the teaching and learning of the English language in India.

Nor does it reflect such rational concerns as those of identifying the levels and areas of professional and public life for which English may be considered necessary and useful and those in which English can be replaced by the regional language and/or by Hindi. Least of all is there any concern about evaluating thirty years of experience of using the mother tongue or a regional language as the medium in schools and the language of administration. The fact is that a radical change has occurred in the basic terms of discourse on the language issue as a whole.

The discourse on the language policy today is primarily a political discourse. Unlike in the late fifties and the early sixties, when cultural identities were linguistically defined, today the discussions on the language policy do not pose a potent threat to such identities. Since the reorganization of states on the linguistic principle, religion, rather than language has become the epitome of the culture of the people. Shorn of rhetoric, disputes concerning the language policy are now more openly stated, to use a hackneyed phrase, in terms of 'who gets what and how in politics'. In more concrete terms, the discourse on the language policy has now been linked (along with other issues such as reservations) to the wider conflict over power in society between two elite groups: the nationally entrenched, pan-Indian English-educated elite and the new but ascendant elites who have lately emerged on the national scene but sans the trappings of an English education.

The former has successfully managed to continue to tighten its hold on the levers of power at the national level since independence. It controls the higher echelons of politics, bureaucracy, the armed forces, corporate business, and the professions. Members of the latter group have, as a result of democratic politics, risen at the regional level and have come to exercise power in the states for the last three decades. They are now attempting to create for themselves spaces in the power structure at the national level (they are known by various names: the regional elite, the rural elite, the 'mofussils', the vernaculars, or simply and crudely the kulaks). The differences between the two are indexed in terms of their urban-rural and caste backgrounds. While there is some overlap between the two in economic terms, the sharp differences between them in socio-cultural terms are marked by the language divide. In the life-world of the former, English occupies a central role; for the latter its role is at best marginal.

The English-educated elites have so far enjoyed the privilege of determining the terms of discourse because they claim to represent a 'national perspective' on every issue; in fact they define what is 'national'. But the regional elites have begun to operate with a newly acquired sense of confidence because of the numbers they represent. In the process, they are seeking to change not only the terms of discourse on the language issue in their favour but are generally proceeding to challenge the role the English-educated elites have been playing since independence, both as norm-setters and pace-setters of India's public life.

This dimension of intra-elite conflict, which has overridden all aspects of the language debate, is not a sudden, fortuitous happening. It is a *denouement* of a longer process of change in the balance of power in society brought about, among other things, by the functioning of open and competitive politics. It will, therefore, be misleading to view the debate merely in terms of intra-elite conflict. At the root of this conflict is the process of further democratization of the Indian polity.

This process begun with the granting of universal franchise by the Constitution of India, the exercise of which was vastly expanded over time. Universal franchise has brought into the political fold groups, which for centuries existed on the peripheries of the Indian political order. For example, the erstwhile Sudras constitute, today, the numerous peasant and intermediate castes; according to the Mandal Commission, they make up over 52 per cent of the Indian population. By deploying their numerical strength and basing themselves on the tradition of social solidarity of groupings among them, they have not only acquired electoral salience in politics but have lately been able to enter the legislatures and other structures of political decision making in fairly large numbers.

In the earlier phase of the 'Congress system' this process was monitored and gradualized, if not contained, through the horizontally factionalized structure of political accommodation and participation— a hallmark of the Congress system. But this structure was subordinated at the national level by the Nehruvian elite. The latter emerged victorious in the elite struggle for power that took place soon after independence, and succeeded in establishing its pre-eminence in national politics. In the process, it insulated the fragile institutional structure of democracy from being overwhelmed by the populist pressures released during the independence movement. But, at the same time, it also resulted in creating a big divide between the elite and the masses which in today's terms is often characterized as the divide between India and Bharat.

Indeed, the Nehruvian elite did not rule by use of raw power. Instead, it established its political hegemony through defining the terms of national discourse for independent India which, along with other forces in its favour, helped it obtain a consent to rule. Although democracy (and modernization) was its credo, the discourse appeared, at best, patronizing and condescending to the vast majority of the neo-literate and illiterate rural masses. They neither had the aptitude nor the language to participate in this discourse. The Nehruvian elite dismissed them as a change-resisting population steeped in obscurantist traditions. The only way the masses could establish their fitness for modernization was by subjecting themselves to self-denigration and unconditionally accepting the modernizing national elite as their saviour.

As was proved later, the problem of modernization had nothing to do with the Indian farmer's resistance to change. The alacrity with which he adopted the new practices of 'scientific' agriculture and took to the monetization of the rural economy firmly repudiated the elite 'theory' of the change-resisting Indian farmer. Bur the same person showed disdain for such abstract ideas as 'modernization', 'secularism' and 'socialism'. For him, these were disembodied ideas with no anchorage in real life. Their embodiment, in real life required that the terms of discourse be adapted to the meaning system and the life-world of the Indian people. Instead they were couched in terms alien to the cognitive and experiential categories used by ordinary Indians. The problem, thus, was not so much with the ideas per se, but with the idiom and the language in which the ideas of change and modernization were packaged. Simply put, modernization became an elite discourse in post-independence India, because it was by and large carried out in English (or at best in some kind of translatese). English became the language of modernity and of moderns in India and the indigenous languages began to be viewed as the medium of traditionalist, even obscurantist thought and lifestyles.

It took about a decade and a half after independence for the subjugated groups to establish their identity as Indian citizens and to express their resentment about the patron-client relationship between them and the Nehruvian national elite. Although this process started in the fifties with the participation of the masses in electoral and party politics, it acquired a big momentum in the decades of the sixties and seventies. It was during this period that the rural-urban and caste-class differences in the society acquired a strong political content and meaning. Several peasant-based and regional parties emerged, some as split-away groups from the Congress; while some old ones acquired a new political salience. The system of one-party dominance came to an end, with non-Congress parties coming into power in several states and collectively posing a serious threat to the monopoly of the Congress party's power at the centre; the threat was first posed in 1967, but it actually materialized in the 1977 elections. The Congress was unable to accommodate or contain the pressures that arose from the base of the polity and thus ceased to be the *system* that it was. It remained a 'national' party, but without strong roots in regional politics. Underlying these developments of the sixties and the seventies was the rapidly expanding process of institutional democratization, which in its first flush brought the large masses of peasant and intermediate castes onto the centre stage of politics. In the process, the upwardly mobile groups among them not only acquired political clout but also a material basis to their power in the rural economy. This significantly changed the balance of power in the society.[2]

While it is true that the politics of this period did not open up avenues to power for the people at the lowest rungs of the traditional social hierarchy, that is, the dalits and the tribals, they at least entered the process by forging electoral alliances with the upper castes—this was the case in the 1971 elections. They are now pressing harder at the gates, in a bid to enter the political process on their own terms. By forming parties (like the Bahujan Samaj), they seek to convert their

[2]For a detailed analysis of the political change brought about during this period through increased participation and assertion of the upwardly mobile rural communities in politics, see writings of Rajni Kothari published around the 1967 elections. Especially see 'The Congress System Under Strain', 'The Political Change of 1967', and 'India's Political Transition', reproduced in Rajni Kothari, *Politics and the People: In Search of a Humane India* (Delhi: Ajanta Publications, 1989), Vol. I, pp. 59–79, 151–65, 166–79, respectively.

numerical strength into a durable political base. Nevertheless, the participation of people as full citizens is still an unfinished process in India and its full impact is yet to be felt at the centre of the political system. But, in the meanwhile, the vernacular elite has entrenched itself firmly in power at the local and regional levels. At the close of the decade of the eighties, the Congress party was removed once again from power at the centre, with the regional elite moving closer to acquiring its hold on the levers of power at the national level. As we enter the decade of the nineties, the Congress has been again returned to power at the national level. This change, however, is least likely to reverse the process of ascendancy of the vernaculars. It is the Congress party which, to survive in power, will have to change its Nehruvian stance on such issues as language, reservations, federalism and those pertaining to the farm policy. Thus viewed, the intra-elite conflict illustrated by the language debate is an outgrowth of the democratic process of politics. The language policy, as also the other economic and social policies, will have to be adapted, sooner or later, to this changing balance of power.

The regional language policy operating on the ground has, either by design or default, produced far-reaching consequences for India's public life, particularly for the educational system—among other things, it has made the status quo regarding English unmaintainable.[3]

One unintended but a major consequence of the manner in which the language policy has been implemented is the mushroom growth of the English-medium schools at all levels of school education—pre-primary, primary, secondary, and higher secondary. The question now being posed by those excluded from the 'public-schools' system is, why is it that the protagonists of English do not take an honest view of this development and do not recommend universal use of English as the medium of instruction in all the schools throughout the country—'public' and 'non-public', private and governmental, and at all levels from pre-primary to the university? If English is so important for

---

[3]For the impact on the educational system created by implementation of the regional language policy in the states, see B.H. Krishnamurti, 'The Regional Language vis-a-vis English as the Medium of Instruction in Higher Education; The Indian Dilemma', in D.P. Pattanayak (ed.), *Multilingualism in India* (Philadelphia: Multilingual Matters Ltd, 1990), pp. 15–24.

development and national integration, they argue, why should access to English education remain restricted to a few? The protagonists of English find any such suggestion 'impractical', even preposterous. Perhaps the idea of universalizing English education in India hurts their pedagogic and nationalist sensibilities: while maintaining the status quo on English not only satisfies their 'noble' sensibilities, it can also be justified on the liberal grounds of freedom of choice. It is a different matter that the choice is not, and cannot ever become, real for the vast majority of Indians! Anyway, the fact remains that despite the increasing spread of English-medium schools, a vast majority of children in India receive, will continue to receive, schooling in the regional language. English can never serve as a vehicle for mass education in India.

Another but by and large an expected consequence of the policy of promoting the regional language for mass education is that it has produced a whole generation of educated youth with little or no exposure to English and whose parents are either illiterate or at best first-generation literate. They are taught English as a subject, but indifferently and at a fairly late stage of their schooling. They show little inclination to use even the little English they may have. When they use it they do so in a halting way, with a strong regional accent. This gives them away as the mofussils they are; they have little chance of getting admitted in the charmed circle of the metropolitan youth, who have acquired their English through its use as a medium of education in 'public schools'. Thus for a vast majority of educated youth, proficiency in English is unattainable and yet they face unequal competition for social mobility in the society in which English continues to be the mark of education.

Today, about 80 per cent of the students graduating from colleges and universities have studied through the medium of a regional language.[4] The 'entrance examinations' or the so-called qualifying tests and 'interviews' they have to take either for jobs or for entrance in the professional institutions are, however, held in English. Even if for pro forma's sake when they are allowed to take such tests in Hindi or other regional languages, their chances of getting jobs and elite positions remain dim in the institutional milieu which is English dominated. A

[4]Out of 185 million students enrolled in all educational institutions in India, 40 million (21.62 per cent) receive instruction through the English medium. Data presented in Mary S. Zurbuchen, 'Wiping out English', *Seminar*, 391, 1992, p. 48.

few gifted ones are able to make an entry, but for the vast majority of educated youth, English has become a barrier to their social and physical mobility. To overcome this disadvantage the non-English educated youth make pathetic efforts by joining 'English-speaking classes' or reading up such books as *The Rapid English Speaking Course*. They do this almost towards the end of their educational career when it is too late for them to make good their 'deficiency'. Obviously, this cannot equip them for competition, but it does bring them the derision usually reserved in society for the parvenus.[5]

It may be a lopsided view, but it contains an element of truth when it is said that the continued dominance of English in India has resulted in the emotional alienation of the non-English educated youth from the national mainstream. This divide between the metropolitan and the vernacular youth brought about by the dual educational streams, has given a new twist to the language issue. The question now being raised is about the future of this mass of population of the non-English educated regional youth in the rural areas whose life-chances are severely affected by their poor knowledge of English. Their frustrations, based on acute status anxiety, find political expression in linguistic and regional chauvinism. This often results in their joining, even founding, regionalist and separatist movements, especially in the non-Hindi regions. In the Hindi-speaking regions, they express such anxiety by vociferously opposing the domination of English and demanding that Hindi take its place; the enterprising ones fancy entering the world of high crime or of 'politics', or organizations like the Bajarang Dal or Shiv Sena, for joining and prospering in which knowledge of English may be a liability rather than an asset.

The continuities of lifestyles and aspirations once informed the relationship between the national political elite and the rural leadership, especially during the independence movement, linking national politics with regional politics. These continuities have been eroded in

---

[5]Peggy Mohan rightly points out that in India, the problem of learning English is not seen as one of acquiring a foreign language. It is seen as making preparation to enter the closely guarded citadel of an exclusive elite class. Learning the language late in one's educational career for instrumental use may be a good pedagogic practice, but not the right strategy for those wanting to make entry into the citadel of the English-speaking elite. See, Peggy Mohan, 'Postponing to Save Time', *Seminar*, 321, 1986.

the course of the last three decades. The neo-colonial elite, having acquired greater, almost exclusive, access to English education, have been able to develop for themselves new techno-managerial skills. In the process, they have struck roots in India's growing metropolises. Their lifestyles and aspirations are now linked to and are more in tune with, the global metropolitan world. This has created a new gap between the so-called national elite and the regional elite. The gap now is not only political but also sociocultural in nature.

While the national elite has kept the regional elite at bay, India's regional politics has also been displacing the upper-caste oriented, English-educated elite from positions of power in the regions. This process is best illustrated by frequent waves of anti-Brahmin movements in the peninsular states of south India and in the western state of Maharashtra. Such movements predate independence, but their nature has changed significantly in the post-independence period, especially since the early sixties. They are no longer the 'protest' movements they once were, expressing strong sentiments, through the symbolism of oppression and exploitation, against what they described as Brahminical domination in the society. The castes, which in the earlier phase were 'in the forefront of these movements, have now acquired political power in these states and are in the process of consolidating it by acquiring economic clout, control over the educational system, and over the job market in the governmental sector. The language and symbolism they now use is of power and not of 'protest'.

The result is that significant sections of the upper-caste elites from these states, equipped with English education, have been elevated to the national level; quite a few among them have also migrated to countries of the developed world. Those who have been left behind are unreconciled to the regionalization of politics brought about by the ascendant middle and intermediate castes and to the consequent loss of their power. In the other states, where there have been no anti-Brahmin movements, regional politics is nonetheless dominated by the caste-class and sectarian factors. In these states, the numerically strong and upwardly mobile groups of the middle and intermediate castes have, by and large, succeeded in casting out the upper-caste elite from positions of power and to some extent from white-collar jobs as well.

This ongoing process operates differently in different states. It is articulated in sectarian terms in states like Punjab and Jammu and Kashmir, and in terms of 'preserving the linguistic and cultural identity' in a state like Assam. In any event, the consequences of this new, post-independence regional polities are similar in all the states in that a certain class of elite is displaced from power, with significant sections from among them moving out into the growing metropolitan world. The process is likely to be intensified in several states of northern and western India with the implementation of the reservations policy for the 'Other Backward Classes'. When fully implemented, total reservations for jobs and college admissions in these states will amount to at least about 50 per cent.

These developments of the last thirty years have not only brought the regional elites into prominence but have radically changed the character and composition of the national elite. The old neo-colonial, upper-caste elite, with a long tradition of education in the language of the ruling elite of the time—this may be Sanskrit or Persian in the past or English today—still constitutes its core. However, the ranks of the 'national' elite have now expanded to include several new groups of castes, by and large of the *dvija* varna, which have acquired access to English education in the post-independence period. This has been made possible by the rapid expansion of English-medium schools which cater to these new aspirants. This development, combined with the push and pull factors described above, has not only contributed to the increase in the numerical strength of this expanded elite, but it has changed the character and function of the elite in society. In this sense, it is a different class of elite from the one which led the independence movement. This new formation is constituted by drawing together different elite elements in the society—the new as well as the old ones. Their commitment to the continued pre-eminence of English in India acts as a binding force for these diverse elite elements. This has not only shaped their attitude and role as the new pan-Indian elite operating in the national arena, but has also detached them from the world of regional politics and cultures. It will be a mistake to confuse this expanded new elite formation at the national level with the regional elites who operate in regional languages but still support the use of English, rather than Hindi, as a second language in their respective regions. Unlike the new national elite their primary commitment is to the regional language and not to English. In effect, their worldview is radically different from that of the pan-Indian elite in whose life-world English has a priority over their mother tongue.

Sociologically viewed, the ranks of the pan-Indian elite are drawn from several groups ousted from their regions, such as Punjabi Hindus, Kashmiri Pundits, and south-Indian Brahmins. Then there are the traditional urban-oriented professional castes such as the Nagars of Gujarat. the Chitpawans and the CKPs (Chandrasenya Kayastha Prabhus) of Maharashtra, and the Kayasthas of north India, whose members have joined the ranks, albeit more through responding to the pull factor than being subject to the push factor. Also included among them are the old elite groups which emerged during the colonial rule: the Probasi and Bhadralok Bengalis, the Parsis, and the upper crusts of the Muslim and Christian communities with a pronounced secular and nationalist persuasion.

Being uprooted from regions, they have become a new somewhat homogeneous all-India group; usually their nationalism is unitary and their idea of the state is that of a centralised and hegemonic political entity. They see a close connection between knowledge and power and use English as a means of exclusion, an instrument of cultural hegemony, by which they seek to defy the logic of numbers in politics and continue their hold over the levers of power at the national level.

Although they operate with the subjective sense of a *national* elite, they lack the self-consciousness, ideological coherence, and the strong will to rule. Their primary concern, it seems, is to somehow retain their hold on the Indian state in the face of radical, and apparently irreversible, changes that have occurred in the balance of power in society. With their lifestyles and aspirations now being hitched to global metropolitanism, they lack a cultural basis to their political power. Theirs is a synthetically manufactured Culture, (with a capital 'C'). While they may continue to give an ideological justification for their rule in terms of modernism, its validation in the wider society has become tenuous.

Although English has become central to the life-world of this national elite, their bilingualism is not of the kind a Gandhi, a Tagore, or a Tilak represented during the independence movement. These leaders used their bilingual facility to transcreate the terms of national discourse in the regional world and thus seek the latter's participation and involvement in nation-building. It is important to remember in this context that the national leadership of the independence movement self-consciously learnt English as a foreign language; it was indeed acquired assiduously and cultivated purposively. But the national leadership lived and, by and large, operated in the milieu dominated by the regional language and culture. It made creative contributions in different fields of knowledge through the medium of a regional language. The national discourse raised by this leadership was addressed to the issues of social reform and political independence and was carried out in regional languages; in the process, it also contributed to the growth of these languages. It was not accidental, for instance, that Gandhiji's *My Experiments with Truth,* Tagore's *Gitanjali,* and Tilak's *Gitarahasya* were written originally, in Gujarati, Bengali, and Marathi, respectively.[6] The post-independence national elites, on the other hand, have become distant from the regional languages and cultures, with English having become virtually their *first* language. Their use of the mother tongue or a regional language is by and large confined to the household or to the bazar. It is a language hardly ever used by them in any serious discourse, not even when the interlocutors among them may belong to the same regional language group. The result is that the political schism which always existed between the 'national' and regional elites has now widened along sociocultural dimensions with the caste-class and rural-urban differences between them being overlaid by the language divide: the 'national' elite by and large operating in English, and the regional elite in the respective regional languages.

The sociolinguistic map of India has vastly changed since the restructuring of the states on the linguistic principle during the period between the late fifties and mid-sixties. It created political units which

[6]In contrast, it is interesting to note that Jawaharlal Nehru, the precursor of the post-colonial English-speaking metropolitan elite, wrote his book, *Autobiography* and *Discovery of India,* in English. On the emergence of literate vernacular cultures through the colonial discourse, led by the bilingual elites, and generally on the relationship between elite power and national discourse, see Sudipta Kaviraj, *On the Construction of Colonial Power, Discourse, Hegemony,* Occasional Papers on History and Society, second series, 35 (New Delhi: Centre for Contemporary Studies, Nehru Memorial Museum and Library, 1991).

became coterminous with large linguistic identities. Identification of the boundaries of a state on the basis of *one* language which was culturally predominant and also numerically preponderant in that region or province, and recognition of that language as the official language of the state created a strong and stable cultural base for the political-linguistic identities in the country. In the process, however, the other smaller languages and cultures in the regions have been marginalized. The 'non-official' languages in the linguistic states do indeed survive today, but more, as 'spoken languages', or as 'dialects', or media of expression for 'folk cultures'. Their role in formal education and in the administration of these states has been almost erased.[7]

This has made regional languages the vehicle of mass literacy, formal education, and generally of public communication in the state. As a result, the regional languages themselves have undergone significant transformation. The sociocultural groups which until recently had little or no access to formal education have now acquired significant levels of education through the medium of an officially recognised regional language. They are now contributing to the evolution of regional languages, bringing with them idioms and perspectives which these languages had shunned when literature was the preserve of the old bilingual elite; in those days, the Sanskritic or English language sources were drawn on for the 'development' of these languages. The growth of dalit literature in several regional languages is one indicator of this change. Added to this is the phenomenal growth of the print media in regional languages which, among other things, has encouraged the participation of new generations of the literate population in a region in the production of signs and symbols relevant for mass politics.[8]

These developments have significantly contributed to making the regional languages more pliable as vehicles of public discourse. The formally adopted language of a state has, in the process, established its primacy not only over the minority languages but also over English.

---

[7]The problem of survival facing many small languages in India, under the threat of increasing linguistic homogenisation of every Indian state through the officially recognised regional languages, is poignantly posed by Sumi Krishna in her *India's Living Languages* (New Delhi: Allied Publishers, 1991).

[8]For data on the growth of print-media in the regional languages, see Sumi Krishna, pp. 139–53.

While English has survived, thanks to the dual education system, its role as the language of cultural hegemony and political domination in the regions is on the decline. But, there is little prospect for several 'mother tongues' or even full-fledged languages within a region to survive, with the predominant language of a region having established itself as the language of formal education and administration in the state. In political terms, this is a development unprecedented in Indian history. It has brought about political and cultural unification within what are today called linguistic states; and it is these that constitute the primary units of the Indian political system.'[9] Several of these political units are larger in population and territory than many European countries.

This particular development has far-reaching implications for the future of Hindi in India. This language has been adopted as the official language in seven Indian states. Four of these states are among India's most populous: Uttar Pradesh, Bihar, Madhya Pradesh, and Rajasthan. The remaining three states of Himachal Pradesh, Haryana, and Delhi are the smaller units. Together they comprise, according to the 1991 census, 43.36 per cent of India's population. Even if we discount the non-Hindi-speaking population in these states, the fact remains that in the 1981 census about 40 per cent of the total household population in India reported Hindi as the language used in their households. As against this picture of spread of Hindi, the census figure for English appears minuscule. Only 52,000 households in the whole of India, comprising about 0.04 per cent of the total household population, reported English as the language used in households. Another 0.5 per cent, population reported English as its second language.

Unfortunately, we do not have data on the third language used by people. It is however common knowledge that the increased proportions

[9]The extent of internal linguistic-cultural cohesion acquired by the states since they were formed on the basis of a predominant language of the region can be inferred from the fact that in the 1981 census 95.58 per cent of India's total household population reported one of the 15 regional languages or its variants listed in the Eighth Schedule (ES) of the Constitution as the language used in their households; 4.42 per cent of Indians spoke the other 106 languages not listed in the ES of the Constitution (figures from Series 1, Paper 1 of 1987). More significantly, the speakers of all the 106 non-schedule languages (except for Garo, Wancho, and Khasi) exhibit a high level of bilingualism far exceeding the national average of 13.34 per cent. See *Census of India, 1981* (Registrar General and Census Commissioner, India), Series 1: 'Population by Bilingualism', Table C-8.

of interstate migrations and particularly out-migration of people from the Hindi belt to other parts of India in recent years, the now vastly expanded networks of the electronic media—the radio and the TV—relaying Hindi programmes, some of which have become quite popular outside the Hindi belt, the reach of Hindi cinema, and the growing integration of the market have all contributed phenomenally to the spread of Hindi in India after independence. Its use as a third language or in the form of a bazar patois seems to have become quite widespread. As such, Hindi has emerged as the one language which is understood and used today by a majority of Indians, albeit with great variations in the degree of comprehension and use. There is thus little doubt that Hindi, in its natural course, has spread to different parts of the country—though more in some and less in others. And such spread has little to do with the work of Hindi proselytisers or with the so-called national policy on Hindi.

Indeed, English has also spread extensively in recent years, figures for which are not adequately reflected in the 1991 census, According to the census data on English, 0.55 per cent of the households use it as either the first or the second language; 0.51 per cent use it as the second language, and only 0.04 per cent as the first language. This however leaves out fairly large numbers of those who may be using English as the third language. For example, an English-educated Coorg will report Coorgi as the mother tongue und Kannad as the second language, while he or she may be quite proficient in English. Similarly a Marathi-, or a Gujarati-, or a Punjabi-speaking Indian who is proficient in English, but uses Hindi in day-to-day transactions vis-a-vis those not knowing his/her mother tongue or English, is likely to report Hindi, rather than English, as the second language. The spread of English is also indicated by the increased circulation figures for English language newspapers and magazines in recent years, by statistics on those listening to news and commentaries in English on the electronic media, and by the number of high school and college graduates who may have learnt English as a subject for a few years of their education. There are also those who may have acquired a smattering of English through the trades they are engaged in such as tourism and hoteliering. Even after taking all these factors into account, the figures for use of English in India continue to remain much smaller, even smaller than say Urdu which is spoken by 5.3 per cent of the Indians.

Such a situation, in which Hindi represents the force of numbers and English the historical power of a small national elite and which is now linked with mobility aspirations of the country's growing literate population everywhere, calls for a change in the perspective and approach of the debate, followed so far, on the language issue. The protagonists of English need to recognize the fact that the regional languages have become a great homogenizing force for the politics and culture of the regions and now also serve as the media for mass education in the country. In light of these developments, English can no longer maintain the kind of hegemony and pre-eminence it has been enjoying in our national life. The protagonists of Hindi, on the other hand, need to change their priorities and concentrate more on its growth than spread. The cause of Hindi will be served better if their interventionist impulses and creative energies are applied simultaneously to the development and standardization of Hindi as a language of the Hindi belt and they leave its spread in the other parts of the country to the ground-level forces which are already at work in favour of Hindi. While the protagonists of Hindi clamour for its national status, they do not seem to pay much attention to its development as the regional language of the Hindi belt covering over 43 per cent of the Indian population. For Hindi to grow as a common language of people across all the states in the Hindi region, and also as the vehicle for serious scholarly discourse, the primary requirement is massive expansion of formal literacy as well as of higher and professional education in the Hindi belt.

Today, only 41.71 per cent of the population in Uttar Pradesh is literate, which is about 11 per cent lower than the national average of 52.11. The literacy rates for Madhya Pradesh, Rajasthan and Bihar are 43.45, 38.81, and 38.54, respectively. In the literacy ranking for all the states and union territories (N = 31), Madhya Pradesh ranks twenty-sixth, and Uttar Pradesh twenty-seventh. Rajasthan and Bihar occupy the bottom most position respectively at 30th and 31st in the rank order.[10]

One reason for this low performance of the Hindi-speaking states on the literacy front is the manner in which the Hindi used in the

[10]Figures on literacy rates are from *Census of India, 1991: Provisional Population Totals* (Registrar General and Census Commissioner, India), Paper-1 of 1991, p. 62.

administration, schools, and the government-sponsored electronic media is sought to be 'standardized'. There is no common policy guiding all these states about the use of basic terminology in administration or for translating concepts and terms from English or other languages into Hindi for their use in the school textbooks. At the same time, standardization is imposed artificially from the top in an ad hoc manner in each state, all relying on opaque Sanskritic terms and often disregarding those in common usage, but each producing a different terminology.[11] The situation is further confounded by the fact that 'official' Hindi is not only confined to the language used by the administration in the state, but it has also invaded the textbooks and the classroom. Being falsely perceived as a literate language, it censors the use of words and phrases—notwithstanding its already narrow vocabulary base—coming from the 'non-standard' sources of Hindi spoken in the households and communities in the Hindi belt. The result is the wide and artificial gap between the Hindi used in the school and the Hindi spoken in homes, in effect, making it difficult for the language to serve as a vehicle for mass literacy. According to the 1981 census, for example, about forty-eight variants of Hindi are being used in the households of the various regions in the Hindi belt. In short, if Hindi has to serve as the medium of mass education in the Hindi states, its standardization will have to be achieved through an evolutionary process rather than through administrative fiat.[12] Meanwhile, at least at the level of the primary school, the distance between the Hindi used in the school and that in homes will have to be minimized.

The pattern of growth Hindi has followed since independence is qualitatively different from its growth during the colonial period as well as from the one followed by other Indian languages. Its growth is being increasingly delinked from a specific linguistic culture with which it was once identified. While this has made it possible for Hindi to become a language used by a much wider population, today, constituting the Hindi belt, it seems to have lost its earlier cultural identity wherein it

[11]See, Krishna, *India's Living Languages*, pp. 58–68.

[12]On the problem of standardization facing Indian languages see Krishnamurti, 'The Regional language vis-a-vis English'.

was territorially confined largely to the western and some parts of eastern Uttar Pradesh and was linguistically fused with Urdu.[13] The result is, as it is written and spoken today, Hindi is not the language of any one identifiable, territorial cultural group. It has evolved, and is evolving as a supra-language, overriding several languages across many Indian states. These are, among others, Avadhi, Bhojpuri, Braj, Marwari, Haryanvi, Maithili, and Urdu. The supremacy of Hindi over these languages has largely been achieved through historical and political processes. Hindi today seems to be groping for a new cultural identity which it can no longer seek in any local culture of the region. Consequently, Hindi has come to be looked upon as the language for political issues, with potential for mass mobilization in the entire Hindi belt. In the process, it has found basis in the mass political culture of the region but is far away from acquiring a distinctive linguistic culture of its own, which it can find only through the growth of literacy and of higher education (through the medium of Hindi) in the entire Hindi region. For its growth as a truly universal language of the entire Hindi belt, and as the second or a third language in other parts of the country, Hindi will have to also develop a capacity to incorporate and draw sustenance from the other cognate languages in the region. Again, for this to happen effectively, the literacy frame will have to vastly expand, such that the increasing ranks of the literate coming from different regions and cultures of the Hindi belt are freely able to enrich Hindi by bringing with them usages and idioms of their various mother tongues, all of which are akin to Hindi. This is how many regional languages in India have grown since the formation of linguistic states.

With a linguistic dynamism thus acquired, Hindi may also become a pliable language for India's literate population outside the Hindi belt. But the resistance to Hindi involves not just the issue of its linguistic capability or incapability. It has also to do with the somewhat negative attitude of the Hindi-speaking population to other Indian languages. This is exhibited by the striking degree of monolingualism prevalent among the Hindi-speaking population. With regard to the proportion of bilingual Indians, as against the national average of 13.34 per cent,

[13]See Krishna Kumar, 'Quest for Self-Identity. Cultural Consciousness, and Education in Hindi Region 1980–1986', *Economic and Political Weekly,* 15 (23), 9 June, 1990, pp. 1247–55.

only 4.74 per cent of the Hindi speakers are bilingual. The only other major language group in India approximating this 'record' of monolingualism are the Bengalis with 5.64 per cent among them having any second language.[14]

In sum, the sociopolitical context of the language issue has radically changed in the course of the last thirty years, but the terms of debate on the issue have yet not adapted to this change. For one thing, the change has severely narrowed down the range of options available to the national elite interested in maintaining the status quo on English. For another, they pose a serious challenge to those interested in making Hindi the lingua franca of India, requiring them to simultaneously develop Hindi as a regional language in the six Indian states and make it acceptable to others in the non-Hindi-speaking regions as the second or a third language. They cannot do this, as I shall presently show, by relying on power of numbers that Hindi represents.

It was by relying on the democratic process that the vernacular elites in almost all the states could convert their numerical strength into political power. They now want to extend the logic of numbers to seek power at the national level. The Hindi-speaking elites among them, however, seem to believe that numbers is the essence of democracy and that they can settle the issue of national language by using numerical strength. They probably do not realize that the game of power in India is quite different at the national level. There the logic of numbers is not decisive. For validation of its power, the national elite must rely on established norms and procedures of the system in which numbers have only a subsidiary role. It is, therefore, not surprising that while the vernacular elites, adept as they are at caste-calculus in elections, could produce electoral victories about twice (1977 and 1989) in the course of the last two decades, they found it difficult to secure continued legitimacy for their rule. Numbers are necessary but not sufficient to make an electoral victory sustainable at the national level.

In reality, power at the national level does not reside in the majority or even in the party elected to form a government. It resides in the

---

[14]Data from *Census of India. 1981*. Series-1: 'Population by Bilingualism'. Table C-8.

apparatus of the state which in India is wielded by the neo-colonial, Nehruvian elite to whom the power was transferred at independence. For its legitimacy, this elite only indirectly depends on numbers, which at the national level remain unaggregated on any issue. Since it is the members of this elite who usually supply terms of definition, the relationship between the merit of an issue, and the weight of numbers behind it is generally kept unarticulated or obfuscated.

It is true that by making connections between considerations of merit and of numbers a democratic leadership can bring about major transformations in the society. The ruling elite in India, however, tends not to make such connections. Instead, it prefers to wield power and seek legitimacy for it through setting broad parameters of the national discourse and by defining terms for issues which acquire prominence in the national politics. In effect, these issues get articulated within a framework of power established by such an elite. The national discourse is thus detached from the logic of numbers; the principle of majority is made to adapt itself to the normative requirements of the system generally laid down by the ruling elite. Indeed, the moment for a revolutionary change comes in a democracy but only when numbers are seen to bear merit or proposition of merit attracts numbers. Such a moment it seems is yet to arrive in Indian politics. Meanwhile, the established power of the ruling elite at the national level will continue to play a decisive role in determining the terms for defining as well as 'settling' any issue considered by them to be of 'national importance'. Its politics is to keep considerations of merit on any such issue unaligned with numbers. The language issue is not an exception to this general rule.

The use of language by the elites as an instrument of social and cultural exclusion and, thus, as the means of their rule in the society is not a new phenomenon in Indian history. In classical times, Sanskrit performed this role. As it was considered the language of deities and celestial beings and their earthly/worldly surrogates on earth, access to it was restricted, by and large, to the two upper varnas of the Brahmins and the Rajanyas. It was the only recognised vehicle of serious thought and scholarship. Even the rules by which the laity was supposed to lead its life, that is, the principles of dharma, were codified and interpreted in Sanskrit, rather than in languages understood by the people. Put differently, by restricting access to Sanskrit, the mechanism of interpretation and mode of application of these rules were securely kept in the hands of the Brahmin-Rajanya dyad, without whose mediation ordinary people could not function in the *dharmic* world. A telling example of this is found in the classical Sanskrit plays in which Sanskrit is spoken by the gods. Brahmins, and Rajanyas (and that too only by the males) and Prakrit is spoken by all others. It is no wonder that the profound thought and high ideals developed by the elite of classical India, but whose medium was not the people's language, almost evaporated with their loss of power. The role of Persian and of English in our history has also been primarily that of serving as an instrument of elite rule.

Of course, such monopoly over knowledge and power exercised through the dominance of an elite language was frontally challenged at least twice in India's history, first by the Buddhist movement and later by the Bhakti movement. But these movements did not quite succeed in breaking the nexus between the elite language and the modes of producing and using knowledge, and between knowledge and power in the society. By rejecting Sanskrit and adopting the people's languages, such as Pali (by the Buddhists) and Ardha Magadhi (by the Jains), as the language of discourse, Buddhism not only flourished for centuries in India, but posed a serious challenge to the elite rule that was associated with the exclusive use of Sanskrit. But equally interestingly, the decline of Buddhism, among other things, was associated with Sanskrit once again becoming the language of discourse for Buddhist thought and metaphysics in the classical and post-classical period. It eventually paved the way for Buddhism's absorption into the mainstream of Vedantic thought. Similarly, the Bhakti movement used local languages for its discourse and opened up the doors of the dharmic world to the masses by challenging the Brahminic monopoly of spiritual knowledge and the Brahmin's role as a mediator in the performance of rites and rituals. However, the Bhakti movement basically did little more than translate the Vedantic discourse and codes of social behaviour associated with it in the language and symbolism of the people. This helped vertical integration of the elite and the masses which was breached when Sanskrit was the predominant language of this discourse, but it only partially succeeded in making a dent in the ideological foundations of the Hindu society characterized by the ritual hierarchy of the varna system.

In our times, we are witnessing a third movement, namely, democratization of politics and through it the ascendancy of the vernaculars. This is different from the previous two movements insofar as it addresses the issue of production and distribution of knowledge—an issue which is integrally linked with the fact of English being an elite language—through effecting changes in the relationships of power and patterns of its distribution in the society. While this is an important historical development, making the continued pre-eminence of English in India a difficult proposition, it remains an open question as to how the void created in this process will be filled. As we have already discussed, the reality of democratic politics is far too complex and cannot be comprehended in terms simply of numbers. While numbers cannot, of course, be ignored in a democracy, the process of democracy gets defeated when numbers are not aligned with larger systemic considerations.

There is another reason why the Hindi-speaking vernacular elites, in their bid to challenge the domination of the English-speaking elite, cannot bring the force of numbers to bear upon the language issue. The numbers supporting the case for Hindi still remain, by and large, territorially confined. In such a situation, if Hindi, because of its numerical strength, is sought to be imposed over the non-Hindi-speaking states, it will produce severe negative consequences for India's unity rather than help the cause of Hindi. This is especially so because the vernacular elite in India as a whole are internally divided on the issue of the 'link' language. On the one hand, the Hindi-speaking elite, which is by and large, monolingual and in effect operates with one-language formula, wants Hindi to be the only 'link language' at the national level. The non-Hindi vernacular elite, on the other hand, although working assiduously towards reducing the pre-eminence of English in their own respective regions, wants to retain English as the only 'link language'; they are loath to concede any ground to Hindi at the national level—not even as second link language, after English.

Such a situation of intra-elite conflict among the vernaculars prevents those who want to downgrade the use of English at the regional levels from aggregating at the national level. In the meanwhile, the metropolitan elite, for whom English has become virtually their first language, has been able to muster support in favour of English vastly disproportionate to its minuscule numerical strength. This support comes from the growing populations of the literate everywhere in India who increasingly look upon English as a means of social mobility. It is another matter that only a few among them actually manage to cross this mobility barrier. In the process, not only have the urban elite succeeded in maintaining their edge in national politics and in the competition for social mobility vis-a-vis the large number of Indians educated in the regional languages, but they have also marginalized the role of the regional languages in the national discourse. As a result, the discourse has lost its dialogic character and has become a political exercise for dominance and hegemony.

In articulating their opposition to the dominance of English at the national level, the Hindi-speaking vernacular elite will, therefore, have to find a common ground with the other regional elites. For this to happen the Hindi-speaking elites have to give up their monolingualism. More importantly, they will have to transcend the numerical and parochial terms in which they tend to define the issue; they must link the language issue with the larger problem of changing the nature and tenor of the national discourse as a whole. It is only then that the exclusivist character of the so-called national discourse, monopolized today by the English-speaking elite, will get exposed. In the long run, what is called for is much greater interaction among the vernacular elites themselves—both the Hindi and the non-Hindi-speaking ones—not just on the language issue but on all issues of national importance. It is through this process that the vernacular elites may evolve a self-consciousness of being a counter-elite or a 'new' *national* elite. So far they have been playing a role at the national level but with the mindset of regional politicians.

Thus viewed, the issue of language in India will have to be treated both by the Hindi and non-Hindi vernacular elites, as well as by the others, not in the antagonistic terms of intra-elite conflict—English versus Hindi—but as part of the larger issue of making democracy, development, and modernity accessible to the majority of Indians. The primary issue, thus, is about the prevailing *bolbala* of English, its pre-eminence in our national life, which by underlining the power of a small class distorts our national priorities and goals. What role Hindi should have at the national level is only a secondary issue.

If, for a moment, the issue of Hindi replacing English at the national level, a proposition which has become a red herring in the language debate, is kept out and Hindi is treated as a regional language which, along with others, seeks spaces in the national discourse, a series of questions arise about the prevailing role of English in India.

Does our woefully bad performance on the literacy front, which is worse than that of many underdeveloped countries, have to do with the dominance of English in our educational system? Has this prevailing dominance distorted our priorities in education, where disproportionately larger allocations are made for English-oriented higher and professional education at the expense of primary education? Has it really resulted in cultivating 'excellence' in various fields of learning or has it only promoted international mobility for a small elite at a cost disproportionate to its claim on the national resources?

Further, has the continued pre-eminence of English helped such causes, avowedly close to the hearts of our modernizing elite, as popularizing science, developing technological skills and instilling 'scientific temper' in our population? Or to achieve these goals is it not desirable to reduce the influence of English and bring upfront the people's own languages in the public discourse on all issues of national importance? (The efficacy of such a measure in our public life is amply demonstrated by such organizations as the Kerala Sastra Sahitya Parishad). Has the continued predominance of English contributed to national integration or to creating a big divide between metropolitan India and mofussil India, between the centre and the regions? These questions acquire great relevance, even urgency, if the language issue is viewed from a truly national perspective, rather than the narrow perspective of a small class of English-educated Indians which, ironically, puts forward its sectional perspective as *the* national perspective.

Viewed in the above context, reducing the pre-eminence of English emerges as the primary requirement for a national policy on the language issue. The case is obviously not about *abolishing* English, although the proponents of English are fond of raising such as scare. Nor is it anybody's case that English should not be taught in schools and colleges as a subject. Even its use as a medium of instruction for certain specified subjects at higher levels of education is not an issue. If the consensus among our educationists is that certain subjects are best taught in English, its knowledge, like competence in mathematics, can be made a prerequisite for offering such courses. Making knowledge of English a blanket requirement for entry into higher education is however not a sustainable policy.

What is at issue is something else: Whether there is any pedagogic or political justification for the continuation of the dual system of education in which one stream of schooling uses English as the medium of instruction from the nursery level all through to the university level while in the other much larger stream its use is either mostly prohibited or introduced at a much later stage and that, too, indifferently.

The growing preference of the middle and lower-middle classes for English-medium schools is, in fact, due to the poor quality of teaching in general, and of English as a subject in particular, in the non-English medium schools; it is not an expression of their preference for English as the medium of instruction for their wards. In order to correct this imbalance, English must be uniformly and efficiently taught *as a subject* at an early stage of schooling in all the states and in all schools, but its use as the medium of instruction has to be discouraged and eventually abolished. Of course, the very small number of Indians whose mother tongue is English should be able to receive education through the medium of English just as those whose mother tongue is, for example, Tulu should have a similar facility.

What we thus need is a national policy on English rather than on Hindi. If such a policy moves in the direction described above, it will considerably weaken, even obliterate, the prevailing dual system of education which cannot be justified either on pedagogical or political grounds. Such a policy will not abolish English altogether. English will survive, but more on functional terms than as an instrument of elite domination. At the same time, as has already happened with vernaculars in other regions, Hindi as a regional language will have to progressively replace English in the Hindi belt. It is intriguing as to why any attempt to replace English by Hindi in the Hindi-speaking region threatens our national elite who see any such attempt as a threat also to national integration! Of course, the spread of Hindi outside the Hindi belt, as we have already argued, should best be left to take its own course and to the ground forces of politics and the market. There, of course, are several complex issues involved in the process, but what is important is the clarity of the direction in which the policy should move.

Clarity about policy options cannot be achieved unless the language issue, guided by our experience of the last thirty years, is formulated entirely in new terms. If conducted as a discourse in dominance, as is the case now, it will remain confined to the narrow terrain of intra-elite conflict where the issue tends to get polarized, articulated in terms of a hegemonistic contest between Hindi and English. It not only ignores the role of the regional languages, of which Hindi is indeed numerically the largest, but also keeps the national discourse on modernization and social transformation inaccessible to the larger masses. Instead, the issue needs to be articulated in truly national terms which are in consonance with democratic politics in general and with the principles of pedagogy in particular.

PART III
LANGUAGE AND THE IDENTITY POLITICS

8

Vanishing Diversities and
Submerging Identities
An Indian Case*

Anvita Abbi

Independent India can boast of ever expanding diversity—cultural, religious, ethnic, linguistic, and now political. The issue to be thought of is how we have survived as a nation with such heterogeneous elements. Paradoxically, the answer lies in this very heterogeneity and diversity. These two factors have been the essence of sustenance—as time and again it has been proved that any coercive method of homogenization under the popular banner of 'national integration' or 'assimilation of cultures' have given rise to agitation and revolt. Our existence and survival has not been in accordance with the 'one nation-state' theory but has been engraved in diversity and multiplicity.

India represents five distinct language families[1] and, 1,652 mother tongues (1961), spoken by a population of more than one billion. When India gained independence, our Constitution makers and planners had a tough challenge to meet, that is, how to devise a communicative network in India which threads together the large and diverse Indian

*This is the final version of the presentation made at Linguapax, Forum 2004, UNESCO, Barcelona, Spain, 20–3 May 2004 in the symposium on 'Dialogue and Language Diversity'.

[1]The latest research by the author has established the sixth language family. Refer to 'Is Great Andamanese genealogically and typologically distinct from Onge and Jarawa?' in *Language Sciences*, 2008. Available online at www.sciencedirect.com.

population. Our planners were not only aware of the existence of the multiplicity of languages in this subcontinent but also of the omnipresent multilingualism of the Indian population. Yet, when they sat down to meet this challenge in 1956, they gave us two magic wands. One was the constitution of the Eighth Schedule (ES) and second was the reorganization of Indian states on the basis of dominant regional languages.

The makers of our Constitution in their wisdom devoted four chapters under part XVII of this document (Articles 343 to 351) to

Table 8.1: Scheduled Languages in Descending Order of Speakers' Strength, 2001

S. No.	Language	Persons who returned the language as their mother tongue	Percentage to total population*
1.	Hindi	422,048,642	41.03
2.	Bengali	83,369,769	8.11
3.	Telugu	74,002,856	7.19
4.	Marathi	71.936,894	6.99
5.	Tamil	60,793,814	5.91
6.	Urdu	51,536,111	5.01
7.	Gujarati	46,091,617	4.48
8.	Kannada	37,924,011	3.69
9.	Malayalam	33,066,392	3.21
10.	Oriya	33,017,446	3.21
11.	Punjabi	29,102,477	2.83
12.	Assamese	13,168,484	1.28
13.	Maithili	12,179,122	1.18
14.	Santali	6,469,600	0.63
15.	Kashmiri	5,527,698	0.54
16.	Nepali	2,871,749	0.28
17.	Sindhi	2,535,485	0.25
18.	Konkani	2,489,015	0.24
19.	Dogri	2,282589	0.22
20.	Manipuri**	1,466,705	0.14
21.	Bodo	1,350,478	0.13
22.	Sanskrit	14,135	N

Notes: *The percentage of speakers of each language for 2001 has been worked out on the total population of India excluding the population of Mao-Maram, Paomata, and Purul subdivisions of Senapati district of Manipur due to cancellation of census results.
**Excludes figures of Paomata, Mao-Maram, and Purul sub-divisions of Senapati district of Manipur for 2001.
N—Stands for negligible.

Table 8.2: 1991 Census: Varieties of Hindi

Languages and Mother-tongues Grouped under Hindi	Number of Speakers
Hindi	337,272,114
1. Awadhi	481,316
2. Bagheii/Baghelkhandi	1,387,160
3. Bagri (Rajasthani)	593,730
4. Banjari	887,632
5. Bharmauri/Gaddi	18,919
6. Bhojpuri	23,102,050
7. Braj Bhasha	85,230
8. Bundeli/Bundelkhandi	1,657,473
9. Chambeali	63,408
10. Chhatisgarhi	10,595,199
11. Churahi	45,107
12. Dhundhari	965,006
13. Garhwali	1,872,578
14. Harauti	1,235,252
15. Haryanvi	362,476
16. Hindi	233,432,285
17. Jaunsari	96,995
18. Kangri	487,999
19. Khairari	14,307
20. Khortha/Khotta	1,049,655
21. Kulvi	152,442
22. Kumauni	1,717,191
23. Kurmali Thar	236,856
24. Labani	13,722
25. Lamani/Lambadi	2,054,537
26. Laria	64,903
27. Lodhi	68,145
28. Magadhi/Magahi	10,566,842
29. Maithili [added to SL category later]	7,766,597
30. Malvi	2,970,103
31. Mandeali	440,421
32. Marwari	4,673,276
33. Mewari	2,114,622
34. Mewati	102,916
35. Nagpuria	777,738
36. Nimadi	1,420,051

(contd.)

Table 8.2 (contd.)

Languages and Mother-tongues Grouped under Hindi	Number of Speakers
37. Pahari	2,179,832
38. Panchpargania	151,599
39. Pangwali	14,780
40. Pawari/Powari	213,874
41. Rajasthani	13,328,581
42. Sadan/Sadri	1,569,066
43. Sanori	11,537
44. Sirmauri	18,280
45. Sondwari	37,958
46. Sugali	113,491
47. Surgujia	1,045,455
48. Surjapuri	370,558
Others	4,642,964

spell out the official language at the level of the union (that is, the central government and the national polity as a whole), at the level of the states, and at the level of the judiciary. The original ES contained fourteen languages but today it includes as many as twenty-two (Tables 8.1 and 8.2). The inclusion, or for that matter, exclusion from the ES is not based on any ideology. The ES was not based on the ideology of fundamental rights or on the principle of equality of opportunity. Nor was it based on the ideology of national integration or invasive assimilation.

THE REDUCTIONIST POLICY: THE GENESIS OF 'MINOR LANGUAGES'

The policy of listing a select few languages as scheduled and embracing a large number of languages under the umbrella of one of the 'Scheduled' languages created an arbitrary cleavage between major and minor languages. The reductionist policy of the Government of India to enlist fewer and fewer languages in the census, for example, the 1,652 languages reported in 1961 were reduced to 122 languages in the census report of 2001, has left a large number of communities speaking unlisted languages as those belonging to minority communities.[2] The so called 'assimilationist goal' while laudable from the 'national' and administrative point of view, is a device to swallow the small fish—the languages not included in the ES. This in turn has led to the loss of identities for many languages and their speakers as language is one of the biggest factors to define an identity issue of an individual.

Consider the case of the Hindi language which subsumes more than forty-seven languages under its fold (Table 8.2). The very practice of herding these forty-seven languages under one banner enforces labels such as 'dialects' or 'minor languages', 'secondary languages', etc. Sometimes two languages sharing very little in common and mutually non-intelligible are grouped as one language. The case in point is Khasi/Jaintia. A recent visit to the Jaintia hills revealed that the speakers consider themselves inferior to Khasi speakers and their independent identity is not granted in the government documents. Some were seen hiding their Jaintia identity while others were rebuked and humiliated by the dominant Khasi speakers as the Jaintia speakers were considerd to be speaking a dialect of Khasi.

Languages in India fall into seven broad categories with varying degrees of socio-economic prestige. Their individual status in the society can be represented in a pyramid figure (Figure 8.1). The most important language from the socio-economic and educational point of view is English, which, ironically, is not listed in the ES. The second language in prestige is Sanskrit, the classical IA language which was dead long ago as a spoken language but is used in rituals by a majority of the Hindu community of the country. The rest of the twenty scheduled languages and their sixty-five dialects come next in the list of prestige. The next in the order of hierarchy are the one hundred non-scheduled languages followed by their large number of varieties, about 149. The lowest in the hierarchy are those speakers who are less than 10,000 (hence are omitted from being reported by the

[2]Ironically the census 2001 reports, 'raw returns of mother tongues has totalled 6661', and this resulted in 1635 rationalized mother tongues and 1957 names which were treated as "unclassified" and relegated to "other" mother tongue categories'. Obviously, the Government does not equate mother tongues with languages.

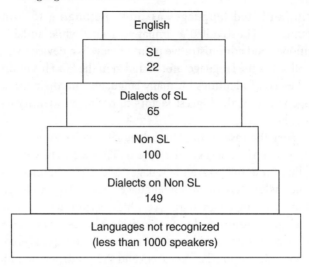

Figure 8.1: Hierarchical Status of Indian Languages and Dialects (336), 2001

government). These are the languages on the verge of being lost either demographically [that is, Andamanese] or linguistically as participants in a major language shift movement.

THE EDUCATION POLICY

Though the ES is discriminatory in nature, the educational policy of the government of India is laudable on paper. It gives enough ways and means to adopt minor languages for various educational purposes. Various Articles listed below are note worthy (Italics are mine).

1. Article 350   *Language of grievances could be any.*
2. Article 350A   *Use of mother tongue at the primary stage of education to children belonging to 'linguistic minority' groups.*
3. Article 350B   *Appointment of a special officer for linguistic minorities. Commissioner for linguistic minorities submit annual report to the President.*

Ample opportunities of exercising linguistic rights such as elicited in the following articles rarely get implemented by the community.

LINGUISTIC RIGHTS

Article 347   *A* substantial proportion *of the population of a State and not only a part thereof, desires the* use of any language *spoken by them to be recognized by that State.*

Article 345   State can adopt *any or more* of the languages in use[3] in a State for all or any of the purpose.

Ironically, these articles are merely statements on paper as the speakers of the so-called minor languages themselves do not wish to educate their children in their respective mother tongues. Nor has a minor language ever been used as the language of grievance, for example, in filing a petition in court, for fear of not being understood by the decision makers.

Similarly, the three-language formula (TLF), which the government of India adopted for imparting education, succeeded to some extent but failed in the Hindi belt (regions exemplified 'by the use of Hindi as a state language), as it was not administered with strict rule. Consider the TLF:

1. In Non-Hindi states:
   Study of Hindi
   Study of a language listed in the Eighth Schedule
   Study of English or any Modern European language
2. In Hindi states
   Study of Hindi
   Study of Modern Indian language especially from South India
   Study of English or any Modern European language

Though the TLF is laudable in its own right, as it takes into account the language diversity and pluri-linguistic and pluri-cultural society that India represents, yet it fails to take cognizance of various minor languages and their learning either as a subject or as a medium of instruction. The TLF gives an option or choice only from among the languages of the ES. There is no motivation to learn or sustain various mother tongues outside the home domain. The latter factor contributing to unlearning these languages in the home domain too.

---

[3]Note: language in use = not less than 15 per cent of population speaking that language in the state.

Our experience of working with various tribal languages speakers of India reveals that tribals in general and those of central India in particular, take pride in forgetting their native languages. While the importance of education cannot be denied, and in fact, it is the birth right of every citizen, it does come with a price. It motivates people to learn the language of education and forget the other languages not used in education.

The Dilemma

We are standing at a threshold. The threshold, to be or not to be! Questions are unavoidable. Should we be compete with the rest of the world and try to educate our masses in select few languages and, in turn, face the inevitable death of linguistic diversity? Or, should we leave our brethren alone and have them use and function in multiple dialects and languages? Should we ignore the long-cherished tradition of orality in the process of imparting literacy? The Indian people who enjoyed the diversity and multiplicity of languages/dialects all through their lives never faced this dilemma of choosing only one, two, or three languages to climb the social ladder. It may appear odd and incomprehensible to the Western world, but the difficult choice of selecting a maximum number of only three languages will ensure a gradual decrease in Indian linguistic diversity. Minority communities, represented by the last three boxes of the pyramid, that is, the non-scheduled languages, dialects of non-scheduled languages, and of those who are represented by less than 10,000 in number, whose languages are not included in the ES nor are considered as medium of instruction, nor are recognized as a subject to be taught, will be forced either to forget their mother tongues or to retain/maintain their respective mother tongues only in the home domain with increasing pressures from the peer group as well as from the seniors of the community to move over to the dominant regional language for intra-community communication. This process of self-proclaimed linguistic suicide has already been witnessed in many tribal communities of central India. The most disturbing fact is the incidence of mass hara-kiri of mother tongues in this belt. Kurux, the Dravidian language, and other Munda languages, barring Santhali, are cases in point. These tribes, as well as the forty-eight varieties of Hindi speakers (Table 8.2), falsely claim Hindi as their mother tongue. What is claimed then is not the reality. Hindi, at best, may be considered only a 'foster mother tongue'. The sense of pride in associating with the dominant regional language is considered as a step towards merging with the mainstream. This implies a direct correlation between the process of submerging identities and the reduction of linguistic diversity. While tribes encourage their children to forget their mother tongues, speakers of other non-tribal minor languages do not do so. At best, these languages are retained in the home domain.

We witness, then, two kinds of submerging identities, one at the state level, when speakers of a language, in the absence of their language being recognized for education purposes, try to identify themselves with the dominant regional language speakers and at best retain their respective tongues only in the home domain. The second type of submerging identity is more serious than the previous one, as it exists at the level of the home domain, where children are discouraged and, at times, punished for using their mother tongues.

The question is how to stop this erosion. These are the tribal languages, most ancient of all, are fully developed and mature. They represent a valuable heritage of the Indian past. The answers to this question are not easy.

Administration of education and literacy programme for a population of one billion, which is multilingual, multidialectal, and pluri-cultural is no doubt a daunting task. It is obvious that all languages cannot be incorporated in our education programmes. Somewhere the line of demarcation has to be drawn on the choice of language used in literacy or educational programmes. Linked to this, then, is the issue of standardization that is decided only after the decision on the choice of language is taken.

As stated earlier, that the TLF, although framed to promote regional languages, does not take into account the non-dominant minor languages of the region. These are the languages whose speakers are willing to commit hara-kiri. To arrest this, one has to provide dignity and honour as well as meaningful functionality to these languages. Among various suggestions that one could put forth, immediate action may be taken in the following areas:

1. The three-language formula may be modified as the four-language formula [FLF].

2. Vitalization and Revitalization of dying languages by holding night classes by the community elders.
3. Incorporation of a language in the scheduled category may be decided by the quantum of speakers.

THE FOUR-LANGUAGE FORMULA

As Hindi is spoken and understood in its various forms, though sometimes far from the standard version, across the major cities and towns of the nation, the study of Hindi, as already included in the TLF, is justified. Considering the impact of the pressures of English in globalization and uplifting the community, its inclusion is also justified. We propose the following formula at education level.

For Hindi Belt:

1. Hindi
2. English
3. Dominant regional language (=Minor language according to the 'Schedule'. This can be either SL or NSL).
4. One language from the south of India (mainly Dravidian).

For Non-Hindi Belt

1. Hindi
2. English
3. Dominant regional language (= major SL)
4. Minor language (of the region, preferably the mother tongue of the large base).

STANDARDIZATION OF LANGUAGES

The clamour for inclusion in the ES and various language movements in the country has forced the government to increase the number of languages in the ES from time to time. The present twenty-two languages listed in the ES are drawn from all four language families, some very new introduction which face the decision making choice of identifying only one out of many scripts available for written purpose.

At present, Indian languages are written in more than fifteen distinct scripts. When Manipuri was included in the schedule, it had to choose between the old traditional Meithei script, which was no longer used by the society, and the current Bengali script. The decision of standardization of an Indian language is a multifaceted decision as it involves narrowing down the diversity at various levels; grammar, pronunciation, and script. Any two varieties of a language may vary at all these levels.

Let us consider the issue of the script for the current discussion. Take the case of Santhali, a Munda language incorporated in the ES recently. Santhali is a tribal language that is spoken in the four adjacent states of Madhya Pradesh, Bihar, Orissa, and Bengal. A line of continuity can be visualized geographically, linguistically, and culturally in an area which was initially to be carved out from four different states under the name of Jharkhand. Santhali, thus, is written in multiple scripts at present. It is written in Devanagari in Madhya Pradesh and Bihar, the two Hindi-belt states, in Oriya script in Orissa, and in Bangla script in Bengal. Moreover, Santhali activists had always promoted Ol Chiki script that was designed to write Santhali. Interestingly, the language is also written in Roman as majority of the Santhals are educated by Christian missionaries.

After the formation of the Jharkhand state, dominated by the Santhals and other tribes, in 2002, which was carved out of southern Bihar, the administration is faced with the dilemma of choosing one script out of the six being used currently. While activists want to promote the Ol Chiki script, the majority want the Devanagari (the script that is used for writing Sanskrit, Hindi, and Marathi) as educated and literate masses are already familiar with it. The old argument that Devanagari is not suited for representing typical Santhali sounds such as vowel length and glottal stop can be overcome by the introduction of specific diacritic marks. Moreover, despite the fact that Jharkhand was separated from Bihar state to give an identity to a large number of the tribal population residing in that part of the state, leaders, administrators, and bureaucrats have not come up with Santhali as the state language nor have decided upon the standard script to be used. At present, Hindi is being used for all official, judicial, and administrative purposes. It is an irony that once the wishes of a separate state and the recognition of the language in the ES is granted, the community at large and activists in particular fail to implement all the necessary changes and inclusion of the language at various realms. They face the opposition within, where masses want to do nothing with the home language being used at the official level. They want to operate in Hindi (or the dominant regional language) and English. The inevitable fears of the tribes about being pushed back in society, desire to rise to the elite and superior languages and amalgamate with the mainstream are the factors discouraging the lower-rung language speakers in exercising their linguistic rights. If this situation persists for another fifty years, a major part of the world's linguistic diversity will be lost.

Revitalization of Vanishing languages and identities

We have to face many glaring questions. How can we arrest the increasingly diminishing linguistic diversity? How can we instil in the community the sense of pride in the use of their native languages? The answer to these questions is far from simple. However, revitalization processes among the dying languages may be started by language activists, linguists, and language users. Revitalization is the only hope for survival of identities and maintaining the diversities. Revitalization finds its existence at two levels: (1) in the home domain and (2) at the official level. The former is related to psychological and emotional issues, whether the community realizes the importance of the language being retained in the home domain or not; whether it satisfies the emotional need of the people who can speak it or not; whether the community finds it essential to retain the language as a heritage of the past or not. If the answer is yes to all these options then there is a will for retention/maintenance of the language in the home domain that result, more often than not, in teaching the children the language of the community. Some of the tribal languages of the Tibeto-Burman group are such examples. The phenomenon of 'night school' is very common where elders teach the children of the village the conversational language, the folk songs, and the folk dances. The participatory involvement of the elders helps in revitalizing the language at the community level. Motivation to learn the language may be provided in the forms of instituting awards and introducing the information about the language in the school history books, and so on.

The next step is to locate the existence of the language at the official level. This comes after the establishment of the first step, that is, revitalizing it in the home domain. It may be introduced at the official level for conducting judicial, legislative, and simple official work, or may be introduced in schools as a subject if not as the medium of instruction. Revitalization of any language at this level depends upon the dynamics of political power and social awareness.

9

Writing, Speaking, Being
Language and the Historical Formation of Identities in India*

Sudipta Kaviraj

A ll civilizations have language but societies do not put this universal
implement to the same use. Historically, language can hardly be
treated as a homogeneous entity. It can be divided in many ways—
into its various strata, its distinct elements, the differing types of
competences which are gathered up into the general notion of a
language. The social functions accredited to different strata of language
in the Indian civilization (though the situation in South India is different
in some important respects) appear to be interestingly different from
the European case; in this paper I shall try to analyze how language
contributes to the formation, and rupturing, of social identities by
focusing primarily on the Bengali speech community.[1] This does not
imply any claim to the exemplary or precedental quality of this
particular case. Though the story of the relation between language and
politics is bound to be different in the different language zones of South
Asia's exceedingly diverse culture, these might reveal some similarity
of processes, though not an identity of the exact line of events. In the

---

*Keynote paper to the Asian section of the German Historical Congress, Bochum,
October 1989. Originally published as 'Writing, Speaking, Being: Language and the Historical
Formation of Identities in India', in Dagmar Hellmann-Rajanayagam and Dietmar
Rothemund (eds), *Nationalstaat and Sprachkonflikte in Sudund Sudostasien* (Franz Steiner
Verlag: Stuttgart, Germany, 1992), pp 25–68.
[1]A standard history of the Bengali language and its literature is Sukumar Sen, *Banglur
Sahitya Itihas* (in Bengali), (New Delhi: Sahitya Akademi, 1965).

last part of the paper, however, I shall speak more generally about the linguistic processes at work in the Indian nation-state.

Language does not only unite people, it also as effectively divides them. Another way of putting this would be to say that language is, socially, not merely a means of communication but also of deliberate incommunication. It causes not only feelings of identity but also of enmity: often the most indestructible barriers among people are 'walls of words'. By this I do not mean merely that the process of formation of one linguistic identity generates a sharper sense of differentiation from others: for instance, the more the people of a particular region become 'Bengalis', their sense of separateness from surrounding languages like Oriya or Hindi must become sharper. This is evidently true; but this is not the only sense in which language creates incommunication. Language divides 'internally' as well, and not to pay attention to this process often distorts historical accounts about linguistic identities.

People 'having' the same language do not have it in the same way. Socially, linguistic competence confers on people capacities, and their absence correspondingly takes them away. Being Bengali is an identity coming out of a person's having the Bengali language; but clearly, all Bengalis do not have this language in the same way or to the same extent. Thus, they enjoy the political 'rights' of Bengaliness to a patently unequal degree; for some rights stemming from Bengaliness must be indivisible, but others are unequal and stratified. The *bhadralok* of Calcutta speak the Bengali standard language, one which has resemblances on one side with the 'high' language in which Tagore wrote his poetry, but also, on the other side of the cultural spectrum, with the language spoken in the bazar by the fisherman, the maid in the babu household, or by criminals in the margins of urban Calcutta. And these are not tightly separated orbits sufficient in themselves— but a complex of words pulled in different directions by the internal logic of each social practice. The historical existence of the Bengali language is a complex fact in which all these sublanguages (or linguistic subpractices) must find adequate and properly judged representation. Language as it is socially used thus has to be broken down into various, subparts—high and low language, literary and common language, the *guru* (high, of greater merit) and the *chalita* (conversational) language (a special distinction of twentieth century Bengali), the literates' and the illiterates' language. Such differences are not merely aural or cultural, but political. Being able to use a language in certain ways enables a person to do certain things socially, others who do not possess such linguistic competence simply cannot perform them. Often, these people are reduced to varying states of dependence on those who are more skilled, and their access to the whole of the social universe is mediated by this latter group who can consequently control this tenuous access.[2]

The use of writing by moneylenders, the scourge of the indebted peasantry, is one example. And the peasants cannot be blamed if they consider writing not as a means of enlightenment but of oppressive mystification. Peasant revolts, historians have argued, show a particular intensity of anger against written records because they relate to the linguistic practice of writing differently. The complexity of the story of language and identities cannot be tackled without a sufficiently complex conception of the gradations of competence in language and its political effect. I shall call this the 'internal economy' of language.

The Structure of the Internal Economy of Language

The manner in which this internal economy was structured in traditional India seems to have been peculiar, and interestingly different from the European case. Jacques Derrida's work has emphasized the primacy in European culture of the grammatological, of the written over the spoken part of language.[3] This is asserted strongly, although in many European cultures the term for language comes from the Latin *lingua* or tongue which might lead one to infer a primacy of the spoken inscribed in the etymology of language about language itself. But there appears to exist a more fundamental difference. The idea of *logos* in the Greek philosophical tradition clearly draws attention to language

---

[2]Bernard Cohn has done pioneering work on these questions: see especially chapters 6 and 10 or his *An Anthropologist among the Historians and Other Essays* (Delhi: OUP, 1987). An excellent discussion of language and political identity can be found in Jyotirindra Dasgupta, *Language Conflict and National Development* (Berkeley: California University Press, 1970). For an insightful study of the relation between language skills and social structure. Satish Saberwal, 'Segmentation and Literacy', *Economic and Political Weekly* (forthcoming).

[3]Jacques Derrida, *Of Grammatology* (translated by Gayatri Chakravorty Spivak) (Baltimore: John Hopkins University Press, 1974). Chapters 1 and 2 argue this against earlier linguistic theories.

as a means of reasoning, of ratiocinative activity, giving this exceptional significance over other things that can be done by means of language. This is related though this is not the place to try to show the connection in detail, to Hans Georg Gadamer's argument about the deep seated privileging of the epistemological in Western cultural tradition.[4] The first difference is that in the classical Indian tradition though a great deal of attention is given to *nada*[5] —the originary form of sound, and, therefore, the source of both language and music—and it is occasionally equated with God himself, it seems to lack a clear equivalent to the typically European concept of the logos—speech, writing, reasoning, episteme, science. By contrast, the Indian philosophic and aesthetic curiosity appears directed towards *vak*—the irruption of the utterance which universalizes language rather than writing. Writing—inscribing something on a receiving medium—is as much to create meaning as to stain virgin space. The Indian tradition's way of treating writing is, in interesting ways, ambiguous. Writing is fixing, giving an idea a kind of material immortality. something that can be done only to the rarest, at least to the most significant, of thoughts, ideas of extraordinary importance in some sense, an exalted fate that common speech does not deserve. It is however possible to argue just the reverse of this case: material things are destructible, to consign ideas to material existence is thus to subject them to the law of decay and destruction. Towards writing the Indian tradition shows a strangely complex combination of reverence and mistrust.

There is a second analytical difficulty. The way Indian culture structures the internal practices of language cannot be adequately captured by a standard distinction between oral and literate cultures. Indian culture arranges the institutional transaction between literate-oral in very complex ways; here the distinction between literate and oral is not homologous to the one between educated and illiterate. Even the educated have their own traditions and institutions of oral performance. It is not that this culture does not know writing; rather, in spite of knowing writing from a very early stage of its history, it clearly

[4]Hans Georg Gadamer, *Truth and Method* (London: Sheed and Ward, 1975).

[5]There are references often in traditional Indian thinking to *nadabrahma*. Nada is the originary meaningful sound which is given great ceremonial significance in two of its cultural forms, the intelligent power of words and the sound of music, its aesthetic side. Theoretical treatises on aesthetics often begin with general considerations of this kind.

uses writing quite sparingly. This peculiar configuration of knowing the gift of writing, yet abjuring its use in social transactions seems to indicate that in traditional Indian culture linguistic practice is governed by a 'theory' of distribution of functions between speaking and writing. Some features of this functional distribution must be noticed before we come to a discussion of more modern history. First, the intimate connection so common in European culture between institutions, that is, the extension in the scale of social practices in time and space, and consigning things to the fixity of writing does not seem to obtain here.[6] Enormous and essential structures of social exchange and communication are entrusted to oral continuity rather than written codification. Although both writing and speaking can create continuity, their manner of doing so are different. In Indian society, except for the vast numbers of the directly productive classes of people, the upper strata depended on literacy and related means of social control. The upper strata required use of literacy for different functional requirements specific to the social practices they engaged in. Trading practices on any large scale required literacy and commercial records, which could not be handled without literacy and numeracy among commercial groups.

Wielders of political power depended on some amount of minimal administrative documentation; occasionally, there was evidence of impressive elaborate accounting of revenue resources of their realms.[7] Brahmins provided some of these services. But they were notoriously selfish repositories of the society's skills of literacy and learning of its practical applications, and they performed two types of essential functions. They lent their knowledge of literacy and its more specialized uses to the Kshatriyas or those who controlled political authority. A two-way traffic results from this caste monopoly of skills and cultural assets. Administrative ordering, deft use of the technical apparatus of legal principles, financial accounting, and book keeping require the use of these relatively rare and jealously monopolized attainments.

---

[6]Some internal diversities in the tradition must be noticed. In the Buddhist tradition there was greater reliance on writing in order to fix the meaning of something especially valuable. The preachings of the Buddha are written down by disciples; but the Hindu tradition by contrast seems in he interested, in inscribing significant ideas on the more quizzical tables of memory.

[7]Both the *Arthashastra* and the *Ain-i-Akbari*, central texts for two different periods point to habitual and widespread use of administrative records.

Those who had formal political power depended on the Brahmins for these essential functional necessities as much as for more general moral legitimation. Caste barriers also constituted effective prevention against possible diffusion of these scarce resources and their increased availability to other groups in society. Secondly, Brahmins also performed the exceedingly important activity of performing rituals which ensured the imaginary continuance of the social order by keeping it supplied with its essential symbolic collective representations and vital concepts for the construction of the collective self.

To be able to perform these materially and symbolically essential functions, the Brahmins had to ensure that the relevant skills were reproduced in undiminished quality within their own caste. Relatively little of this function of institution maintenance was given over to writing or writing-based forms of training. Although Brahmins had to be literate, a surprisingly large part of this training came to be not ratiocinative and written but passive and mnemonic.[8] Memory is never an unfailing implement for perfect or reliable reproduction. Dependence on oral continuity gave to these practices a peculiar character which may be read wrongly by social scientists. They confer on these continuing institutions the solidity and relative immobility common to similar institutions in written cultures. Here, because the internal mechanism was oral, and because there were rarely standardized written institutional histories, institutional continuity could be compatible with great flexibility. The eternal religion (*sanatana dharma*) can therefore keep constantly changing. Though this may not have ensured continuity the way writing would have done, it did have a compensating advantage. Reliance on memory fulfilled the historical need for flexibility within a formally rigid structure in a subtle and partly covert fashion. In reasoning activities, no mnemonic reproduction could be perfect, a reproduction without variation, without slippages caused by simple incompetence, inadvertence, interpretation, or deliberate intent. Indeed, quite often, the key to understanding the unchanging structures is the astonishing amount of unannounced change which these sanction. Rigid formal rules of social conduct were meant to ensure

---

[8]The difference is between the ability to think through a problem and the ability to reproduce from memory standard recipes. Even current Indian educational practice shows over-reliance on memory-oriented skills.

a remarkable degree of conformist continuity. Since these rules were uncodified and worked through an oral tradition, they afforded those who directed society considerable space for informal amendments. Sometimes a reputation for rigidity accomplished things in subtle ways which an actual immobility would not have done.[9] No wonder the record of Indian history is marked by a paradox—a rhetoric of immutability (as for instance in sanatana dharma, an eternal religious order invented in the nineteenth century) cut through by historical evidence of silent and surreptitious change. A good example is provided by the fascinatingly mobile history of the supposedly immutable order of castes.[10]

Traditional Indian society thus had a highly literate culture, but inside it, literacy was guarded with great jealousy through institutional arrangements which strictly prevented its extension, so that it was always a strong sellers' market in literacy. Ordinary unlettered people carried on their daily existence through spoken vernacular dialects. In the nature of things, these vernaculars varied a great deal, and in most cases did not have standardized written scripts of their own before the tenth century. Above these productive and oral classes presided a bilingual elite which commanded the use of an esoteric language which could not be mastered by others because of caste prohibitions. The elite could carry on their own internal discourse (which could be either theological or political) in a language which had the strange quality of

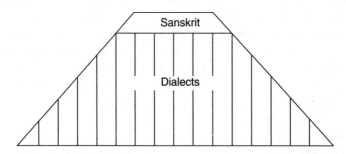

Figure 9.1: Alterations in Linguistic Structures during Medieval Times

[9]The difference the two forms of the caste system—of varna and jati might have something to do with this.

[10]The sociological controversy about caste is instructive in this respect. Without denying Dumont's general claim that what is essential to caste is the ideological *form* of hierarchy, one can still admit the evidence of historical change through the process known after Srinivas as sanskritization.

a partial publicity, with the dual quality of being public and secret at the same time.[11] It was public to insiders, but closed, esoteric, secret to outsiders who did not have the requisite skills. This has significant political results, because it made the scale of possible collective action or consultation asymmetric between the elites and the subaltern social groups. While elite discourse could range across the entire subcontinent, the discourse of the subordinate groups necessarily remained trapped in the closed boundaries of their vernacular dialects. Thus, while conservatism and reaction could be subcontinental in spread, dissent was condemned to be mostly local. Only those reform initiatives were likely to succeed which used the implements of the elite discourse itself against its ideological structures.

Alterations in Linguistic Structures during Medieval Times

Social and political changes in medieval times brought some alterations in the structure of language and literacy, but these were not so fundamental as to introduce changes in the linguistic economy. Two types of change occur. Owing to the political power of Muslim rulers—a reality Brahminical Hindu society could not ignore—Arabic and Persian came to slowly occupy a part of the exalted position of the earlier esoteric language—Sanskrit. But it was more a situation of power than of authority. As Muslim power became entrenched in north India, especially those social groups and specialized castes which traditionally used literacy in the administrative service of the government now extended their skills to the new language of power.[12] It must be

[11]Considerations of such things get unnecessarily embroiled in controversies about nationalist pride, accusations of orientalism and such other judgmental disputes. Few social scientists in India have, for instance, pursued the question of what is the exact relation between what is indubitably common and what is conceptually public. Existence of commonness does not mean that this would be conceptualised as public space, or public interest, or public institutions. The work of Satish Saberwal raises this question (though not in this language); Satish Saberwal, *India: The Roots of Crisis* (Delhi: OUP 1989).

[12]This linguistic configuration continued undisturbed down to the time of Ram Mohan Ray who was proficient in both Sanskrit and Arabic–Persian, besides his native Bengali and colonial English. It is remarkable how quickly this heteroglossia is destroyed by the cultural processes of colonialism. By the time of Bankimchandra or Tagore, proficiency in Arabic–Persian language or familiarity with Islamic culture are not required as marks of a cultured Bengali. The Bengali bhadralok elite had decided to give themselves a resolutely Hindu past.

recognized, however, that this does not seem to have threatened the privilege of Sanskrit. Hindu society responded to the reality of Muslim rule partly through an attempt to marginalize the power of the state and eject it out of the circle of Hindu social practices, a move which succeeded in part due to the pragmatism of the rulers themselves. Although this could not wholly succeed, it did result in a sharper hiatus between the political power of the state and social dominance inside Hindu communities.[13] Power and prestige inside these communities remained intimately related to real or supposed competence in Sanskrit; officiating Brahmins may have had a tenuous grip on the intricacies of Sanskrit grammar, but this hardly mattered, since the effectiveness of these practices were symbolic not grammatical. Indeed, stable political power of Muslim rulers and the process of conversion to Islam of those who used this to escape the repressive rigidity of the caste system set in motion two contrary responses in Hindu society. On one side, this gave rise to a more frantic traditionalism, but, on the other, also to types of exchange with Islamic culture. A tendency towards utilitarian secular exchanges was discernible in the practices of castes like the Kayasthas who were given to government employment traditionally, or the trading groups who tended to treat all men equally as long as this served the objective of commercial expansion. But there were also the more intellectually grounded proposals for religious exchanges advocated by bhakti doctrines—at the same time more ambitious and vulnerable.

Religious developments have an intimate relation to our story of languages. Throughout this period there occurred a slow development of vernacular languages through the gradual separation of their emerging literatures from the high Sanskrit tradition. Comparatively little research has been done on this process; but the lines of development and their basic interconnections are clear. And it is instructive to dwell on this process, because the radicalism of the reform religions displays some peculiar features. Emergence of a vernacular literature does not indicate an immediate change in the narrative or imaginative content of literary culture, or a sharp, dramatic, conscious rupture with the

---

[13]I have suggested elsewhere that the pre-colonial state was marked by the twin features of being spectacular and marginal. 'State Society and Discourse in India', in James Manor (ed.), *Rethinking Third World Politics* (London: Longman, 1991).

classical tradition, however striking the disjunction may appear in retrospect. They arise haltingly, always making reverential genuflexions in the direction of the high tradition and its texts, which they were eventually to undermine. These are not seen or begun as revolts against the logic of exclusion of the common people from aesthetic and religious seriousness built into the classical Hindu tradition. Rather, their first and most impressive texts are attempts to stretch the riches of this high culture towards the lower, culturally deprived orders. Their implicit justification would have been that, if religiosity and aesthetics were significant and valuable for all human beings, those without the use of Sanskrit should not be deprived of these values. As a consequence, these literatures assume a consciously subaltern relation between themselves and the high classical texts. The narratives around which these literatures grew up were in most part old esteemed narratives from the classical tradition—the Ramayana, the Mahabharata, or similarly modelled stories of what in Bengal were called the *Mangalkavyas*, which, though exalting unknown and upstart deities, do it in a style and form too easily recognizable as derived.[14]

One of the great texts of this translation of religiosity into a popular register was the *Ramcharitmanas* of Tulsidas,[15] and many of the complex and ambivalent properties of this new vernacular literature could be found in this, its acknowledged masterpiece. In neighbouring Bengali regions, too, similar texts were composed: the Ramayan by Krttivas and the Mahabharat of Kashiramdas were written out of similar cultural impulses, though in artistic quality they do not compare distantly with Tulsidas's text. But Tulsidas himself, like a number of other lesser poets, was no mean composer of Sanskrit lyrics, and vernacular writers often had to legitimate their claim to serious attention by writing in the more exalted language.[16]

[14]*Mangalkavyas* were composed in honour of neoclassical Hindu deities like Manasa, the snake goddess, Chandi, and one of the best known texts in this tradition is Mukundaram Chakrabarti's *Chandimangal*.

[15]Several English translations of the *Ramcharitmanas* are available: for instance, *Ramacharitamanas*, edited and translated by R.C. Prasad (Delhi: Motilal Banarasidass, 1989), and *The Holy Lake of the Acts of Rama*, translated by W. Douglas, P. Hill (Bombay: OUP, 1971).

[16]A good example from Bengal, though in a later period, is Bharatchandra who wrote some wonderfully innovative metric poetry apart from his larger works. *Annadamangal* and *Vidyasundarkavya*; but he, too, established his claim to poetic recognition by insignificant versification in Sanskrit.

Despite this, vernacular literatures and poetic traditions began an undeclared revolution. Within the formal terms of continuity with classical traditions in terms of narratives, forms, and texts, these 'translations' in vernaculars were hardly passive cultural creations; and they gradually produced an alternative literature which told the same stories with subtle alternative emphases to alternative audiences. It founded a cultural strand that Namwar Singh has elegantly called a *dusri parampara,* a second tradition.[17] It has been pointed out quite often that the *Ramcharitmanas* was in several respects a deeply innovative text. Its ambition of taking the classical narrative to a common audience forced some alterations in the narrative and characterological structures. The humaneness of the idol is reinterpreted from a serenity that befits the almighty to an intimacy of a more accessible kind. As the epic is rewritten into the bhakti register, this gives a softness and sentimentality to the characterization which was lacking in the classical original. Modern interpreters of these texts sometimes make an anachronistic mistake by conceiving them in a style common to modern heterodoxies. Modern rebellions announce themselves even before they are wholly successful; revolutions in traditional cultures tended to hide the fact of their being revolts. They pretend to respect a continuity, which they do not in fact practise. By declarations of continuity, however, they circumvent the censorship: precisely by their submission, they create a space for themselves in which the narrative axis, patterns of denouement, delineation of characters, all undergo a subtle transformation. Krishna, the incomparable warrior of the high tradition becomes Krishna the incomparable lover. Ideas about union with god and his availability to his devotee go through the most radical change.[18] All the while this is accompanied by formal declarations of continuity apparently testified to, indubitably, by the sameness of the narratives, the figures, the tropes, and the symbols. Yet at the same time, in a slow, undeniable, open process, these religions and their observance become public spectacles of a kind of defiance and heterodoxy.

[17]Namwar Singh, *Dusri Parampara ki Khoj* (in Hindi) (Delhi: Rajkamal Publications, 1975), in which his argument partly follows the critical work of Hazari Prasad Dwivedi, specially his reading of Kabir.

[18]I have discussed this with reference to Krishna and Radha in my *Unhappy Consciousness,* (Delhi: OUP, forthcoming).

These new texts could do this because they were practising an activity which was tolerated by the Hindu canonical tradition. Ascription of texts to mythical all-seeing sages was clearly a sanctioned device of collective writing, of having open-ended texts which went through constant proposals of embellishments and extension. This must happen of course in oral retelling of stories; but it does happen in written cultures like India's in peculiar ways. Nameless poets tried to smuggle their favourite works into great texts to savour the ironical taste of an unnamed immortality.[19] Oral incantation made this possible to an even greater extent, creating something like a latent market of interpolations of which only those favoured by a wide public eventually made it into the text itself. Accumulations of this kind sometimes changed the narrative structure, *rasa* structure, flavour, or even the meaning of the work. Hinduism had a tradition of such kumbhilakas, of this strange form of plagiarism in reverse, of people claiming not someone else's work as their own, but their own as someone else's. Bhakti literature in its celebrated translations used this general sanction of free retelling to interpret a new religion into existence.

Gods and goddesses of the classical tradition retain their audience at the cost of this alteration of their character. The stateliness of the central divine characters is replaced by their accessibility and humaneness.[20] This principle of accessibility extends to the formal poetics of the compositions. The verses are composed in a simple dignified language, in the most accessible of metres, in Bengali the *payar*, for instance, the language and rhymes most suited for oral incantation by common people. Literary creations of the vaishnava cult around Chaitanya displayed similar attributes and converted the figure of Krishna into a figure of love. Krishna's physical form, the idol itself is transformed: the warrior form with four arms displaying the *shankha, chakra,* and *gada* somewhat softened by the residual *padma,* is replaced by the anthropomorphic symbol of the child, Gopal, or the adolescent Krishna of pleasurable and excusable transgressions. The predominant rasa is changed from *aishwarya* to the one of *vatsalya* or *shringara—*

[19]The Sanskrit word for such writers is *kumbhilaka.*
[20]Though both in the Valmiki's Ramayana and in the *Uttararamacharita* of Bhavabhuti, Rama is seen moved to tears, a demeanour not considered incompatible with his status as a hem or an *avatara* of Narayana.

both in their different ways vehicles of nearness and indistinction. The language considered adequate for this religiosity is the vernacular. Like Buddhism much earlier, the bhakti movements favoured the lower language; but since these were touched by religiosity, this gave these tongues a new dignity. It will be historically misleading, however, to exaggerate this point; the extrication from Sanskrit remains incomplete in several significant ways. The Bengali *vaishnava padavali* literature shows this ambivalence with remarkable clarity. Its poetic compositions hover between the clear folkishness of the language of Chandidas or Jnanadas on one side and the comparatively sanskritized Bengali used by Govindadas. Both are equally indispensable parts of a single literary trend. Most interestingly, this linguistic tension is also reflected in the ways in which Chaitanya's life story is told by his biographers. Vrindavandas's *Chaitanyabhagavat* chronicles it in anthropomorphic terms, the extraordinariness of his acts marked by his miraculous humaneness. By contrast, Krishnadas Kaviraj's *Chaitanyacharitamrta* emphasizes the divinity of this existence, and sees in every act a metaphor of the order of the universe. It is hardly accidental that Vrindavandas writes in a limpid Bengali, while Krishnadas's work is only formally written in Bengali: in its more sombre moments it reminds us that we are in the presence of God himself by lapsing into appropriately complex Sanskrit, heightened by the erudite compositions in the more complex metre, *mandakranta*, although Chaitanya is an avatara of Krishna, he is saved from the heaviness of the classical type by the infusion into his image of Radha (because he is, according to Vaishnava theology, *radhabhava krishnaswarupa*). The figure of the feminine in the Indian tradition is often the symbol of the approachable, the popular, the proximate, the unthreatening, and accessible. Because Chaitanya combines in himself the features of Krishna with the lovability of the feminine, he is an androgynous god, the deity of a popular religion which can capture the imagination of relatively subaltern peasant elements in the Hindu society of eastern India.

This indicates a further interesting fact about how people thought of themselves, and conferred self-descriptions on their relevant community. It is not only that the disengagement from Sanskrit is yet incomplete, and the continued popularity of the work of Jayadeva demonstrates its unassailed position as the norm for Vaishnava poetic compositions. More importantly, for my central hypothesis, the poetry of Vidyapati from neighbouring Mithila is considered an inalienable part of the Vaishnava heritage. Given the later linguistic identity of this region as Bengali, both Jayadeva and Vidyapati would have raised problems of subsumption, as the first was an inhabitant of Orissa and the second of Mithila. If anything, this shows that despite the unmistakable beginnings of a distinctive vernacular literature, people's identity must have been primarily determined by their belonging to a religious sect rather than the one of common speech.

This suggests the following hypothesis. Between the two great layers of language, the upper layer of Sanskrit and the lower layer of dialects in medieval times, a slow process of differentiation had begun. But the vernaculars were still held together in linguistic intelligibility in a linguistic structure marked by the commonness of Sanskrit at the high end and the easy neighbourly intelligibility of the dialects below.

Gramsci said a language contains a certain conception of the world. To put it another way, there is usually a strong historical connection between a natural and a conceptual language. Seen this way, the origin of vernacular languages appears to be intimately linked to an internal conceptual rebellion within classical Brahminical Hinduism. Along with the emergence of a new conception of religiosity, based on a more intimate relation between man and his deity, this movement required a new type of language. To fulfil its functions, it had to be a language of transparency and nearness rather than of inaccessibility and distance. If the purpose of the act of worship was to underline the inequality between God and man, His infinitude against the vulnerable finiteness of all human capacities, the inaccessible sonority of Sanskrit achieved that perfectly. Bhakti Hinduism, like strands of European Protestantism, sought to destroy the brokerage of the Brahmins between the devotee and his god. The philosophical argument behind this was, as is well known, that the act of worship, the most significant act of attunement of man to God's universe, must be transparent and meaningful, and against the earlier semiotics of forbidding distanciation bhakti religion brought in a whole new semiotic of nearness and informality. All this could be accomplished only in a language which, although still distanced by the question of literacy, was closer to actual common speech in two senses. It was, first, a literature in vernacular. Secondly, it was a vernacular written, though with an ineffable elegance, like common spoken word. The idea was, in its ideal, utopian, perfect phases, like a pedagogy of the oppressed: poetry spoke a language of the people, expecting that over the long term popular language of worship and sensibility would he exalted by this poetry.

Later, when vernacular literatures were fully formed in colonial times, some of them, like Bengali, would often seek to confer upon themselves a history with a suitably impressive antiquity. In constructing these images of their pasts, they constantly gerrymander historical frontiers. Histories of Bengali literature, a required segment of the formation of 'cultured' Bengalis, standardly claim Vidyapati (from Mithila) and Jayadeva (from Orissa) as parts of their own history. Unlike what Gellner says about the histories nations construct of themselves, there is nothing really fraudulent about this,[21] for these were truly part of the genetic process of the formation of these cultures. But this also shows something equally and vitally true: that there was no Bengal in the modern sense. There was already perhaps an identity of the language, but no linguistic identity. Linguistic identity is not formed by the simple objective fact of some people having a common language: it lies in a more deliberate choice to see this fact as the essential criterion of their identity. The primary reason for this mild paradox: why the language existed without a linguistic identity of its people, I shall suggest, was due to the fact that it was a different kind of social world altogether. My argument is not that this social world 'lacked' some of the features that the modern world has; but that it was a world of a different kind, which we must try to understand by historical inference.

LANGUAGE IN A FUZZY WORLD

Elsewhere I have tried to approach this problem through a distinction between a fuzzy and an enumerated (in the sense of being counted) social world.[22] Traditional society is made up of a structure of groups which are, in some crucial cases though not in all, fuzzily conceived,[23]

---

[21]Ernest Gellner, *Nations and Nationalism* (Oxford: Blackwell, 1983).

[22]Sudipta Kaviraj, 'On the Construction of Colonial Power', in Shula Marks and Dagmar Engels (eds), *Foundations of Imperial Hegemony* (Oxford: Oxford University Press, 1991).

[23]Social groups have fuzzy ends of edges in a world in which differences are organized as spectrums rather than divided by boundaries. Arguments of this kind, though conceptualized differently, are found in Richard G. Fox (ed.), *Realm and Region in Traditional India* (Delhi: Vikas, 1977). See especially the papers by Burton Stein, Bernard Cohn, and Ainslie T. Embree.

of fuzzily conceived space,[24] and fuzzily sensed and imaged time.[25] It is impossible to develop a full argument here about the diverse ways in which the social world, social space, and social time are fuzzy conceptions, and, further, how these conceptions are interlocked. Indian society, as anthropologists have argued, is of course segmented. But these segments of the lived world do not seem to have boundaries as in any organization of modern social space. Villages do of course begin and end, and therefore have their boundaries, though here, too, in the most immediate form of lived space, there is a certain approximateness and indeterminability. Boundaries of villages, it has been pointed out for many regions of the pre-colonial world, were not drawn the way states would be represented in maps. It is important to stress that this traditional world is a world without maps, and is therefore devoid of a special mentality, inextricable from modernity, which thinks in terms of mapped spaces, and its corollary, measured distances. Inhabitants of the traditional world may thus be said to have a conception of farness rather than of calibrated distance.[26] Beyond the village, the boundedness of regions, subregions, languages, kingdoms are undetermined or indeterminable with modern precision. 'Boundaries' do exist, things, spaces, groups, do begin and end. But they tend to shade off, merge, graduate. It is a different way of organizing difference from the modern one with which we are familiar.

Language illustrates this principle of organization of difference very clearly. In the area lying between, say, Banaras to Puri, a traditional observer would have heard dialects slowly and imperceptibly changing, such that, with historical clairvoyance these could be ascribed to what would eventually become three distinct vernaculars Hindi, Bengali, and Oriya. But it would be impossible, within that world, to determine where Bengali ended and Oriya began; in any case, the change would be decisively different from the standard modern organization of linguistic difference as they are fixed on to maps. Differences would shade off the

---

[24]Spatial perception could be similarly rendered into a traditional idea of farness against the modern sense of distance.

[25]Anthropological work provides sufficient evidence about a sense of time that is linear in relatively short spans, but whose edges become vague before and after a few generations.

[26]What I mean is that they may think of place X as 'far' and Y as 'farther'. They would not have the means, much of the time, to say that X is 500 miles, and Y is 5000.

way as distinctly different colours are arranged in a spectrum. It is a world, to put it dramatically, of transitions rather than of boundaries.

Some other ontological features of this social world are of serious consequence for any understanding of politics. First, not merely are the boundaries hazy or spectrum-like, people and objects inhabiting this world are radically uncounted. It is also an unenumerated world. In this world, again, Hindus and Muslims would have perceived their difference (though I doubt they would do it in the modern way); Bengalis and Oriyas do so as well, just as do Shaivas and Vaishnavas. But they do not live in a world in which the knowledge of how many Hindus, or Muslims, or Vaishnavas, or Bengalis are there is a part of the commonsensical social knowledge determining patterns of social action. This has a crucial political, corollary. Self-identifications are in some senses fuzzy and uncounted; thus Vaishnavas do not know how many of them are there in the world, and they are crucially incapable of considering what they can do to force the structure of their social world to their collective benefit, if all who are like themselves act together.[27] Distinct languages can thus exist in this society without uniting or dividing people in the manner in which we familiarly see these processes in modern contexts.

COLONIALISM AND THE GROWTH OF LINGUISTIC IDENTITY

British colonialism introduced decisive and irreversible changes in the structure of traditional society in this respect. Establishment of colonial power created a different structure of culture by a combination of deliberate policy and unintended consequences. Colonialism had to force social behaviour into recognizable institutional forms, which could be done only by introducing a new type of discourse. Colonialism did not allow to subject Indians any option in this matter; they were obliged, differentially according to their social status, to respond to its demands, identifications, and actions. Colonial laws and rules restructured Indian society in fundamental ways. Behind these laws there was a more fundamental conception of what laws were, how they related to the facts of the social world, a primarily bourgeois-rationalist discourse of legality. To understand and practically respond

[27]Kaviraj, 'On the Construction of Colonial Power'.

to the colonial legal, it was imperative for all Indians to understand this discourse; but it follows that the need was more intense according to their intimacy and involvement with colonial power. Sub-Brahmin groups seeking quick upward mobility through the pathways opened by colonial administration, newly endowed landlords under the permanent settlement, and those armed with a university degree who could get professional placements in the new society had more to do with this system, and therefore showed understandable eagerness to enter schools, pass public examinations, read European history, and get a grip on these conceptual assumptions on which the colonial institutional system was founded. For understandable reasons, they themselves, and to a lesser extent their colonial patrons, acclaimed this as their acquisition of the difficult, yet potentially universal principles of rationalism. By contrast, other groups which, by choice or circumstances, had less to do with the colonial institutions acquired less of this conceptual language, and eventually came to be derided by the babus for lack of rational inclinations. Interestingly, it is not only the poorer and culturally deprived social groups which fell into this ignominy, but also those who, on grounds of cultural pride or other such non-maximizing grounds, remained within the institutions and practices of traditional culture. However, in general, colonialism imposed on society a radically new, unfamiliar discourse, a conceptual grid, an alphabet, without which these institutions were uninhabitable, unworkable, and unintelligible. Institutions are after all the external superstructure of practices, and by altering the logic of institutional functioning, colonial rule also forcibly altered the structure of traditional practices and the social understandings that went with them.

Though early colonial administrations, by and large, followed a policy of non-interference in cultural affairs, there were strict limits to this tolerance. Colonial administrations could hardly dispense with one essential prerequisite of effective rule: intelligibility of this world to the rulers themselves. As a result of the unanswerable power that attached to the moves of the colonial administration in its days of dominance, even though sometimes these moves were misidentifications, they had real consequences. Gradually, colonialism introduced into this social world entirely unfamiliar processes and institutions drawn from the enormous cognitive apparatus that rationalism had by this time created in the West by which alone the colonizers could make this world cognitively and practically tractable. Surely, colonialism was an enterprise of introducing modernity only in truncated forms.[28] However, one particular aspect of modernity the colonial state did introduce with effectiveness—the modem imperative of setting up social connections on an unprecedentedly large scale. Extension of scale of social action brought in, as sociological research has amply shown, pressures towards standardization in varying forms.[29] European missionaries of the Srirampur College sought to fashion printed alphabets for Bengali, and by 1800, religious tracts meant to popularize Christianity were being printed at their press. These foreign pioneers of printing chose from among various styles of calligraphy, keeping in mind technical constraints, but once this contingent choice was made, it came to have decisive standardizing effects on even Bengali writing. Ironically, the way generations of modern Bengalis would read and write their own tongue was fatefully decided by choices made by a peculiarly skilled Englishman.

The most significant standardization, however, occurred in the areas of spoken and literary language; and this begins the mysterious process by which a high literature which they would never be able to read nonetheless confers an identity on the illiterate. Calcutta, an unknown village before the advent of the British, came to acquire as the colonial capital an unprecedented economic, administrative, and commercial eminence. The prime beneficiaries of the colonial social transformation either came from the society in Calcutta or journeyed there to remain close to the source of all colonial beneficence. The social elite resident in that city thus came to enjoy an eminence unknown in earlier times, and, indeed, structurally impossible. In a matter of less than a hundred years, the Calcutta babu came to acquire an unequalled capacity to do social and cultural norm-setting, growing out of his opulence and to screen demands made on the colonial administration. Slowly, the language of the Calcutta bhadralok, with occasional skilful mixtures from areas which had a reputation for particularly mellifluous accents

[28]The economic aspect of this argument—that colonialism did not introduce a capitalist economy of the Western type, but a peculiarly distorted form—is too well known to require special mention.

[29]Bernard Cohn, 'Census, Social Structure and Objectification in South Asia', in his *An Anthropologist Among the Historians and Other Essays* (New Delhi: Oxford University Press, 1987).

came to be regarded as the norm language for bhadralok Bengalis for all regions of this linguistic area. Of course, this norm-setting process could not have been completed without the print media. One of the reasons for lack of standardization in earlier language was the lack of scale-extension of any particular speech form. Arrival of printing altered this fact by exerting two types of pressures on its users. First, language had to be standardized not only at the material level of letters to be used in print, but, also, this standard Bengali could then be dedicated to modern uses as the vehicle of high literature, of science, of serious intellectual instruction. Second, once this standard or norm language became established, elites or aspirants to elite status from other, more outlying, regions began to emulate its accents and written idioms. The gentry of Medinipur, presumably content in earlier times with speaking a dialect which kept them in close ties with their local lower-order brethren, and, more significantly, in intelligible proximity with Oriyas, now began to read and speak as in journals written in the norm language of Calcutta. Any claim to linguistic distinction in the traditional language economy rested on the command of esoteric languages. Dialect Bengali would be spoken the same way by all social groups. Now the marks of distinction had to be entered into the vernacular itself. Traditionally, though, the two languages, Sanskrit and Bengali, may have been placed in a relation of hierarchy, each language was internally more equal. Two changes now occurred in this structure; English quickly displaced Sanskrit from the status of esoteric language: Sanskrit was relegated to the position of an archaic tongue. More significantly, the internal economy of the Bengali language itself became distinctly more hierarchical. As an aspiring high language, Bengali, in its increasingly sophisticated form, came to have interestingly complex relations with Sanskrit and English, the two languages from whose tyranny it was supposed to emancipate its cultivated speakers. The resources of the colloquial language of the street, its early literary masters, like Vidyasagar and Bankimchandra, felt, were too meagre and insubstantial to carry the burden of such tasks. The more Bengali would replace Sanskrit as a high language, therefore, the more it would 'become' like Sanskrit in a sense, both in the direct sense of borrowing from its vocabulary and being less accessible. Indeed, the new 'high' Bengali took on board a whole range of attributes from both Sanskrit and English, the two languages with which it existed in a relation of cultural contestation. Further, its internal economy would open up greater possibilities of hierarchy through the infinite refinement of 'literary' writing styles, and of 'cultured' pronunciation, an unfailing marker of increasing social differentiation.[30]

Sometimes this emergence of a standard Bengali and a culture of transaction of high functions in this language rather than in Sanskrit or English is treated absent-mindedly as a democratization of the linguistic field, a judgment that has to be taken with some caution. Within its incontestably democratic trends were lodged sharper inequalities of a new kind. The peasantry, the Hashim Sheiks and Rama Kaivartas of Bankim's famous essay, stood no chance of comprehending the argument in which they figured, and which was made on their behalf—for no other reason but they could hardly understand its Sanskritic grace.[31] Ironically, a speech community certainly grew up in nineteenth-century Bengal as Bankim's *Vande Mataram* illustrated—with seven crores of Bengalis, a vast majority of them illiterate, prepared to worship their linguistic motherland, extending to her a form of reverence earlier reserved only for scriptural deities. Yet, though this produced a sense of political community around language or speech, it was anything but a community of the same speech.

This historical sketch, though obviously crude and minimal, helps us to put to rest some prejudices that social science analyses of identity formation have uncritically picked up from later nationalist discourse. Both in mature nationalism and in social science, it is customary to seek systemic differences between traditional and modern identities. A vulgar Weberianism which almost always subtly informs nationalist thinking on this question often makes it out as if linguistic identities are primordial, while the national identity of India is modern.[32] This

[30]Subsequently, Bengali showed an interesting line of development on this count. Through the radio and the great popularity of the Bengali film, the 'cultured' way of speaking Bengali has become since the sixties very widespread. While this may have extended the 'civilising' process in a certain sense, the diction and accent have become distinctly less significant social markers.

[31]Bankimchandra Chattopadhyay, *Bangadesher Krshak, Bankim Rachanavali*, Vol. II (Calcutta: Sahitya Samsad, 1964), p. 288.

[32]Nationalism in India has had a particularly strong connection with modernist developmentalism. As it develops, nationalist discourse decisively sides with modernity and sees everything modern with approval and things 'traditional' with suspicion, if not with straightforward hostility. Additionally, it often tends to consign all pre-modern forms to

view is false, it appears, on two different counts: (i) the identities of region and nation are both products of the same historical-cultural processes which produced a mapped world out of the earlier fuzzy one. Political identities based on language are therefore equally modern though the languages on which they are based have distinct historical existence from much earlier times. (ii) This historical imperative— that is, both these are modern and historically intertwined making it difficult to play one against the other—makes for a peculiar configuration of a two-layered identity for individuals and groups. A regional identity is subsumed in a larger national one—a fundamental historic fact that later, more anxious and simple-minded forms of nationalist ideology have often sought to deny.[33] Within Bengali fiction, Bankimchandra's work is fascinating, I have argued elsewhere, because he shows quite precisely how this consciousness is formed; how some crucial cultural choices are made, how within the newly formed intense consciousness of being Bengali critical weaknesses are perceived.[34] Suffering of political humiliation and rightlessness are felt not to be a peculiar problem of the Bengalis, but common to all those who lived under British rule. Besides, if a credible political coalition was to be built up, which could effectively menace British power, a regional identity of Bengalis alone was unlikely to impress them. Authors like Bankim display what I have termed an anti-colonial consciousness before they chose their nation.[35] After considerable hesitation, and a few false starts, Bengali creative writing, by the middle of the nineteenth century, accomplishes a substantial gerrymandering of the boundaries of its imagined community. Initially, it appears that the 'we' who should oppose the British are to be Bengalis; but after considering proposals of making Hindus their nation, they eventually choose to be Indians. Reflecting this process graphically, Bankim breaks the boundaries of

---

primordiality (in the derogatory sense of an aboriginal primitiveness). But it is useful to distinguish between two distinctions widely used in the literature. Primordial/modern is in one sense a chronological historical distinction. In a related but quite distinct sense, this may also mean a taking/making of identities: primordial identities are those people have to take, modern ones are those they make on their own, or so they would like to believe.

[33]This is a point that has been made consistently by radical left parties against the grain of mainstream nationalism.

[34]Kaviraj, *Unhappy Consciousness*, chapter 4.

[35]What I mean is that their decision to oppose British colonialism comes chronologically before they decide who this 'We' were—Bengalis, Hindus, Indians?

his initially restricted Bengali regional identity and begins to represent Rajputs, Sikhs, and Marathas in their saying of 'we', in their collective self-description. As parallel processes go on in other parts of the country, this contributes, by the beginning of the twentieth century, to the making of the familiar contours of Indian nationalism. Still, under this nationalistic configuration of self-consciousness, other identities of language, occasionally linguistically perceived ones of religion or subregional cultures are always present in an indistinct and politically inactive state.[36] Much of current Indian politics revolves around how nationalism decides to deal with them—to attack and destroy them as competing attractions or to give them a place within its own internal architecture. Precedents of European nationalism through which Indian nationalists initially sought to understand and think through their own world, presented an immediate problem. Successful European nations created, in most cases, culturally homogeneous states based crucially on the unity of one language. Indian national identity seemed to 'lack' one of the main prerequisites of a modern nation, a feature which helped them to weather periods of political adversity.[37] Indian nationalism and its state inherited from its inception a 'language problem': that is, the problematicity of its cultural formation in the absence of a single unifying language. Two ways appeared to be open to it and the state it aspired to establish after independence was achieved. One arguable, but unlikely, road was to pursue a single-minded strategy of cultural homogenization based on the primacy (others would call it domination) of a 'majority' language. This would have implied trying to solve the cultural problem by a Soviet model: the only drawback was that the conditions for its practical realization did not exist. Hindi did not have a statistical absolute majority in India, nor was its political supremacy firmly established by the cultural processes of nationalist politics. It was therefore the

---

[36]The connection of Urdu with Islam, and of Punjabi more recently with Sikhism. Yet, it is interesting to note, with Khubchandani, that Urdu, especially Hindustani is the language of a culture rather than of a religion. Similarly, those who equate Punjabi too closely with the Sikh religion forget that there is a Punjabi-speaking people in Pakistan, and there is a Punjabi 'diaspora'. Lachman M. Khubchandani, *Language, Culture and Nation-building*, Indian Institute of Advanced Study (Shimla and Delhi: Manohar Publications, 1991).

[37]Curiously, any historical or social feature that Indian society has that is different from standard forms in European history is seen as a feature it does not have: its presence is seen as a lack and theorized consistently in this fashion.

second solution which was taken up by the national movement—a strategy of accepting the legitimacy of linguistic self-identifications of people in their regions, giving it a place in a second-order identity of Indian nationalism and using a critically significant political diglossia.

THE NATIONALIST DIGLOSSIA

The nationalist movement used two cultural devices to solve this difficulty of according legitimacy to regional identities but still requiring a second-order self-identification of people as Indians. In its mature stages, it generated a plausible and powerfully articulated narrative of India's immemorial past, a logic of cultural unification lodged in the essentials or the depths of Indian history, into which, through the creation of a 'composite culture', Muslims were integrated in the medieval times. Nehru's *Discovery of India* was of course the classic of this narrative construction, which saw the imagining of India as having been accomplished in the past.[38] As a part of an anti-imperialist ideology, it had an understandably powerful appeal, though in my judgment, the exclusive reliance on this narrative for solving all problems after independence has had a deleterious effect on political thinking. This logic of creating unity within plural strands, the ecumenical tolerance which gradually absorbed others into an extended notion of the self, was felt to have created this imagination and its practical institutions already in the past; British colonialism disturbed its continuity only temporarily. This implied that once the national state was achieved, this deep-lying cultural imagination of India would again come into its own. This became a deeply held and widespread belief that undergirded much nationalist practice of mobilization and state-building. Nehru's text, written at the moment of its imminent triumph, was a systematic and passionate statement of this narrative of culture; and I think Nehru's curious inattentiveness to cultural construction cannot be explained without understanding how seriously his generation believed in the story they had told themselves. As I said earlier, as an empowering narrative for the nationalist movement this picture of India's past was immensely powerful. For rational reconstruction

---

[38]For a critical discussion of this narrative structure see Sudipta Kaviraj, 'The Imaginary Institution of India', in Partha Chatterjee and Gyanendra Pandey (eds), *Subaltern Studies VII* (Delhi: OUP, 1994).

of the state, in the less romantic period after freedom, this narrative was more a hindrance to realistic policy than a help. It put the process of the cultural construction of the nation in the past, rather than in the future; it saw that as an accomplished task rather than as a requirement to be fulfilled, if India was to stay together as a nation-state. It encouraged forgetfulness and negligence about the cultural reproduction process in all its forms—in everyday life, social practices, and education, its most significant institutional form.[39]

But this narrative structure was supported by a deeper cultural arrangement that was more directly linguistic, which determined and mediated crucial political relations and decided who could, literally, speak to whom. To rejoin my earlier argument, the mixed elite drawn from the educated, bilingual intelligentsia of different regions found themselves within a triangle of cultural or discursive exchange—exchanges with the lower orders of their regional people, with peoples of other regions through their leaders, who were culturally and politically similarly placed, and exchange with the British, apart from the more general and exalted need to receive information about scientific developments in the Western world. The most effective and economical means of dealing with this set of discursive demands was a diglossia or cultural bilingualism.[40] Through political experimentation, the national movement came to settle on this device of political culture quite fundamentally. Common training in English education, with a common syllabus, common cultural preferences and tastes, common biases provided the preconditions for this situations, but this was cemented by the evident functionality of this arrangement for the growth of an Indian political movement.

Some consequences of this invisible cultural fact deserve some mention. This ensured in an oblique and unobtrusive way a kind of elite domination of the higher levels of nationalist mobilization, even though subaltern dissent against colonialism was more extreme and visceral and middle-class defiance more careful and circumspect. The linguistic economy partly guaranteed that despite this, it was only the

---

[39]Though there is no space for outlining this here, my argument requires as a complement a critical discussion about educational structures, practices, and policies.

[40]Any observant student of Indian culture would notice the common prevalence of diglossia and heteroglossia. After the coming of colonialism, the' typical structure of Indian bilingualism is English-vernacular rather than vernacular 1 and vernacular 2.

middle-class elements who would provide the all-India leadership. Vernacular speakers could storm into the leadership of linguistically homogeneous areas, but there their political stars stopped climbing. Compulsions of this kind, working not through the explicit and usually resented logic of social class or status but the subliminal agencies of language and communication, introduced an elitist counterweight into the inherent populism of the nationalist movement.

This diglossia was also politically rational in a narrower sense. Indian culture, it is often remarked, is characterized by an easy heteroglossia. After the entry of English education on a large scale, the situation stabilized into a fairly common structure of diglossia among the educated. A pure Indian bilingualism (that is, using two Indian languages equally fluently for serious intellectual activity) was not very common among the elite; bilingualism rather meant ability to use a vernacular and English. This meant that a bilingual person was not thickly aware of cultural or political development in only two areas; under this arrangement, he was, of course, thickly aware of his own vernacular-based regional culture, but also thinly of all others. Success of nationalism was made possible by political conceptual coordination between the various vernacular regions. However, often this bilingualism was internally uneven, those who could use these languages were unequally fluent in them. This yields a structure similar to the flower-shaped arrangement suggested by the Dutch sociologist of language, Abram de Swann, with the inconvenience of having widely irregular sized petals.[41] The petal representing Hindi would account for about 40 per cent of India's population next to those of comparatively small languages like Kashmiri or Manipuri. Recent admission of the political significance of some languages which cannot be ascribed specific regional or spatial location like Nepali or Sindhi would make the structure of actual linguistic exchanges still more complex. Additionally, such bilingualism is bound to be in individual cases asymmetric: a speaker would not have equal competence in both, and since competence confers and abridges rights and capacities, each would thus support the cause of

---

[41]The floral model is used in Abram de Swann, *In Care of the State* (Cambridge: Polity Press, Cambridge 1988), chapter 3, and used in a discussion on India in his draft paper. 'Political and Linguistic Integration in India: Monopolistic Mediation versus Language Integration', at a seminar on Changing Relations between State and Society in India and Trends towards an Emerging European State, IDPAD, New Delhi, 5–9 March, 1990.

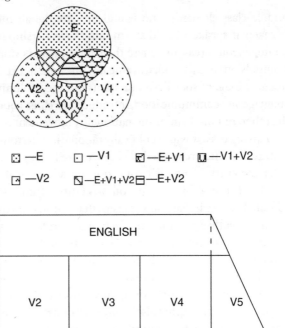

the language he is more proficient in. For individuals, thus, we should write not only that person X has E+V, but also indicate a certain slope or precedence: E/V or V/E, because these would, in political action, make a material difference.

Language thus acted as a necessary process of filtration, or 'gatekeeping', it would filter out inconvenient, extreme, radical, intransigent demands from subaltern social groups from reaching higher bodies. This was no small factor in enabling the higher decision-making bodies to maintain their immaculate middle-class ambience of restraint and polite gentility. This gives rise to a certain paradox of participation. Certainly, the English-knowing bilingual elite represented the largest number of people from all vernacular regions; but this implied an inverse relation between the extent or width of representation and its intensity or intimacy. Conversely, seen from the point of view of ordinary people living in the dialect or vernacular spaces of the pyramid of speech, the further their demands were carried into the political world by their representatives the lesser the control they could exercise over them.[42] The Indian people became, like democratic people elsewhere, the generalized reason, the universal justification for things done in their name, which they would have found largely incomprehensible. The greatest example of this paradox was the Constitution. It was apparently part of their tryst with destiny to give themselves the longest, the best, and the most intricate constitution in the world; there is a minor irony considering the fact that over 70 per cent of this people were illiterate and had no clear idea of what they had given themselves. Making a constitution of this kind was a strange, but historically inevitable, a mixture of giving them unprecedented rights and also keeping them securely out of their reach.

LANGUAGE AND POLITICS AFTER INDEPENDENCE

What is remarkable in this story of language and conferment of identity is a paradox that emerges in a comparison between pre-independence years and the time after independence. Abstractly, it appears that cultural problems of nationalism can be handled better when the ideological force of nationalism is assisted by the material power of the modern state. Yet, on a historical view, it seem that the Indian national movement, when it had to contend with the enmity and obstructiveness of the colonial state tackled some cultural processes better than the nation-state. In certain ways, the guiding logic of the complex network of culture, language, identities, discourses seems gradually to slip out of the grasp of the state, leading to a further paradox. The state is becoming increasingly powerful in technical and material terms and, at the same time, abjectly ineffective in regulating, let alone solving, cultural conflict.

The Nehruvian elite, which inherited effective control after independence, faced a complex initial situation. Indeed, the issue of an official or 'national' language occasioned some of the most

[42]In democratic theory a distinction is commonly made between delegation and representation. Something like this also exists in the Indian national movement, though this is seen as two pragmatic forms rather than two theoretical positions engaged in explicit debate.

acrimonious debates in the Constituent Assembly. Its proceedings also showed another ironical fact: how deep the influence of European precedents was on the minds of the Indian intelligentsia. On the language issue, the Assembly saw a division between moderates and Hindi extremists centred on three major issues: (i) whether India should have a national language, and if it did whether it would be the broad ecumenical form of Hindustani, or a sanskritized Hindi, (ii) what would be the status of English, how quickly this mark of foreign subjugation was to be phased out and replaced by the national language; and (iii) the largely symbolic problem about the system of numerals to be adopted. A nation, it was argued by those who favoured Hindi, must have a national language; and this could only be an Indian language. Of the various Indian languages, since there was, 'unfortunately', no clear majority language, this place should go to Hindustani or Hindi as the language spoken by the largest plurality. Strong and insistent demands were also made in the Constituent Assembly for having a Hindi version of the Constitution adopted as the original in place of the English one. Interestingly, even moderates on the language issue conceded the idea of having a single language being a precondition of firm, unassailable nationalism. Eventually, however, the Assembly adopted a more complex, if less decisive, line in favour of what was known as the Munshi-Ayyangar formula which pragmatically reflected the structure of discursive exchange which underlay the national mobilization.[43]

The influence of European examples was so deep that it determined the manner in which the constitution makers framed their question. A single language, one of the prime features of European nationalism, was missing in the Indian case: the nation-state lacked a common language. Pragmatically, with their comparative knowledge and historical sense, however, the Nehruvian leadership realized that the cultural form of Indian nationalism must be different from the European norm. Nehru's government pursued a policy of gentle exhortation on the significance of Hindi as an official language for the union government and communication between states. Actual use of languages in government, however, diverged substantially from its declared policy.

---

[43]For an excellent account of the debates on the language issue in the Constituent Assembly, Granville Austin, *The Indian Constitution: the Cornerstone of a Nation* (Oxford: Clarendon Press, 1966), chapter 12.

Introduction of large-scale economic planning, and the related emphasis on science, technology, processing of standardized information naturally increased the subtle forms of power exercised by the high bureaucracy simply by their inabilities and preferences. They could converse more easily in English and carry on these intricate activities more conveniently without the acute problems bound to be raised by impeding translations many times over between vernaculars. English became more entrenched in the bureaucratic and private managerial echelons after independence, because the earlier political compulsion of using vernaculars to underline self-respect had less relevance. To those outside the charmed circle of English education, this gave ground for complaint that India was reconquered for English after independence.[44] The language of India's nation-building was unfortunately, English.

The first wave of regional disturbance that the new state faced was not of its own making; it may have contributed to its occurrence only by forgetfulness about the promises the Congress had made. Congress acknowledged during the freedom movement that administrative boundaries instituted by British rule were arbitrary and had to be reordered after independence. After 1920, the Congress organization decided to work on the basis of linguistic provinces rather than of administrative boundaries, implicitly reinforcing the commitment. Events at the time of partition and the experience of constitution framing may have made the ruling group more cautious in this regard. However, the original organization of states was by the mid-fifties, facing serious disaffection in some parts of India. The structure of this disaffection is interesting. Initially, regional discontent did not arise in all parts of the country simultaneously, but only in those parts in which some communities had, under the colonial dispensation, enjoyed subcolonial advantage over others. Early opportunities of colonial employment had imparted a peculiar class structure to the Bengali society, since Bengalis had supplied the entire demand for

[44]One of the telling examples of this was the alteration in the structure of school education. A strong emphasis on symmetrical bilingual education in the period from the thirties to the sixties produced a fairly distinctive school system in the areas that had enjoyed the differential advantages of colonial education. This was gradually replaced by a flourishing privileged private sector of English-medium schools and an underprivileged state sector of vernacular schools. Because of the strong correlation between the acquisition of English language and chances of good middle-class employment, there has been a constant demand for rapid expansion of these 'public schools'.

middle-class bilingual professionals not only for the Bengali-speaking areas, but the entire northern and eastern parts of the empire. In the Madras Presidency, Tamil has enjoyed largely similar superiority for similar reasons. Linguistic groups who were disadvantaged by this, naturally, hoped that with the end of colonialism, such privileges would also disappear. Strong regionalist sentiments arose over the Congress's tardiness and hesitance. Although this caused temporary embarrassment to Nehru's government, some peculiarities in the situation made the eventual transition to linguistic states remarkably easy and smooth. The actual grievance was against the regionally superordinant cultures rather than the central government. The moral strength of the case of these regions was matched by the weakness of their adversaries. Besides, constitutional rights, unlike material resources, were not scarce or restricted things, and thus the achievements of the rights of one group instead of threatening furthered the claims of others.

Interestingly, although the Nehru government conceded these demands, and gave it a generalized form by instituting the States Reorganisation Commission, Nehru himself expressed some forebodings. First, he thought living in mixed, multilingual administrative units would provide education in common living and reduce linguistic chauvinism.[45] Second, he anticipated difficulties in administratively applying the principle: areas like the North-East have in fact proved chronically difficult to settle linguistically.[46] Yet Nehru agreed lo linguistic reorganization because of the undeniable force of the argument of democracy—that use of the vernacular in administration would bring government closer to the people, because, that was the language they were literate in. In case of the demand for a Punjabi *Suba*, he persistently refused to grant it because he thought this was merely a communal divide under a thin subterfuge of language.

Reorganization of states on the basis of language still left major difficulties. In some areas like Assam, linguistic groups were too mixed to allow for their clear administrative disentanglement without making

---

[45]Occasionally, such ideas went to an unpractical extreme—as in ease of the intensely unpopular suggestion for the merger of Bengal and Bihar. For Nehru's thinking on linguistic states, see S. Gopal. *Jawaharlal Nehru*, Vol. 2 (Delhi: OUP, 1979), chapter 12.

[46]Professional linguists sometimes argue that the idea that there should be sharply defined territorial boundaries not only for nation-states but also for linguistic units inside them was unsuited to the Indian situation and bound to cause problems. Khubchandani.

the units too small. Even such reordering has not, much afterwards, solved the question of enclaves within majority languages. Hindi remained anomalously placed inside the constitutional structure, since it was stretched from Bihar to some parts of Punjab. This might have encouraged some kind of interest coalition among them, and since their resources taken together would have been quite substantial, this may have renewed the conflicts of the Constituent Assembly once more. A potentially difficult situation was avoided precisely due to the internal divisiveness of the Hindi-language area. Hindi was historically less standardized than other vernaculars,[47] and several of its subregional forms[48] could claim to be much more than mere dialects of some general norm language, though khadi boli from early on made known its pretensions to that, status.[49] Apart from the problem of the standard, Hindi was riven by the acrimonious dispute between a sanskritized Hindi and a persianized Urdu tearing apart the spontaneous historical form of the Hindustani, the language in which most people actually spoke in north India. That was also the form which was more easily intelligible to neighbouring vernacular speakers, and in which much of high literature was written. Internal dissensions within Hindi led to a circumstance which turned ironically to he beneficial to the new state. The potential mobilization for Hindi as a 'national' language which would compulsorily replace English, and make India look more like a unilingual European nation-state failed to gather momentum, because it was hard to decide which kind of Hindi would enjoy these privileges of universal aggrandizement. After 1956, the union government has faced infrequent difficulty from this direction, except for some areas like the North-East where linguistic determination of state boundaries has remained intellectually unconvincing and politically contested.

One of the major features of Nehru's development policy that has escaped serious critical attention was its economism: a superstitious

[47]For a discussion or the issues involved in the Hindi–Urdu–Hindustani debate. Khubchandani, *Language, Culture and Nation-Building*, and an earlier account in Dasgupta, *Language, Conflict and National Development*, chapters 2 and 6.

[48]Maithili has caused endless debates on this count—whether it was a dialect of Hindi or a separate but closely related language.

[49]Even this has to be qualified, because during the early development of modern Hindi literature eminent figures tike Bharatendu Harishchandra had suggested khari boli as the form of prose and *brajabhasha* as the form for poetry.

belief in the powers of economic growth to dispel all evils like rays of light in enveloping darkness of traditionalism. Thus, although individual members of that early governmental elite had impressively high cultural attainments, their dedicated economism made them deeply negligent about processes of culture. While economic processes were minutely analysed, alternative policies assessed and debated, they did not see cultural processes or institutions as serious objects of either historical reflection or of deliberate policy, except in terms of budgetary allocations. Unattended cultural reproduction processes, left to the violence and malignancy of both a vicious market and unprincipled state manipulation, have now produced something like a massive counter-revolution of culture. In the rest of this paper, I shall try to present a bare outline of this process, and its relation to the crisis of the state.

If states, to be durable, have to depend on something like a common consciousness, the Indian national state faced an obvious difficulty, not so much because of the multiplicity of its languages, as owing to the fact that there were two rather different types of 'common sense' about the world that were lodged in the English and the vernacular segments of its culture. True, serious transactions had begun between these two orbits of common sense in the nineteenth century and during the freedom movement. But such exchanges remained unfinished and irregular. As India did not have a natural coincidence of a common culture and a common language, the quotidian self-recognition of its citizens depended crucially on an argumentative and ratiocinative process which could be fashioned by education and deliberate cultural policies. Such a self-recognition of Indianness is primarily a conceptual construction and is to be produced and maintained by means of cultural arguments quite different from the easy recognition of a collective self given in the mere utterance of a natural language. It has to be an indirect, second-order process, quite distinct from the process of linguistic self-recognition, of creation and stabilization of a political common sense. Identity in India must have more than one layer. From this point of view, Nehru's government and its successors have consistently misconstrued the historical function of education. Owing to their deeply economistic reasoning, they considered education an input in the creation of skills necessary for a modern economy and entirely missed the more fundamental common-sense-forming role. These roles are performed by different levels of the educational structure. Technological education was given nearly exclusive priority, including science education as its base, and naturally also higher education. This led to a state of affairs in which, while a large number of middle-class graduates were trained to be engineers, medical practitioners, or planners, the large majority were not trained in being Indians. Such training, sorely missed in recent years, has been left to the canned patriotism provided abundantly and free of charge with the television news.

Later evolution of Indian politics has shown such superstitious belief in the enlightening powers of economic processes to be fallacious. Economically upwardly mobile farmers have not become more kindly towards other rural classes—their traditional neighbours in the daily life of the countryside.[50] Professional middle classes have not shown increased comprehension of others' justified demands on the resources of the state.[51] Under the primitive capitalist conditions that exist in India, greater economic prosperity does not seem to increase a group's understanding of the overall requirements of distributive justice; rather an insensitivity to distributive questions may produce the drive for strong commercial enterprise. In general, economic growth simply failed to radiate the kind of illumination and understanding expected of it by the development model.

Cultural defaults of the nation-state begun in the absent-mindedness of Nehru's government, were intensified by successor regimes. While all governments paid ceremonial attention to high culture and art, made larger budgetary allocations to higher education, they considered their responsibility completed by such exertions and showed little interest in organizing social reflection on the relation between democracy, poverty, and culture. These delicate processes were thus left to an increasing chaotic and iniquitous market of cultural skills and goods whose spontaneous trends were 'corrected' by an increasingly arbitrary state which specialized in correcting injustices

[50]The demands of rich farmers show this insensitivity quite dramatically.

[51]The middle class's hostility to any suggestion of redistributive moves was reflected in its violent reaction to the declaration that the recommendations of the Mandal Commission would be partially implemented.

by other injustices rather than the unaccustomed intellectual practice of following a judicious policy over a long term.[52] Indian cultural life saw the emergence of a progressive intelligentsia, whose only vocation in life, after pursuing individual self-interest, was to lead the Indian people, especially the indigent, to liberation, but it had forgotten to pick up their language. Those who spoke those languages often had political horizons too narrow to consider national interests, and were mired by pulls of regional or subregional selfishness. The contradiction between the two common senses, lodged largely in the English and the vernaculars, has now assumed close to crisis intensity, bringing the conceptual basis of the Indian state to great strain. The process of the imagining of India has fallen a victim to quietly effective processes of bifurcation and heterogeneity. Neglect of education and leaving it to the market meant the difference between high and low culture, incompatible with the logic of democratic politics, persisted. Entrant elites at the state levels of the Indian federation, drawn from farmer groups, perceived this system, with some justification, as a system of cultural or linguistic untouchability, an English-based caste system. On the other hand, the urban elite, systematically withdrawing from the diglossia into exclusive use of a coarsening functional English, reacted negatively, often showing their paradoxical belief that only those who could not speak in any Indian language could be safely called Indian nationalists; others were assigned derogatory ethnicities like Punjabi, Bengali, Bihari, Tamil, etc. Unplanned and unorganized spread of vernacular education, which is often distinctly inferior in quality, accentuated this process. The diglossia that had formed the cultural basis of the national movement has tended to fall apart. Educational differentiation has led to a situation in which a monolingual, English-using elite is faced by an equally monolingual, vernacular aspirant group contesting its power with increasing urgency. Both languages suffer coarsening in this friction, though it is the slow slide of English into a

---

[52]This is reflected in the irrationalities of the schools system. Public schools, run on lines of merciless private enterprise, treat these institutions as business propositions with high fees, impossible entry criteria, and a quality of training which is hardly commensurate with the expenses or the advertisement. Government schools, starved of basic resources and plagued by bureaucratic controls are not allowed to stabilize into any reasonable pattern by the appallingly arbitrary way in which changes are made in their educational schemes.

functional inelegance which is most observable.[53] Thus the discursive structure of nationalism is being broken down in two ways. First, the English-using managerial elites at the top of the pyramid are getting distanced from the vernacular-using lower slices, failing to perform the task of creating and disseminating a nationalist common sense which must not be an ossified collection of ideas from the past nationalist leaders but an active configuration of ideas which can negotiate real problems and pick its way through the political world. Second, since in our model the major part of the exchanges between the vernacular segments did not occur laterally, but through the bilingual top, these vernacular sections are coming into increasing friction.[54]

By and large, till recently, the Indian state has faced relative infrequent difficulty from linguistic separatism. Common people's quotidian linguistic identities seem to lie quiescent in a pleasant, inoffensive, taken-for-granted kind of way, until they become vehicles for other types of grievance through a malignant elective affinity.[55] Though both the Assam and the Punjab problems have pronounced linguistic aspects, in these disturbances the linguistic demand exists in interestingly complex relation with others.

In recent months, one can glimpse the emergence of a different sort of problem in Indian politics, which might revive the question of Hindi chauvinism in a new form. Since Indira Gandhi's victory in the general elections of 1971, directly populist rhetoric had been rather faint in Indian political discussion. Since the last elections, populism

[53]I would argue against some enthusiastic linguists that while the Indian way of using English must be legitimately different, the question of linguistic elegance should not be confused with this. Elegance or distinction is achieved when language rises above mere functionality and can express complexity and subtlety of ideas. From this angle one can find a clearly perceptible coarsening of the linguistic culture. And it is not the inadequately bilingual speakers who are responsible but the parasitic, culturally sterile, imitative, whose only language is this vulgarized, subliterary English.

[54]It must be seen, however, that this model is meant to be an ideal-typical construction. Exchanges took place bilaterally between regional cultures, e.g., Bengali literature (especially the novels of Bankimchandra Chatterjee, Rabindranath Tagore, and Saratchandra Chatterjee) were widely translated in other languages. My point is that the primary political exchange happened systematically through the bilingualism of the elite.

[55]Khubchandani, makes this point about Punjab; *Language, Culture and Nation-Building*. Despite the creation of Bengali-speaking Bangladesh, there was no noticeable urge on either side for a sentimental merger.

has seen a great revival, forcing democratic issues on the political agenda of the nation, mixed in a distinctly Tocquevillesque fashion, with dangerous disregard for norms of institutional circumspection. Gandhi spoke in the name of the great majority of the poor; parties now speak in the names of the equally great majorities of the 'backward castes', of the neglected Hindus, or the insulted, disprivileged speakers of Hindi, the language of the majority of Indians. We saw earlier how the question of what to do with Hindi was alleviated by the other one of what was Hindi. Since independence, the situation has changed in several ways. The first is the noticeable retreat of Urdu into the cultivated middle-class parlour under the assault of a state-patronized sanskritized Hindi. Because of the evident disruption of the nationalist diglossia it has become possible now to claim that the division of the rich and the poor, of the urban exploiters and the rural sufferers, the upper castes and lower ones are all translatable into the symbolic divide between English, the language of the undeservingly privileged, and Hindi, the speech of unmerited suffering. A significant recent development was the declaration of four chief ministers of the northern states that Hindi should displace English in official administrative functions. They explicitly demanded that it should be used in interstate communication, and as the exclusive language for entrance examination of various types of government and semi-government bureaucracy. Its major supporting argument is that insistence on English artificially and unjustly wrongfoots speakers of Indian languages—an entirely understandable idea up to this point. But their demand is not that linguistic inequity should be ended, but that it should be turned to the favour of the native Hindi speakers. They should enjoy the privilege that belonged to English-users because they constitute the ironical majority of 40 per cent of the Indian population. Clearly, this would not be perceived as equitous by those who do not speak Hindi, only a proposal to disadvantage others. English, they would claim, is more equitous because it places all Indians in a position of equality of disadvantage.

Undoubtedly, in the past forty years, India has seen a process of uneven but also unprecedented enfranchisement of common people. Language rights constitute a vital part of this process—the right to protest becomes attenuated if it is not right to protest in one's own language. Through the processes of democracy, identities have undergone rapid reconfiguration, and political groups are naturally trying to split and recoalesce identities in ways preferable to themselves. Communal elements have put forward the considerable appeal of a Hindu majoritarianism. In response, the Janata Dal advanced a consolidation, also majoritarian, of backward castes splitting the potential Hindu coalition on caste lines. The proposals for Hindi majoritarianism, though statistically on somewhat weaker grounds, bear interesting connections with Hindu communal sentiments. Historically, the trend most dangerous for survival of Indian democratic government will be a process of mutual attraction, a fatal elective affinity between various forms of majoritarianism, a coalition struck between differently grounded majoritarian demands. Indeed, as some people have argued at different points in recent history, the majority demand of a Hindu state, instead of the present one based on 'Western' secularism, and the majority demand for a Hindi-dominant state can coalesce, because the two groups of beneficiaries of such privilege would overlap to a large degree. 'Being Indian' has been historically a multilayered identity in which the upper and more general identification subsumes, but does not nullify, the less general and particular ones. The new majoritarian trends threaten this historical form and the specific equilibrium the nation-state has tried to give it. In a major irony of history, although most of these forces and their political leaders see themselves as being uncompromisingly anti-English and anti-Western, they wish, despite their strident indigenous rhetoric, to replay a European paradigm of nationalism in which being Indian must find confirmation in speaking Indian and writing Indian. If such a convex majoritarianism gradually takes shape, convex because this puts the majoritarianism of religion on top of that of language, compensating the statistical inadequacy of Hindi by the overwhelming dominance of the Hindu, this can really fatally threaten the cultural presuppositions of the Indian nation-state. That would illustrate the disruption of a democratic state by unqualified and uncomprehending application of an equation between democracy and majority rule. For democracy cannot exist without rule of the majority, but, equally, it cannot exist as only majority rule, unmodified by other subtler, juster, latent, equitable principles which make it not only the most acceptable, but also the most delicate and perishable among forms of modern governance.

GLOSSARY OF BENGALI/SANSKRIT TERMS
IN ORDER OF APPEARANCE

Kumbhilaka—a plagiarist or one who interpolates his own work surreptitiously into someone else's

Payar—a metre used in Bengali verse compositions, one of the simplest

Shanka—the conchshell

Chakra—the disc, a weapon always associated with Krishna

Gada—the mace used in warfare

Padma—Lotus

Gopal—literally means cowherd, but in case of the iconography of Krishna it refers to his child form

Aishvarya—grandeur

Vatsalya—love of parents for their child

Shringara—or adirasa, erotic love

Vaishnava padavali—a tradition of verse compositions by vaishnava poets

Mandakranta—a metre associated particularly with the classical Sanskrit poet, Kalidasa

Avatara—incarnation

Radhabhava krishnaswarupa—one who is the real self of Krishna but with the attributes of Radha

Jayadeva—a great Vaishnava poet who composed the classic text, Gitagovindam, which constitutes a part of the literary canon of Vaishnavism in Eastern India

Shaivaj—worshippers of Shiva

Babus—Western-educated middle-class Bengalis

Bhadralok—literally, gentlefolk, but actually referring to the Western-educated middle class

Vande Mataram—literally means, in Sanskrit, let us worship the Mother. This was the title of a song in Bankimchandra Chatterjee's novel, *Anandamath*, and this came to be one of the most popular nationalist songs in India

Suba—was the term used to mean administrative territorial units in pre-British times. Here, it means a state within a federation

10

Talking the National Language
Hindi/Urdu/Hindustani in Indian Broadcasting and Cinema*[1]

David Lelyveld

Nearly twenty years ago, when I first looked into the history of broadcasting and cinema, I was drawn to what I took to be a sharp dichotomy that had emerged in the sort of language that was called 'Hindi' in either of them. The Hindi on the radio was characterized by a heavy use of *tatsama*, that is, unmodified Sanskrit words and various morphological markings that distinguished it from Urdu, such as the distinction of singular *vaha* and plural *ve* for the third person nominative and demonstrative pronoun, rather than the undifferentiated *voh*. In films, one was unlikely to come across such strongly marked Hindi expressions, except as parody, and far more

*Originally published as 'Talking the National Language: Hindi/Urdu/Hindustani in Indian Broadcasting and Cinema', in Sujata Patel, J. Bagchi, and M.K. Raj (eds), *Thinking Social Science in India: Essays in Honour of Alice Thorner* (New Delhi: Sage Publications, 2002), pp. 355–66.

[1]This paper expands on a series of related studies, I am grateful to the American Institute for Indian Studies, the Social Science Research Council, and the National Endowment for the Humanities for supporting my research over the years; David Lelyveld, 'Transmitters and Culture: The Colonial Roots of Indian Broadcasting', *South Asian Research*, 10 (1), 1990; 'The Fate of Hindustani: Colonise Knowledge and the Project of a National Language', in C. Breckenridge and P. van der Veer (eds), *Orientalism and the Post-Colonial Predicament: Perspectives on South Asia* (Philadelphia: University of Pennsylvania Press, 1993); 'Upon the Sub-dominant: Administering Music on All-India Radio', in C. Breckenridge (ed.), *Consuming Modernity: Public Culture in a South Asian World* (Minneapolis: University of Minnesota Press, 1995).

likely to encounter words of Persian or Arabic origin associated with Urdu, frequently phonologically and morphologically marked as such.

I wanted, and want here, to explore some of the implications of this distinction between *filmi* and *akashvani* Hindi, but first I should note the bewildering transformations that have taken place since I first embarked on this research. As I was arriving in the Delhi airport in the fall of 1982, I noticed that there were large areas filled with cartons of imported television sets. Prime Minister Indira Gandhi was promoting television, most immediately in anticipation of the forthcoming Asian Games. The following year, the American space shuttle, Challenger, took up India's satellite, INSAT, one of whose purposes was to enable the Government of India to establish a far-flung, centrally controlled television system to reach the vast majority of the population. For the first time, after some sixty years of small-scale interest, the government was putting major resources into broadcasting. Within three years, television reaped its first great popular success: the serialization of the Ramayana. As I will point out later, the language of the Ramayana, highly sanskritized and virtually free of Arabic and Persian words, was the culmination of a long, frequently frustrated effort to mount this sort of Hindi as a national language for India. In the eyes of many observers, it also was an important event in a historical process of defining the nation as 'Hindu' and excluding non-Hindus, especially Muslims, from the mainstream of national identity. In the meantime, video cassettes and, more recently, private international satellite television (TV) enterprises have further complicated the world of mass communications.

The pre-partition debates on Hindi/Urdu/Hindustani were not only indexes, they were boundary markers of other social and cultural divisions, Hindu versus Muslim. The battle to define a national language was a matter of staking out claims to far-reaching authority, who could speak and who could be spoken to. Ultimately it was a question of what sort of socialization, what scholastic disciplines a person would have to undergo in order to qualify as a member of the nation, to participate in the emerging public sphere. A national language was more than an emblem, it was a very specific set of practices. Pierre Bourdieu has argued that only when the making of the 'nation', an entirely abstract group based on law, creates new usages does it become necessary to forge a *standard* language, impersonal and anonymous like the official uses it has to serve.... The *normalized* language is capable of functioning outside the constraints and without the assistance of the situation, and is suitable for transmitting and decoding by any sender and receiver, who may know nothing of one another. Hence it concurs with the demands of bureaucratic predictability.[2]

Establishing a national language, Bourdieu maintains, is an act of 'symbolic domination', enforced through codes of correctness, carefully inculcated by the educational system, and maintained in a wide range of cultural practices as 'legitimate language'.

In the early 1930s, at the same time that the Indian National Congress declared full national independence as the unambiguous goal of the national movement, two forms of communication appeared on the scene that raised the issue of a national language in new ways. Radio broadcasting and sound motion pictures made it possible to imagine reaching truly national audiences without relying on the more complex mechanisms of literacy and printing. From a purely technological point of view, film and radio speech did not require written texts; they might have been purely oral, free to speak in many voices without conforming to the rigours of a literary education. They appeared particularly suitable to a society still overwhelmingly illiterate and characterized by substantial linguistic variation. But in actual practice, the language of both radio and television in India were conceived in the first instance as written, carefully constructed according to literary criteria that summoned up the full measure of controversy about cultural authority, in particular the appropriate educational background one would have to have to participate as speaker or even as audience. Hovering over this controversy as a model of public language, the place that any future national language would have to occupy was the very substantial role of standardized British English.

Though the development of mass communications now seems of immense political importance, it would be anachronistic to imagine

[2] Pierre Bourdieu, 'The Production and Reproduction of Legitimate Language', in John B. Thompson (ed.), *Language and Symbolic Power*, translated by Gino Raymond and Mathew Adamson (Cambridge, Massachusetts: Harvard University Press, 1991), p. 48.

that such issues were placed high on many political agendas at the time. Although the official records of British administration indicate fairly extensive discussions of the politics of broadcasting, a wider public interest is hard to locate, particularly among the established leaders of Indian nationalism. The cinema, on the other hand, received little official attention after the pre-talkie inquiry of the Indian Cinematography Committee of 1927–8 and the Film Enquiry Committee of 1950, neither of which were concerned with linguistic issues.[3] Films were a matter of considerable popular interest, especially in urban areas, but again were not something that attracted attention by political leaders until a later era when film stars themselves entered politics.

Language policy, however—the language of schools and universities, of courts and government offices—was a matter of long-standing debate. Prompted in particular by Gandhi, from the time of his advent on the Indian scene in 1916, the Indian National Congress had formulated what was intended to be a language policy that would include and satisfy the largest number of constituencies.[4] A good statement of that policy was set out by Jawaharlal Nehru in 1937 in his capacity as president of the Congress and later reprinted in a book of his essays entitled, significantly, *The Unity of India*.[5] In this essay, Nehru foregrounded the controversy between Hindi and Urdu and the need for cultivating a national language. As for the other major languages of India—he listed twelve—these were to be accommodated by a reorganization of political boundaries according to linguistic lines, so that education and government business might be conducted in them, a transformation that Nehru as India's prime minister, was to resist, unsuccessfully, two decades later. He expressed a hope, already long advocated by Gandhi, that all of these languages would eventually adopt a common script, Devanagari. But the Hindi-Urdu question was at a different level. Like Gandhi, Nehru believed that for the foreseeable future it was necessary to recognize both Hindi and Urdu as legitimate

[3]Erik Barnouw and S. Krishnaswamy, *Indian Film*, 2nd edn (New York: Oxfrod University Press, 1980).

[4]M.K. Gandhi, *Our Language Problem*, Anand T. Hingorani (ed.) (Bombay: Bharatiya Vidya Bhavan, 1965).

[5]Jawaharlal Nehru, 'The Question of Language', in *The Unity of India: Collected Writings 1937–1940*, 2nd edn (London: Lindsay Drommond, 1942), pp. 241–61.

literary languages, written in their respective scripts. Nehru went on to say that there was nothing wrong with both Hindi and Urdu proceeding to develop their separate vocabularies to express modern needs. The vitality of literary development required an open door to new words and expressions. Ultimately the enrichment of one language would feed the other. Such developments could not be matters of government policy.

In a characteristic argument, Nehru states that the distinction between Hindi and Urdu, with its communalist implications, was just a temporary historical phase. What was really important was the promotion of change, of 'mass education', and of national unity. 'Most of our present troubles are due to highly artificial literary languages cut off from the masses.' But if writers 'think in terms of a mass audience...., this will result automatically in a simplification of language.... Language which is to make appeal to the masses must deal with the problems of those masses ...' It was Nehru's faith that language serving such purposes would evolve into a greater unity.

In the meantime, the task of enhancing communication among the people of India might be advanced by creating a 'basic Hindustani', modelled on the schemes of C.K. Ogden and I.A. Richards for Basic English. Such a language could suffice with a lexicon of about 1,000 words, Nehru thought—Basic English was constructed on 800—and a simplification of grammatical forms, such as gender agreement. Such a language could be founded, Nehru appeared to think, on what was common to both Hindi and Urdu.

From Broadcast Hindustani to Akashvani Hindi

Although Nehru only made passing reference to radio and film, his proposal and that of the Congress for the promotion of Hindustani was taken up with enthusiasm by the British official brought out that year from the BBC to establish a national radio broadcasting system.[6] The following year, 1938, following Congress victories in most of the provincial elections under the new Government of India Act, Lionel

[6]Lionel Fielden, *Report of the Progress of Broadcasting in India up to the 31st March 1939* (Delhi: Manager of Publications, 1940).

Fielden took what was, from the perspective of British bureaucratic ethos, a bold move in seeking to project radio broadcasting into the heart of national political controversy. It was, however, a controversy that radio broadcasting could hardly avoid since it was a matter of the language to be used in its own broadcasts. What Fielden proposed was a well-publicized broadcast forum on the issue, 'What is Hindustani?'

Apart from the general interest that All India Radio has in movements that aim at a greater unity amongst the various sections of the people in this country, any attempt towards creating and popularizing a common language is of special significance to broadcasting ... whose constant aim is to make itself intelligible to the largest possible number of people.[7]

Six speakers were invited to give fifteen-minute talks on consecutive days, followed by 'an objective summing up' on the seventh. Under All-India Radio censorship policy, the talks would have to be submitted in written form, and the invited speakers were given the opportunity, unusual at the time, to record them. The programmes would be broadcast from the five major north Indian stations—Peshawar, Lahore, Delhi, Lucknow, and Calcutta. The six-speakers were Rajendra Prasad, Abul Kalam Azad, Zakir Husain, Tara Chand, Abdul Haq, and Narendra Dev—two of them, by the way, future presidents of India. As Rajendra Prasad wrote to Fielden, however, the list of speakers was overwhelmingly skewed in favour of Urdu and made no room for the advocates of a more restricted definition of Hindi, those who felt that All-India Radio was giving unwarranted prominence to Urdu at the expense of Hindi, 'and that the Hindustani that it has encouraged is of the Urdu variety'. He suggested that All-India Radio invite a speaker from 'the more orthodox school' of Hindi writers connected with the Hindi Sahitya Sammelan in Allahabad.[8]

The Hindi Sahitya Sammelan was indeed the major thorn in the side of All-India Radio in the decade before partition. Founded in

---

[7]Lionel Fielden to Jawaharlal Nehru, 17 November 1938 (Nehru Papers, Nehru Memorial Museum and Library, New Delhi). When Nehru refused, Fielden sent the identical letter to Rajendra Prasad, 8 December, 1938; Valmiki Choudhury, *Dr Rajendra Prasad: Correspondences and Select Documents*, Vol. 1 (1934–8) (New Delhi: Allied Publishers, 1984). For Fielden's relations with Congress leaders and his failure to interest them in the possibilities of broadcasting, see his other correspondence with Nehru, Nehru Papers, and his autobiography, *The Natural Bent* (London: Andre Deutch, 1960).

[8]Prasad to Fielden, 13 December 1938, see Choudhary, *Dr Rajendra Prasad*, p. 170.

1910, partly to mobilize pro-Hindi responses to the forthcoming census, the Sammelan included major leaders of a Hindu-oriented nationalism, such as Madan Mohan Malaviya and Purushottam Das Tandon. Part of a long-standing Hindi movement based in Allahabad since the early 1880s, the Hindi Sahitya Sammelan worked not only to promote Hindi in education, journalism, and government offices, but to oppose Urdu as a legitimate language, particularly with respect to any sort of official recognition, from courts to coins.[9] The establishment of All-India Radio in 1936, along with elected provincial governments the following year, gave the Hindi movement a new focus of concern. The fact that Lucknow rather than Allahabad, was selected as the only broadcasting headquarters between Delhi and Calcutta, contrary to the technical recommendations of a BBC engineer, had skewed broadcasting production away from the major centre of Hindi advocacy and literary activity to one long associated with Urdu. In fact, the leadership of the All-India Radio throughout the pre-partition period was associated with Lahore, recruited by Ahmad Shah Bokhari 'Patras', a former professor of English, student of I.A. Richards at Cambridge and prominent writer of elegant and witty Urdu prose. The major architect of All-India Radio's language policy, Bokhari struggled to appease diverse constituencies, while working all the while to create a unified language, Hindustani, at least for north India, that would draw upon both Hindi and Urdu.

In 1940, Bokhari initiated what turned out to be a five-year project to prepare a lexicon with over 8,000 entries to be used for the preparation of Hindustani news broadcasts. He assigned to this project two prominent literary figures, Sachchidananda Vatsyayan 'Ageya', a major Hindi poet, and C.H. Hasrat, an Urdu journalist, both from Lahore. The procedure was to list English words that appeared in the initial news copy from which the vernacular translations were prepared. The Hindi expert prepared a list of Hindi equivalents, his Urdu counterpart set down the Urdu ones; then the two worked out a compromise based on what they considered to be most common, most precise and, if possible, most neutral. Each of the entries gave multiple options for translating a single English term.[10]

[9]C.A. Bayly, *The Local Roots of Indian Mines: Allahabad 1880–1920* (Oxford: Clarendon Press, 1975), p. 218.

[10]AIR (DG) PZ–3/42, 1942; P(I)Z–6/45–I, 1945; P(I) 2–15/46, 1946; P(I) Z–2/46 II; P(I) Z–34/49, 1949 (All-India Radio, New Delhi); interview with Vatsyayan, Bombay, 1982.

The Hindi and Urdu entries were, in fact, not necessarily divided on Sanskrit versus Persian-Arabic lines and often overlapped. They were listed under the heading 'Equivalents in Hindi and Urdu Journals'. The compromise terms were listed under 'Proposed Simple Equivalent'. For example, translations of 'prime minister'—cross-referenced to 'premier'—overlapped in Hindi and Urdu. The first word on the Hindi list, in Devanagari, is *mukkyamantri*, but it appears fourth on the Urdu list. The first word on the Urdu list is *vazir-i a'zzam*, which is second on the Hindi list. The 'simple' compromise is *bara vazir*—the big minister.

Another example is the translation of 'nation'. The Hindi list starts with *jati*, a word that anthropologists have been pleased to translate as 'caste'. The next word, Arabic in origin, is *qaum*, a word that has come to mean 'community' in its special South Asian sense of Hindu versus Muslim. It is spelled in Devanagari with a dot under the/ka/to give it the characteristically Arabic sound/q/. The third word on the Hindi list is *rashtra,* the word used by the Hindu 'nationalist' Rashtriya Swayamsevak Sangh (RSS). The words listed for Urdu were the same, except that *millat* comes third in place of *rashtra*. The suggested 'simple' word is *qaum*. On the other hand, 'community' (as in communalism) is translated as *sampradaya* in Hindi, *firqa* in Urdu, and, again, *firqa* or *biradari* (lineage) in the suggested 'Hindustani'.

The linguistic experiments of All-India Radio only created greater dissatisfaction. In 1943, the Muslim League supported a resolution to trim the broadcasting budget in protest of what were considered excessive concessions to sanskritized Hindi, as in the use of the words *yudh, andolan,* and *diya,* mixed in with Urdu. 'The language which is used by the All-India Radio', said Liaquat Ali Khan, '... is neither Urdu nor Hindi nor English nor Sanskrit but it is a hotch-potch of all these languages'. Ignoring the principles of Muslim separatism and the prospect of Pakistan, Liaquat and others maintained that Urdu was the appropriate national language of India, 'the result', said Zafar Ali Khan, 'of thousands of years of inter-language impact'. Urdu, said another Muslim League speaker, was the language of 'the teeming millions'. With the Congress leadership largely in jail, Hindu participants in the debate countered that All-India Radio made far too many concessions to Urdu—words like *shikayat* and *kamyabi*—because, in fact, it was controlled by Muslims. Urdu was the language of the Mughal court and its army, not of the people of India.[11]

Ahmad Shah's younger brother, Zulfiqar Ali Bokhari, was also an important official in the broadcasting service, serving as station director in Bombay, before going off to work under George Orwell in the war-time Indian service of the BBC.[12] After partition he became Director-General of Radio Pakistan. In his autobiography, published in 1966 and free of any need to placate Hindi interests, he states the kind of linguistic attitude that the supporters of Hindi had attributed all along to pre-partition All-India Radio. According to him, to know Urdu properly one must know Arabic and Persian. Muslims were more likely to have the necessary educational background. In response to the Government of India's policy to balance recruitment among religious communities, it was appropriate to have more Muslims in charge of programming, leaving the technical side to Hindus. As for Hindustani, Bokhari says, 'If the Hindustani language had any dictionaries, if there existed any literature in the Hindustani language, then we could have said, *chalo bhai*, let's pick the Hindustani language.' But such was not the case.[13] When K.M. Munshi, a minister in the Congress government complained about the Arabic-Persian vocabulary of the Hindustani broadcasts, Bokhari replied, fine, but then they would be unable to mention his name on the radio, since *munshi* was an Arabic word.[14]

Suspicions of such attitudes as well as responses to the actual practice of broadcasting, especially with reference to the news, led to boycotts by Hindi writers, debates in the Legislative Assembly, and fierce polemics. The major spokesman for the Hindi Sahitya Sammelan on this issue was an Allahabad academic named Ravi Shankar Shukla, who wrote a series of books and pamphlets in Hindi and English during the mid-1940s, all directed against the very concept of Hindustani and, in particular, the formulations of All-India Radio. According to Shukla, Urdu was a separate literary style of Hindi, associated with

---

[11]Legislative Assembly, 9 March 1943.
[12]Sayyid Zulfiqar Ali Bokhari, *Sarguzasht* (Karachi: Ma arif Limited, 1966).
[13]Ibid., pp. 119–20.
[14]Ibid., p. 129.

nawabs and maulvis and unknown to the vast majority of India's population. Granting legitimacy to Urdu, he argued, was like recognizing 'Babu Hindustani', that is, a version of Hindi laden with English vocabulary. Although Urdu had now to be recognized as an accomplished fact in the life of a significant number of Muslims, it was essential to keep it sequestered. Shukla quotes a remark attributed to Robert Southey that use of Latin and French expressions in place of 'pure old English' was an act of 'high treason'. Not only the vocabulary, but the whole literary culture of Urdu was 'foreign' and dangerous. Teaching Urdu to the young could only undermine a really Indian outlook. 'Hindi charges Urdu with "high treason"'.[15]

Shukla also condemned the various proposals for 'basic Hindustani'.[16] What was needed was a national language capable of complex expression to take the place of English in Indian life. It was entirely appropriate to use Sanskrit words, especially when the alternatives are Persian, Arabic, or English. If Muslims refuse to adopt this language, then this is only a sign that they have opted out of Indian national life. The Hindustani of All-India Radio, whether conceived as an amalgamation of Hindi and Urdu or as a rudimentary 'basic' language, amounted to a conspiracy, initiated by British rulers and a small Muslim elite, to undermine Hindi. If nothing else, Hindi had to be recognized as a regional language and deserved at least the same status as Bengali, Marathi, Tamil, and the others. But, instead, broadcasting authorities chose to make it available only in a corrupted form. If Hindi was not to be given its rightfully dominant place, it should at least be allowed a fair quota of time on the air alongside Urdu and whatever concoction of Hindustani the government might choose to sponsor. But to broadcast Hindi properly it was necessary to recruit properly educated personnel and to write scripts in Devanagari so that Hindi words could be pronounced correctly.[17]

---

[15]Ravi Shankar Shukla, 'Language Policy of A.I.R.' (Allahabad: Provincial Sahitya Sammelan, 1944) p. 12.

[16]In addition to Nehru, see Suniti Kumar Chatterji (1942: 229–35, 240–48). Correspondence between Ahmad Shah Bokhari and S.N. Aggarwal of the Hindustani Prachar Sabha, Wardha, in P(l)2–5–5/45, 1945 [All-India Radio, New Delhi].

[17]Ravi Shankar Shukla, 'The "National" Government and A.I.R.'s Language Policy,' in Durga Das (ed.), *Sardar Patel's Correspondence 1945–50*, Vol. IX (Ahmedabad: Navajivan Publishing House, 1972), pp. 320–34. See also Shukla, 'Language Policy of AIR'.

Shukla's writings provided the background and expansion for repeated legislative debates and bureaucratic infighting. Bokhari had to organize responses to these criticisms, including answers to parliamentary questions about the comparative number of Hindus and Muslims employed in the programming sections of All-India Radio, the extent to which they were literate in Hindi as opposed to Urdu, the amount of time devoted to texts read from Hindi and from Urdu scripts. Compromises were negotiated, as in naming the cardinal directions, north, south, east and west, or the days of the week, or the use of *adab arz* as a greeting. Periodic conferences of station directors, followed by orders from headquarters in New Delhi, took up matters of vocabulary. Bokhari also made continued efforts, only partially successful, to recruit well-known Hindi writers to read their works on the radio.[18]

In 1945, Rajendra Prasad attempted to mediate between the Hindi Sahitya Sammelan and All-India Radio by asking Bokhari to send him actual scripts that would show that changes had, in fact, been made to meet the pro-Hindi demands. Bokhari sent eighteen scripts, commenting, 'During the last ten years ... the language of our news bulletin has been shifting backwards and forwards towards Urdu at one time, towards Hindi at another time according to the storms of public opinion.' Finally, he wrote, the question of whether there should be a common language or separate Hindi and Urdu broadcasts was a political, not a linguistic question.[19]

In October 1946, Vallabhai Patel, Minister of Information and Broadcasting as well as Home Minister in the interim government, forced Bokhari's resignation in response to dissatisfaction with his language policy.[20] All India Radio's *khabren* now became *samachar*.[21]

---

[18]'Hindustani language policy of All India Radio,' PLG-/40–II, 1940; 'General policy of All India Radio, regarding Hindustani,' PZ–1/42–I, 1942; see also files relating to parliamentary questions: PQ-3/44, PQ–6/44, PQ–7/44 (AIR, New Delhi). An excellent account, partially based on these records as well as personal experience of a long time A.I.R. employee is H.R. Luthra, *Indian Broadcasting* (New Delhi: Publications Division, 1986), pp. 258–69.

[19]Bokhari to Prasad, 24 October, 1945, P(l)Z–l/45 (AIR, New Delhi).

[20]For indications of Patel's motives see V. Shankar, *My Reminiscences of Sardar Patel*, Vol. 1 (Delhi: Macmillan, 1974), pp. 24–5; Shiva Kumar Tripathi, 'This is All India Radio ...', *The Statesman*, 24 October 1982; a response, defending Bokhari, is contained in a letter by his close friend, S.N. Chib, who was Delhi Station Director at the time. *The Statesman*, 8 November 1982; interviews with Chib, New Delhi, 1982.

[21]Tripathi, 'This is All India Radio ...'.

For a time, news bulletins were broadcast in Hindi, Urdu *and* Hindustani, all overseen by separate advisory committees; time was to be allotted according to regional census statistics.[22] Shukla of the Hindi Sahitya Sammelan kept up the pressure, and in response, on the eve of partition, Patel took further steps to advance the cause of sanskritized Hindi.[23] The new Director General of broadcasting, P.C. Choudhuri, was an ICS man with a strong background in Sanskrit and literary-Hindi as well as ancient Indian history. After consulting a number of major Hindi writers and pro-Hindi politicians, Choudhuri appointed a noted scholar of Hindi literature, Dr Nagendra, to institute the new language policy. During the Bokhari years, Nagendra had encountered what he took to be an anti-Hindi bias when he had occasionally read essays and poems on the radio. One programme assistant who tried to get him to eliminate Sanskrit words was the important Urdu poet N.M. Rashid. Now he was determined to set things right. Broadcasters were now selected by examinations, testing their ability to prepare correct Hindi scripts. Nagendra coached and rehearsed announcers on pronunciation, enforcing the distinction between sibilants/ś/and /ṣ/, as represented in Devanagari but not Urdu script. Similarly, it was Nagendra who replaced *ye* and *voh* with *yaha/ye* and *vaha/ve*.[24] When Urdu words were used, Nagendra insisted that they be pronounced according to Urdu phonology. A new lexicon came a few years later when S.H. Vatsyayan 'Ageya' returned to broadcasting as *salabkar*, language supervisor, to the news department. The task now, as Vatsyayan saw it, was not to find a compromise between Hindi and Urdu, but to identify words, generally from Sanskrit, that would be common to the regional languages of India.[25]

FILMI HINDI: THE ALL-INDIA LANGUAGE

In 1941, All-India Radio consulted a different set of 'experts'. Asked to study broadcast Hindustani with respect to its 'dignity' and whether

[22]Luthra, *Indian Broadcasting*, pp. 268–9.

[23]Shukla, 'The "National" Government and A.I.R.'s Language Policy,' pp. 60–91.

[24]Interview with Dr Nagendra. Delhi, 1982: for in attempt to identify phonological distinctions between Hindi and Urdu, see Ashok K. Kelkar, *Studies in Hindi-Urdu. 1: Introduction and Word Phonology* (Poona: Deccan College Postgraduate Research Institute, 1968).

[25]Vatsyayan interview; *Akashvani sabdakosa* (A.I.R. Lexicon) (New Delhi: Publications Division, 1970).

or not it could be understood 'by the great majority of the people in this country', the 'experts of Bombay Talkies' endorsed the language of the radio. That endorsement had special authority, they claimed, because films, unlike radio, had to meet the test of the market. 'Their box-office takings ... are a clear indication of whether the people can, in fact, readily understand the language used and will pay their hard earned annas to listen to it.' Even more important than comprehensibility, however, was its authority: 'among those who could not themselves speak even reasonably good Hindustani there were very many who could recognize when it was well spoken and who would resent the use of undignified language'.[26]

The sources for studying the language of the Hindi cinema differ significantly from those for radio, particularly in the early period. For one thing, there are very few actual radio scripts and virtually no recordings available. One must rely on bureaucratic records, parliamentary debates, pamphlets, newspapers, and, of course, the lexicons that broadcasters were supposed to use. In the case of film, there is virtually no official discussion of language issues, but the films themselves are available, as well as a good deal of commentary in film magazines. I will confine myself, for present purposes, to some of this commentary, what some people said about film language, as opposed to the more substantial task of analyzing actual film dialogues. The distinction of course is between the language of the state and the language of the market. Films Division documentaries and Radio Pakistan news broadcasts should also be a part of this study. But there is also a distinction between the linguistic demands of fiction and fantasy and those of official pronouncements, so that one might expect greater linguistic variety in broadcast drama and poetry than in news bulletins.

Having said all that, however, it would be a mistake to imagine that the language of the cinema was not calculated and constructed by people who had ideological agendas alongside the profit motive. Bombay Talkies had its experts, generally north Indian literary figures who wrote the scripts and coached the actors on how to pronounce the words according to appropriate literary standards.[27] As with radio,

[26]Sir Richard Temple to N.A.S. Lakshmanan, Station Director, Bombay, n.d., in PZ–1/42–I, 1942 (AIR, New Delhi).

[27]See for example, Agha Jani Kashmeri's, autobiography of a script writer and dialogue coach from Lucknow; *Sahr Hone tak* (Delhi: Imperial Press, 1964). One colleague featured

the authority of film language was authority conferred by literary education, an education that has remained inaccessible to the majority of people who are said to speak Hindi.

In 1955, Khwaja Ahmad Abbas, journalist, critic, novelist, scriptwriter, and director, claimed that film dialogues 'have done more than any person or institution to propagate and popularize the national language'. That language, created by 'commercial instinct' was admittedly 'artificial'. Neither 'elegant' not 'literary', it was 'a curious mixture of Hindi words like prem, ashirvad and lagan and Urdu words like mohabat, manzil and mehfil, certainly an artificial language but a language that had a chance of being understood in Calcutta and Bombay as well as Allahabad or Lahore and even to some extent in Mysore and Rangoon'. Such a language made it possible for a film to be 'produced by a Gujerati producer in Bombay and starring a Bengali hero and a Tamilian heroine, both speaking Hindustani dialogue written by a Punjabi'.

But shifting his stance, Abbas went on to speak from the privileged position of the *ahl-i zuban,* people of the language, that is literati of the Delhi region, whose speech and writing claimed to be the model of correct and elegant usage.[28] The task of the film writer was to exemplify 'the beauties, the subtleties and the profundities of language and literature'. More than that, the language of films could serve as the standard of ordinary speech throughout a united India. 'Film dialogue must become the speech of our people', not the other way around. For all the talk, then, of linguistic compromise and uneducated audiences, the standard and concept of language remained literary.[29]

One type of evidence of the criteria used for linguistic decisions, for creating and evaluating film dialogue, can be found in statements about language in contemporary reviews. For the pre-independence period, the reviews that I have managed to look at are unfortunately from a highly disreputable source, *Filmindia*, published out of Bombay

---

in this book is Hameed Butt, uncle of Salman Rushdie, who is only slightly fictionalized in *Midnight's Children*.

[28]I have discussed this in 'Eloquence and Authority in Urdu: Poetry, Oratory and Film,' in K. Ewing (ed.), *Shariat and Ambiguity in South Asian Islam* (Berkeley: University of California Press, 1988); 'Zuban-i Urdu-i Mualla and the Idol of Linguistic Origins,' *Annual of Urdu Studies*, 9, 1994.

[29]R.M. Roy (ed.), *Film Seminar Report* (New Delhi: Sangeet Natak Academy, 1955).

by a notorious Hindu chauvinist, Baburao Patel. Patel's reviews were characterized by anti-Muslim bigotry and overtly vociferous denials that his opinions were negotiated by bribes and blackmail. A Maharashtrian with no special authority with respect to Hindi or Urdu, Patel demanded above all simplicity and uniformity of speech. The stories of the films, at least as recounted in the reviews, suggest at least a few possible social variables that might have been reflected in language, but Patel hardly ever complained about inappropriate uniformity in the face of male-female, urban-rural, rich-poor, Hindu-Muslim or untouchable characters, or different historical periods and regional settings. Overriding any serious attention to representation was the need of comprehensibility on the part of people who were assumed to have limited command of the language. Thus a common complaint is that a film's Urdu is too 'high flown' or its Hindi too 'jaw-breaking'. He objected to idioms and proverbs because they were 'vulgar', but also because they were likely to be misunderstood.

Like Patel, the sponsors, producers, and directors of Hindi films did not come from the linguistic community or educational background associated with the language of their all-India productions. Nor did most of the performers, as *Filmindia* repeatedly pointed out. The major centres of Hindi films were Calcutta, Poona, Bombay, and later Madras. But, contrary to Khwaja Abbas's later statement, Patel insisted on what he considered authentic and correct language. Muslim writers who used sanskritized vocabulary were taken to task, but so were Hindus. Despite his communalism, at least as marked as Ravi Shankar Shukla's, Patel felt the appropriate language for films was Hindustani, which he defined as 'simple, popular Urdu'. He was concerned that it be pronounced properly and took some trouble to denounce Punjabi as well as Maharashtrian, Bengali and Anglo-Indian accents. This concern for 'correct' speech suggests the enduring prestige of Delhi and Lucknow. Even Baburao Patel, who spoke of the Mughals with loathing, deferred to the style of language associated with Mughal culture.

The demand for a standardized and simplified language for the films seems to ignore the special opportunities of expression generally associated with cinema. If one considers film as a representational art, attempting to present something other than itself, its attraction lies in the pretence that one is in the presence of real people and places. Cinema claims an extraordinary power of defining the limits of what is available in this world. But popular Indian cinema has always had other aims. Songs, dance, preposterous settings and ridiculous stories, a deliberate neutrality of language, region, ethnicity and class—all this is taken as a sign of rootlessness. It would be more accurate to say that the 'reality' and 'roots' of popular Indian cinema lie elsewhere, perhaps in dreams, perhaps within a self-contained world of the cinema itself. The way to connect that self-referring reality to other worlds is to ask about the processes of bringing it into being and experiencing it, the making and the receiving of it by people who do, after all, have other roots and realities—and many other languages—in their lives. From that point of view, the artificiality of Indian films, the fact that they are so palpably made things, may be their saving grace.

The distinction, then, between akashvani Hindi and filmi Hindi, may lie above all in the difference between government decrees and the world of fantasy. But what happens when those two streams flow together, when the state takes up the power of fantasy, rooted in religion? Is that what made the Doordarshan Ramayana such an important, perhaps even ominous, event?

REFERENCES

Akashvani Sabdakosa (A.I.R. Lexicon), 1970. New Delhi: Publications Division.

Barnouw, Erik and S. Krishnaswamy, 1980. *Indian Film,* 2nd edn. New York: Oxford University Press.

Bayly, C.A., 1975. *The Local Roots of Indian Politics: Allahabad 1880–1920.* Oxford: Clarendon Press.

Bokhari, Sayyid Zulfiqar Ali, 1966. *Sarguzasht.* Karachi: Ma arif Limited.

Bourdieu, Pierre, 1991. 'The Production and Reproduction of Legitimate Language', in John B. Thompson (ed.), *Language and Symbolic Power,* translated by Gino Raymond and Matthew Adamson. Cambridge, Massachusetts: Harvard University Press, p. 48.

Chatterji, Suniti Kumar, 1942. *Indo-Aryan and Hindi.* Ahmedabad: Gujarat Vernacular Society.

Choudhury, Valmiki, 1984. Dr *Rajendra Prasad: Correspondences and Select Documents,* Vol. I (1934–38). New Delhi: Allied Publishers.

Fielden, Lionel, 1940. *Report of the Progress of Broadcasting in India up to the 31st March 1939.* Delhi: Manager of Publications.

———, 1960. *The Natural Bent.* London: Andre Deutsch.

———, 1984. Letter to Dr Rajendra Prasad, 8 December 1938, in Valmiki Choudhary (ed.), *Dr Rajendra Prasad: Correspondences and Select Documents*, Vol. I (1934–38) New Delhi: Allied Publishers, pp. 168–70.

Gandhi, M.K., 1965. *Our Language Problem*, ed. by Anand T. Hingorani. Bombay: Bharatiya Vidya Bhavan.

Kashmeri, Agha Jani, 1964. *Sahr Hone tak*. Delhi: Imperial Press.

Kelkar, Ashok R., 1968. *Studies in Hindi-Urdu. I: Introduction and Word Phonology*. Poona: Deccan College Postgraduate Research Institute.

Lelyveld, David, 1988. 'Eloquence and Authority in Urdu: Poetry, Oratory and Film', in K. Ewing (ed.), *Shariat and Ambiguity in South Asian Islam*. Berkeley: University of California Press.

———, 1990. 'Transmitters and Culture: The Colonial Roots of Indian Broadcasting', *South Asian Research*, 10(1).

———, 1993. 'The Fate of Hindustani: Colonise Knowledge and the Project of a National Language', in C. Breckenridge and P. van der Veer (eds), *Orientalism and the Post Colonial Predicament: Perspectives on South Asia*. Philadelphia: University of Pennsylvania Press.

———, 1994. 'Zuban-i Urdu-i Mualla and the Idol of Linguistic Origins', *Annual of Urdu Studies* 9.

———, 1995. 'Upon the Sub-dominant: Administering Music on All-India Radio', in C. Breckenridge (ed.), *Consuming Modernity: Public Culture in a South Asian World*. Minneapolis: University of Minnesota Press.

Luthra, H.R., 1986. *Indian Broadcasting*. New Delhi: Publications Division.

Nehru, Jawaharlal, 1942. 'The Question of Language', in *The Unity of India: Collected Writings 1937–1940*, 2nd edn., pp. 241–61. London: Lindsay Drommond.

Roy, R.M. (ed.), 1955. *Film Seminar Report*. New Delhi: Sangeet Natak Academi.

Shankar, V., 1974. *My Reminiscences of Sardar Patel*, Vol. I. Delhi: Macmillan.

Shukla, Ravi Shankar, 1944. Language Policy of A.I.R. Allahabad: Provincial Sahitya Sammelan.

———, 1947. *Lingua Franca for India (Hind)*. Lucknow: Oudh Publishing House.

———, 1972. 'The 'National' Government and A.I.R.'s Language Policy', in Durga Das (ed.), *Sardar Patel's Correspondence, 1945–50*, Vol. IX. Ahmedabad: Navajivan Publishing House.

11

Language and the Right to the City*

Janaki Nair

Kavery neeru kudiyuva munna Kannada kali!
Sign on the back of an autorickshaw, 2002

For three days between 30 July and 2 August 2000, a pall of silence fell upon the city of Bangalore, when its streets were emptied of noise, traffic, and frenetic crowds.[1] Not even the 'virtual' city entirely escaped this spell of silence as many homes lost their cable connections and the busy hum of the internet parlour was stilled. The abrupt shutdown of city life was informally imposed by a set of forces that had gained increasing visibility in the city for at least two decades. This display of anger was against the kidnapping of the leading cultural icon of the Kannadigas, Rajkumar, by the notorious forest brigand Veerappan in the early hours of 30 July 2000. The helpless anger of a wide range of Rajkumar fan clubs and Kannada associations that spread across the city and the state was only heightened by the fact that the film star, who had come to represent pride in the Kannada language itself, was kidnapped by a man who shed his image as a sandalwood and ivory poacher to take up the cause of Tamil nationalism.

*Originally published as 'Language and the Right to the City', in *The Promise of the Metropolis: Bangalore's Twentieth Century* (New Delhi: Oxford University Press, 2005), pp. 234–70.
[1]'Mob Fury Brings Bangalore to a Halt', *Deccan Herald*, 1 August 2000.

Right across the city, the violence took the form of bringing public transport to a halt, forcing people to abandon their private vehicles and walk home as a mark of solidarity with the abducted hero.[2] More important, it was a moment when, by his very absence, the entire city was made aware of Rajkumar's larger-than-life presence within the world of Kannada, his place in a cultural universe that had thus far embraced only a section of people in the city. Not always was this a voluntary recognition of his fame. When roving bands of young men vented their anger and grief on new glass and steel structures that have an insistent presence in commercial areas of the city, vulnerable business establishments and car owners quickly declared their allegiance to the Kannada hero by pasting his picture on the glass. Violence against property and people was low key—though one person was stabbed to death for not complying with those who ruled the streets that day—but there was a menacing threat from those who brought the city temporarily under their rule.

The unity of silence that was thrust on Bangalore by the roving bands and the police alike, briefly made for a withdrawn and watchful space of the city.[3] Industry analysts and others were quick to calculate the economic costs of such disruption,[4] while the film industry imposed a *bandh* on itself, refusing to open theatres, undertake productions, or release new films until the star was released.[5] Yet throughout Rajkumar's tedious 108-day captivity, the fan clubs, Kannada organizations, film institutions, and the 'first family' (as Rajkumar's wife and children were referred to in the press) retained a focus on the predicament of the star by organizing rallies, bandhs, *urulu seves*, pujas, meetings, and days of prayer.[6] In this, they were amply aided by the taped messages and news reports of Rajkumar's life in the jungle at the mercy of his abductor Veerappan. The star's eventual release from

[2]Ibid.

[3]Schools were closed for 15 days, bars and liquor stores for weeks, and cinema theatres for nearly two months.

[4]'Karnataka's Image Takes a Beating', *Indian Express*, 13 August 2000; 'Riots in the New Economy', *Times of India*, 8 August 2000.

[5]Pradeep Belave, 'A Downhill Journey', *Deccan Herald*, 13 August 2000; 'Stark Reality on Celluloid Screen', *Deccan Herald*, 21 August 2000.

[6]'Kannada Chaluvali Men Stage Dharna for Raj's Release', *Times of India*, 21 August 2000; 'Raj Fans to Take out Procession Today', *Indian Express*, 21 August 2000; 'Massive Show of Solidarity', *Deccan Herald*, 22 September 2000.

Figure 11.1: The Reigning Cultural Hero of the Kannadigas:
Rajkumar's Cutout Dominates the Front of the Kapali Theatre
at the Screening of the Film Shabdavedi. (Clare Arni, 2000)

captivity on 15 November 2000 brought relief to a capital city that
had been precariously poised on the edge of full-scale riots.[7] Yet, not
even Rajkumar's release from captivity, which happened only after

[7]'Gopal's Empty Handed Return Puts Bangalore Police on Fresh Alert', *Indian Express*,
7 August 2000. Trouble was anticipated particularly in areas of west and northwest Bangalore,
and some parts of the east.

repeated rebuffs by Veerappan of the Tamil journalist and emissary Gopal, and after several reversals in the court, resulted in anything more than a carnival of joy (Figure 11.1).

The abduction of Rajkumar was not just a criminal act of a forest brigand, but was staged as a dramatic encounter between two nationalisms, Kannada and Tamil, that had over the past two decades come into violent conflict over issues relating to land, jobs, and water in the southern regions of Karnataka and particularly Bangalore city. It was striking then that the Tamils and other citizens of Bangalore more generally were not exposed to violence that conformed to these established patterns. The restraint was all the more significant given the provocations of Rajkumar's captors, who bargained with state authorities in both Karnataka and Tamil Nadu on issues concerning the fate of Tamils in Karnataka and of some Tamils in Tamil Nadu itself. In his list of ten demands that was handed over at the time of abduction, Veerappan and his new-found allies in the forest, the Tamil National Liberation Front (TNLF), included several that were previously the cause of violent clashes between the two linguistic groups. Among those that concerned Karnataka in particular, he included: a permanent solution to the Cauvery water dispute, adequate compensation to all Tamil victims of the Cauvery riots of 1991, the inclusion of Tamil as an administrative language in Karnataka, the installation of the Thiruvalluvar statue in Bangalore, and a vacation of the stay on the Sadashiva committee which investigated atrocities of the Special Task Force in the forest.[8] The demands included several that addressed both sides of the border at once: thus both states were asked to implement minimum daily wages of Rs 150 for plantation workers.

This mixture of economic and cultural demands blurred the battle lines between the two linguistic groups, and in many ways diffused the tension, producing new loyalties and alliances. Bangalore Tamils were quick to distance themselves from the actions of a forest brigand, refusing to acknowledge that he represented their interests. There was even some bitterness at how readily the state government was prepared

[8]*Indian Express*, 7 August 2000. The other demands were addressed to the Tamil Nadu government: to raise the procurement price of Nilgiris tea, release the five Veerappan associates from jail, and solve the problems of the Manjolai estate workers, who had been on a long strike.

to acquiesce to Veerappan's demands: R.S. Maran of the Tamil Sangham said it was an insult that government was heeding Veerappan's demands rather than the petitions of Tamil organizations in Bangalore. Nearly all the issues that were raised in the demands of Karnataka state had left their scars on a city that was deeply divided on the question of language and its implications for a right to the city. Veerappan and his allies chose to address the state on issues that had long slipped out of its grasp, and had become the battleground of groups and associations in Karnataka. Maran's plea was that the state reassert its power and rein in these non-state organizations.

For those long involved in the Kannada movement, the predicament of Rajkumar was in fact the predicament of Kannada itself, held hostage to what was perceived as the more robust nationalism of the Tamils. Clearly, the triumphant march of computer languages such as Java and C++ through every neighbourhood of Bangalore, and some other parts of Karnataka, had done nothing to resolve or render irrelevant the crisis within which the Kannada language and the state found itself, and may only have accentuated it. Indeed, 'When the capitalists give Kannada a sidelong glance (*kadeganninda noduthiruvaga*), Kannada itself becomes capital to some', said the Kannada Development Authority chairman Bargur Ramachandrappa, in his plea for recasting Kannada pride.[9] A similar anguish marks the speech of nearly all those who have been involved in the Kannada movement over the past few decades.

This chapter traces some of the ways in which Bangalore has been re-territorialized by those who lay increasing claim to the city as a regional, rather than a national or international metropolis. It develops a framework for understanding language issues in the city by tracing the broader contours of the language question as it emerged in pre-independence and immediate post-independence years. It then traces the successive stages through which the Kannada movement has passed, particularly as it has reconfigured specific domains of life in the city, such as work opportunities, access to land, or governmental power. Finally, there is a consideration of the prospects of Kannada nationalism in a time of rapid but uneven capitalist development.

[9]Bargur Ramachandrappa, 'Kannadaabhimanada Katuvaasthava', *Prajavani*, 31 October 2000.

CONCEIVING THE KANNADA NATION

From its tentative start during the colonial period, Kannada nationalism measured itself and its inadequacies not against the overarching triumphs of the imperial power, but against the more modest successes of other linguistic nationalisms within India itself.[10] Alura Venkat Rao's anguished response in 1917 to the nationalist imperative, 'We don't have a history! We must have a history!!'[11] recognized that it was only through a recast history of the Kannada people that the Indian nation could be imagined. Even more important, he deplored the fact that his effort came a full forty or fifty years after his Bengali, Marathi, and Telugu counterparts had made their heroes and historic triumphs part of the nationalist common sense.[12] The absence of a unified administration under which the Kannada people could develop continues to haunt even contemporary historical accounts.[13]

Since the narrativization of Kannada's modern identity had been somewhat overwhelmed by the sense that it is unoriginal, weak, and even imitative,[14] the massive and indisputable presence of the state in envisioning modernity, particularly the old Mysore state, has been overlooked. By the late nineteenth century, the bureaucracy of the princely state forged a paradigm of development which, while unmistakably nationalist, strove to usher in a legal and economic

[10]As M. Chidanandamurthy has said, 'A survey of historiography in Kannada during the 19th century clearly shows the lack of a nationalist outlook among the Kannada people, more so among the south Karnataka (old Mysore) people'. Chidanandamurthy, 'Historiography in Kannada during the 19th Century', in Tarashanker Banerjee (ed.), *Historiography in Modern Indian Language, 1800–1947* (Calcutta: Naya Prakashan, 1987), p. 168.

[11]As Bankimchandra exclaimed in *Bangadarshan*, cited by Ranajit Guha, *An Indian Historiography of India: A Nineteenth Century Agenda and its Implications* (Calcutta: K.P. Bagchi, 1988), p. 47.

[12]Alura Venkat Rao, *Karnataka Gatha Vaibhava* (Bangalore: Kannada Sahitya Parishat, [1917] 1982), esp. pp. 1–6. Also, *The Karnataka Handbook*, printed and published for the editorial board of the Karnataka Pradesh Congress Committee (Bangalore, Sreenivasa Iyengar, 1924), p. 10.

[13]Kannada speakers were scattered across five administrative regions in colonial India: apart from the princely state of Mysore, the single most cohesive entity, they included Bombay-Karnataka, Hyderabad Karnataka, Madras Presidency, and Coorg. R.R. Diwakar, *Karnataka Through the Ages: From Pre-historic Times to the Day of Independence of India*, Vol. II (Bangalore: Government of Mysore, 1968), p. 889.

[14]Early Kannada novels were usually translations of Marathi and Bengali ones.

modernity through the instrumentalities of the state.[15] The state thus absorbed the nationalist agenda and restricted the conditions of possibility for the development of a public sphere, tending, as Sudipta Kaviraj says, 'to suffocate non-state institutions of civil society by theoretically equating the principle of public good with the institutional form of state control'.[16] There were, for instance, a number of caste associations whose scope remained limited until at least the 1930s.[17]

For a long time in Mysore, the state loomed large in the imagination of cultural nationalists searching for patrons and sponsors of a rejuvenated Kannada: thus B.M. Srikantia (B.M. Sri) made the plea in 1915 at the Mysore Economic Conference that

Governments concerned with Kannada areas will, as they have been doing already, encourage writers systematically and on settled principles, and may even see the way to establish a sort of academy with power to lay down general principles to map out a course of production and to reward any work that is done in an excellent manner and to print and distribute it if necessary among the people at large.[18]

It is no surprise then that the Kannada Sahitya Parishat was set up in 1915 as a part of Dewan Visvesvaraya's overall vision of Mysore's material progress and welfare.[19] B.M. Sri's was among the many voices that argued for a Kannada adequate to the tasks of modern industrial and scientific life.[20] Yet he too made the point feebly, acknowledging instead the sphere within which Kannada was condemned to circulate,

[15]I have considered some of these initiatives in *Miners and Millhands: Work Culture and Politics in Princely Mysore* (Delhi: Sage, 1998); 'Prohibited Marriage', *Contributions to Indian Sociology*, (n.s.) 29 (1&2), 1995, pp. 157–88; 'The Devadasi, Dharma and the State', *Economic and Political Weekly*, 29 (50), 1994, pp. 3157–67.

[16]Sudipta Kaviraj, 'On the Structure of Nationalist Discourse', in T.V. Satyamurthy (ed.), *State and Nation in the Context of Social Change*, Vol. I (Delhi: Oxford University Press, 1994), p. 327.

[17]Speaking of the Mysore Lingayat Educational Fund Associations (1905) and the Vokkaligara Sangha (1906), James Manor argues that these associations failed to become 'the new type of public organization since they were governed according to the logic of the old private polities'. Manor, *Political Change in a Princely State*, p. 46. For a list of caste associations in the early twentieth century, see Thimmaiah, *Power, Politics, and Social Justice*, pp. 70–2.

[18]B.M. Srikantia, *The Improvement of the Kannada Language* (Bangalore: B.M. Srikantia Memorial Foundation [1915] 1969), p. v.

[19]Ibid., p. iv.

[20]Ibid., p. 7 and 9.

envisaging a division of labour where English 'our cultural and political language', Sanskrit 'our spiritual and classical language', and Kannada 'our native and speaking language' could coexist.[21] It is striking that the language of the economy did not figure in the division of labour envisaged by B.M. Sri, who attached cultural and political rather than economic dominance to a language like English. This was to change dramatically in the post-independence years, when the international hegemony of English only increased. The division of labour between languages which B.M. Sri envisaged was untenable in a situation which strongly tied English to the historic emergence and expansion of capitalism itself in a country like India. With the market strongly on its side and the growing demands of the new economy, English-medium schools have burgeoned in a city like Bangalore: attempts to stall this march have usually been through an appeal for state intervention.[22]

Kannada protagonists have attempted to forge stronger links with the cultural world through private and state bodies such as the Kannada and Culture Department. We shall consider in some more detail the consequences of this for the field of culture, and the contests it has generated in the Bangalore context. Notwithstanding widespread acknowledgement of its dominated status, there has never been, in the past or today, a widespread movement to promote literacy or encourage reading, as happened in the library movements of Kerala and the Andhra Mahasabha during the colonial period.[23] The obvious limits of promoting the growth of a language through its literary texts have been recognized by several Kannada intellectuals,[24] and even the

---

[21]Ibid., p. 18.

[22]In January 2002, the Karnataka government sanctioned 300 new English-medium primary schools in the state of which 150 were in Bangalore; strong objections from the chair of the Kannada Development Authority, Bargur Ramachandrappa, led to a withdrawal of the order. However it is well known that English-medium schools are supple enough to respond to the demand of the market, and resort to all kinds of subterfuge in order to exist rather than conform to the dictates of the state.

[23]See for instance, Dilip Menon, *Caste, Nationalism and Communism in South India: Malabar 1900–1948* (Cambridge: Cambridge University Press, 1994), esp. pp. 143–51. There were smaller innovations in Bangalore: in the late 1960s, several batches of volunteers of the Kannada Sahitya Prachara Samiti went around the city with pushcarts urging people to buy books rather than crackers for Diwali. 'Makkala koota in Chamrajpet', *Deccan Herald*, 10 November 1969.

[24]Mahadev Banakar, *Safeguards for Linguistic Minorities in India: Karnataka Sets a Model* (Bangalore: Anubhav Publications, 1982), p. iii.

leadership by a renowned writer, Bargur Ramachandrappa, of the Kannada Development Authority in 2000–2 did little to recast this link.

If, like all Indian languages under colonialism, Kannada bore the burden of domination, it sometimes translated into a very material marginalization. Despite its wry humour, B.G.L. Swamy's description of the Kannada department as it was when it first took shape in 1917 in Central College, Bangalore, suggests that self-effacement was thrust upon the language:

Unlike the other departments, the Kannada department had no architectural pretensions. Neither a house nor a stable, nor a block, nor a hut, it was unique in its own way. Two rooms of the building in the northern corner with an adjoining one to the west constituted the department.

There were doors, one on the western wall of the twin rooms and one on the eastern wall. The door on the western wall was used by the other language departments for entry and exit. The door on the eastern wall was used by the Kannada department.

It is my hunch that this decision was taken because the road in front of the western wall was used by most of the people coming into or going out of the college and by customers of Narayan's hotel. Or because of a sense of humility the Kannada people with its ideal of living one's life as a forest bloom away from the pomp and people's gaze.[25]

The Kannada teacher had a comparatively lower status, for as N. Lakshman Rau recalled of the time when he was student of Central College in the 1930s, 'Kannada professors were big men but their salaries were so low they were looked down upon. Their position was not so good. The Kannada scholars were given poorer chambers ... students failed in Kannada and passed in other subjects'.[26] The dominated status of the language had its effects on the psychology of its speakers too, as Nittoor Srinivas Rao, former chief judge of the high court, and one of the pioneers of the publishing trade in Bangalore remembered:

... we had pundits in Maharaja's college in Mysore and in Bangalore, not only in schools and colleges, [but] elsewhere, very great scholars in Kannada, but they were all called Munshis and their salary was 40 rupees and 50 rupees

---

[25]B.G.L. Swamy, *Panchakalagopura* (1964), pp. 19–26; translation of this excerpt by Ramachandra Sharma in *Sunday Herald*, 13 May 1990.

[26]Interview with N. Lakshman Rau, 22 July 1998.

while a man like me passed B.Sc. and [when I] was appointed as demonstrator in Central College, I got 75 rupees. That was the position of our Kannada....

The domination of Kannada within the colonial order had much to do with the emerging division of labour between languages, as English occupied a hegemonic presence as the language of science, technology, and indeed capitalism, while Kannada strove to make its presence felt in the politico-cultural sphere. Yet it was still a time when English was only one among the languages that the nationalist intelligentsia knew and used, although it had already made inroads into the spheres of intimacy and private life. Nittoor Srinivasa Rao, who came to Bangalore in 1919 for higher studies, captures the gradual growth of English hegemony in private life:

In regard to what we consider to be sophisticated important ideas we think in English. And I used to write letters to my father [in Kannada] and he would write back to me in English, writing in Kannada was considered a departure. I may tell you that even as high school students we used to talk to each other mainly in English and even if we spoke in Kannada there was a large mixture of English words. Very important operative words were taken from English and as a matter of fact, [when we became] part and parcel of the Kannada movement, now we had sort of evolved a rule amongst ourselves that we would pay a fine of one paise for the use of English words in the course of our conversations.[27]

In fact, the debate about whether Kannada should be the medium of instruction was still raging, and was far from settled until at least 1940. Kannada high schools preparing students for the upper secondary examination at the turn of the twentieth century 'did not flourish in competition with English' and were therefore abolished in 1935 although Kannada was made the medium of instruction that year.[28] Only in 1919 were girls' schools reluctantly made bilingual from the middle grade on, despite the belief that English was 'intrinsically bound up with information offensive to native tradition'.[29]

The few isolated efforts made by nationalist intellectuals did little to change the restricted domains of Kannada as a literary or domestic

[27]Interview with Nittoor Srinivasa Rao, 14 July 1998.
[28]Diwakar, *Karnataka Through the Ages*, p. 814.
[29]S. Chandrasekhar, *Colonialism, Conflict and Nationalism* (Delhi: Wishwa Press, 1995), p. 47.

language: Nittoor's decision to teach both mathematics and physics in Kannada 'which I regarded as a great departure from what was happening all over' was indeed a refreshing attempt to reverse the downslide. This was, however, a losing battle as English began invading the private sphere as well, sometimes restructuring the self, at other times appearing as a means to address the nation in the making. It sculpted new subjectivities that allowed for a confident use of the new language even to record one's own life history: the accomplished Karnataka painter, K. Venkatappa, who maintained diaries from as early as 1913, chose to keep them largely in English.[30] However, the need to command the language of the masters often overshadowed other concerns: Nittoor Srinivasa Rao remembers his disappointment when, at their first meeting, the great B.M. Sri spoke to him in English.[31]

Nevertheless, in the period before independence, the language question was figured more in terms of the political and literary successes of languages such as Marathi, Telugu, and Bengali: Tamil and Urdu were barely visible on this horizon. At least two other elements made their appearance only in the decades after independence: the increasing recognition that the hegemony of English cannot be easily challenged led to a displacement of demands on to the political cultural sphere, that called for the intervention of the agencies of the state which at this time was a far from insignificant distributor of resources. Second, questions of demography and geography became central to the imaginary of Kannada nationalism, which ranged itself against subaltern groups in southern Karnataka, particularly in its chief metropolis, Bangalore. After all, as Partha Chatterjee points out, following Foucault, the concept of population, 'differentiated but classifiable, describable and enumerable', has been crucial to the emergence of modern governmental technologies.[32] Census data of the state and of the city reveal much that could become the basis for rallying people to the cause of language on both sides of the language divide: it has been

[30]K. Venkatappa Private Papers, KSA. See also, Janaki Nair, 'Drawing a Line K. Venkatappa and his Publics' *IESHR*, 35 (2), 1998, pp. 179–210.

[31]Interview with Nittoor Srinivasa Rao, 18 July 1998. Indeed, as Nittoor pointed out, it is striking that the field of Kannada literary criticism has become the, monopoly of English professors: A.N. Murthy Rao, the pioneer of the Kannada essay, and P. Lankesh, who ran the popular newspaper, *Lankesh Patrike*, for instance, were professors of English.

[32]Chatterjee, 'Beyond the Nation? Or Within?', p. 31.

one of the major basis for seeking state intervention to alter terms which are determined by an emerging linguistic market.[33]

LANGUAGE AND POWER AND THE REORGANIZATION OF STATES

If, following Pierre Bourdieu,[34] we adopt the notion of a 'linguistic market', an economy within which particular language competencies take on value, we may discern the deeply segmented and far from unified linguistic market which has developed in Karnataka through

Figure 11.2: Reterritorializing the City: Kannada Signs being Added to the Popular Lakeview Coffee Bar and Icecream Parlour on Mahatma Gandhi Road. (T.L. Ramaswamy, 15.5.1970)

---

[33]Thus, Kannada Shakti Kendra specifically requested the government to appoint Kannada-speaking officers in Bangalore and border areas, where large numbers of other language speakers reside, presumably to ensure accurate enumeration of all populations. *Deccan Herald,* 12 January 1990.

[34]Pierre Bourdieu, *Language and Symbolic Power* (Cambridge: Harvard University Press, 1994), p. 45. Bourdieu's chief concern is the emergence of a standardized French that triumphs as an official language over the patois.

the twentieth century. It is a linguistic market that sustains a division of labour between different languages and language competencies, defining a very restricted sphere within which Kannada may circulate. The restrictions imposed by such objective factors as geography and demography appear then as far less crucial in defining the predicament of Kannada than those imposed by the economy or the organization of the political sphere. The overwhelming dominance of English as an internationally hegemonic language, in the commercial, financial, scientific, or IT fields, or the dominance of Hindi and Tamil in the cultural spheres (for example, TV and cinema) leaves Kannada to its lonely reign over the literary sphere, or within the space of domesticity. Strenuous attempts to make Kannada the administrative language of the region have done little to recast the segmented linguistic market or compensate for the division of labour between languages that has emerged. Although Kannada has been the official language of the state since 1963, and is by and large the language of governance, this does not sufficiently remedy its dominated status (Figure 11.2).

The overwhelming success of economic nationalism in the colonial period compared with the more modest gains of cultural nationalism is crucial to any discussion of the predicament of Kannada today. Rather than being a latecomer to linguistic and communal identities, Karnataka has fashioned a different path to modernity, fraught with anxieties that have violently manifested themselves in the past two decades. This violent renegotiation of the terrain of development occurs between those who are poised to benefit most from Karnataka's new economies, particularly in the field of information technology, and those who seek a stake in it. Moreover, the post-independence years have been marked by a diglossia in crisis,[35] where a nationalist elite which was thoroughly bilingual (moving between English and the regional language) has yielded space to two or more resolutely unilingual groups.

One of the earliest attacks on Tamils in the city followed the Talwadi incident, when Kannada Chaluvali leader Vatal Nagaraj was arrested for demanding that a part of Tamil Nadu be joined to Karnataka. 'Leaderless, disorganized mobs' stoned several cinema houses, shops, and buses including one belonging to Tamil Nadu in protest and an

[35]Kaviraj, 'On the Structure of Nationalist Discourse', p. 324.

effigy of the Tamil Nadu Chief Minister M. Karunanidhi was carried in a mammoth procession to the Gandhi statue.[36] The main areas to be affected were the older Tamil areas of the city such as Laxmipuram, Okalipuram, and Magadi Road. By the late 1990s, Mysore's unique multilingual character was seen as a burden, and mild disturbances of the 1970s gave way to citywide upheavals and unprecedented acts of violence against the lives and properties of linguistic minorities.

Has the early nationalist *vision* of Karnataka come to grief, close to turning into a *nightmare* in the hands of some groups in the 1980s and 1990s? This was D.R. Nagaraj's chief concern in an article that discussed the emergence of a more strident Kannada nationalism, particularly in the last two decades of the twentieth century. He distinguished between a 'fear-centred nationalism' as represented by the writings of M. Chidanandamurthy (and the activity of Kannada Shakti Kendra) and the 'spiritual nationalism' of earlier writers such as Alura Venkata Rao. Consider Alura Venkata Rao's message on the occasion of Karnataka unification in 1956:

In short, we should not forget that Karnataka is a much broader entity than Kannada. Not only the speakers of dialects, we should also not forget the minorities who speak other (neighbouring) languages—in the construction of united Karnataka this is a principle to be kept in mind. In other words, Kannada has the dominant status. But knowledge is welcome from all sides. As someone who keenly conducted the Karnataka movement, I never forget this. Thus, once when the Marathi library in Dharwar was facing closure, I took it over, added the collection to my own Bharata Pustakalaya, ran it for some years and when the Marathis here came forward to manage it, I handed it over to them.[37]

Chidanandamurthy's activist prose, and the copious outpourings of Kannada Shakthi Kendra, on the other hand, are marked not just by fear but by envy of the more muscular Tamil nationalism.[38] Indeed, the self-confidence of Venkat Rao in the early twentieth century was

[36]*Deccan Herald*, 2 February 1970; 3 February 1970; 4 February 1970; 6 February 1970.

[37]Aliru Venkat Rao, *Kamatakatvada Vikasa* (1980, p. 148) as cited in Nagaraj, 'The Nature of Kannada Nationalism'.

[38]See, for instance, Ra Nam Chandrasekhar, *Kannada Shakthi* (Bangalore: Kannada Shakthi Kendra: 1998); also his '"Kannada Jagruthi Varsha" Saadisideno?' (mimeo); also *Kannada-Kannadiga-Karnataka* (Bangalore: Kannada Pusthaka Pradhikaara, 1996). This last text draws obvious inspiration from the menacing slogan 'Hindi-Hindu-Hindusthan.'

largely replaced by an aggressively defensive stand by the end of the century, allowing a more fragile presence for a writer like P. Lankesh who occupied a 'secular socio-political' space. This 'secular socio-political space', which values the multiple strands that make up contemporary Karnataka, has consistently opposed the 'language of violence and militancy' as a solution to the predicament of Kannada, and indeed Karnataka itself.[39] It was sorely tested on more than one occasion over the last two decades, and in particular in 1991 and 1994 when two different minorities, Tamils and Muslims, were singled out for attack. One might however go further to suggest that the identity of Karnataka itself is endangered when its constituent elements are threatened, for who will hesitate to acknowledge Karnataka's debt to the literature and labour of Marathi, Urdu, Telugu, and Tamil speakers?

It is impossible to understand the predicament of Kannada without an understanding of the language's dominated status within Karnataka. This, the votaries of Kannada Shakti Kendra would have us believe, is to be understood in demographic terms. We may note here that the experience of 'wounds inflicted by geography' (especially the experience of Kannada speakers remaining fragmented under different administrative authorities in the colonial period) gives way to a reckoning of citizenship by numbers. Commenting on D.R. Nagaraj's critique of his activism as a Kannada supporter, Chidanandamurthy was reported to have defended his own position by claiming that his position 'stems from very real memories as well as contemporary realities. He was only trying to point out that in two or three decades there would be no Kannada left in Bangalore. Soon Kannada would [be evicted from] other parts of Karnataka as well.'[40]

[39]I have discussed these positions briefly in '"Memories of Underdevelopment": Language and its Identities in Contemporary Karnataka', *Economic and Political Weekly*, 31 (41 and 42), 12–19 October 1996, pp. 2809–16. Several Kannada intellectuals (writers, teachers, journalists, and artistes) who represented the strand of 'secular polities' took a clear and uncompromising stand against the more aggressive and violent actions of several Kannada groups during the Gokak agitation (1982), the agitation against the removal of the Kannada test for Class II and Class IV employees (1984), the Thiruvalluvar episode and Cauvery riots (1991). They included writers like G.K. Govinda Rao, Marulsidappa, D.R. Nagaraj, Ki Ram Nagaraj, S. Siddalingaiah, Vijaya, Shudra Srinivas, Agrahara Krishnamurthy, and U.R. Ananthamurthy. Their stand on the riots against the Urdu telecast (1994) was less unambiguous although here too the violence against Muslims was severely condemned.

[40]*Deccan Herald*, 26 March 1992.

Not a small part of the effort of Kannada Shakthi Kendra, headed by Chidanandamurthy, has gone into a careful charting of demographic imbalances within the city of Bangalore. Such an understanding is seriously flawed as it is translated into a programme for redressal that turns against minorities in the state. In demographic terms, after all, the estimated 20 per cent of Bihari Hindi speakers in Calcutta[41] or the substantial number of Malayalam and Telugu speakers in Chennai has done nothing to challenge the hegemony of Bengali or Tamil respectively in Bengal and Tamil Nadu. Clearly, something other than mere demography or geography is necessary to come to terms with the present crisis. An exclusive focus on demography thus avoids engagement with the most important factors which have resulted in Kannada's dominated status, which is largely due to the structuring of opportunities by the market, rather than the state, and in the consequent privileging of English over other languages.

DOMINATION AND ITS EFFECTS

'The name is Karnataka, now let the breath be Kannada' (*hesaraayithu Karnataka, usiraagali Kannada*) was the rallying call of poet Chennavira Kanavi, who recognized that the linguistic reorganization of states in 1956, an administrative act, did not automatically bring linguistic dominance in its wake (Figure 11.3). Clearly, the state machinery has a large role to play in making this a reality, and as Sumathi Ramaswamy's recent work has shown, even such a robust nationalism as that of Tamil could not do without the state's support in making Tamil the de facto language of the state.[42] Karnataka is unusually rich in the number of languages that are spoken within its borders. While Kannada is spoken by about 65 per cent of its inhabitants, languages such as Konkani, Tulu, and Kodagu (which are identified with subregions of Karnataka), and Marathi, Telugu, and Tamil (identified with other linguistic states), are among the important minorities. During the four significant moments in the history of language politics in the past two decades, that is, the Gokak agitation (1982), the Cauvery agitation (1991), the

[41]Jean Racine et al., *Calcutta 1981*: there were 61 per cent Bengali speakers, 20 per cent Hindi speakers, and 9 per cent Urdu speakers in 1981, p. 111.

[42]Sumathi Ramaswamy, *Passions of the Tongue: Language Devotion in Tamil Nadu 1891–1970* (Delhi: Munshilal Manoharlal, 1998), pp. 161–8.

Figure 11.3: Asserting Linguistic Pride: Kuvempu's Ramayana Darshanam being Taken in Procession on an Elephant from the Kempegowda Statue. (T.L. Ramaswamy, 8.1.1969)

anti-Urdu telecast agitation (1994), and finally the crisis produced by Rajkumar's kidnapping (2000), the geographical spread of the movement has narrowed to become more closely identified with southern Karnataka, and Bangalore in particular. An impressive all-Karnataka affair in 1982 (Gokak), with an organizing nucleus based in Hubli-Dharwad, was restricted, during the Cauvery agitation, to a struggle over jobs, land, and water in southern Karnataka.[43] Indeed, the Cauvery agitation shifted from the Cauvery basin to the city of Bangalore within a few days, becoming virulently anti-Tamil in ways that were unforeseen and unprepared for.[44] The anti-Urdu agitation, which revolved around the question of Kannada's visibility as an official language, was more or less confined to Bangalore and Mysore.

Associations such as Vatal Nagaraj's Kannada Chaluvaligaru, Kannada Shakthi Kendra, or Rajkumar Abhimanigala Sangha, to name a few, maintain a vigil against real and perceived threats to the language in its home state. The city of Bangalore has become emblematic of the dominated status of Kannada: by the 1991 census only 35 per cent of the people declared Kannada as their mother tongue, followed by Tamil (25 per cent), Urdu (19 per cent), and Telugu (17 per cent). This demographic deficit is produced as humiliation in nationalist discourse. Thus, Chidanandamurthy recalls asking for a ticket in Kannada in a cantonment cinema theatre and being threatened by the manager: more humiliating than the threat was the fact that other 'Kannadigas were [reduced to] mute witnesses'.[45] The Kannadiga is here a 'local refugee', said Ra Nam Chandrasekhar, an HAL employee who has produced some of the most detailed analyses of the demographic data to prove that Kannada has only a marginal presence in the state capital.[46] This is both a result of, and a cause for, the 'Kannadiga's lack of self respect and the limitless tolerance of others' needs' which have been represented as 'positive' attributes (the 'large heartedness of the Kannadiga' or the 'civilized Kannadiga') to trick the guileless Kannadiga into a state of contentment.[47]

---

[43]At the height of the Cauvery agitation, a farmer from Bidar, a dry district far removed from the state capital said, 'Where is Cauvery? What has It to Do with this Backward District?' *Hindu*, December 1991.

[44]*Deccan Herald*, 12–13 December 1991.

[45]M. Chidanandamurthy, *Nanna Baduku: Ondu KiruChitra* (Dr M. Chidanandamurthy Gourava Samputa 'Samshodana' dalli Prakatagonda Lekhanada Mel Acchu, n.d.), p. 942; see also Ve Srinivas, 'Kannada Chaluvali Nadedubanda Daari', in *Kannada Kanmani* which describes the humiliation experienced by Ma Ramamurthy when the demand for the screening of Kannada films in Majestic was made.

[46]Interview with Ra Nam Chandrasekhar, 7 and 11 October 1998; see also the chapter 'Valase' in *Kannada-Kannadiga-Karnataka*, pp. 163–8. 'Ekathegondu Savalu: Antharajya Valase', in *Saarthaka*, n.d., 152–62.

[47]Chidanandamurthy, 'Kannadadha Samasyegalu', in *Kannada-Kannadiga-Karnataka*, p. 51.

The 'cosmopolitanism' which is hailed by the city's bourgeoisie and the English press in particular thus takes on a pejorative meaning in Kannada writings: says G. Narayana, former mayor of Bangalore, 'Bangalore is today a "cosmopolitan city". If this situation continues [the whole of] Karnataka itself may become "cosmopolitan"'.[48] The demographic lack, these writers suggest, may be redressed in a number of ways: by encouraging migration into the city from north Karnataka,[49] for instance. This has, however, already been enabled by the new modes of labour mobilization, particularly in the construction industry. By the 1950s, inter-state migration was overshadowed by intra-state migration, and the trend has not been reversed. Nevertheless, the protagonists of Kannada suggest that the wounds inflicted by geography must be redressed in other ways.[50] Since Bangalore is located near the borders of two other states, Andhra Pradesh and Tamil Nadu, it attracts many of their workers. This situation can only be avoided, Sa Ra Govindu, the President of the Rajkumar Abhimanigala Sangha declared, by banning new industries in Bangalore.[51] During the Cauvery agitation, Siddaiah Puranik, a litterateur who feared 'losing Bangalore to outsiders', suggested that Bangalore should be made a 'Kannadiga city'.[52]

The use of demographic data is an attractive stratagem as it abundantly lays bare the dominated status of Kannada in Karnataka and particularly Bangalore, compared with other state capitals such as Chennai, Trivandrum, or Hyderabad.[53] However, the Kannada movement did not owe its origins to the activities of the Shakti Kendra (begun in 1988), nor the Rajkumar Abhimanigala Sanghas (begun in 1982). Nor do these groups today monopolize the struggle to build a new identity for Kannada. What then were the Kannada movements'

[48]G. Narayana, 'Bengaluru Nagarada Mukhya Samasyegalu', mimeo, 19–97, p. 2.

[49]Chidanandamurthy, 'Kannadadha Samasyegalu'.

[50]The States Reorganisation Committee (1956) acknowledged the particularly fragmented political status of Kannada speakers, who were reduced to minorities in three of the administrative divisions of colonial Karnataka.

[51]Interview with Sa Ra Govindu, president, Dr Rajkumar Abhimangala Sangh, 23 October 1998.

[52]*Hindu,* 14 December 1993; *Deccan Herald,* 14 April 1992. A newly laid out extension came to be called 'Little Karnataka', as it had people from Bombay and Hyderabad–Karnataka, as well as old Mysore, *Deccan Herald,* 18 July 1966.

[53]Ra Nam Chandrasekhar, 'Ekathegondhu Savalu', p. 153.

early forms after state reorganization and how have these been transformed since the 1980s to raise not only new demands but adopt new strategies in the achievement of its goals? How do other groups, such as Karnataka Vimochana Ranga for instance, envisage and work towards *another Kannada nation* and with what success? The rest of this discussion will focus on specific sites where Kannada's dominated status is revealed in recent struggles over space in Bangalore. Contentious struggles have occurred in a variety of sites, over the language of liturgy, work opportunities in the formal and informal economies, or access to power in the city.

LANGUAGE AND CULTURE

In the early 1960s, the Kannada movement in Bangalore had two principal aims: to build up cultural resources that drew on and strengthened the Kannada language, and to secure jobs for sons-of-

Figure 11.4: Asserting Linguistic Pride: Writer Aa Na Kru (in dark glasses) and Others Take the Kannada Bhuvaneswari in a Motorcade.
(T.L. Ramaswamy, 1970s)

the-soil. As old Mysore and particularly Bangalore withdrew from its cultural dependence on Madras Presidency,[54] there was a vigorous call to support indigenous (Karnataka) cultural productions. Aa Na Krishna Rao (Aa Na Kru) and Ma Ramamurthy of the Karnataka Samyuktha Ranga were among those who demanded that Kannada singers be given a place in the annual Ramotsava cultural festivals, then dominated by artistes from Tamil Nadu (Figure 11.4).[55]

Cinema too emerged as a site of struggle from the 1960s. At one level, leaders of the Kannada movement objected to representations of Karnataka in Tamil films. In *Kanchi Thalaivan* (1963), a Tamil film, the humiliation of Mayurvarman, the Kadamba king, at the court of the Pallavas at Kanchi was taken as a humiliation of the entire Kannada nation, and the movie was withdrawn from circulation.[56] At another level, there were growing demands that more Kannada films be screened in the city. At the start of his political career, Vatal Nagaraj threatened to shut down, through violence if necessary, the theatres where Tamil films were being shown, particularly in the Majestic area of Bangalore city.[57] Finally, in order to stress the separation of the new linguistic state from its earlier cultural moorings in Madras Presidency, there were appeals to actors such as Kalyan Kumar to restrict themselves to acting in Kannada language films.

The quest for a way to dominate the sphere of culture has passed through many phases, though by no means is culture the unalloyed domain of Kannada. The struggle over films that are screened in the city is illustrative of the dominated status of the language. A national culture, which has been purveyed throughout the country via the medium of Hindi, has rarely been questioned and has even been strengthened through the wide spread of the televisual medium. In fact, tolerance of Hindi is a badge of honour, compared with the

[54]Susan Lewandowski shows that Madras became a more homogeneously Tamil city as a consequence of the development of other state capitals after Independence. See Lewandowski, *Migration and Ethnicity in Urban India*, p. 75.

[55]*Samyukta Karnataka*, 28 April 1962.

[56]'Kannada Chaluvali Nadedhu Banda Dari', in *Kannada Kanmani*; interview with Ra Nam Chandrasekhar, 11 October 1998; 'Chidanandamurthy elevates what was perhaps no more than a small wrestling match into a historic event' says D.R. Nagaraj, commenting on the use of this episode in constructing a history of the Kannada nation. 'The Nature of Kannada Nationalism.'

[57]*Deccan Herald*, 28 December 1960; 20 February 1962, 8 September 1962.

virulent opposition to the language in Tamil Nadu. Mahadev Banakar cited the Tamil objection to the use of the term 'Akashvani' as a symptom of its anti-national stance, a position from which he was anxious to distance Kannada.[58] Even the demand to replace the broadcast of Hindi news with Kannada at prime time was raised by the regional Tamil AIDMK party in Bangalore.[59] Instead, when there were protests against Hindi tele-serials such as Sanjay Khan's *The Sword of Tippu Sultan*[60] or Ramanand Sagar's *Ramayana*,[61] it was because the dubbing of such films, rather than their remake, reduced opportunities for jobs in the film industry.

Even when Kannada films have a more assured presence in the city, periodic protests against the dubbing of other language films or 'remakes' have continued. Dubbed films are the lowest in a hierarchy which places films originally made in Kannada at the top; 'remakes' continue to maintain a substantial hold along with original films and dubbed ones as there is an acknowledged 'lack of story lines and even directors'. In a mid-1990s recurrence of this crisis, the Karnataka Film Producers' Association and Karnataka Film Directors' Association under the leadership of the Rajkumar Abhimanigala Sangha demanded that Bangalore exhibitors reduce theatre rent for Kannada films and show Kannada films for at least six months in a year. It also asked the government to impose a twelve month ban on the release of non-Kannada films.[62] Exhibitors however claimed that it was difficult enough to run Kannada films for more than two to three weeks. The self-imposed shutdown of the film industry during the kidnapping crisis dealt a body blow to an industry already in decline. Neighbouring states such as Tamil Nadu and Andhra Pradesh were at an advantage as they 'had a huge ready viewership outside their respective states', assuring them of audiences (and therefore film budgets) that Kannada could only dream about.[63]

Notwithstanding a measure of pride in the fact that 'films in six languages are shown in the state', the insistence, particularly during

---

[58]Banakar, *Safeguards for Minority Languages*, p. iii.
[59]*Deccan Herald*, 8 July 1994.
[60]Ibid., 12 December 1994.
[61]Ibid., 30 August 1994.
[62]*Lankesh Patrike*, February–March 1996, *Hindu*, 21 February 1996.
[63]*Deccan Herald*, 13 July 2000.

moments of crisis, that only Kannada films be seen in theatres in Bangalore and that DD1 and DD9 telecast only Kannada at peak times are a sign of Kannada's limited reign over the field of culture. During the debates in the legislature, Chief Minister J.H. Patel jocularly declared that it was not the job of the government to teach film artistes to sing and dance as well as their Hindi or Tamil counterparts.[64] In other words, no government action could compensate for the preference of cinema viewers for Hindi or Tamil films: that was to enter the thickets of taste, a point to which I shall return below.

Kannada seeks to monopolize the state channels knowing that it is powerless against the myriad private channels that beam programmes in English, Hindi, and Tamil throughout the day. The aspiration to monopolize the official channel is part of a wider effort to acquire legitimacy in a situation where dominance has been denied: there were times, as in 1976, when suggestions were made for the nationalization of theatres to promote the Kannada industry.[65] Thus, the violent agitation which broke out against the introduction of Urdu news at prime time was a consequence of the desire to monopolize, by force if necessary, the symbolic face of the state on television. From its early days, Kannnada programmes on the national channel had been a contentious issue, many preferring programmes from Madras and resentful of the subtle imposition of Hindi.[66] The periodic protests also point to a very specific relationship between religion and language that has been a part of the Kannada movement to this day. Most recently, the renewed conflict over water-sharing in a distress year, which led to fresh hostilities between the two states in September 2002, was immediately effected as a ban on Tamil movies and television channels in Karnataka's capital city.

RELIGIOUS AND LINGUISTIC SPACES

Elsewhere I have discussed the way in which the dominated status of Kannada has been narrativized by early nationalists: the epistemological

[64]*Deccan Herald*, 2 March 1996.
[65]'Takeover of Cinemas Urged', *Deccan Herald*, 19 April 1976; 'No Takeover of Cinema Houses Now', *Deccan Herald*, 14 April 1976.
[66]'Why this Hindi Imposition on Bangalore TV?', *Deccan Herald*, 3 December 1983; 'City TV Fans Favour Kannada and Delhi Relay', *Deccan Herald*, 9 December 1983.

violence of colonialism in the nineteenth and twentieth centuries in these accounts is considered less important than the waning fortunes of the Vijayanagara empire and the rise of the Adil Shahi/Bahmani sultanate in the sixteenth century.[67] The commonsensical link between Karnatakatva and Hindutva was most evident during the outbreak of violence against Muslims during the agitation against the Urdu news telecast in 1994. Once more, Kannada protagonists in Bangalore and Mysore acted on a version of history which identified Urdu speakers in Karnataka as Muslims, choosing to ignore Kannada's links with Urdu and, indeed, Karnataka's historic encounter with Islam. If the Tamil speaker is envied for an extra-territorial loyalty, for an allegiance to the politics of a neighbouring state, the Urdu speaker is feared for her excessive identity which guarantees the language a space in governmental discourse despite its lack of a territorial location. Both these languages thus survive, and even flourish, without an official political structure to patronize their community of speakers.

Envy and fear of the languages of minorities, and usually subaltern minorities such as Tamil and Urdu speakers, often, though not always, devolves on the question of jobs created for people within the space that is officially Karnataka. The pattern of such demands in Bangalore has followed well-established patterns set by groups in Bombay and Madras through the 1960s and 1970s. Susan Lewandowski has analysed the riots against Malayalis in Madras and several cities of Tamil Nadu during 1974: Malayali establishments were attacked and even cinema houses were not spared. This was followed by a state government effort to reserve up to 80 per cent of jobs for Tamils and domiciled Tamils. Importantly, however, she points out that Madras remained relatively free of bitter ethnic conflict owing to the long history of Malayali involvement in the non-Brahmin movement, and the numerical dominance of Tamils in Madras.[68]

The case of Bombay bears closer parallels to the history of Bangalore. Thomas Hansen's recent study shows that although Marathi speakers were far from reduced to minority status, 'sharpened competition over middle class, white collar jobs' in the 1970s paved the way for the rise of a sons-of-the-soil movement led by the Shiv

[67] See Nair, 'Memories of Underdevelopment', p. 2813.
[68] Lewandowski, Migration and Ethnicity in Urban India, pp. 82; 175 ff.

Sena that targeted south Indians.[69] Indeed, the self-perception of Marathi language speakers as a dominated 'minority' bore a close resemblance to the emerging identity of Kannada speakers as a similar minority. Moreover, the tussle over government jobs, and public sector jobs in particular, were the breeding ground of Kannada nationalists through the 1960s and 1970s.

When the Ramakrishna Hegde government relaxed the compulsory Kannada examination for Class III and IV employees in 1984, as a concession to Muslim government servants, the Rajkumar Abhimanigala Sangha demanded a restoration of the compulsory examination.[70] Despite government explanations for the decision, the sangha organized a citywide bandh which turned violent, and there were attacks on the property of Tamils and Muslims in the western part of Bangalore, as well as on government property.[71] Yet it was a moment when the government succeeded in sticking to its decision: the more virulent attacks on Tamils and Muslims were the 1991 and 1994 attacks, respectively, when the Rajkumar Abhimanigala Sangha had the tacit support of the state government (1991) and of groups such as the Kannada Shakti Kendra and the Hindu Jagarana Vedike in 1994.

In October 1994, the telecast of a ten-minute Urdu news bulletin at prime time (7:45 to 7:55 p.m.) was taken as a direct provocation to those committed to deepening the presence of Kannada. It was viewed as being just as a step away from 'making Urdu the second language of the State'.[72] It was the public face of Urdu on the state-run TV channels that was most resented. Thus Chidanandamurthy, in an interview with the People's Democratic Forum declared: 'Let there be Urdu news on Doordarshan (DD) 2 but not on DD1 or DD9.'[73] Indeed, 'there are enough Urdu programmes on TV' but Chidanandamurthy's primary objection was to the timing: 'why should Urdu news be telecast only during the prime time from 7:30 p.m. onwards?' Although the

[69]Hansen, Urban Violence in India, p. 47.

[70]'Raj to Head Panel on Kannada Row', Deccan Herald, 14 January 1984.

[71]'Three Killed in Bandh Violence: Curfew Clamped on Some City Areas', Deccan Herald, 19 January 1984.

[72]A statement signed by several intellectuals made this specific charge: Go. Ru Channabasappa, Prof. G.S. Shivarudrappa, H.S. Doreswamy and Prof. M.H. Marulsiddappa released the statement on 5 October 1994. People's Democratic Forum, 'Medium' for Communalism: A Report on the Anti-Urdu Communal Riots, December 1994, p. 4.

[73]Ibid., p. 26.

programme was not the result of a popular Muslim demand, riots that followed targeted Muslim-owned homes, businesses, and shops.

The identification of Muslims with Urdu is achieved with greater ease than the identification of Christianity with any one language. The Kannada movement's focus on Christians has therefore taken the form of asserting a Kannada presence in a Tamil-dominated church. The substantial presence of the Christian church in Bangalore, and its role as distributor of charity and resources has been well recognized both within and beyond the church. Throughout the nineteenth century, as the Protestant church gained ground, the flock in Bangalore and nearby Kolar Gold Fields was composed largely of lower-caste Tamil speakers who moved to the more profitable Bangalore region.[74] The language of liturgy of many churches, particularly in the Cantonment area, was Tamil, though industrial workers settled to the west of the city were quicker to assimilate the local language for worship.[75] A similar linguistic preference is true of the Catholic church in the city, with some congregations remaining wholly or predominantly Tamil while others were more mixed.

The predominance of Tamils in both the Protestant and Catholic churches has made for a very great source of tension in the past few decades. If the Protestant church has been free of the acrimonious exchanges between church functionaries and congregations, it is a result of an informal arrangement that appoints a Kannada-speaking bishop for each of its dioceses in the state. The principal focus of Kannada nationalist attention has therefore been the Catholic church. In the early 1980s, the Karnataka Catholic Christhara Sangha became a significant presence, as it was felt that there were not enough Kannada catechists or even priests to meet the needs of the minority.[76] Writers and other intellectuals who jumped into the fray, such as V.K. Gokak,

[74]Muthaiah David Appavoo, *The Effect of Migration on the Churches of Bangalore* (Bangalore: C1SRS, 1965), pp. 2, 10, 17.

[75]Ibid., pp. 19–20: among the more exceptional churches noted by Appavoo was the St Barnabas church of HAL where workers from different backgrounds endeavoured to maintain the unity of the spirit by worshipping in four different languages. Thus, the author concludes, 'industrial life obliterated language differences' and produced a new sense of belonging. For a different reading of this phenomenon, see J.R. Henry, 'A History of the Tamil Churches in Mysore Diocese' (thesis submitted for the College Diploma of UTC, Bangalore, 1962).

[76]'Letters', *Deccan Herald*, 3 November 1980.

commented on the way the Catholic church was imposing Tamil on Kannada Catholics, often by simply not providing services in Kannada. Indeed, there was growing resentment that there were Kannada services only in twelve of twenty-three parishes in the Bangalore metropolitan area, while daily services in Tamil and English were most common. One aspiring priest, Thomas Puttaswamy, said that 'The Karnataka youths that are barred from priesthood had to go to Mysore Diocese to fulfill their vows and Karnataka women are blocked from nunneries'.

Such openly voiced resentment found supporters among the more strident sections of the Kannada movement who based their objections to the language of liturgy, especially during major festivals. Begun as a movement to declare the Bangalore diocese as a Kannada diocese, members of Christhara Sangha attempted to stop the Latin Special (Easter) Mass at St Xaviers' Cathedral in Bangalore east in 1981 and assaulted (the Tamil) Reverend Arokiaswamy. The demand for a mass in Kannada infuriated the Tamil majority congregation.[77] There was another attack on the church in Briand Square to the west of the city to demand that Kannada and not Tamil be adopted as the language of the high mass, despite the fact that the congregation was mostly Tamil.[78]

Kannada writers who threw themselves into the agitation declared that it was a problem of culture and language and not religion. The fact that Tamil songs and liturgies were being printed in Kannada and imposed on Kannadigas showed that the church was trying to create a mini-Tamil Nadu.'[79] Once more, the protagonists resorted to the use of numbers to make their respective claims: Kannadigas wanted the Bangalore diocese to be declared a Kannada diocese, while Tamils did not want even a single Tamil mass to be reduced, and even asked for an increase of masses where the majority were Tamils. After all, of the 200,000 Catholics in Bangalore, 75 to 80 per cent were Tamils.[80]

In 1988, the church issued a special circular 2188 declaring a three-language formula of Kannada, Tamil, and English services, which the Kannada Catholics refused to accept.[81] As a result, almost every year,

---

[77]'Clash in Cathedral: Archbishop Gheraoed', *Deccan Herald*, 17 April 1981.

[78]'33 Held after Disturbance in Church', *Deccan Herald*, 4 May 1981.

[79]'Writers Back Kannada Catholics Demands', *Deccan Herald*, 2 July 1981.

[80]'The Catholic Church and Language', *Deccan Herald*, 3 June 1983.

[81]'Church to Stick to Three Language Formula', *Deccan Herald*, 2 May 1988; 'Church Circular on Language Rejected', *Deccan Herald*, 4 May 1988.

protests are organized during Easter against the language of liturgy.[82] Writers and artistes participated in these protests out of concern not only for the language but for its speakers 'since the use of Tamil or any language other than Kannada ... meant that all the jobs in the churches and various related offices would not go to Kannadigas'.[83] In some ways symbolic victories have been won, as the Archbishop is now chosen from within Karnataka.

The controversy over the language of liturgy cannot be reduced to concern over the power and opportunities for advancement that are offered by the church. Nevertheless the access of the Kannada Christian to opportunities for work in the church has fuelled many such interventions. For the right to the city has been materialized in its most important sense as a right to jobs in the city. It is in this domain that the Kannada movement may have recorded its most important successes.

REALM OF WORK IN THE CITY

If the protests against the status of Kannada in the cultural sphere and as the language of liturgy have made largely symbolic gains, there is another sphere in which the Kannada movement has been relatively more successful. This is in the realm of public sector jobs, which were important entitlements not only to a salary but a whole new way of life in the city (Figure 11.5). Public sector companies paid good wages for fairly undemanding work. The perquisites are equally important, and include housing, transport, subsidized canteens, etc., all of which were gains consolidated by a left-wing trade union movement. The Big Four units, HAL, BEL, HMT, and ITI, employed largely Malayali and Tamilian workers: the Kannadiga presence was rather muted until the 1960s when a combination of demographic shifts, management policies, and new cultural politics began to gain ground. The public sector units were also important locations of well-funded cultural and fine arts groups, initially monopolized by Malayalis and Tamils. One might even say that these were the languages of cultural organizations and trade unions well into the 1970s.[84] The Tamil Mandram, Kerala

[82]*Samyukta Karnataka*, 18 April 1992.

[83]These were the words of G.S. Siddalingaiah, president, Kannada Sahitya Parishat. 'Agitation for Kannada in Church to be Stepped Up', *Deccan Herald*, 4 June 1990.

[84]Interview with Ra Nam Chandrasekhar, 7 and 11 October 1998.

Figure 11.5: Not Just Jobs for the 'Sons-of-the-Soil': Women on the
Assembly Line at the HMT Watch Factory. (T.L. Ramaswamy, 28.10.1971)

Samajam, and Telugu Mithrulu registered their presence well before
the Kannada Sanghas were started. Many realized the limits of
such activism: as industries minister in 1973, S.M. Krishna urged
Kannadigas not to remain content with cultural troupes and instead
start industries.[85]

Since the formation of the linguistic states, migration from
erstwhile Presidency areas into Bangalore has been gradually overtaken
by flows from areas of rural Karnataka. As the new linguistic state
consolidates its resources, simultaneously redrawing and restricting
the sphere of influence of the Presidencies, labour mobility (of the Tamil
versus the Kannadiga labourer for instance) has been transformed,
slowing down inter-state and enhancing intra-state migration.[86] The
state has, however, been a net gainer from immigration in comparison
with the other three southern states which are net losers of population.

[85]Krishna made this suggestion while inaugurating HAL's Kannada Sangha; *Deccan
Herald,* 23 August 1973.

[86]Johnson Samuel and M. Lingaraju, 'Migrants in Bangalore', ISEC Working Paper 13,
1989, p. 13.

These migration patterns were offset by recruitment policies: in BEL, for example, the strength of the AITUC was challenged in 1967 by the Workers' Unity Forum, which consisted primarily of new Kannadiga (middle peasant caste) migrants, who were encouraged by a management anxious to curb left-wing militancy.[87]

At the height of the seventy-seven-day public sector strike, when workers of seven public sector units decided to stay off work in March 1981, posters appeared under the signature of INTUC threatening to 'socially boycott Tamilians and Keralites' if they were not expelled from the state in a week: the implication was that as strike organizers, they were keeping hard-working Kannadigas from rejoining work.[88] The letter from the National Student's Union of India, which was reproduced in the INTUC posters, threatened to cut off water and electricity in workers' colonies, as 'the heritage of our beloved Karnataka is at stake ... the Employee's State Insurance Scheme is being misused by Keralites and Tamilians in large numbers'.[89] The 'treacherous' Tamil or Malayali was thus pitted against 'peace-loving, loyal' Kannadigas, whose desire to work was being thwarted by the outsiders.

Though this had no strike-breaking impact, and even embarassed the Congress government into disavowing the offensive posters, it had important effects on the psyche of the leadership. Michael Fernandes, a member of the Joint Action Front (JAF) heading the strike declared that this was a ploy of the state to divide the working class on lines of language and regionalism where it had failed to divide it on the grounds of caste and religion as had been tried in BEL and HMT.[90] Yet the poster incident forced Fernandes to defensively declare that 'four of the joint convenors of the JAF were Kannadigas'.

[87]Interview of M.S.L. Rao by Dilip Subramanian, June 1981.

[88]'Posters Under Fire'; 'Uproar in Lok Sabha Over City Posters'; 'Nip it in the Bud', *Deccan Herald,* 10 March 1981. In its hard-hitting editorial, the *Deccan Herald* said 'the chauvinist call of the NSUI patterned on the Kannada Chaluvali philosophy is not only stupid and impractical but will only set one linguistic group against another in a fragile society as obtains in cosmopolitan Bangalore'.

[89]Subramanian, 'The Bangalore Public Sector Strike', 1980–81, Part II, p. 852. The reference to the use of ESI funds was true: many workers made ends meet through the long strike period by claiming sickness benefits from the two ESI centres, ibid., p. 844, Predictably the ESI act was amended soon after the strike in such a way as to bar workers on strike from making sickness and disablement claims.

[90]'Posters under Fire', *Deccan Herald,* 10 March 1981.

Fernandes's response was an acknowledgement of the scrupulous attention that Kannada groups were paying to the recruitment policies of institutions and agencies within the city. The audit of institutions from the perspective of language had begun as early as 1973, when it was discovered that the newly started Indian Institute of Management, which had procured land and other resources from the state government, was not employing a fair proportion of Kannadigas.[91] The real battleground continued to remain the public sector units, although by the mid-1980s it was clear that Kannada speakers easily formed the majority.

The large number of Kannada Sanghas which participated in the Gokak Chaluvali of 1982 was ample indication that the tide had turned in favour of the Kannadigas. Indeed, the decision of the Devaraj Urs government to make the Kannada test compulsory for Class 2, 3, and 4 employees in government even led to a temporary decline in the activities of the Chaluvaligars.[92] So much so, that the Sarojini Mahishi Committee report which recommended that 100 per cent of the Group D jobs, with proportionately lower percentages for the other categories, be reserved for Kannadigas, came just when the Kannada speakers were a growing majority in nearly all public sector units. The statistics submitted to the Sarojini Mahishi Committee were revealing, though they failed to satisfy Kannada organizations (Table 11.1).[93]

Table 11.1: Language Spoken in Public Sector Units, 1984

Unit	Kannada Speakers	Other Language Speakers
ITI	13,826	4,418
HAL	16,670	1,848
HMT	8,858	2,800
BEML	9,622	3,622
BHEL	2,539	150

Source: Deccan Herald, 16 May 1984.

[91]'Furore Over Jobs for Kannadigas in IIM' despite land granted by state government. Also, 'Minister Clarifies IIM Affairs', Deccan Herald, 25 September 1973.

[92]Joseph, 'Politics of Recruitment in Public Sector Undertakings', pp. 69, 168.

[93]'Kannadigas in Central Sector: Workers Dispute Official Figures', Deccan Herald, 16 May 1984.

The Hegde government's decision to reverse the policy of a compulsory Kannada test in 1984 led to the first agitation on the question of jobs headed by the Rajkumar Abhimanigala Sangha.[94] The Gokak Chaluvali of 1982, initially a movement of litterateurs, artistes, and academics centred in the Hubli-Dharwar region, which also included significant numbers of women, brought a fresh and positive unity to the Kannada movement, while drawing a whole range of new groups to its fold of which Rajkumar Abhimanigala Sangha was the most important. The entry of Rajkumar into the Gokak Chaluvali truly made it a mass movement, with the actor addressing meetings all over the state.[95] In turn, the emergence of Rajkumar Abhimanigala Sangha signalled a new stage in the movement, with the unhesitating use of violence against public property.[96]

By the time the Wheel and Axle plant was set up in Yelahanka in the early 1980s, '50,000 from all over Karnataka took out a procession' under the leadership of the Rajkumar Abhimanigala Sangha to complain against the injustice done to the Kannadigas in recruitment. The Sarojini Mahishi Committee was a result of this agitation, so that, as Sa Ra Govindu asserted, it soon became a unit that employed 60 per cent Kannadigas. Thus, the local language speaker became a forceful presence in the organized sector and was willing to assert his claim to the privileges of blue-collar work. The 'sons-of-the-soil' policy was deliberately gendered male, since women did not form a part of the Kannada imaginary at any level as we shall see below. Yet such triumphs occurred just when the public sector itself was shrinking, and major changes in the economic profile of the city were underway.

[94]Interview with Sa Ra Govindu, 23 Oct. 1998; interview with R. Radhakrishna, President, Jaga Mechida Maga, Dr Rajkumar Abhimanigala Sangha, 20 July 1999.

[95]'Raj Jumps Intro Fray', *Deccan Herald*, 17 April 1982; 'Rajkumar V Fight for Kannada Supremacy', *Deccan Herald*, 12 May 1982; 'Stir Will Continue to Kannada Gets Primacy—Raj', *Deccan Herald*, 17 May 1982.

[96]'Kannada Stir Turns Violent', *Deccan Herald*, 18 April 1982. The deaths in 1982 of Muslims at Chitradurga and Tamils at Kolar Gold Field (KGF) occurred as a result of police firing on those who opposed the proposed language policy: such opposition also took the form of violence against public property. For instance, the five persons from KGF who were killed in police firing had set fire to the post office and some other mining property.

INFORMAL ECONOMIES AND 'POLITICS IN A NEW KEY'

Two simultaneous processes in the 1980s altered the composition course and strategies of the Kannada movement: the marginalization of the public sector and its (usually left wing) trade unions, and the increasing privatization and informalization of the economy. When the long and bitter public sector strike ended in 1981, the eclipse of this sector as prime employer was already under way. Only sporadic protests could take place on the question of jobs, for after all, how could the same pressure be put on the private or largely informal sector? The 1984 agitation against the Hegde government order on Kannada tests for government jobs, and the later demand for the Wheel and Axle Plant or the Railway headquarters in Bangalore were protests largely aimed at the government. Yet, the gradual eclipse of well-established arenas of working-class action, such as trade unions, made the informal networks (neighbourhood youth groups, Kannada Sanghas and Abhimanigala Sanghas in particular) even more important sites of political activity. Large numbers of those who belong to Abhimanigala Sanghas for instance are service providers in the city: autorickshaw drivers, tempo drivers and mechanics, recycling job workers, petty shopkeepers, and KEB or BWSSB employees.[97] Not surprisingly the more important arena of action in the 1980s was the symbolic reterritorialization of the city: red and yellow Kannada flag poles that mushroomed all over the city after 1982 were compensating *visually for* what was an *audible* absence.

Even so, the contentious question of language in the city was not serious enough to warrant the attention of the state apparatuses. The Deputy Commissioner of Police (intelligence) confessed before the N.D. Venkatesh Commission inquiring into the violence against Tamils in 1991 that 'for purposes of collection of intelligence he had made some classification such as labour problems, communal problems, etc., but he is certain that *linguistic relationships with the City population* was not a subject for gathering information.'[98] The violence against Tamils in the old Mysore region, and particularly in

[97]Interview with members of Jaga Mechida Maga Dr Rajkumar Abimanigala Sangha, 20 July 1999.

[98]Report of the N.D. Venkatesh Commission of Inquiry, Vol. 1, p. 52 (emphasis in original).

Bangalore in 1991, was indeed unprecedented and, further, came at a time when the issue of jobs for Kannadigas was less important than the questions of rights to the land and water. Steen Folke's study of the agricultural uses of the Cauvery river in both Karnataka and Tamil Nadu points to a wide range of bitter disputes over water rights, usually between head—and tail-end users within the same village and between villages, with caste and class (rather than language) playing an important role in deciding water allocations.[99] Nevertheless, the Cauvery water dispute has since the 1980s increasingly been staged as a dispute between two linguistic regions and nationalisms.[100] The centrality of land and water rights both within and beyond the city thus became crucial to the way in which the language question was framed in the 1990s.

The historical conjuncture at which the violence against Tamils occurred in 1991 is of some importance: it was a time when the right to land within the city and beyond had become more uncertain and yet more critical as a resource in an informal economy. Conflicts over land rights within the city had heightened in the decade when the population increased by a massive 76 per cent (1971–81). The geographies of violence, both during the riots of 1991 and 1994 against Urdu-speaking Muslims reveal a very interesting congruence. They were both concentrated in the western parts of the city, where land rights were most precarious, a terrain that was fully occupied by illegal constructions, and, further, hilly ground that made surveillance difficult. The riots did not affect older settlements of Tamils to the east of the city. The Venkatesh Commission noted that the 1991 violence was confined to thirteen police station limits, all of which were contiguous and in the western part of the city.[101] In the 20 sq. km falling to the Basaveshwaranagar and Kamakshipalaya police stations, 'there existed several revenue pockets and slums mostly inhabited by labour class and migrant poor people considerable number of whom were linguistic minorities'.[102] In the anti-Urdu

[99]Steen Folke, 'Conflicts Over Water and Land in South Indian Agriculture: A Political Economy Perspective', *Economic and Political Weekly* 33 (7), 1998, pp. 341–7.

[100]S.G. Balekundry, 'Injustice to Karnataka in Regard to Cauvery Waters' (Bangalore, 1991).

[101]Report of the N.D. Venkatesh Commission of Inquiry, Vol. l, p. 2.

[102]Ibid., pp. 59, 64.

telecast riots of 1994, the properties and businesses of Muslims were singled out for attack in the same western divisions of the city off Mysore Road.[103]

This area, as Benjamin and Bhuvaneswari's work has shown, boasts of one of the most vibrant informal economies in Bangalore city, but ironically in an area which has the most tenuous of rights to property and where ownership is constantly in a state of flux.[104] The authors say of Azadnagar, near the KR Market,

The land supply system in Azadnagar comprises of a variety of subsystems— free sites formed by state agencies and distributed to poor groups, revenue plots, Gramthana or layouts on village land and squatter settlement. Valmikinagar one of the largest layouts in the ward, for example, was developed partly by the State for free sites and partly by private developers. Azadnagar, another large layout in the ward evolved on gramthana land. In addition, there are a large number of smaller private revenue layouts in the ward— Markandeya layout, Vittal nagar layout, Adarshnagar, Rudrappa garden, etc., Besides, the Bande Squatter settlement emerged on 'marginal' land in the abandoned quarry area, low-lying land in the ward. The different land settings encompass the variety of economic activities and its actors.

Property here has economic value not merely as housing but also as a source of livelihood. Further, as locations outside the master planning area, 'claims are established not only via markets, but also [via] ethnic and political routes'. Such fragile and complex economies have been most vulnerable during the riots of the 1990s.

Both in 1991 and in 1994, the property and livelihoods of Tamils and Muslims respectively were subjected to far more sustained attack than the bodies of these inhabitants. Of the twenty-three deaths that are believed to have occurred in 1991, seventeen were due to police firing and six due to mob violence.[105] Property loss in these riots was put at Rs 17 crores in both Tamil Nadu and Karnataka by the Indian People's Human Rights Tribunal.[106] The Venkatesh Commission put the estimate

---

[103]People's Democratic Forum, *Medium for Communalism: A Report on the Anti-Urdu Communal Riots* (Bangalore: People's Democratic Forum, 1994), pp. 5, 7.

[104]Solomon Benjamin *et al.*, 'On Valmikinagar/Azadnagar', in 'Urban Poverty and Governance in Bangalore'. An amended longer consideration is in Benjamin and Bhuvaneswari, 'Democracy, Inclusive Governance and Poverty in Bangalore', pp. 49–53.

[105]*Report of the N.D. Venkatesh Commission of Inquiry*, Vol. 1, pp. 2–3.

[106]*Indian People's Human Rights Tribunal Report*, Annex. IV.

Figure 11.6: A Steadily Growing Informal Economy: Roadside Welding
Shop in Tilakanagar. (G. Raghav, 1999)

of losses variously at Rs 3 crores (state and central government losses) at Rs 15.5 crores (according to the Department of Commerce and Industries) and Rs 20.5 crores (according to police estimates).[107] In the anti-Urdu riots, 25 were killed, an equal number dying as a result of police firing and stabbing injuries. These are shocking statistics for a city that had no previous history of such deadly violence. However, the statistics relating to the loss of private property and livelihoods and the threat to certain social groups in the western part of the city were indicative of more enduring strategies by which claims to an area or neighbourhood were altered (Figure 11.6).[108]

Kannada speakers are preponderant in north-west and west Bangalore, according to recent analyses of slum populations, indicating that the migration of people from other districts of Karnataka has been most sustained in these areas.[109] This contrasts with successive waves of migration to the city of Bangalore from areas in Tamil Nadu. Tamil migrants, despite their substantial contribution to the economic profile of the city, particularly in the informal sector, are culturally viewed as inhabiting slums, a visible blot on the city landscape. Mahadev Banakar, at the height of the Gokak agitation, said that a disproportionate number of Tamils live in the slums of Bangalore: 'they seem to be happier in Karnataka than Tamil Nadu'.[110] Even less charitable were the versions of Tamil migration that were attributed to Tamil Nadu's prohibition policy.[111] Town planners and officials, who may not share this hostility to Tamilians, nevertheless reinforce the idea that migration is the cause of the city's problems, as the 'bulk of the migrants are illiterate and would accept substandard existence in the city'.[112]

As suppliers of goods and especially services that are vital to the survival of the city, slums render the boundaries of linguistic states irrelevant. Bangalore is the preferred destination of migrants from

[107]Report of the N.D. Venkatesh Commission of Inquiry, Vol. 1, p. 3.

[108]This has also been noted in other instances of communal violence, as for instance in Ahmedabad, Surat, and Bhopal in 1993: see Mehdi Arslan and Janaki Rajan (eds), Communalism in India: Challenge and Response (Delhi: Manohar, 1994).

[109]De Wit, 'Remote Sensing and Slums in Indian Cities', p. 58.

[110]Banakar, Safeguards for Linguistic Minorities, pp. 31–2.

[111]Interim Report of the Committee of Legislators on the Slum Problems of Bangalore, (draft). This reference was later deleted, p. 7.

[112]Report of the Review Committee on BDA, Vol. VIII, p. 30–1.

Tamil Nadu, particularly from the districts of North Arcot and Chingleput: Gertrude Woodruffe's 1959 study of migrants to a segregated slum of 207 Adi Dravida families in Bangalore showed that though the city was 125 miles away from the migrating village, and Madras only 75 miles away, 'no one in either cheri has ever gone to Madras except en route to Penang'.[113] This, she explains, is a 'self reinforcing process which is both the result of and results in villagers going to places they have heard about often in detail or where they have relatives'.

More recent studies also confirm that the attractions of Bangalore as a destination for migrants have not been tarnished by the episodes of violence directed against Tamils. A majority of the hawkers at KR Market are migrants from villages in South Arcot. Kattupaiyur has sent many of its families to work in Bangalore. Benjamin and Bhuvaneswari found that

families prefer to go to Bangalore because of the diversity of employment opportunities enable them to generate greater surplus. Those who have moved to Madras can find only low grade work as coolies in the airport or as unskilled industrial workers in North Madras. They have less mobility as compared to employment in Bangalore. Also in Madras, women do not find much opportunity to earn an income, and have to usually work as domestic servants with a low pay and less upward mobility. In Bangalore, in contrast, both men and women are involved in hawking and are able to generate enough surplus to send remittances and also make investments back home.[114]

Even as jobs within the organized sector are shrinking, the burgeoning opportunities of the informal sector are an attraction enough for new migrants who find the city a source for capital accumulation, even when the cultural conditions may not be as hospitable as they may have been. The population of the slums in Bangalore is changing, as more intra-state migrants enter the city competing for the opportunities offered at the lower end of the scale for economic mobility and accumulation. This has produced politics in a new key, and the dangers of equating the urban poor with certain linguistic groups (Tamil or Urdu) poses political perils that are only gradually being recognized.

[113]Woodruffe, 'An Adi Dravida Settlement in Bangalore India', p. 71.
[114]Benjamin and Bhuvaneswari, *et al.*, 'Urban Poverty and Governance in Bangalore', pp. 75–7.

A 'rather grand scale' government policy of slum improvement in the early 1990s fixed a cut-off point which qualified older slums for 'improvement' and younger slums for 'clearance'. The programme was called off when it was discovered that it would have led to the improvement of predominantly Tamil slums and the clearance of more recent Kannada ones.[115]

The definite link between the growing violence of language politics in the past two decades (particularly in the 1990s) and transformations within the economic sphere, however, must not obscure the work of ideologically constituting and mobilizing the Kannada people in the name of linguistic nationalism. An account of the role of language politics in defining the right to the city in economic terms alone would clearly be inadequate in understanding the meaning and scope of politics in the new key since the 1980s.

MODES OF MOBILIZATION

It would be tempting to see in the actions of Kannada activists since the 1980s a mimicry of the styles and strategies of Tamil nationalism. Yet not always was the image of nationalism in Karnataka one that was subordinated to language. At a mammoth rally in Shivajinagar on the occasion of Annadurai's birthday addressed by the then Tamil Nadu Chief Minister M. Karunanidhi, the CM asked the DMK (Dravida Munnetra Kazhagam) state unit to 'identify with Karnataka and fight for the supremacy of Kannada'.[116] A similar sentiment had earlier been voiced by the ideologue of the Dravidian movement, E.V. Ramawamy Naickar, on a visit to Bangalore, when he called on Tamilians 'to live as Kannadigas' in Karnataka.[117]

In the 1960s, the relative political quiescence of the Kannadiga was deplored by those Bangalore Tamils who threw themselves into the anti-Hindi protests:[118] there is an apocryphal tale of Tamils sending the shaming 'gift of bangles' to their Kannadiga counterparts to goad them into opposing Hindi. The 'emasculated Kannadiga' here is contrasted

[115]De Wit, *Geographical Information Systems*, p. 58.
[116]*Deccan Herald*, 12 October 1969.
[117]*Samyukta Karnataka*, 15 November 1964.
[118]Anti-Hindi protests were most conspicuous in the Tamil-dominated areas of the city such as Srirampuram, Ulsoor, Murphy Town, etc.

with the 'virile Tamil', and structures the response of the Kannadiga, leaving language conflicts gendered on both sides of the border.

For language itself is 'feminized,' personified as Kannada Bhuvaneswari/Tamilttay, while her supplicants, devotees, and protectors are overwhelmingly male.[119] Mobilization on the question of language and state identity has remained resolutely and aggressively male: not only has participation in fan clubs or language associations been male, the female has been mobilized within this discourse as a revered but weak personification of language itself, calling for the constant vigilance of her protectors.[120] Tejaswini Niranjana's scrutiny of the cultural productions—cassettes, tabloids, and the like—focused on the kidnapping of Rajkumar by Veerappan reveals an overwhelmingly masculinized discourse, which called on Kannada *abhimanis* to shed their historic timidity. The new masculinity, nevertheless, valorized Rajkumar as a cultured and urbane figure compared with Veerappan. The two men and their respective linguistic nationalisms were made to stand for the dichotomy between village, or more correctly forest and city/state *(kaadu* and *naadu)*. Most of the cultural productions and periodic public utterances of the first family therefore urged the abhimani to exercise self-restraint, in what Niranjana calls a 'double performance' which was 'necessary for the preservation of Kannada pride'.[121]

The woman is figured not as 'citizen' in this discourse, but an embodiment of regional/linguistic honour. Neither Chidanandamurthy nor Sa Ra Govindu recognized the need to draw more women into their organizations, still less recast this profoundly gendered discourse. On his part, D.R. Nagaraj, while characterizing 'virile politics' as entirely a modern invention, a weapon of the Hindu nationalists, falls back on valorizing Gandhi as the embodiment of an Indian ideal of 'ardhanareeswara'.

The commonalities between the gendered discourses of both Kannada and Tamil may be understood within the broader context of nineteenth-century nationalist mobilizations that strove to correct the

[119]On the feminizing of the Tamil language, see Ramaswamy, *Passions of the Tongue,* esp. pp. 79–134.

[120]Thayinadu Prema Thayi Pritiashte Shrestha, *Kannada Kanmani,* November 1993.

[121]Tejaswini Niranjana, 'Reworking Masculinities: Rajkumar and the Kannada Public Sphere', *Economic and Political Weekly,* 35 (47), 2000, pp. 4147–50, esp. p. 4150.

colonial stereotype of the emasculated Indian male. Rather than the Kannada linguistic movement being simply imitative of the Tamil model, there are quite often common sources for modalities of mobilization, as Niranjana has shown in her discussion of the construction of masculinity following Rajkumar's abduction. There are, however, other discernable debts to the political energies of Tamil activists. S. Siddalingaiah, dalit poet, teacher, and former MLC, recalls his early tutelage by RPI activists from Tamil Nadu (who were also vehemently anti-DMK) and the support of the Tamil dalits during the *busa* agitation of 1973 when he was himself under attack.[122] This was a time when Dalit or trade union politics was unmarked by an exclusivist emphasis on language. The gradual evolution of a stress on (exclusivist) pride in the Kannada language has thus had serious repercussions on the tolerance for minorities. Suggesting that multilingualism was a 'mistake' rather than a virtue, Chidanandamurthy says, 'at the same time we too have erred, we know it, we have been too good, we have been addressing Tamilians in Tamil, Malayalees in Malayalam, without initiating them into our language.'[123]

Fortunately, even the Rajkumar abduction crisis did not dim the pride that many people of Karnataka took in their multilingualism: Deputy Chief Minister Mallikarjun Kharge spoke in the chaste Urdu of his native Gulbarga to his NDTV interlocutors; Rajkumar and his family themselves did not hesitate to use the language of the captors in their appeals. This is why the politics that brandishes numbers in its support may be somewhat misleading, since, as K.S. Singh's *Peoples of India* project has shown, there is overwhelming indication of the multilingualism of many Indians (as much as 66 per cent in that sample). Knowledge of Kannada in Bangalore may be far more widespread than is admitted in mother tongue counts; the only sections who may afford the luxury of ignorance may be the English speakers.

However, while it is quite possible to legislate on the language of administration, employment, or education, there remains the stubborn question of taste. D.V. Gundappa, writing to R.R. Diwakar in 1950, despaired over the relative unpopularity of Kannada songs:

[122]Interview with S. Siddalingaiah, December 1999.
[123]Interview with M. Chidanandamurthy, 9 October 1998.

We are now supposed to have as many as five AIR centres for Karnataka. But there is not even one among them which is doing what is necessary to encourage the singing of Kannada songs. Even the Mysore station prefers to provide Tamil and Telugu pieces as recorded music and the Mysore Palace artist T. Chowdiah prefers to render a Tamil Pallavi rather than a Kannada or a Sanskrit one.[124]

More recently, Radhakrishna, president of the Jaga Mechida Maga Dr Rajkumar Abhimanigala Sangha, expressed similar dismay over the preference of Kannada speakers for the more lavish productions of the Tamil or Hindi film industry. For the price of a cinema ticket, the audience is transported to Simla, Kashmir, or Washington, whereas the Kannada film shows 'the same Nagarhole, the same Bandipura, the same Mysore Palace'.[125] Nor is this merely a consequence of the smaller population of Kannadigas in the country. What cannot be achieved through the mechanisms of persuasion is therefore achieved through the modalities of compulsion: the compulsory screening of Kannada films in all theatres for a fixed number of weeks per year has thus been a repeated demand of the Kannada movement.[126]

Events of the last two decades have hardened the position of both Kannadigas and Tamils who may formerly have been political allies within the trade union, the dalit movement, or even the linguistic movement. Let us recall, for instance, that many left-wing groups in the public sector responded in the early 1960s to the contentious issue of language by promoting Kannada literature and celebrating Kannada's ascendance. Forced to respond to the mobilization of workers on linguistic lines in BEL during the late 1960s, the AITUC devised programmes for the sale of books by Kannada writers, talks, and other cultural programmes in Kannada as a means of playing down the management emphasis on the regional origins of left-wing

[124]D.V. Gundappa Private Papers, Karnataka State Archives (KSA) Bangalore.

[125]Interview with R. Radhakrishna, 20 July 1999.

[126]In his recent article, Bargur Ramachandrappa discusses the futility of struggles based so narrowly on the language of cinema, arguing for a more liberal definition of culture and cultural resources. His studious avoidance of any discussion of Tamil nationalism, choosing instead to speak of Marathi, Bengali, and Malayalam successes, is however a reminder of how closely tied are the modalities of nationalism on both sides of the border; 'Kannadaabhimanada Katuvaasthava'.

trade union organizers. Celebrations of Karnataka's Rajyotsava, meanwhile, were increasingly resembling large-scale Ayudha pujas, forcing work stoppages and promoting the worship of Kannada Bhuvaneswari at factory locations.

The defensive Tamil response to the relentless campaign against migration into the city has been to produce a mythicized past that speaks of Tamils as the 'original inhabitants' of the Bangalore and Kolar districts. Even Kempegowda, the founder of the city, it is claimed, 'was a Tigala who belonged to the Tamil Vanniyar caste'.[127] Many solidarities were broken, says the Tamil Sangham report, citing attacks by dalits in Siluvepura as a sign that in addition to myths of Hindu, Dravidian, or class identity, even a 'caste based unity of Dalits' has begun evaporating in the minds of Tamils.[128] This, despite the fact that there were many voices raised against the ferocious attacks on Tamils and Tamil properties by a range of organizations and individuals in Karnataka—Karnataka Rajya Raitha Sangha, Karnataka Vimochana Ranga, women's groups in Bangalore such as Vimochana, and sections of Rajkumar Abhimanigala Sangha themselves. Could these alternative positions, no matter how weak, be taken as resources for a envisaging another Kannada nation?

Another Kannada Nation

Never before in Karnataka's history has the economic value of English education been as visible as in the opportunities offered by the new economy. Infosys Chairman N.R. Narayana Murthy's plea for a massive expansion of English education to wrest the opportunities offered by the global market for software production has been matched by an equal and opposite response among Kannada protagonists. U.K. Ananthamurthy's inaugural address at the 69th Kannada Sahitya Sammelan in February 2002 remarked on the imbalance which keeps Kannada as a language 'confined to the kitchen':

Children who attend the modern schools in Bangalore do not know the work of DVG; Kuvempu, Bendre, Kumara Vyasa, Karanth. If caste was the most

---

[127]A Mute Genocide: A Report on the Gory Incidents of Violence on Karnataka Tamils. During the Black December 1991 (Bangalore: Bangalore Tamil Sangham, 1992), pp. 39, 40.
[128]Ibid., p. 41.

unequal division of our society in the past, today it is the possession of English that produces inequalities.[129]

Ananthamurthy inveighed against the 'mindboggling tolerance' of Kannadigas, and called for 'meaningful resistance' to protect the language, culture and civilization of Karnataka.[130] The identification of the hegemony of English as resulting in Kannada's beleaguered status was evident in the statement of those Kannada intellectuals who were pained by the anti-minority direction in which the 1982 Gokak agitation was developing: if English was the 'prestigious enchantress', Kannada was the 'sobbing mother'.[131] The state, meanwhile, elides the issue by citing the exigencies of law which have interfered with implementing its policy of compulsory education in Kannada from standard 1–5.[132]

At the height of the Gokak agitation, K.N. Harikumar, the young editor of the *Deccan Herald,* himself under siege for having criticized the 'conservative integrationism' of the pro-Kannada movement, produced a lengthy critique of the movement in his own newspaper. In his analysis of the language agitation, its protagonists and beneficiaries, from a strictly Marxist perspective, Harikumar made a useful observation:

Because the Kannada intellectual tradition is largely literary, the role of Kannada in particular and languages in general is highly overplayed. The role and meaning of non-linguistic identities, modes of perception and expression, and of wider social and political forces, is neglected or at best seen as subservient to the role of language, i.e. Kannada.

Furthermore, the obsession of the Kannada intelligentsia with language—be it Kannada, English, or Sanskrit—forces them to view

[129]'Jati Jagadalli English: Asamaanathege Bunadi', *Prajavani,* 16 February 2002.

[130]'Do not Sacrifice Karnataka's Interests', *Hindu,* 16 February 2002. This plea for protection of Kannada lay itself open to the obvious criticism that writers such as Ananthamurthy had benefited from globalization and from English translations of his writing. See, for instance, the words of the then State Information Technology Minister B.K. Chandrasekhar, 'Litterateurs' Remarks Lamented', *Hindu,* 23 February 2002.

[131]These were the words used by several Kannada intellectuals who raised their voice against the increasingly violent trend of the Gokak agitation. 'Letters', *Deccan Herald,* 18 April 1982.

[132]'Bhashaabhimanada Hesaralli Prachara Tantra: Krishna Vishada', *Prajavani,* 22 February 2002.

everything from this perspective so that 'they are unable to ... see that in certain areas of intellectual activity, for example, in music, painting, mathematics, modern science etc., and of life itself, for example, Harijan oppression, marriage, untouchability, trade union struggles etc., language or the differences between language has no role or plays a very different role'.[133] Throughout this article, Harikumar was careful to distinguish between different phases and sections of the language agitation, although his critique pointed to the impossibility of conceiving a democratic culture founded only on the ethnocultural unities of language. Nevertheless, the real link between language and democracy was ignored, the fact that language is not a neutral medium, and that access to the very instruments of democracy—the law or education, for instance—was enabled in and through language.

In an important study of the historical cleavage between patriotism and nationalism as it developed in Europe, Maurizio Viroli suggests that though 'patriotism' and 'nationalism' compete on the same terrain, they are antithetical to each other.[134] Identifying the former with republican ideals and fights for freedom rather than a singular language or ethnicity he says, 'properly understood, the language of republican patriotism could serve as a powerful antidote to, 'nationalism'. However,

the ethnocultural unity [of nationalism without a republican liberty] may translate into civic solidarity, if a culture of citizenship is erected on it; or better, if the sense of belonging based on common culture and common ethnic descent is translated into a culture of citizenship. Without a political culture of liberty, ethnocultural unity generates love of one's cultural uniqueness (if not superiority) and a desire to keep it pure from external contamination and intrusion. We would have the nation but it would not be a nation of citizens ... Democratic polities do not need ethnocultural unity; they need citizens committed to the way of life of the republic.[135]

Such an opposition between the sites of patriotic (democratic) actions and (modern) nationalisms (and sub-nationalisms are hardly exempt from the monstrosities of the full-fledged nationalisms, as we well know) may be relevant in delineating the strands of the Kannada movement.

[133]K.N. Harikumar, 'Language and Democracy: Towards a Democratic Culture in Karnataka', *Deccan Herald,* 13 August 1982.
[134]Maurizio Viroli, *For Love of Country: An Essay on Patriotism and Nationalism* (Oxford: Oxford University Press, 1997), p. 8.
[135]Ibid., p. 175.

At the present time, there is no doubt that the dominant strand is one that calls for the kind of ethnocultural unity that Viroli warns against. There are, however, many signs of political activities in Karnataka that complicate the picture of a resolutely ethnocultural nationalism.

Even such an apparently unified movement as the Rajkumar Abhimanigala Sangha was composed of multiple strands. Until 1987, said Radhakrishna, president of Jaga Mechchida Maga Dr Rajkumar Abhimanigala Sangha, the sanghas were intolerant, particularly of the large minority of Tamils.

After 1987, we realized we were wrong. By this time, a lot of gaps had grown between Kannada and Tamil brothers. After 1987, our viewpoint changed. People who live in Karnataka are called Kannadigas. Kannadiga is not the one who knows Kannada ... Those who live here, who migrated for the sake of livelihood ... they also are the people of the state.

He urged that 'Both [Kannada and Tamil speakers] should join our movement [which opposed the rapacious forces of the market in globalized consumption—for example, the struggle against Kentucky Fried Chicken—and the appropriation of livelihood resources in return for only an image—for example, the ongoing struggle against the Bangalore–Mysore Infrastructure Corridor.'[136]

There is recognition among such groups as the Karnataka Vimochana Ranga (KVR) that the only language that the Karnataka state is actively promoting is the language of capitalism, and resistance to that calls for a critique of the development paradigm itself: to what use must the resources of Karnataka be put? to benefit which people? The KVR, as Ramesh Bairy's research has pointed out, is possessed of a different vision of Karnataka, one that questions and restructures the frames within which the language question may be posed.[137] The current campaign to halt work on the massive acquisition of land for the Bangalore–Mysore infrastructure project has been joined by respected Gandhians such as H.S. Doreswamy, environmental activists, KVR, dalit groups, and branches of the Rajkumar Abhimanigala Sangha.

Other critiques of the dominant voices on the predicament of Kannada have come from unexpected quarters, and adopt alternative

---

[136]Interview with R. Radhakrishna, 20 July 1999.
[137]Ramesh Bairy, 'Competing Constructions of Kannada Identity'.

strategies of mobilization. Karnataka Rajya Raitha Sangha, though not unambiguous in its agenda, has consistently questioned the emerging 'sovereignty of the market', which has begun to reduce the role of the state to that of 'service provider'. Further, its critique of the absorption of rural resources by cities has sometimes led to untenable demands that no more Cauvery water should be allowed to flow into the city of Bangalore. A strong feminist critique of the gendered discourse of linguistic politics has laid bare the inadequacies of norming the subject of the Kannada nation as male. Also, although Karnataka's dalit groups have wavered more recently on whether they must support the strident calls to defend Kannada identity, they remain only uneasily aligned with the clearly pro-Hindutva version of Kannada nationalism. Thus, Karnataka Samata Sainik Dal, at the height of the protests against the unveiling of the Thiruvalluvar statue, detected an upper-caste plot to keep a dalit hero (Thiruvalluvar) from occupying public space in the city.[138]

Indeed, Rajkumar himself has remained loyal to another nation in his increasing distance from the activities of the majority of his fans' associations. In 1978, he went into hiding to avoid being dragged into standing for elections against Indira Gandhi in Chikmagalur. In 1984, he condemned the violence during the bandh, and refused to serve on the government panel which the Hegde government set up to solve the issue of Kannada examinations for Class III and IV jobs, though he declared the cause just. By the late 1980s, the activities of 'fan clubs' were a positive embarrassment to him when they took to violent road and rail *rokos:* the 1987 rail roko campaign which was meticulously organized to press for a Southern Railway Centre in Karnataka, led him to publicly stage a break, saying that he was in no way related to fans' associations. It was at that moment that many Abhimanigala Sanghas publicly declared *their* autonomy. 'It is like, in a poster somewhere, a beedi is kept in [Rajkumar's] mouth,' explains Radhakrishna. 'Does that mean he is smoking a beedi? No. So like that we will keep his name, we have that right. *When he has come into public life we have the right to use him.*' Thus, the man who wished to represent the aspirations of '3 crore Kannadigas' in 1982 has been increasingly distanced from the very organizations that invoke his name.

[138]Pamphlet of Karnataka Samata Sainik Dal, n.d.

Conclusion

Between June and November 2002, the districts of southern Karnataka were once more convulsed when the failure of the southwest monsoon resulted in a crisis of water-sharing between Karnataka and Tamil Nadu. Karnataka's reluctance to comply with the Supreme Court order to release at least 8000 cusecs per day to Tamil Nadu, following the death of a farmer in the Kabini reservoir, invited the charge that the Karnataka CM S.M. Krishna had committed contempt of court. Meanwhile, Veerappan struck once more, taking as hostage a former MLA, Nagappa, who tragically died in captivity. The conjunction of events once more raised the spectre of a confrontation between two irreconcilable nationalisms, which, however, spared the city of Bangalore from violence. Antagonism against Tamil Nadu instead took the form of shutting down Tamil TV channels, thus banning the screening of Tamil films. Once more the conflict over scarce water resources was mapped on to a linguistic difference with important consequences for the relationship between the two communities.

Undoubtedly there was widespread support for the programmes and activities of the more extreme linguistic nationalisms, especially during the Rajkumar abduction which was increasingly (and dangerously) read as an 'encounter between two nationalisms'. Such readings sweep complex histories out of sight, leaving the borders of the administrative state as the final space within which such identities may unfold. Nothing could be further from the fanciful wish of the advertisement for BPL mobiles which proclaims 'Geography is history'. Yet it is possible, even in these globalizing times, to detect the anguish about the destiny of a language threatened by the votaries of globalization in Bangalore. Karnataka's unique state formation, geography, and history may be the starting point for conceiving a different kind of nation, one that grasps both ends of a slippery pole to 'achieve universality through being specific', as D.R. Nagaraj has suggested, by placing these gathering passions at the service of a new democratic citizenship. Meanwhile, the contest over territories, and the territories of Bangalore in particular, continue to mark a range of struggles and contests of the last few decades. This becomes clearer when we turn to the many contests over symbolic spaces, as the city is reterritorialized in ways that bring many mental-imaginative maps to life.

Select Bibliography

Abbi, Anvita (ed.), 1997. *Languages of Tribal and Indigenous People of India*. Varanasi: Motilal Banarsidas Publishers Private Limited.

Abu-Lughod, Lila and Catherine A. Lutz (ed.), 1991. *Language and the Politics of Emotion*. Cambridge: Cambridge University Press.

Acharya, K.P. (ed.), 1987. *Pidgins and Creoles as Languages of Wider Communication*. Mysore: Central Institute of Indian Languages.

Acharya, Poromesh, 1986. 'Development of Modern Language Text-Books and the Social Context in 19th Century Bengal', *Economic and Political Weekly*, 26 April.

———, 2000. 'Santhal Education: Language and Literature in West Bengal', *Journal of the Anthropological Society in India*, 49 (4).

Anderson, Benedict, 1991. *Imagined Communities: Reflections on the Origin and Spread of Nationalism*. London: Verso.

Angel, M.Y. and Peter W. Martin, (ed.), 2005. *Decolonization; Globalization; Language in Education Policy and Practice*. Clevedon: Multilingual Matters.

Annamalai, Jernudol and Rubin (eds), 1983. *Language Planning*. Mysore: CIIL.

Annamalai, E. (ed.), 1984. *Language Movements in India*. Mysore: CIIL.

———, 1999. 'Language Choice in Education: Conflict Resolution in Indian Courts', *Language Science*, 2 (1).

———, 2001. *Managing Multilingualism in India: Political and Linguistic Manifestations*. New Delhi: Sage Publications.

———, 2003. 'Language Policy for Multilingualism: A Reflective Essay', *Language Policy*, 2 (2).

Ananthamurthy, U.R., 2001. 'Towards the Concept of a New Nationhood:

Languages and Literatures in India', in Peter, de Souza (ed.). *Contemporary India*. New Delhi: Sage Publications.

Apte, Mahadev L., 1976. 'Multilingualism in India and Its Socio-Political Implications: An Overview', in William M. O'Barr and Jean F. O'Barr (eds), *Language and Politics*. Paris: Mouton.

Austin, Granville, 1966. *The Indian Constitution: Cornerstone of a Nation*. Oxford: Clarendon Press.

Bach, Emmon and Robert Harms (ed.), 1968. *Language, Sense and Nonsense*. Oxford: Blackwell.

Badre, Narayan, 2002. 'Deconstructing "Official": Language, Identity and Politics', *Indian Journal of Federal Studies*, 3 (1).

Bain, Bruce (ed.), 1983. *The Sociogenesis of Language and Human Conduct*. New York: Plenum Press.

Barbour, Stephen and Cathie Carmichael (eds), 2001. *Language and Nationalism in Europe*. New York: Oxford University Press.

Basu, D.D., 1996. *Shorter Constitution of India*. New Delhi: Prentice-Hall of India Private Limited.

Beams, J., 1866. 'Outlines of a Plea for the Arabic Element in Official Hindustani', *Journal of the Asiatic Society*, 1 (1).

Beer, W.R. and J.E. Jacob (eds), 1985. *Language Policy and National Unity*. Totowa, NJ, USA: Rowman and Littlefield.

Bell, David A., 1995. 'Lingua Populi, Lingua Dei: Language, Religion and the Origins of French Revolutionary Nationalism', *The American Historical Review*, 100 (5).

Benjamin, Walter, 1986. 'On Language as Such and on the Language of Man', in Peter Demetz (ed.), *Walter Benjamin, Reflections: Essays, Aphorisms, Autobiographical Writings*. New York: Schocken Books.

Bhabha, Homi K. (ed.), 1990. *Nation and Narration*. London: Routledge.

Bhaktavatsalam, M., 1978. *The Absurdity of Anti-Hindi Policy*. Madras: Perumal Udayar.

Bolinger, Dwight L., 1980. *Language—the Loaded Weapon*. London: Longman.

Bourdieu, Pierre, 1991. *Language and Symbolic Power*. Cambridge: Harvard University Press.

_____, 1977. 'The Economics of Linguistic Exchange', *Social Science Information*, 16.

Brass, Paul R., 1974. *Language, Religion and Politics in North India*. London: Cambridge University Press.

_____, 1990. *The Politics of India Since Independence*. Cambridge: Cambridge University Press.

Breton, Roland J.L., 1991. *Geolinguistics: Language Dynamics and Ethnolinguistic Geography*. Ottawa: University of Ottawa Press.

———, 1996. 'The Dynamics of Ethnolinguistic Communities as the Central Factor in Language Policy and Planning', *International Journal of the Sociology of Language*, 118.

———, 1997. *Atlas of the Languages and Ethnic Communities of South Asia*. New Delhi: Sage Publications.

Brown, W. Norman, 1958. 'Religion and Language as Forces Affecting Unity in Asia', *Annals of the American Academy of Political and Social Science*, Vol. 318.

Burghart, Richard, 1993. 'Quarrel in the Language Family: Agency and Representation of Speech in Mithila', *Modern Asian Studies*, 27 (4).

Burke, Peter, 1987. *The Social History of Language*. Harvard: Cambridge University Press.

Caie, Graham D., 1987. 'Nationalism, Language and Cultural Identity in Fourteenth Century England', *Culture and History*, Vol. 1.

Cameron, Deborah, 1990. 'Demythologizing Sociolinguistics: Why Language Does not Reflect Society'. in John E. Joseph, and Talbot J. Taylor, (eds), *Ideologies of Language*. London: Routledge.

———, 1992. *Feminism and Linguistic Theory*. New York: St Martin's Press.

———, 1995. *Verbal Hygiene*. London: Routledge,

———, 2006. 'Ideology and Language', *Journal of Political Ideologies*, 11 (2).

Carberera, Miguel A., 2001. 'On Language, Culture and Social Action', *History and Theory*, 40 (4), December.

Chandrasekhara Rao, R.V.R., 1979. 'Conflicting Roles of Language and Regionalism in an Indian State: A Case Study of Andhra Pradesh', in Taylor David and Yapp Malcolm (eds), *Political Identity in South Asia*. London: Curzon Press.

Chartier, Roger, 1987. *The Cultural Uses of Print in Early Modern France*, Translated by Lydia G. Cochrane. Princeton: Princeton University Press.

——— (ed.), 1989. *The Culture of Print: Power and the Uses of Print in Early Modern Europe*. Princeton: Princeton University Press.

Chatterji, Nandlal, 1965. 'A Nineteenth Century Controversy on the Teaching of Hindustani', *Journal of Indian History*, 42 (1).

———, 1953. 'The Problem of Court Language in British India', *Journal of Indian History*, 3 (3).

Chatterjee, Partha, 1993. *The Nation and its Fragments: Colonial and Postcolonial Histories*. Princeton: Princeton University Press.

Chomsky, Noam, 1981. 'Knowledge of Language: Its Elements and Origins', in *Philosophical Transactions of the Royal Society of London*, Series B.

———, 2004. *Language and Politics: Political Aspects*. California: A.K. Press.

Coates, Jennifer and Deborah Cameron (eds), 1988. *Women in Their Speech Communities: New Perspectives on Language and Sex*. London: Longman Publishers.

Cohn, Barnard, 1987. *An Anthropologist among the Historians and Other Essays.* New Delhi: Oxford University Press.

Cooper, Robert L., 1989. *Language Planning and Social Change.* New York: Cambridge University Press.

Coulmas, F. (ed.), 1984. *Linguistic Minorities and Literacy: Language Policy Issues in Developing Countries.* New York: Mouton Publications.

Crane, Robert I. (ed.), 1981. *Language and Society in Modern India: Essays in Honour of Prof Robert O. Swan.* New Delhi: Heritage Publishing.

Dalmia, Vasudha, 1998. *The Nationalization of Hindu Traditions: Bhartendu Harishchandra and Nineteenth Century Banaras.* New Delhi: Oxford University Press.

Das, S.K., 1991. *A History of Indian Literature, Vol. VIII, 1800–1910: Western Impact: Indian Response.* New Delhi: Sahitya Akademi.

Dasgupta, Jyotirindra, 1970. *Language Conflict and National Development: Group Politics and National Language Policy in India.* Berkeley: University of California Press.

———, 1976. 'Practice and Theory of Language Planning: The Indian Policy Process', in William M. O'Barr and Jean F.O' Barr (eds), *Language and Politics.* Paris: Mouton.

Dasgupta, Probal, 1993. *The Otherness of English: India's Auntie Tongue Syndrome.* New Delhi: Sage Publications.

———, 2000. 'Sanskrit, English and Dalits', *Economic and Political Weekly*, 35 (16).

———, 2004 'Language, Public Space and an Educated Imagination', *Economic and Political Weekly*, 39 (21).

Dass, Dayal, 1956. 'Language Controversy a Century Ago', *Indian Historical Records Commission*, 32 (2).

Daswani, C.J. (ed.), 2001. *Language Education in Multilingual India.* New Delhi: UNESCO.

Devotta, Neil, 2004. *Blowback: Linguistic Nationalism, Institutional Decay and Ethnic Conflict in Sri Lanka.* Standford University Press.

Dil, Anwar S. (ed.), 1972. *The Ecology of Language: Essays by Einar Haugen.* Standford: Standford University Press.

Dimock, Edward C., Kachru Braj B. (eds), 1992. *Dimensions of Sociolinguistics in South Asia: Papers in Memory of Gerald Kelly.* New Delhi: Oxford University Press.

Dua, Hans Raj, 1985. *Language Planning in India.* New Delhi: Harnam Publications.

———, 1993. 'The National Language and the Ex-Colonial Language as Rivals: The Case of India', *International Political Science Review*, 14 (3).

———, 1994. 'Hindi Language Spread Policy and Its Implementation', *International Journal of the Sociology of Language*, 107.

Duranti, Alessandro, 1997. *Linguistic Anthropology.* Harvard: Cambridge University Press.

Eckert, P. and S. Macconnell-Ginet, 1992. 'Communities of Practice: Where Language, Gender and Power All Live', in *Locating Power: Proceedings of the Second Berkeley Women and Language Conference.* Berkeley: University of California.

Errington, Joseph, 2001. 'Colonial Linguistics', *Annual Review of Anthropology*, Vol. 30.

Fabian, Johannes, 1986. *Language and Colonial Power: The Appropriation of Swahili in the Former Belgian Congo 1880–1938.* Cambridge: Cambridge University Press.

Fairclough, N., 1995. *Critical Discourse Analysis: The Critical Study of Language.* London: Longman.

Fishman, Joshua A., C.A. Ferguson and J. Dasgupta (eds), 1968. *Language Problems of Developing Nations.* New York: John Wiley.

———, 1999. 'The New Linguistic Order', *Foreign Policy*, Winter.

Fishman, Joshua A., 1996. 'Perfecting the Perfect: Improving the Beloved Language', in Laura Garcia-Moreno and Peter C. Pfeiffer (eds), *Text and Nation: Cross-Disciplinary Essays on Cultural and National Identities.* Camden House: Columbia.

Ford, Caroline C., 1993. 'Which Nation? Language, Identity and Republican Politics in Post-Revolutionary France', *History of European Ideas*, 17 (1).

Forrester, Duncan B., 1966. 'The Madras Anti-Hindi Agitation, 1965: Political Protest and Its Effects on Language Policy in India', 39 (1–2).

Francis, John De, 1950. *Nationalism and Language Reform in China.* New Jersey: Princeton University Press.

Gal, Susan, 1989. 'Language and Political Economy', *Annual Review of Anthropology*, Vol. 18.

Gal, Susan, and Irvine, Judith, 1995. 'The Boundaries of Languages and Disciplines: How Ideologies Construct Difference', *Social Research*, Winter.

Gal, Susan, 1991. 'Between Speech and Silence: The Problematics of Research on Language and Gender', in M. Dileonardo (ed.), *Gender at the Crossroads of Knowledge.* Berkeley: University of California Press.

Gandhi, K.L., 1984. *Problem of Official Language in India.* New Delhi: Arya Book Depot.

Gandhi, M.K., 1938. *Hind Swaraj or Indian Home Rule.* Ahmedabad: Navajivan Publication House.

———, 1965. *Our Language Problem*, edited by Anand T. Hingorani. Bombay: Bhartiya Vidhya Bhawan. Karachi 1942.

Garvin, Paul L., 1993. 'A Conceptual Framework for the Study of Language Standardization', *International Journal of the Sociology of Language*, 100/101.

Gavaskar, Mahesh, 2002. 'Politics of Language', *Economic and Political Weekly*, 37 (52).

Gerow, E. and M.D. Lang (eds), 1973. *Studies in the Language and Culture of South Asia*. Seattle: University of Washington Press.

Ghosh, Kunal, 1997. 'Origin of Sectarian Nationalism, Language Factor and Indian Polity', *New Quest*, Vol. 124.

Ghosh, Partha S., 1996. 'Language Policy and National Integration: The Indian Experience', *Ethnic Studies Report*, 14 (1).

Gopal, Ram, 1966. *Linguistic Affairs of India*: New York: Asia Publication House.

Gordon, David C., 1978. *The French Language and National Identity, 1930–75*. Haque: Mouton Publishers.

Gramsci, Antonio, 1985. 'Language, Linguistics and Folklore', in David Forgas and G.N. Smith (eds), *Antonio Gramsci: Selections from Cultural Writings*. Cambridge: Harvard University Press.

Grierson, George, 1927. *Linguistic Survey of India*, Vols 1–11. Calcutta: Superintendent of Government Printing Press.

Grillo, R.D., 1989. *Dominant Languages: Language and Hierarchy in Britain and France*. Cambridge: Cambridge University Press.

Grossman, Jeffrey, 1997. 'Wilhelm Von Humboldt's Linguistic Ideology: The Problem of Pluralism and the Absolute Difference of National Character or Where do the Jews Fit in?', *German Studies Review*, 20 (1).

Gumperz, John J., 1971. *Language in Social Groups*. Standford: Standford University Press.

———, (eds), 1982. *Language and Social Identity*. Cambridge: Cambridge University Press.

Gupta, R.S., Anvita Abbi and Kailash S. Aggarwal (eds), 1995. *Language and the State: Perspectives on the Eighth Schedule*. New Delhi: Creative Books.

Handa R.L., 1983. *Missing Links in Link Language*. New Delhi: Sterling Publishing Private Limited.

Harris, Roy, 1981. *The Language Myth*. New York: St Martin Press.

Harrison, Selig, 1960. *India: The Most Dangerous Decades*. New Jersey: Princeton University Press.

Haugen, E., D.S. Thompson, and J.D. McClure (eds), 1981. *Minority Languages Today*. Edinburg: Edinburg University Press.

Hobsbwam, Eric, 1996. 'Language, Culture and Identity', *Social Research*, 63 (4), Winter.

Hooks, Bell, 1996. 'This is the Oppressor's Language/Yet I Need to Talk to You: Language a Place of Struggle', in A. Dingwaney and Carol Maier (eds), *Between Languages and Cultures: Cross Cultural Texts*. Oxford: Oxford University Press.

Houben, Jan E.M. (ed.), 1996. *Ideology and Status of Sanskrit: Contributions to the History of Sanskrit Language*. Leiden: J. Brillo.

Hudson, Richard A., 1980. *Sociolinguistics*. Cambridge: Cambridge University Press.

Hymes, Dell (ed.), 1964. *Language in Culture and Society*. New York: Harper and Row.

Inglehart, Ronald F. and Margaret Woodward, 1968. 'Language Conflicts and Political Community', *Comparative Studies in Society and History*, Vol. 10.

Irvine, Judith T., 1989. 'When Talk isn't Cheap: Language and Political Economy', *American Ethnologist*, 16 (2).

Jalal, Ayesha, 1995. *Democracy and Authoritarianism in South Asia: A Comparative and Historical Perspective*. Cambridge: Cambridge University Press.

Jernudd, Bjorn H. and Michael J. Shapiro (eds), 1989. *The Politics of Language Purism*. New York: Mouton de Gruyter.

Jespersen, Otto, 1954. *Mankind, Nation and Individual from a Linguistic Point of View*. London: George Allen and Unwin Ltd.

Ji, Fengyuan, 2004. *Linguistic Engineering: Language and Politics in Mao's China*. Honolulu: University of Hawaii Press.

Jindal, K.B., 1993. *A History of Hindi Literature*. New Delhi: Munshiram Manoharlal Publishers Private Ltd.

John, Edwards, 1985. *Language, Society and Identity*. London: Basil Blackwell.

Joredom, Tem, 2001. 'Language and Libertarianism: The Politics of Cyber Culture and the Culture of Cyber Politics', *Sociological Review*, 49 (1).

Joseph, John E. and Taylor, Talbot J., 1990. *Ideologies of Language*, London: Routledge.

Joshi, Svati (ed.), 1994. *Rethinking English: Essays in Literature, Language, History*. New Delhi: Oxford University Press.

Joyce, Patrick, 1991. 'The People's English: Language and Class in England c 1840–1920', in Peter Burke and Roy Porter (eds), *Language, Self and Society: A Social History of Languages*. London: Polity Press.

Judson, Pieter M., 2006. *Guardians of the Nation: Activists on the Language Frontiers of Imperial Austria*. Cambridge: Harvard University Press.

Kamat, A.R., 1980. 'Ethno-Linguistic Issues in Indian Federal Context', *Economic and Political Weekly*, 14–21 June.

Kandian, Tiru and John Kwan Terry (eds), 1994. *English and Language Planning: A South East Asian Contribution*, Singapore: Times Acedemic Press.

Karve, D.D., 1960. *The Linguistic Problems of India*. Berkeley: University of California Press.

Kathryn, A. Woolard and Bambi Schieffelin, 1994. 'Language Ideology', *Annual Review of Anthropology*, 55–82 (23).

Keshari, B.P., 1997. 'Present Situation of the Jharkhandi Language', *Journal of Anthropological Survey of India,* 46 (4).

Khubchandani, Lachman M., 1991. *Language, Culture and Nation-Building: Challenges of Modernization.* Shimla: Indian Institute of Advanced Study and Manohar Publications.

____, 1997. *Revisualizing Boundaries: A Plurilingual Ethos.* New Delhi: Sage Publications.

King, Christopher, 1994. *One Language, Two Scripts: The Hindi Movement in Nineteenth century North India.* New Delhi: Oxford University Press.

King, Robert, 1997. *Nehru and the Language Politics of India.* New Delhi: Oxford University Press.

Kramer, Chris, Thorne Barrie, and Nancy Henley, 1978. 'Perspectives on Language and Communication: Review Essay', *Sign: Journal of Women in Culture and Society,* 3 (3).

Krishna, Sumi, 1991. *India's Living Languages: The Critical Issues.* New Delhi: Allied Publishers.

Krishnamurti, B.H. 1998. *Language, Education and Society.* New Delhi: Sage Publications.

Kymlica, Will and Alan Patten (eds), 2003. *Language Rights and Political Theory.* New York: Oxford University Press.

Laitin, David D., 1989. 'Language Policy and Political Strategy in India', *Policy Sciences,* 22 (3–4).

____, 1992. *Language Repertoires and State Construction in Africa.* Cambridge: Cambridge University Press.

____, 1993. 'The Game Theory of Language Regimes', *International Political Science Review,* 14 (3).

Lakshmanan, M., 2001. 'Language and the Nationality Question in Tamil Nadu', *Indian Historical Review,* 28 (1–2).

Lambert, Richard D., 1959. 'Factors in Bengali Regionalism in Pakistan', *Far Eastern Survey,* 28 (40).

Language Atlas of India, 1991–2004. New Delhi: Controller of Publications, Government of India.

Laponce, Jean, 1987. *Languages and Their Territories.* Toronto: Toronto University Press.

Lazear, Edward. P., 1999. 'Culture and Language', *Journal of Political Economy,* 107 (62).

Leaf, Murray J., 1976. 'Economic Implications of the Language Issue: A Local View in Punjab', *The Journal of Commonwealth and Comparative Politics,* 14 (1).

Lelyveld, David, 1993. 'The Fate of Hindustani: Colonial Knowledge and the Project of a National Language', in C. Breckenridge and Peter van der Veer, (eds), *Orientalism and Post Colonial Predicament*. New York: Oxford University Press.

———, 1994. '*Zuban-e-Urdu-e-Mualla* and the Ideology of Linguistic Origins', *The Annals of Urdu Studies*, Vol. 9.

Lihani, John, 1992. 'Review of Brian Weinstein', *Language Problems and Language Planning*, 16 (3).

Macfany, Joan-Lluis, 2004. '"Minority" Language and Literacy Revivals', *Past and Present*, Vol. 184, August.

Mah, Harold, 1994. 'The Epistemology of the Sentence: Language, Civility and Identity in France and Germany, Diderot to Nietzsche', *Representations*, Vol. 47.

Majeed, Javed, 1995. 'The "Jargon of Indostan": An Exploration of Jargon in Urdu and East India Company English', in Peter Burke and Roy Porter (eds), *Languages and Jargons: Contributions to a Social History of Language*. London: Polity Press.

Maloney, Clearence and Ishwaran K. (eds), *Language and Civilization Change in South Asia*. Leiden: Brillo.

Manoharan, S., 1999. 'Scheduled Tribes of India and Their Language: A Study on Language Loss and Maintenance', *Journal of Anthropological Survey of India*, 48 (2).

Mansoon, Sabiha (ed.), 2004. *Language Policy Planning and Practice: A South Asian Perspective*. New Delhi: Oxford University Press.

McCormack, William C. and Wurm, Stephen A., 1974. *Language and Society: Anthropological Issues*. Mouton: The Hague.

McConnell-Ginet, Sally Ruth Borker, and Nelly Furman (eds), 1980. *Women and Language in Literature and Society*. New York: Prager.

Miri, Mrinal (ed.), 1993. *Tribal India: Continuity and Change in Tribal Society*. Shimla: IIAS.

Mitra, Subrata K., 2000. 'Language and Federalism: The Multiethnic challenge', *Indian Journal of Federal Studies*, 1 (2).

Mohanty, Nivedita, 2005. *Oriya Nationalism: Quest for a United Orissa; 1866–1956*. Bhubneshwar: Prafulla Press.

Montaut, Annie, 2005. 'Colonial Language Classification, Post-Colonial Language Movements, and the Grassroot Multilingualism Ethos in India', in Mushirul Hasan and Asim Roy (eds), *Living Together Separately: Cultural India in History and Politics*. New Delhi: Oxford University Press.

Naregal, Veena, 2002. *Language Politics, Elites and the Public Sphere: Western India under Colonialism*. London: Anthen Press.

Nayar, Baldev Raj, 1969. *National Communication and Language Policy in India*. New York: F.A. Praeger.

Nigam, R.C., 1972. *Language Handbook on Mother Tongue in Census*. Census Centenary Monograph, No. 10.

O'Barr, William M. and Jean F. O'Barr (eds), 1976. *Language and Politics*. Paris: Mouton.

Oommen, T.K., 2001. 'Civil Society: Religion, Caste and Language in India', *Sociological Bulletin*, 50 (2).

_____, 2004. *Nation, Civil Society and Social Movements: Essays in Political Sociology*, New Delhi: Sage Publications.

Ostler, Nicholas, 2005. *Empires of the Word: A Language History of the World*. New York: Harper and Collins.

Ozolins, Uldis, 1996. 'Language Policy and Political Reality', *International Journal of the Sociology of Language*, No. 118.

Pai, Sudha, 2002. 'Politics of Language: Decline of Urdu in Uttar Pradesh', *Economic and Political Weekly*, 37 (27).

Pandharipande, Rajeshwari V., 2002. 'Minority Matters: Issues in Minority Languages in India', *MOST: Journal of Multicultural Societies*, 4 (2). Paris: UNESCO.

Pandit, P.B., 1978. 'Language and Identity: The Panjabi in Delhi', *International Journal of the Sociology of Language*, 16.

Parker, Ian, 1983. 'The Rise of Vernaculars in Early Modern Europe: An Essay in the Political Economy of Language', in Bruce Bain (ed.), *The Sociogenesis of Language and Human Conduct*. New York: Plenum Press.

Pattanayak, D.P., 1981. *Language and Social Issues*. Mysore: Central Institute of Indian Languages.

Patten, Alan, 2001. 'Political Theory and Language Policy', *Political Theory*, 29 (5).

_____, 2003. 'Liberal Neutrality and Language Policy', *Philosophy and Public Affairs*, 31 (4).

_____, 2006a. 'The Humanist Roots of Linguistic Nationalism', *History of Political Thought*, 27 (2).

_____, 2006. 'Who Should Have Official Language Rights?', *Supreme Court Law Review*, 31.

Paulston, Christina Bratt, 1997. 'Language Policies and Language Rights', *Annual Review of Anthropology*, Vol. 26.

Paxman, David B., 1993. 'Language and Difference: The Problem of Abstraction in Eighteenth Century Language Study', *Journal of the History of Ideas*, 54 (1).

Pei, Mario, 1956. *All about Language*. London: Bodely Head.

Pendekure, Krishna and Ravi Pendekure, 2002. 'Language as Both Human Capital and Ethnicity', *International Migration Review*, 36 (1), Spring.

Phillipson, Robert, 1992. *Linguistic Imperialism*. New York: Oxford University Press.

_____ (ed.), 2000. *Right to Language Equity, Power and Education: Celebrating the 60th Birthday of the Skutnabb Kangas*. New Jersey: Lawrence Erlbaum Associates.

_____, 2003. *English-Only Europe? Challenging Language Policy*. New York: Routledge.

Pollock, Sheldon, 1998. 'India in the Vernacular Millennium', *Proceedings of the American Academy of Arts and Sciences*, 127 (3).

_____ (ed.), 2003. *Literary Cultures in History: Reconstructions from South Asia*. New Delhi: Oxford University Press.

Prakash, Karat, 1972. 'The Role of English-Educated in Indian Politics', *Social Scientist*, 1 (4).

_____, 1973. *Language and Nationality Politics in India*. Delhi: Orient Longman.

Rahman, Tariq, 2002. 'Language, Power and Ideology', *Economic and Political Weekly*, 37 (44–5).

Rai, Alok, 2001. *Hindi Nationalism*. Hyderabad: Orient Longman.

Rajan, Rajeswari Sunder (ed.), 1993. *The Lie of the Land: English Literary Studies in India*. New Delhi: Oxford University Press.

Ramaswamy, Sumathi, 1997. *Passions of the Tongue: Language Devotion in Tamil India, 1891–1970*. Berkeley: University of California Press.

Rani, Asha, 2004. 'Language as a Marker of Religious Difference', in Imtiaz Ahmad and Helmut Reifeld (eds), *Lived Islam in South Asia: Adaptation, Accomodation and Conflict*. Delhi: Social Science Press.

_____, 2002. 'Politics of Linguistic Identity and Community Formation in Colonial North India,1900–1947', Ph.D thesis. Chicago: University of Chicago.

Robin, Joan (ed.), 1973. *Language Planning: Current Issues and Research*. Washington: Georgetown University Press.

Rossi-Landi, F., 1973. *Ideologies of Linguistic Relativity*. Hague: Mouton.

Roy, Harris and Ben Rampton, 2003. *The Language, Ethnicity and Race: Reader*. London: Routledge.

Roy, Porter and Peter Burke (eds), 1991. *Language, Self and Society: A Social History of Language*. London: Polity Press.

Rundle, Stanley, 1946. *Language as a Social and Political Factor in Europe*. London: Faber and Faber.

Ryang, Sonia, 2005. 'How to Do or Not Do Things with Words: The Case of Koreans in Japan', *Asian Ethnicity*, 6 (3).

Rao R.V.R., Chandrasekhara, 1979. 'Conflicting Roles of Language and Regionalism in an Indian State: A Case Study of Andhra Pradesh', in Taylor

David and Yapp Malcolm (eds), *Political Identity in South Asia*. London: Curzon Press.

Safran, William, 1992. 'Language Ideology and State Building: A Comparison of Policies in France, Israel and Soviet Union', *International Political Science Review*, 13 (4).

Samarin, William J., 1989. 'Language in the Colonization of Central Africa, 1880–1900', *Canadian Journal of African Studies*, 23 (2).

Sarangi, Asha, 2004. 'Ambedkar and the Linguistic States: A Case for Maharashtra', *Economic and Political Weekly*, January 14.

____, 2004. 'Ritual of Political Rhetoric', *Seminar*, July.

Schiffman, Harold F., 1996. *Linguistic Culture and Language Policy*. New York: Routledge.

Shapiro, Michael J., 1981. *Language and Political Understanding: The Politics of Discursive Practices*. New Haven: Yale University Press.

Singh, K.S. and S. Manoharan, 1993. *Languages and Scripts*. New Delhi: Oxford University Press.

Singh, Rajendra (ed.), 1995. *Explorations in Indian Sociolinguistics*. New Delhi: Sage Publications.

Singh, Udaya Narayan, 2003. 'Social Aspects of Language', in Veena Das (ed.), *The Oxford Indian Companion to Sociology and Social Anthropology*. New Delhi: Oxford University Press.

Sinha, K.K., 1958. *Modern India Rejects Hindi*. Calcutta: Association for the Advancement of the National Languages of India.

Smith, Olivia, 1984. *The Politics of Language, 1791–1819*. Oxford: Clarendon Press.

Smith, Philip M., 1985. *Language, the Sexes and Society*. Oxford: Basil Blackwell.

Sonntag, Selma K., 1995. 'Elite Competition and Official Language Movement', in James W. Tollefson (ed.), *Power and Inequality in Language*. Cambridge: Cambridge University Press.

Spender, Dale, 1980. *Man Made Language*. London: Routledge.

Spolsky, B. (ed.), 1986. *Language and Education in Multilingual Settings*. Clevedon: Multilingual Matters, Vol. 25.

Srivastava, Gopi Nath, 1970. *The Language Controversy and the Minorities*. Delhi: Atma Ram and Sons.

Steiner, George, 1975. *After Babel: Aspects of Language and Translation*. London: Faber and Faber.

Swann, Abram De, 2001. *Words of the World: The Global Language System*. Cambridge: Polity Press.

Tambiah, S.J., 1967. 'The Politics of Language', *Modern Asian Studies*, 1 (30).

Taylor, Charles, 1985. *Human Agency and Language: Philosophical Papers*, Vol. 1. Cambridge: Cambridge University Press.

The Census of India 1961. *India and States.* New Delhi. Census Commissioner, India.

———, 1991. *Language, India and States,* Series 1, New Delhi. Registrar General & Census Commissioner, India.

———, 2001. www.censusindia. gov. in/Census Data 2001/Census Data Online/ Language/Statement 4.htm

The Constitution of India, 1991 (third edition). Delhi: Government of India.

Thorlac, Turville Petre, 1996. *England the Nation: Language, Literature and National Identity,1290–1340.* London: Clarendon University Press.

Tharakeshwar, V.B., 2004. 'Translating Nationalism: The Politics of Language and Community', *Journal of Karnataka Studies,* 1.

Tollefson, W. (ed.), 1995. *Power and Inequality in Language.* Cambridge: Cambridge University Press.

Trautmann, Thomas R., 2006. *Language and Nations: The Dravidian Proof in Colonial Madras.* Berkeley: University of California Press.

Trivedi, Harish, 1995. *Colonial Transactions: English Literature and India.* Manchester: Manchester University Press.

Varma, Direndra, 1945. *Hindi Basha aur Lippi.* Prayag: Hindustani Academy.

Venkatachalapathy, A.R, 1995. 'Coding Words: Language and Politics in Late Colonial Tamil Nadu', *South Asian Bulletin,* 15 (2).

Venkatachaliah, M.N., 1999. 'Language and Politics: Status of Urdu in India', *Economic and Political Weekly,* 34 (26).

Verma, Shivendra K. and Dilip Singh (eds), 1996. *Perspectives on Language and Society,* Vol. 1. New Delhi: Kalinga.

Wardhaugh, Ronald, 1987. *Language in Competition.* Oxford: Basil Blackwell.

Viswanathan, Gauri, 1989. *Masks of Conquest: Literary Study and British Rule in India.* New York: Columbia University Press.

Warsi, M.J., 2000, 'Politics of Language in India', *Third Concept,* 14 (163).

Washbrook, David, 1991. '"To Each a Language of His Own": Language, Culture and Society in Colonial India', in P.J. Corfield, (ed.), *Language, History and Class.* Cambridge: Basil Blackwell.

Waswo, Richard, 1987. *Language and Meaning in the Renaissance.* Princeton: Princeton University Press.

Weedon, Chris, Andrew Tolson, and Mort Frank, 1980. 'Theories of Language and Subjectivity', in Stuart Hall, Dorothy Hobson, Andrew Lowe, and Paul Willis (eds), *Culture, Media, Language: Working Papers in Cultural Studies, 1972–79.* London: Hutchinson.

Williams, Collins H. (ed.), 1991. *Linguistic Minorities: Societies and Territory.* Cleaveldon: Multilingual Matters.

Windmiller, Marshall, 1954. 'Linguistic Regionalism in India', *Pacific Affairs,* 27 (4).

Wodak, Ruth (ed.), 1999. *The Discursive Construction of National Identities.* Edinburgh: Edinburgh University Press.

Woolard, Kathryn A. and Bambi B. Schieffelin, 1994. 'Language Ideology', *Annual Review of Anthropology*, Vol. 23.

Xaxa, Virginius, 2005. 'Politics of Language, Religion and Identity: Tribes in India', *Economic and Political Weekly*, 40 (13).

Yagnik, Achyut, 2005. 'My Mother Tongue', *Seminar*, Vol. 470, October.

Contributors

ANVITA ABBI is Chairperson and Professor, Centre for Linguistics, School of Language, Literature and Culture, Jawaharlal Nehru University, New Delhi, India.

GRANVILLE AUSTIN is a constitutional analyst who has written extensively on the Indian constitution. He lives in New York, USA.

PAUL R. BRASS is Professor Emeritus of Political Science and South Asian Studies, University of Washington, Seattle, USA.

SUDIPTA KAVIRAJ is Professor of Indian Politics and Intellectual History, Columbia University, New York, USA.

DAVID LELYVELD is Professor, Department of History, William Peterson University, New Jersey, USA.

JANAKI NAIR is Professor of History, Centre for Historical Studies, School of Social Sciences, Jawaharlal Nehru University, New Delhi, India.

SUMATHI RAMASWAMY is Professor of History, Duke University, Durham, USA.

ASHA SARANGI is Associate Professor, Centre for Political Studies, School of Social Sciences, Jawaharlal Nehru University, New Delhi, India.

JOSEPH E. SCHWARTZBERG is Professor Emeritus, University of Minnesota, Minnesota, USA.

D.L. SHETH is National Fellow, Indian Institute of Advanced Study, Shimla, India.

SELMA K. SONNTAG is Professor, Department of Government and Politics, Humboldt State University, Arcata, California, USA.

K.WARIKOO is Professor and Director, Central Asian Studies Programme, School of International Studies, Jawaharlal Nehru University, New Delhi, India.